WITCH HUNTING, MAGIC AND THE NEW PHILOSOPHY:

An Introduction to Debates of the Scientific Revolution 1450–1750

WITCH HUNTING, MAGIC AND THE NEW PHILOSOPHY:

An Introduction to Debates of the Scientific Revolution 1450–1750

BRIAN EASLEA

Lecturer in History and Social Studies of Science, University of Sussex

THE HARVESTER PRESS • SUSSEX

HUMANITIES PRESS • NEW JERSEY

First published in Great Britain in 1980 by
THE HARVESTER PRESS LIMITED
Publishers: John Spiers and Margaret A. Boden
16 Ship Street, Brighton, Sussex

and in the USA by
HUMANITIES PRESS INC.
Atlantic Highlands, New Jersey 07716

British Library Cataloguing in Publication Data

Easlea, Brian
  Witch hunting, magic and the new philosophy.
  (Harvester studies in philosophy; 14).
  1. Science—Social aspects—Europe
  2. Science—Europe—History
  I. Title
  301.24'3'094   Q175.52.E/

  ISBN 0–85527–908–7 (cloth)

Humanities Press Inc.
ISBN 0–391–01806–X
        0–391–01808–6 pbk

Printed in Great Britain by
Redwood Burn Limited, Trowbridge and Esher

CONTENTS

It was not 'pure reason' or the 'absolute spirit' which at the beginning of the modern age sketched out the tremendous program of a comprehensive mechanistic explanation of nature and man... but the new will to power over nature and the desire to work upon her on the part of the rising bourgeoisie.

MAX SCHELER

The source of science is not the will to power over things (though such power has in fact occasionally had a stimulating effect on science) but the will to truth.... The will to truth, this source of human dignity, is the origin of modern science and its character; it is the sovereignty of man's freedom to know.

KARL JASPERS

[S]cience, *by virtue of its own method* and concepts, has projected and promoted a universe in which the domination of nature has remained linked to the domination of man.... If this is the case, then the change in the direction of progress, which might sever this fatal link, would also affect the very structure of science.... Its hypotheses...would develop in an essentially different experimental context (that of a pacified world); consequently, science would arrive at essentially different concepts of nature and establish essentially different facts.

HERBERT MARCUSE

Marx's notion of a human appropriation of nature retains something of the *hubris* of domination....[Nature] may well be hostile to man, in which case the relation [between man and nature] would be one of struggle; but the struggle may also subside and make room for peace, tranquillity, fulfillment. In this case, not appropriation but rather its negation would be the nonexploitative relation: surrender, 'letting-be', acceptance.... the faculty of being 'receptive', 'passive' is a precondition of freedom: it is the ability to see things in their own right....This receptivity is itself the soil of creation: it is opposed, not to productivity, but to *destructive* productivity. The latter has been the ever more conspicuous feature of male domination; inasmuch as the 'male principle' has been the ruling mental and physical force, a free society would be the 'definite negation' of this principle—it would be a *female* society.

HERBERT MARCUSE

*

Now let me put a feigned case...of a land of Amazons, where the government public and private, yea the militia itself, was in the hands of women. I demand is not such a preposterous government (against the first order of nature, for women to rule over men) in itself void, and to be suppressed? I speak not of the reign of women, (for that is supplied by counsel and subordinate magistrates masculine,) but where the regiment of state, justice, families, is all managed by women. And yet this last case differeth from the other before; because in the rest there is terror of danger, but in this there is only error of nature.

FRANCIS BACON

Then the reign...of a queen that lived solitary and unmarried and yet her government so masculine, as it had greater impression and operation upon the states abroad than it any ways received from thence.

FRANCIS BACON

PREFACE

SEVERAL introductory texts are available on the scientific revolution of the sixteenth and seventeenth centuries. Why have I written another? Principally for two related reasons. First, because many introductions ignore problematic features of the 'new philosophy' and consequently make the scientific revolution appear far too straightforward a triumph of 'reason' over 'prejudice' and 'superstition'. What I have therefore tried to do is to present through the eyes and words of leading protagonists a *critical* account of this momentous but also problematic revolution, thereby giving students an opportunity to assess for themselves the extent and nature of its rationality. Second, many texts concentrate almost exclusively on either the 'scientific' features of the revolution or on its social context. However, as I hope this text demonstrates, such a dichotomization prevents an understanding of the always relevant and at times *decisive* interplay between the 'internal' technical arguments advanced by the revolution's protagonists and their often passionately advocated or defended 'extra-scientific' commitments. My aim has therefore been to provide 'blow by blow' accounts of the development and 'resolution' of major debates of the scientific revolution taking into account the often very important (reciprocal) impact of social, political and religious institutions on the protagonists' different and competing constructions of natural reality. In this context, it is relevant that while the names of Popper, Kuhn, Lakatos and Feyerabend are not to be found in the following pages, the 'Popper-Kuhn debate' and its aftermath have continually informed the writing of this book, thereby making it, I hope, a useful companion text to introductory courses on the philosophy of science. More generally, since an introduction to the scientific revolution ought to be useful not only for students of science concerned with the origins of modern science but also for students of anthropology, history and philosophy undertaking a study of Western man's new and dramatically effective perception of the cosmos and of his relationship to it, I have attempted to provide that degree of technical detail which, while it does sufficient justice to the scientific revolution, also keeps the various 'technical' arguments and debates accessible to non-science students.

In several ways this essay can also be seen as an extension and elaboration of some of the arguments and themes first developed in my book *Liberation and the Aims of Science*. It is also an enlarged extract, complete in itself, of an essay I am currently writing which focuses on the 'male female relation' and its relevance to an understanding of the general development and application of scientific knowledge, a theme developed in a preliminary manner in the present work.

The text opens by presenting a 'world picture'—a cosmology —widely prevalent in sixteenth-century Europe in which the earth is conceived as lying at the centre of a finite cosmos with Christians continually under attack by Satan and his (in)human, mostly female, allies; the aim of Chapter 1 is to examine the developing debate concerning the reality of Satanic witchcraft which by 1600 ended in an emphatic victory for demonologists and witch-hunters. If Chapter 1 presents a picture of no change—or change towards the consolidation of an oppressive cosmology—Chapter 2 presents an account and analysis of a series of arguments and discoveries which by the 1640s had convinced many natural philosophers of the falsity of the Aristotelian-Ptolemaic cosmology. The relative success of the heliocentric world system, however, still left undecided the question of the kind of world this is—in particular the nature of matter and the existence of supernatural forces. Chapter 3 tackles these questions head-on, arguing that it was not obvious in the 1650s whether proponents of a purified natural magic or mechanical philosophy would eventually triumph, thus posing the problem of accounting for the victory by the turn of the century of the extremely implausible cosmology of mechanical philosophy and preformationist *emboîtement*. Chapter 4 resumes the theme of 'occult' forces and seeks to trace important social influences on the work of Isaac Newton, both demonstrating the undoubted explanatory power of Newtonian theory (within the framework of its own explanatory principles), yet making intelligible the source of the particularly deep antagonism to Newton's ideas that prevailed on the Continent until nearly half a century after the publication of the first edition of the *Principia*. Chapter 5 takes up where Chapter 1 left off, arguing that witchcraft trials disappeared during the second half of the seventeenth century as a result of the increasing stability and confidence of privileged classes, their adoption of (a variant of) the mechanical philosophy, and their determination to appropriate the natural (mechanical) world; of relevance to this theme, the cosmology of a man who first and foremost sought to achieve a just social world is contrasted with the cosmology of a major spokesman for the new bourgeois social order. That the new social order was one in which the 'new philosophy' could not be used for the 'relief of man's estate' is strongly suggested. The book ends by emphasizing the relevance of social and sexual stratification for the development of science and the project to appropriate the natural world.

Obviously in the space available to me I have not been able to do more than *sketch* the main outlines of *some* of the debates central to the scientific revolution. However, I trust that the references at the end of the book will enable students to turn to the work of the relevant specialists and at the same time to follow up their own ideas. The book, I hope, will in this way prove to be a stimulating first read. (Parenthetically I might add that whenever I have used and quoted from original sixteenth and seventeenth–century sources I have not attempted, except in one or two cases, to modernize the spelling or punctuation; the original punctuation and spelling help readers, I think, to be more aware that they are studying times very different from their own.)

As will be apparent to any specialist in the period, I am greatly indebted to many historians who have published works on early modern Europe and the scientific revolution. In particular, I should like to mention Christopher Hill, Keith Thomas and Frances Yates whose works, especially *The World Turned Upside Down, Religion and the Decline of Magic,* and *Giordano Bruno and the Hermetic Tradition,* have been sources of continual inspiration. There are also many other historians whose work I have drawn on and to whom I am greatly indebted, in particular E.J. Aiton, I.B. Cohen, A.G. Debus, B.J.T. Dobbs, S. Drake, E.J. Dijksterhuis, J. Farley, J.R. Jacob, M.C. Jacob, A. Koyré, T.S. Kuhn, H.C.E. Midelfort, E.W. Monter, P.M. Rattansi, D.P. Walker, C. Webster and R.S. Westfall, to name but a few. My debt to other authors will, I hope, be apparent from the notes.

In conclusion I wish very much to thank friends and colleagues with whom I have discussed ideas and who helpfully commented on an early draft of this book, especially Bob Golub, Robert McCutcheon, Jerry Ravetz, Keith Roby and Graham Thomas. In particular I owe very special thanks to my friend Francisco Coutinho for his never failing help, criticism and encouragement. I should also like to thank the editor of the Harvester Studies in Philosophy Series, Maggie Boden, for accepting the book in her Series and for making many useful comments on an early draft. I have also benefitted greatly from the efficient and helpful services of the librarians of the

Inter-Library Loans Service of Sussex University Library, the Library of the Wellcome Institute for the History of Medicine in London, and the British Museum Library. I wish as well to thank Peter Morris for drawing the diagrams and Gillian Holmes and Sally Petch for typing sections of one draft. Above all, however, without the constant helpfulness, leg-pulling and matchless typing ability of Freda Williams this book would not even have reached its first typed version, let alone the version the publishers took from me. I hope very much the book is worthy of her kindness and effort.

Chapter 1

THE EXISTENCE OF WITCHES

> Witchcraft is a notion so foreign to us that it is hard for us to appreciate
> Zande convictions about its reality. Let it be remembered that it is no less
> hard for Azande to appreciate our ignorance and disbelief about the subject.
> I once heard a Zande say about us: 'Perhaps in their country people are not
> murdered by witches, but here they are'.
> E.E. Evans-Pritchard, *Witchcraft, Oracles and Magic among the*
> *Azande*, 1937.

> Human collectivities, large and small, certainly are capable of grotesque and
> monstrous deeds—no century has proved it more abundantly than our own.
> Nevertheless, there is no good reason to think that [sabbats] ever happened:
> we have examined case after case, and have found hardly any where the
> accusation did not include manifestly impossible features.
> Norman Cohn, *Europe's Inner Demons*, 1975.

IN 1500 educated people in western Europe believed themselves
living at the centre of a finite cosmos, at the mercy of
(supernatural) forces beyond their control, and certainly continually menaced by Satan and his allies. By 1700 educated
people in western Europe for the most part believed themselves
living in an infinite universe on a tiny planet in (elliptical) orbit
about the sun, no longer menaced by Satan, and confident that
power over the natural world lay within their grasp.

Such a dramatic transformation in human thought and confidence appears even more remarkable when we bear in mind that
for the greater part of these two centuries God-fearing citizens
participated in a ferocious campaign to combat Satanic maleficia
by executing Satan's servants. Although opponents of witch
hunting certainly existed, by the end of the sixteenth century they
had been decisively defeated by the beleaguered defenders of
Christendom. It is indeed the failure of these opponents of witch
hunting—the principal theme of this chapter—that sets the stage
for the profound revolution in Western educated thought which
did occur between roughly 1600 and 1700, a revolution which
ultimately entailed rejection of belief in the possibility of Satanic
witchcraft.

1 *'Superstition' versus 'Reason'*
Let us suppose it might have been the case that God had

1

enchained Satan for a period of 1000 years after the death of Christ before eventually turning him loose for several centuries on a sinful mankind. Certainly there were many people living in western Europe in the seventeenth century who felt that the times could never have been so bad. Mercifully, however, the worst was held to presage the final redemption and comforting prophecies were widespread that Christ would soon return in glory to the earth. Indeed one such belief was that the *annus mirabilis* of 1666 would mark the beginning of the end of the world—a date determined by adding the thousand years' binding of Satan to the number in years of the Beast as given in the Book of Revelation.[1] However, the Second Coming—still awaited by the faithful—was not to be in the seventeenth century. But how were people to know this before the years of 1666 and after had come and gone without witnessing the reign of Christ on earth? Should such believers never have believed in the first place? The evidence supporting such apocalyptic predictions appeared very uncertain even to contemporaries. A sixteenth-century French lawyer, Jean Bodin (who is to be a central protagonist of this chapter), wondered just how it was that men of great authority had felt so confident in interpreting the Bible's obscure apocalyptical writings according to their own particular lights.

But whether or not men and women were living in the last age of the world, witnessing the decay of nature, and waiting for the Divine Restauration, it was clear that they were living in a very terrible age, trapped as they believed themselves to be at the degenerate, corrupt centre of the cosmos. Constant grinding poverty and often famine for the masses, plague and disease, peasant rebellions and millenarian movements, civil wars, wars between emerging nation states, the Protestant challenge to the Catholic Church, the Counter-Reformation, even attacks on the common knowledge of the order of the cosmos: all these phenomena made living in the sixteenth and seventeenth centuries, if a time of creative achievement for a few, a misery and rack for the many. It is with sympathy for the plight of the common man and woman that a social historian appropriately refers to the hundred and ten years between 1550 and 1660 as 'The Iron Century'.[2]

There were, of course, explanations for much of the misery of this age, especially that misery inflicted on the masses of the people and in particular on the peasantry. The Devil was held to be loose in the world and was working in his traditional way through that weaker, more susceptible half of mankind, womankind. Unbelievable wickedness though it was, old peasant women —but other women too—only too readily allied themselves with the Devil in his indefatigable attempts to spread death and desolation among God's people. One could argue over fine details but the generally accepted features of the gigantic conspiracy seemed clear enough. Prolonged frosts and severe storms, disease and unexpected death, male impotency and female barrenness—all these afflictions were caused by evil women using powers given them by Satan in return for their souls on death. During their earthly lives, moreover, Satan and demons would satisfy the depraved carnal appetite of these women with nocturnal intercourse, and at least weekly Satan would preside over an orgiastic sabbat of carnality and wickedness to which the witches (thanks to the power of Satan) would fly on broomsticks lubricated with an unguent derived from the flesh of unbaptised babies.

Against such unmitigated evil both Church and lay authorities, Catholic and Protestant alike, acted without kid gloves. Suspects denounced by neighbours would be tortured into confessing their crimes and, more importantly, into betraying the names of their accomplices. Arrested and tortured in turn, the accomplices would invariably also confess and name yet more accomplices. In this way, by constant vigilance and ruthless procedures, the Holy Office and lay magistrates attempted to obey God's commandment to Moses—'thou shalt not suffer a witch to live'[3]—and to stamp out or at least to keep in check the diabolical conspiracy with which they believed themselves confronted. Indeed, during the sixteenth and seventeenth centuries more women were executed for the crime of witchcraft than for all other crimes put together, the total number of victims reaching tens of thousands, perhaps hundreds of thousands of people, mostly women.[4] In the middle of the nineteenth century, the historian W.E.H. Lecky appropriately commented (and I think his words still hold good) that perhaps never in human history had victims died in such extremes of physical agony and mental anguish: rejected by their next of kin, almost universally hated, perhaps believing themselves truly guilty of witchcraft or knowing themselves to have condemned innocent people to a trial similar to their own, all the time undergoing protracted suffering in custody, the victims of the witchcraze prepared to meet their Creator in a death that was seldom quick and often made deliberately slow.[5]

The witchcraze of the sixteenth and seventeenth centuries which, let us remind ourselves, were the two centuries of the Copernican-Newtonian revolution represents an extreme antithesis to a rational, non-oppressive, non-violent world. Two questions demand answers. What brought the witchcraze to an end and why did whatever brought it to an end not bring into being a society antithetical to the irrationality and sadism characteristic of the witch hunting?

Certainly the beliefs and derivative practices associated with belief in Satanic magic have led several historians to express gratitude for the concurrent rise of science. If we postpone for the moment asking what we mean by 'rational' and 'science', we may note that from the second half of the seventeenth century onwards, reason, rationality, science—call it what you will—has often been acclaimed as bringing to an end the hideous persecution of old women and others for crimes they could not possibly have committed, even if—let us grant—a (very) small percentage of those executed might have wished to commit such crimes or even tried very hard to commit them.

It is worth quoting in full an eyewitness, Thomas Sprat, as he praises what he sees as this particular achievement of the 'real philosophy'—the abolition from people's minds of a world populated and dominated by ghosts and demons and their devilish mischief. In his celebrated *History of the Royal Society of London,* Sprat first identifies the culprits responsible for seducing people's minds into superstition—Homer, Virgil and Ovid in particular—and then he acclaims the agent of liberation:

The *Poets* began of old to impose the deceit. They to make all things look more venerable than they were, devis'd a thousand false *Chimaeras*; on every *Field, River, Grove,* and *Cave,* they bestow'd a *Fantasm* of their own making... And in the modern *Ages* these *Fantastical Forms* were reviv'd, and possess'd *Christendom,* in the very height of the *Scholemens* time: An infinit number of *Fairies* haunted every house; all Churches were fill'd with *Apparitions;* men began to be frighted from their *Cradles,* which fright continu'd to their *Graves,* and their Names also were made the causes of scaring others... But from the time in which the *Real Philosophy* has appear'd, there is scarce any whisper remaining of such *horrors*: Every man is unshaken at those Tales, at which his *Ancestors* trembled: The cours of things goes quietly along, in its own true channel of *Natural Causes* and *Effects.* For this we are beholden to *Experiments;* which though they have not yet completed the discovery of the true world, yet they have already vanquish'd those wild inhabitants of the false worlds, that us'd to astonish the minds of men. A Blessing for which we ought to be thankful, if we remember, that it is one of the greatest Curses that God pronounces on the wicked, *That they shall fear where no fear is.*[6]

What is remarkable about this passage is the confidence with which it is asserted that 'Experiments' have already shown what does *not* exist; it apparently only remains to find out what *does* exist in nature as its course (determined by God) proceeds without possibility of interference from non-material spirits. These are claims, to be sure, of the very greatest importance —but claims that are nowhere substantiated by Sprat!

In the following century of Enlightenment, as executions for witchcraft disappeared accompanied by the removal of the crime itself from statute books, Voltaire, the promulgator of Newtonian cosmology in France, mocked the once widely held belief that incantatory control over the natural world is possible. Of almost household familiarity is his devastatingly cutting remark that it is 'unquestionable that certain words and ceremonies will effectually destroy a flock of sheep if administered with a sufficient portion of arsenic'. Above all, Voltaire explicitly identified the specific agent of human liberation from what had become the cruellest of superstitions: 'Never has there been a more universal empire than that of the devil'. 'What has dethroned him?' Voltaire answers in one word, 'Reason'![7]

In the twentieth century historians have not neglected what they perceive to be this liberating, spectacular, achievement of modern science. In a not atypical passage one historian writing in the 1930s confidently asserted that the force that killed off witchcraft was 'the spirit of science with its revelation [!] of a new world of law and reason in which there is no place for either magic or devil'. More recently the historian Hugh Trevor-Roper has similarly asserted that 'what ultimately destroyed the witch-craze . . . was the new philosophy, a philosophical revolution which changed the whole concept of Nature and its operations'. Trevor-Roper explains further: 'That revolution did not occur within the narrow field of demonology . . . It occurred in a far wider field, and the men who made it did not launch their attack on so marginal an area of Nature as demonology. The attack was directed at the centre; and when it had prevailed at the centre, there was no need to struggle for the outworks—they had been turned.'[8]

Now this may be the case. If belief in Satanic witchcraft did not wither away 'of its own accord', then something destroyed the belief of two centuries' duration together with the associated practices of extirpating the unfortunate people believed to be Satan's agents. That something may very well have been the 'new philosophy' even if, as will be argued later, the witchcraze was in part exacerbated, not attenuated, by the predominant Christian response to some of the claims of the scientific revolution's first protagonists—the natural magicians. Be this as it may, it does appear plausible that an examination of the rise and decline of belief in Satanic witchcraft will serve to throw valuable light on factors underlying the scientific revolution. But this is not the only reason for beginning an investigation into the rise of science with a discussion of the witchcraze. For since (I agree with Herbert Marcuse) the desire to reduce human suffering is an essential cornerstone of any rational endeavour, the end of belief in the possibility of Satanic witchcraft is of paramount importance, and an examination of the 'pseudo-science' of demonology thus becomes an integral part of a discussion of the scientific revolution.[9] Superstition versus reason? Let us see.

2 Feminine Evil and Satanic Powers: Believers and Sceptics

The witch-hunters' case: Kramer and Sprenger
In 1486 a book was published that was to become a landmark in the growing debate concerning the reality of and measures to be taken against Satanic witchcraft. Entitled *Malleus Maleficarum* (*The Hammer of the Witches*), this *magnum opus* by two Dominican inquisitors was a searing indictment of what the priests believed to be female evil and Satan's conspiracy against the Christian faithful. These two priests, Henry Kramer and James Sprenger, had been appointed by Pope Innocent VIII as special inquisitors to root out witchcraft and it was with the Pope's Bull that Kramer and Sprenger began their account of the new and virulent form of witchcraft with which they maintained Christianity had been recently afflicted.

The Pope in his Bull listed the crimes of the witches against Christianity, principal accusations being that they destroy crops, cause illness, render men impotent and women barren. Innocent VIII required his two inquisitors to be offered every possible help in their task of identifying and punishing Satan's servants.

The argument of *Malleus Maleficarum* has the following central features. In the first place, because of Biblical testimony it is heretical to doubt the existence of witches. Apart from the fact that the wisdom of all ages acknowledges their unwelcome reality, the Bible would obviously not command witches to be put to death if they did not exist. Would that there were no witches living in present times but unfortunately such is not the case; indeed they have increased greatly 'in this twilight and evening of the world' and their crimes and evils are evident. The inquisitors lament that 'we dare not refrain from inquiring into them lest we imperil our own salvation'.[10]

The witches are held to perform their evil deeds with the assistance of Satan and demons. Although the existence of demons is never doubted by Kramer and Sprenger, they do refer in passing to the heretical belief that demons do not exist and that so-called encounters with them are only the figments of imagination of deluded brains. However, such an opinion obviously runs directly contrary to the Bible, the Church Fathers and, once again, to the wisdom of the ages. Demons are omnipresent. In particular, as Succubi, they visit male witches at night whose semen they use, now as Incubi, to impregnate female witches and hence increase the number of Satan's servants. Despite the undoubted importance of Satan and his demons in witchcraft, Kramer and Sprenger acknowledge that it is still necessary to refute the arguments of those who insist that the crimes witches commit arise not from the actions of Satan and demons but either from the witches' knowledge of the occult properties of things or as a result of the incantations they mutter under a favourable influence of the stars. The first argument, however, scarcely needs refutation given that the crimes of witches are in general well beyond the powers of natural bodies, although not beyond the powers of Satan since he has knowledge of *all* of nature and can work effects that have the appearance of being miraculous but, of course, are not so. (Only God can work true miracles by causing effects *outside* the bounds of nature.) Also and very importantly, from Isaiah, c 28: v 15, it is known that witches enter into a formal pact with Satan: 'Because ye have said, we have made a covenant with death, and with hell are we at agreement.' All witchcraft is necessarily *Satanic* witchcraft. As to the second argument, the Dominican priests declare that witches' incantations have no power in themselves but are directed at planetary Intelligences. However such Intelligences desire the good of mankind and hence in no way cooperate with witches in the committing of their crimes. The conclusion again follows that witches achieve their malevolent, destructive effects only with the aid of Satan and demons. But are *all* violent storms and severe illnesses the result of witchcraft? Obviously not, and care must be taken to distinguish diabolically caused from natural phenomena. In the case of illness, this is relatively easy for when an illness fails to respond to or even gets worse under treatment, or when an illness suddenly strikes down a previously healthy person, then the presence of witchcraft is indisputable. But cannot the Devil work on his own? In general God permits Satan and demons to achieve destructive effects only with the collaboration of humans —nearly always women—who *of their own free will* give themselves to the service of mankind's and God's enemy. Erroneous therefore is the claim that demons both commit the crimes and deceive mentally ill old women into believing that the horrendous events have been caused by them, not by the demons. Witches must be adjudged guilty of intent, cause and effect.

But why are the overwhelming number of witches women? The two Dominicans explain that women more than men tend to extremes in both spiritual goodness and depravity. It is a sad reality, however, that in general women tend to only one of these two extremes—the one abhorrent to both God and man. This is only partly because of woman's inferior intellect. The real reason, Kramer and Sprenger insist, is because of her excessive carnality, the two priests reiterating an indictment of women that would become commonplace in the sixteenth century:

All witchcraft comes from carnal lust, which is in women insatiable. See Proverbs XXX: There are three things that are never satisfied, yea, a fourth thing which says not, it is enough; that is, the mouth of the womb. Wherefore for the sake of fulfilling their lusts they consort even with devils.[11]

Whatever else it is, the *Malleus Maleficarum* is a misogynist's textbook. The reader is informed that innumerable is the number of girls who sleep with their lovers in the expectation of marriage, and, when disappointed and everywhere despised, then turn to demons and witchcraft both to gain revenge and to satisfy every sort of lechery. Married women, too, seek first and foremost carnal rather than maternal satisfaction in that shameful act necessary for procreation. Although a husband may piously say to his wife after intercourse that he hopes she conceives, only too often does the good man hear the evil reply 'May the child go to the Devil!'[12] Even when conception does follow intercourse, women's evil is far from over. For midwives 'who surpass all others in wickedness' have an excellent opportunity to kill the unfortunate baby and to make use of its body for Satanic purposes—a crime that is apparently as widespread as it is loathsome and abominable.[13]

Do witches fly? There are those who assert that they do so only in their imagination or in vivid dreams, backing up their prejudice with reference to a misunderstood *Canon Episcopi* of the fourth century which claimed that women do not really fly at night. Now, of course, not all flights are real and it is necessary to distinguish carefully between illusion and reality. But those who maintain that the Devil cannot transport people by air are heretically wrong—the Devil transported Christ himself (with God's permission) to the top of first a temple and then a mountain. Furthermore the confessions of women convicted of witchcraft amply reveal that they undergo bodily transportation. While it may be true that husbands have sometimes sworn that supposedly absent wives were all the time asleep in the marital bed, this objection has no force at all, such are the powers of deception of Satan and demons. For demons can easily assume the shape of the absent women and thus deceive husbands and other watchers. Kramer and Sprenger ominously inform the reader that 'In the same way all other objections can be answered.'[14]

Having thus established to their satisfaction that witches really can fly, the two Dominicans explain how such flights are achieved: 'They take the unguent which...they make at the devil's instruction from the limbs of children, particularly of those whom they have killed before baptism, and annoint with it a chair or a broomstick; whereupon they are immediately carried up into the air, either by day or by night and either visibly or, if they wish, invisibly; for the devil can conceal a body by the interposition of some other substance...'.[15]

Kramer and Sprenger next advise inquisitors on how best to answer some of the doubts that misguided but well-meaning laymen are likely to raise. God permits evil in the world, they have already explained, because if men were not able to choose between good and evil, then they would not possess free will and this gift by God is a most precious and desirable possession, even if it is one that gives rise to the existence of evil. But from the evil that God thus permits, much good is subsequently generated which would not be possible were there no evil: for through the persecution of Christians came the patience of the martyrs and 'through the works of witches comes the purgation or proving of the faith of the just'. As to why witches do not become rich, the answer is because the Devil likes to show his contempt for God by buying witches at the lowest possible price; and also, Kramer and Sprenger add, 'lest they should be conspicuous by their riches'.[16] As to why witches do not succeed in killing off all their enemies and wreaking even more havoc than they do, this is simply because God does not permit it; and, very importantly, God does not permit witches any power at all against those men who prosecute them and administer justice (although it is still wise to take certain precautions).

How best to contain, hopefully to extirpate, this Satanic conspiracy? Kramer and Sprenger explain that it is virtually useless to rely on normal judicial procedures which require an accuser either to prove her or his case against the accused or to suffer the talion, a punishment which could be exceedingly severe. Since by the nature of the crime of witchcraft conclusive proof is extraordinarily difficult to establish, inquisitorial procedures must be used if victims of witchcraft are to have sufficient courage to voice their suspicions and offer evidence. Under such procedures, not only does the law of the talion not apply but members of communities are required to identify suspected witches as a duty while it is the inquisitors who assume responsibility for ensuring that witches answer to the law of God. Accordingly, Kramer and Sprenger advise that the process of witch hunting should begin with a general citation displayed in parish churches or town halls of the following nature (the witchcraze was a persecution started 'from above'):

WHEREAS, we, the Vicar of such and such Ordinary . . . By the authority which we exercise in this district, and in virtue of holy obedience and under pain of excommunication, we direct, command, require, and admonish that within the space of twelve days . . . they should reveal it unto us if anyone know, see, or have heard that any person is reported to be a heretic or a witch, or if any is suspected especially of such practices as cause injury to men, cattle, or the fruits of the earth, to the loss of the State.[17]

The procedures to be used in the interrogation of a suspected witch are complex but may be summarized as follows. Although apprehension of the suspect is not a dangerous undertaking when carried out by officers of the law, certain precautions should be taken such as removing the suspect from contact with the ground by placing her in a basket or on a plank of wood. Lest her glance bewitch and soften a judge's heart, wherever possible she should be led backwards into the courtroom. A person gravely suspected of witchcraft because of her activities and notoriety has thereby convicted herself and the judge must ensure that she is not allowed to escape. In particular no advocate is admitted on behalf of a gravely suspected witch. However, since common justice demands that a witch confess her crimes before being sentenced to death, a confession must be extracted, where appropriate, by the use of torture.[18] Although Kramer and Sprenger advise that torture must not be indiscriminately used since people vary greatly in their sensitivity to pain, some people falsely confessing to crimes at the 'very gentlest' tortures such as being suspended by their thumbs, nevertheless such evil people as witches will confess their crimes under torture only when compelled to do so by a holy angel or if and when they are abandoned by the Devil because of their failure to give themselves totally and wholeheartedly to him.[19] It is a matter of common sense that care should always be taken to shave the suspect's body and to remove all concealed charms that may hinder the efficacy of torture. Torture is permitted for three consecutive days, but is not to be immediately repeated 'unless there should be some fresh indication of its probable success'. Those who still preserve their silence to the end are truly the Devil's own. Indeed, a 'gravely suspected' person who does not confess after such torture is to be kept imprisoned and periodically tortured, or can be sentenced to death without confession.[20] Since, however, the overwhelming majority of witches do confess, the truth of the accusations is thereby proved.

So much for the arguments, or rather assertions, of the *Malleus Maleficarum.* Between 1487 and 1520 the book was reprinted 14 times but thereafter was not reprinted again for nearly 60 years.[21]

It should be noted that, landmark though the book became and encyclopedic its content, there were two extremely important features of witchcraft and Satanic magic that Sprenger and Kramer did not discuss, although both features were prevalent in demonology before 1487 and very much more so during the sixteenth century. The first feature is the mark that the Devil was supposed to leave on his servant after the pact had been formally concluded; discovery of the mark—a major means of identifying a witch—was made possible by the claim that the mark is insensitive and fails to bleed when punctured with a sharp instrument. The second feature the *Malleus* failed to discuss was the witches' sabbat, the nocturnal rendezvous of witches in celebration of Satan who usually presided in the form of a goat. It was to obtain information about accomplices present at sabbats that suspects were subjected to yet more torture after confession of their own guilt. Thus the first major opponents of the witchcraze in the sixteenth century found themselves confronted not only with the beliefs elaborated in the *Malleus Maleficarum* but also with belief in the reality of sabbats without which there would have been no chain reactions of cases as confessed witches proceeded under duress to name accomplices. Ironically enough, before dissenters such as Johann Weyer published in the second half of the sixteenth century, witch hunting had been a rather sporadic activity; but after the 'refutations' by demonologists of the dissenters' arguments, the witchcraze reached a greatly increased level of intensity, particularly in the 70 years between 1580 and 1650. Let us examine this debate.

The witchcraft debate to 1600
In the first place why should any educated person during the sixteenth century have doubted or denied the overall claims advanced in the *Malleus Maleficarum*? To the extent that prosecutions were mostly restricted to old peasant women, educated people were not provoked into dissent by fear that they might be accused of Satanic witchcraft. In any case, accusations against respectable citizens would not necessarily have brought into question the reality of Satanic witchcraft but only the reliability of procedures for identifying witches.

Illness and sudden death, storms, droughts and frosts—these phenomena were as undesirable as they were real, frightening and unwelcome. But were witches responsible? If we recall that nearly all societies have believed in the reality of witchcraft together with flights of witches to nocturnal gatherings, educated belief in the reality of witchcraft in early modern Europe is perhaps no longer surprising. Christianity had, however, added to witchcraft the new and lethal ingredient of belief in the Devil and his malevolent powers. Any denial of Satanic witchcraft therefore smacked very much of heresy, if not of outright atheism, and it is difficult to see how any sincere Christian could have brought herself or himself to doubt the menace of Satan and his servants. Nor why any sincere Christian should have been motivated to so doubt.

Nevertheless, disagreement over fine but important details was clearly possible. Did Satan cause the storms and deceive witches into thinking they had done so or had Satan truly given such power to his servants? If the latter, what was the nature of that power? Could witches really fly and attend sabbats or did such phenomena exist only in the imagination of evil women? Or of ill, senile women? If the latter, ought not the women to receive the help of physicians rather than the attentions of the executioner? Could even voluntary confessions be taken at face value? Any educated person who had appreciable doubt that *all* convicted witches were evil-minded people who had freely become enemies of Christianity would surely have had to wrestle with a troubled, heavy conscience, given the severity of the trial and the often automatic execution. And reason for doubt there obviously was. On the other hand, doubt of this kind would not necessarily have called into question the necessity of legal action against witches, but would rather have given rise to a demand to ensure a 'fair' trial for the accused. With these preliminary remarks in mind, let us look at the impassioned protest of perhaps the most famous dissenter of the sixteenth century, Johann Weyer.

Against witch hunting

Johann Weyer (1515?–88) was a Protestant physician at the Rhineland court of Cleves who could not bring himself to believe that senile, uneducated people—least of all women whose minds and understanding are weaker than those of men—could ever be sufficiently empowered by the Devil so as to be able to generate storms or cause illness. This belief underlies his influential book *On the Tricks of Demons*, published in 1563, and on this belief his case rested.

The Devil was ubiquitous in the world, especially now 'in the last days', and with God's permission could raise storms and undertake similar, apparently marvellous, always malevolent actions.[22] While educated magicians could by their elaborate esoteric procedures conjure, summon and command the Devil and his demons (and should be severely punished for so doing), this was obviously beyond the power of old, stupid peasant women. If it was the case that such women really believed that they had caused storms, this could only be explained by the Devil's trickery. Knowing that a storm was approaching or having (with God's permission) brought it into being, the Devil would encourage his senile servant to mutter an imprecation whereupon, the storm appearing, the old woman would congratulate herself on her power and wickedness. There was even the very real possibility that the old woman had made no pact at all with the Devil but that the Devil had taken advantage of melancholy and illness to deceive the old woman into thinking she had done so. In both cases Weyer recommended that Christian mercy and forgiveness should follow successful medical treatment provided the witch truly repented for any small part she may have freely played in encouraging the Devil's attention. As Weyer later pointed out—or rather asserted (in a letter to a Dr Johann Brenz)—God is merciful and sinners and heretics at the Last Judgment 'will not be severely punished if they repent, confess their error, and abandon it'.[23]

The same divine mercy, however, would not necessarily be shown to the lawyers, judges and executioners who so brutally tortured these helpless old women into confessing whatever ridiculous crimes they were accused of. 'Thus it is', Weyer complained bitterly, 'that recently a poor old woman was so broken by torture that after condemnation to the stake, she confessed that she had caused the intense and continued cold of the preceding winter of 1566'. But nothing could be as absurd as this confession, Weyer protested; these old women when tortured will confess anything. Indeed there is no escape for them: even if they die under torture the joyful cry goes up that the Devil has claimed his own. 'But', Weyer cried out eloquently, 'when the great Searcher of Hearts, from whom naught is hidden, shall appear, your deeds shall be made manifest, oh cruel tyrants, blood-thirsty judges, butchers, torturers, and truculent robbers, who have cast off humanity and know no mercy. Thus I summon you to the tribunal of the Great Judge, who shall decide between you and me where the truth which you have trodden under foot and buried shall arise and confound you, demanding vengeance for your robberies.'[24]

The truth of the matter, Weyer insisted, is that these old women are not capable of doing anything. But could the Devil transport them to their sabbats? Weyer is inconsistent on this point. Obviously Satan has the power to transport bodies —witness his transportation of Christ, and Weyer himself has seen a person being transported by a devil. Nevertheless Weyer is adamant that the sabbat is a diabolical illusion and so are witches' flights. Certainly the Devil's unguent has no power in itself to transport witches on their notorious broomsticks. As to the witches' removal of children's corpses from their graves in order to make the unguent from their thighbones, this is an action possible only by those who have cast aside any trace of human sentiment: '[I]t is', pleaded Weyer somewhat ingenuously, 'so inhuman, horrible, cruel, and hard to believe, that even if I saw it with my own eyes I would rather believe that my eyes were charmed by the spell of such a spectacle than confess to seeing this wicked and ultra-tragic thighbone, which surpasses all belief'.[25]

As for those physicians who claim witchcraft is responsible for illnesses they cannot cure, or whose incompetence merely exacerbates illnesses, Weyer has nothing but contempt. Senile uneducated women, no matter how much the women believe otherwise, cannot cause illness; those illnesses that are untreatable because of our ignorance can be treated only by prayer. Catholic counter-magic, claimed Weyer, is as blasphemous as it is useless. Indeed, the Protestant physician's book was not only a polemic against witch hunting; it was also, and very dangerously so, a polemic against what Weyer believed to be the (useless and idolatrous) magic he found so pervasive in Catholicism.

Weyer's heartfelt, closing recommendation to his fellow Christians was unambiguous, 'Love men, kill errors, fight for the truth without any cruelty', advice he reinforced by repeating St Augustine's warning that men who are cruel in their cruzading zeal 'do not know with what pain truth is discovered, and with what great difficulty one guards oneself against errors'.

If Weyer's book had convinced his educated contemporaries, Protestant and Catholic alike, that the suicidal confessions of old peasant women were necessarily the consequence of either torture, illness or both, that they could in no way be believed, and that in any case ignorant, senile women were incapable of committing any crime (except that of common poisoning), then the witchcraze would never have occurred. At most there would have been sporadic burning of luckless individuals. Certainly this long book of over 170 chapters was widely promulgated: four Latin editions appeared between 1563 and 1568, German and French translations appeared in 1567, the book was republished in an enlarged Latin edition in 1577 and two years later the enlarged version was translated into French.[26] But Weyer's series of assertions failed to convince. Above all, Weyer's masterpiece provoked a towering rebuttal from Jean Bodin, one of the foremost intellectuals of early modern Europe.

For witch hunting
It would take us too far astray to trace Jean Bodin's intellectual

achievements before he turned his public attention to the question of witches. Suffice it to say that in 1568 he had published a tract arguing the reality and nature of the inflation that had overtaken Europe, following this success in 1576 with his *Six Bookes of a Commonweale*, a classic of political theory that ran to 28 editions in five languages within 30 years of publication. Yet this sophisticated political and economic theorist was the man who was so largely responsible for annulling the ideas of Weyer and for putting the European witchcraze firmly back on its vengeful course. His book *On the Demonic Madness of Witches*, to which he appended an explicit refutation of Weyer, was translated into German and French in 1581, only one year after its publication in Latin, and, in all, ran to 15 editions in four languages in 25 years.[27] What, then, was Jean Bodin's conception of the cosmos and why was he so sure that Weyer was not only wrong but a diabolical double-agent? We are fortunate in that a year before his death in 1597 Bodin published his *Drama of Universal Nature* and three years earlier completed an unpublished *Colloquium of the Seven about Secrets of the Sublime*. The elements of Bodin's world view were thus mapped out by Bodin himself in considerable detail.

Above all else, Bodin desired and appreciated order: 'There is nothing in the world', he writes, 'pleasanter to behold, or which more deliciously revives the mind, or which serves us more commodiously, than order'. It therefore follows that any religion, no matter how superstitious, is infinitely better than atheism: 'For that superstition how great so ever it be, doth yet hold men in feare and awe, both of the laws and of the magistrates, as also in mutuall duties and offices one of them towards another; whereas meere Atheisme doth utterly root out of mens minds all the feare of doing evill.'[28] This being so, how utterly detestable and loathsome is witchcraft, that deliberate rejection of God in favour of Satan—provided, of course, the rejection is deliberate and of the witches' free choice.

Is, then, Weyer correct in his assertion that old peasant women convicted of witchcraft are all either ill with melancholy and thus not responsible for their actions or entirely innocent but forced to confess to deeds they have not committed because of torture? Bodin opens his *Demonic Madness of Witches* by recounting the case of one Jeanne Harvillier of which he had personal knowledge. At the age of 50 Jeanne Harvillier had freely confessed to the practice of witchcraft since the age of 12 and had been known for years by her neighbours to be a witch. Could she have been a melancholic all that time? The idea is as ridiculous as the belief that throughout history all those women that had freely confessed to witchcraft had been melancholics. In any case, it is well known that women are in general healthier than men because once a month they are able to expel bad blood. Bodin cites the ancient authorities Hippocrates and Galen to refute Weyer: women simply do not suffer from melancholia (there is no discussion as to what might happen to women after menopause). Weyer is either ignorant or very wicked. But he is a physician and therefore not ignorant!

But what of confessions produced under the duress of torture? Bodin claims that in the first place, a suspect does not find herself questioned under torture because she has been seen to have enjoyed a blameless life but, on the contrary, because she has been accused of witchcraft by her neighbours. Furthermore, although Weyer is quite correct to stress that little attention should be paid to confessions 'unless these deal with things that are true and possible', Bodin points out that Weyer's 'assumption that nothing is possible in law that is not possible in nature is not only wrong but wholly impious'. For it is obvious that while hail and thunderstorms cannot be made by natural means, 'since nothing is so alien to nature as that which happens violently and recklessly', they can be and are made diabolically. If regrettably Satan cannot be brought into court, nevertheless the duty of judges is to 'diminish the scope of his power by taking from him those witches who help him, pray to him, pay obeisance to him, and carry out his instructions'.[29]

Moreover, since the Bible, ancient authorities, and the Church Fathers all confirm that Satanic magic and witches exist, it is apparent that witches' confessions refer to phenomena that are possible, not impossible. Conversely, the free confessions of witches, Weyer notwithstanding, confirm the reality of Satanic magic. Indeed, these witches confess that their carnal intercourse with demons takes place while they are awake, not asleep, thus proving the reality of their diabolical experiences. Likewise, the witch's pact with Satan is a reality, so are witches' flights and their sabbats. Weyer's tortuous reasonings on the matter of witches' flights do not pass unappreciated by Bodin: 'It is thus extreme folly for Weyer to confess that Simon the Sorcerer flew through the air, and to maintain that the other Sorcerers deceive themselves in thinking they are transported through the air to their assemblies.' Weyer admits the Devil transported Christ to the summit of a temple and then to a mountain: 'Has the Devil less power now than he had then?' asks Bodin. (A few years later Reginald Scot will take very careful note of these remarks.) In his *Tricks of Demons* Weyer writes that he himself in broad daylight before an audience had witnessed the levitation of a witch into the air; he gives several other examples of diabolical transports and declares that such things are certain; yet, Bodin notes, Weyer says exactly the contrary in his later work *De Lamiis*. 'In this', mocks Bodin, 'one can see a light brain which gets confused on every topic'.[30] Bodin agrees that of course witches' flights *seem* incredible but they must not be disbelieved on mere grounds of incredibility. For since many natural things are incredible and some of them incomprehensible, 'how much more incomprehensible are the powers of supernatural intelligences and the actions of spirits'. In particular, 'those who say that it is impossible that an evil spirit carry a man 100 or 200 leagues from his house have not considered the fact that the heavens and all the great celestial bodies make their movement [around the earth] in twenty-four hours'.[31] Although the senses do not allow one to deny this phenomenon, it is nevertheless incomprehensible. Who then dares deny the diabolical transport of bodies on grounds of incomprehensibility? Sceptics, Bodin writes in the Preface to his *Demonic Madness*, should not be so obstinate as to deny the reality of a phenomenon merely because they cannot perceive the underlying cause.

Again, the results of witches' sabbats is confirmed by witches' confessions. Not only that, it is widely known that on one occasion three intrepid spies secretly observing a sabbat were discovered by the Devil and beaten to the point of death, surviving just long enough to tell their unfortunate story. A participant in Bodin's unpublished *Colloquium* speaks for all when he declares: 'Indeed, I have been overcome before this with an incredible desire to view with these eyes the flights of witches and the meeting with demons. However, when I had compared all the writings on this subject of the ancients, Greek and Latin, and all the divine and human laws from the most remote antiquity with the accounts of fortune tellers, the charges, confessions and depositions of witnesses to such associations, I decided I must give assent at the least to their existence. I also thought I ought not to set my life in jeopardy as to whether the things which were being commonly reported were true or not.' And he concludes thoughtfully: 'Furthermore, I was mindful of Aesop's fox who, when invited by the lion, refused to go to his cave to dine "because footprints that lead all in one direction and none in the other terrify me".'[32]

Convinced of the reality of witchcraft and Satanic magic, Bodin explains in his refutation of Weyer why it is that 'for every male witch there are fifty female witches'. It is certainly not because women are frail for—more so than men—they often remain stubbornly silent under torture. Neither is it because they lack sense and intelligence. Bodin agrees with Sprenger and Kramer:

it is because women far more than men suffer from 'bestial cupidity', and it is for this reason that the great Plato placed woman between man and the brute beast.[33] Women in general, Bodin believes, bring men to ruin: there can be no greater curse wished upon an enemy than that he be ruled by women.

Since women who disobey and betray their husbands deserve death (and Bodin believes it necessary to grant husbands authority of life and death over their wives), how much more do women—and men—deserve death who renounce God to serve Satan, thereby committing the most grievous crime of all. Prosecution must be rigorous in the extreme since not one witch in a million would be accused and punished if the procedure were governed by ordinary rules. Moreover, because failure to prosecute and execute witches can only further offend God and provoke His wrath, leniency towards witches is a crime as great as witchcraft itself and is invariably the action of secret witches. In Bodin's opinion, human punishment of witches should serve to remind the faithful of the divine punishment of eternal damnation. A gruesome observation follows: 'Whatever punishment we can order against witches by gradually roasting and burning them over a fire', concludes Bodin, 'is very little in comparison with . . . the eternal agonies which are prepared for them [in hell], since the fire here cannot last for much longer than an hour before the witches are dead'. Whereas, it would seem, Weyer's Christian God is merciful given true repentance, Bodin's Old Testament God administers absolute justice. This is highlighted by the fact that whereas Bodin necessarily sees Weyer as a witch protecting where he can his diabolical accomplices, Weyer's Protestant colleague Erastus excuses Weyer on the grounds that his fellow physician had been overcome by 'misplaced, sentimental humanitarianism'.[34]

Contemporaries, it would appear, judged that the case had now been won by believers in the reality of witchcraft and by proponents of severe punishment. Weyer had been shown up as, at best, a muddled misguided do-gooder, at worst, a diabolical double-agent. Indeed, as a specialist in European witchcraft has emphasized, the central feature of witchcraft trials is their remarkable extension after 1580. For in nearly all regions of Europe the intensity of witch hunting peaked dramatically at some time between 1580 and 1650.[35] I therefore conclude this brief introduction to the witchcraft debate by looking at two opponents of the witchcraze writing in the 1580s, the Protestant Englishman Reginald Scot and the Catholic French lawyer and essayist Michel de Montaigne. This is followed with an exposition of the successful arguments of a French judge, Nicolas Remy, who personally tried and condemned to death over 800 people for the crime of witchcraft. But first the opposition.

Against belief in Satanic power
Four years after the publication of Bodin's *Demonic Madness* a radical attack on belief in the reality of Satanic magic appeared in England. Written by Reginald Scot, a Kentish county squire and hop grower, educated at Oxford University but without taking a degree, this work not only attempted to deny the essential feature of witchcraft beliefs, namely belief in the ability of the Devil to cause marvellous effects, but in addition came dangerously close to denying belief in the reality of the Devil himself.

Like Weyer, Scot could not bring himself to believe that uneducated, senile women had the power, no matter how obtained, to cause illness, raise storms, and to fly on broomsticks or other missiles. Whereas Weyer's argument had foundered, however, because Weyer admitted the reality of Satan's magic and of the ability of educated male magicians to command demons, Scot attempted to remove Satan and demons lock, stock and barrel. From a Christian writer *The Discoverie of Witchcraft* is a devastating attack on witch-hunters and it takes Scot to the very brink of atheism. One more step and all is nature and natural magic.

Scot's God is omnipotent and basically generous. He ordered nature in its course and all storms and illnesses are either natural phenomena or sent by God and by God alone as punishment for sins. To suggest that witches have the same power as God is blasphemous indeed. Certainly evil old women exist as do insane ones. But to suppose that God would not forgive the former upon true repentance is to have a mean and false opinion of God.

Scot can scarcely find words appropriate enough to express his sense of outrage at what he sees as the credulity and cruelty of educated men. Although it may well be that the witch-hunters are 'not of the inferior sort of writers', nor are they all 'papists', nevertheless it can only be their names that give credit to their cause, certainly it is not their writings. For the witch-hunters agree among themselves only in 'cruelties, absurdities and impossibilities'. Yet, such is the authority of the witch-hunters, their 'monsterous lies' will not be easy to suppress. Scot, however, tells his readers that he has on his side 'reason and common sense' and the credulity of the witch-hunters he will deride with laughter. But their cruelty he will only be able to lament with tears. Before Scot commences on the main argument he makes a vital claim: no matter how ancient an opinion is, 'truth must not be measured by time: for everie old opinion is not sound'.[36] A battery of ancient authors all testifying to the same opinion will not therefore impress Scot unless, of course, good arguments are advanced as well. In the case of the witch-hunters, however, the arguments are pathetic and the evidence marshalled totally inadequate to warrant such extreme consequences.

It is obvious, says Scot, why many of the old women come to believe themselves witches and to be believed by neighbours to be witches. They are uneducated and poor, they beg, sometimes they are refused charity and they curse. Inevitably, sooner or later, one of the people thus cursed suffers a mishap. He or she puts it down to the scolding old woman, the old woman does likewise. After a few such chance events both become convinced: the old woman knows herself to be a witch and the neighbours likewise know her to be a witch. Trial, conviction and execution follow. But Scot wants to know how good Christians can believe that such crimes are possible. There are all kinds of causes for mishaps and misfortunes. Why, then, must the cause of calamities be attributed to witches? 'Such mischeefes as are imputed to witches', Scot writes, 'happen where no witches are; yea and continue when witches are hanged and burnt: whie then should we attribute such effect to that cause, which being taken awaie, happeneth neverthelesse?' Scot drives his point home. If all the devils in hell were dead and all the witches in England executed, there would still be rain, hail and tempests just as there are now. Then again, Scot adds, 'if all the old women in the world were witches; and all the priests, conjurers: we should not have a drop of raine, nor a blast of wind the more or the lesse for them'.[37]

Scot certainly agrees that there really exist old women who wish their not so neighbourly neighbours ill and even wish a plague on the entire community. What should be their punishment? Scot reminds his fellow Christians of the offence of Peter, privileged to have lived with and to have been instructed by Christ Himself, and yet, though forewarned only a few hours previously, 'forsooke, thrise denied, and abandoned his maister'. Yet Christ forgave Peter and continued to love and trust him. But an old woman confessing to witchcraft cannot possibly fall as far as Peter fell 'bicause she never ascended halfe so manie steps'. Illiterate, destitute and alone, Christian duty towards her is clear. At the very least, pleads Scot, 'I see not, but we may shew compassion upon these poore soules; if they shew themselves sorrowfull for their misconceipts and wicked imaginations'.[38] Needless to say, this is just the sort of attitude that Bodin believed so dangerous.

As for the pact with the Devil, all this is nonsense. Neither are voluntary confessions to be believed. Scot gives an example known to him personally of a woman, low in spirits, who confessed to her husband to having 'bargained and given hir soule to the divell, to be delivered unto him within short space'. Furthermore, she confessed to having bewitched her husband and children. Her husband, however, comforted her by declaring that no harm could come to him or the children because of their faith in God, and that Christ would 'unwitch' them all. At the midnight hour that the Devil was to come for the woman's soul, terrible sounds were heard outside the window but the husband's and woman's prayers, they believed, prevented the Devil from entering the bedroom. Now, concluded Scot, Bodin would have had no hesitation in executing the woman and if any harm had happened to either husband or children few judges would not have attributed the misfortune to bewitchment. But, argued Scot, the woman was guilty of nothing even though she believed herself worthy of death. She had done harm but that was only to herself. As for the terrible noise, it turned out that a trapped sheep had been eaten by a dog outside the window! The woman recovered, 'remaineth a right honest woman, far from such impietie, and ashamed of hir imaginations, which she perceiveth to have growne through melancholie'.[39]

However, women confess not only to making a pact with the Devil but also to carnal acts with demons and flights to sabbats. Scot is almost speechless at the folly of people's credulity. There is only one explanation of the first phenomenon: 'this *Incubus* is a bodilie disease... although it extend unto the trouble of the mind'. Likewise the killing of children, the boiling down of their fat to make potions, the subsequent flights to sabbats—such confessions are the result of torture. No human beings are *that* evil. Scot writes in anguish (paraphrasing Weyer): '[I]t is so horrible, unnaturall, unlikelie and unpossible; that if I should behold such things with mine eies, I should rather thinke my selfe dreaming, dronken or some waie deprived of my senses; than give credit to so horrible and filthie matters.' To prove that Satanic transport of witches is possible, the witch-hunters all refer to Satan's transporting of Christ to the temple summit and mountain top. But does this prove, asks Scot, that the Devil would do the same for witches? In any case, adds Scot, it is to be hoped that the witch-hunters do not suppose 'that Christ had made anie ointments, or entred into anie league with the divell...'.[40] Scot wisely refrains from asking Christians if they suppose Christ to have made the trips on a broomstick. The most probable interpretation of the entire episode, Scot concludes, is that with God's permission Christ witnessed a vision in which the Devil tempted him as described. Scot is clearly determined to give the witch-hunters not a single pillar on which their elaborate demonologies can remain standing. Certainly God performed miracles as related in the Bible but since Christ's resurrection no more miracles have been or will be performed. This is because the Christian religion has been sufficiently established. The belief that God permits witches very remarkable if not supernatural powers is as false as it is blasphemous. God is the sole magician who transcends nature. Spiritual and demonic magic do not exist.

Whereas, as we have seen, Weyer believed in the magic of educated male practitioners, Scot offers only withering sarcasm. Such conjurors 'deale with no inferiour causes: these fetch divels out of hell, and angels out of heaven; these raise up what bodies they list, though they were dead, buried, and rotten long before'. And their means are most impressive: 'These are no small fooles, they go not to worke with a baggage tode, or a cat, as witches doo; but with a kind of majestie, and with authoritie they call up by name, and have at their commandement seventie and nine principall and princelie divels, who have under them, as their ministers, a great multitude of legions of pettie divels.' Scot then lists and describes the various devils, and with which signs, images, charms and incantations they may be called and bidden to carry out the conjuror's commands. But the Kentish gentleman can hardly control his derision: his very exposition of these means is, he thinks, their sufficient refutation. For what the reader will observe is a 'disordered heap' of blind, superstitious ceremonies 'which are so far from building up the endevors of these blacke art practitioners, that they doo altogether ruinate and overthrow them, making them in their follies and falshoods as bare and naked as an anatomie'. Scot rocks with mirth as he relates that Bodin had quailed before the ceremonies described by Weyer in his book and had not dared to read them 'least (belike) the divell would come up, and scratch him with his fowle long nailes'. He, Scot, made of sterner stuff than Bodin, had read through their conjurations but the only devils he had ever seen were in a play. Bodin, of course, would declare Scot's failure to conjure devils to be because the devils know that Scot is not in good faith. Why, then, is Bodin afraid? Might it be...? Scot brings the mirth-taking to an end: 'But oh absurd credulitie!'[41]

Spiritual and demonic magic impossible, words, characters, charms, images all useless, how then is the Christian to aid nature in producing works of benefit for all. It is through, and only through, the pursuit of 'naturall magicke'. In explaining what this means Scot at the same time cautions: 'Howbeit, such things as God hath laid up secretlie in nature are to be weighed with great admiration, and to be searched out with such industrie, as may become a christian man: I meane, so as neither God, nor our neighbour be offended thereby.' Knowledge of natural magic enables practitioners to achieve very remarkable effects which the ignorant ascribe falsely and foolishly to witchcraft: 'And yet in truth, naturall magicke is nothing else, but the worke of nature.'[42] The aim of natural magicians, explains Scot, is to understand the secret properties of things, the 'strange effects of Sympathia and Antipathia'. Some such properties are already well-known and therefore taken for granted but they are marvellous none the less, for example, 'that a draught of drinke should so overthrow a man, that never a part or member of his bodie should be able to performe his dutie and office', and then there is the strange and marvellous property of the loadstone 'so beneficiall to the mariner'. Scot is somewhat reluctantly prepared to take other properties on trust for he dares not deny (much as he would like to) the authority of 'so manie and so grave authors' (oh absurd credulitie?), for example, that the *echeneis remora* fish, but six inches long, can stop in its tracks a 'mightie ship with all hir loade and tackling, and being also under saile', that the wound of a murdered man 'reneweth bleeding; at the presence of a deere freend, or of a mortall enimie'.[43] There is certainly much in nature that lies hidden—truly remarkable properties—and the exploration of nature undertaken in truly Christian spirit will enable Christians to achieve remarkable and marvellous effects.

In the concluding section to his book Scot sums up his arguments against belief in the reality of Satanic magic. Ridicule is his final weapon. Since Satan does not offer his followers great stores of 'a thing which would procure him more disciples than any other thing in the world', namely money, Satan's general level of intelligence is to say the least suspect; and a bargain whereby an old woman, soon to die anyway if not earlier dispatched by a hangman, should 'for nichels in a bag' sell her soul to be tormented in hell fire is a bargain that hardly seems to offer her either the best life in this world or in the world to come.[44] The reason and common sense that Scot referred to in his preface—plus his sarcasm—allow him only one possible verdict.

In *A Discourse upon Divels and Spirits,* published together with his *Discoverie,* Scot tackles the central question hitherto evaded in his major work: do devils and spirits really, truly, physically exist? In meeting this question head on, the Christian Scot is not, it would seem, treading on very thin ice, he is attempting to tread on water. His opening lines emphasize the danger: 'There is no question nor theme . . . so difficult to deale in, nor so noble an argument to dispute upon, as this of divels and spirits. For that being confessed or doubted of, the eternitie of the soule is either affirmed or denied.' He agrees that belief in the immortality of the soul minimizes the importance of this earthly life and makes it easier for Christians to bear whatever hardships occur and even loss of life itself: 'whereas, if the soule were mortall, all our hope and felicitie were to be placed in this life, which manie Atheists (I warrant you) at this daie doo'. As a good Christian he, Scot, must condemn the Sadducees and Aristotelians who deny the existence of devils and spirits; yet he cannot bring himself, he writes, to believe in the foolish and superstitious works of Plato and Plotinus or of the absurd opinions of Kramer, Sprenger and Bodin who populate the cosmos with spirits and demons everywhere. Of course Scot does not deny that there are spirits and devils 'of such substance as it hath pleased GOD to create them' but they are neither corporeal, nor visible. In fact spirits and devils for Scot become suspiciously like the entities of the Sadducees he has just criticized. When in the Bible it is stated that God sent an evil spirit we are to understand by this, Scot asserts, that God sent 'the spirit of hatred, and not a bulbegger'. As for the seven devils cast out of Mary Magdelene, by this is meant an uncertain number of vices, not 'seven corporall divels'. Scot concludes: 'In summe, this word [Spirit] dooth signifie a secret force and power, wherewith our minds are moved and directed; if unto holie things, then is it the motion of the holie spirit, of the spirit of Christ and of God; if unto evill things, then is it the suggestion of the wicked spirit, of the divell, and of satan.'[45] One more step it would seem, and Reginald Scot's reason, common sense and compassion would take him into the abyss of atheism.

Scot, it is clear, has been greatly influenced by Weyer but he is much more radical. While Weyer is 'sexist', 'agist' and 'elitist' —uneducated old women cannot possibly command demons but the matter is very different for educated male magicians—Scot is uncompromising. All phenomena are natural or the result of God's intervention. *All* claims to be able to practise Satanic magic are either made in bad faith or are the result of self-deception. With respect to diabolical phenomena, the English hop-grower will believe in nothing that is not found among his hops, and much personal searching for demons and demonic magic has produced the expected result—absolutely nothing at all. Evil old women—and they have much cause to be angry—are to be forgiven by true Christians (unless the women are poisoners). Bodin and all the witchmongers are not merely fools, they are sadistic fools.

For the modern reader Scot's work shines like a beacon. One wants almost to embrace him and recommend everyone to take up hopgrowing if (galleon-stopping little fish, etc. apart) such honest empiricism and compassion be a necessary concomitant or consequence. But nevertheless it is necessary to question the plausibility of Scot's position. In good faith or bad, Scot does not deny the existence of a supreme spirit of infinite goodness and power. Quite the contrary! How then can he be so sure that there are not lesser spirits of finite and varying goodness, badness and power, and that they do not interact with human beings according to the intentions of the would-be magicians and the level of their esoteric knowledge? That *Scot* has failed to detect demons is no absolute guarantee of their non-existence, nor that other people are lying or deceiving themselves when they claim to have contacted them. Scot's position of absolute certainty—nature is marvellous and full of occult secrets, God certaintly exists but demons certainly do not—is one that his fellow Christians, to say the least, would not find convincing. Let us therefore turn our attention to the more 'moderate' position of the last anti-demonologist we look at in this chapter, the sceptic Michel de Montaigne.

The benefit of the doubt
Ironically enough, in his collection of essays published in 1580 (and certainly without having read the *Demonic Madness of Witches*), Montaigne praised Bodin's way of thinking as similar to his own, adding later that Bodin was endowed with unusual judgment, and most deserving of our consideration.[46] Even more ironically, Montaigne then proceeded to take Bodin to task for incredulously refusing to accept Plutarch's story that a boy who had stolen a fox, and hidden it under his clothes, silently allowed the fox to gnaw through his stomach and intestines rather than reveal his theft. If Bodin wishes to indict Plutarch for accepting 'things incredible and entirely fabulous', this particular example is ill-chosen, Montaigne complains, for it is much more difficult to know the limits of human mental powers than physical. In any case, on the grounds of our own experience, Montaigne argues, we can be absolutely sure of nothing at all.[47] In an earlier essay Montaigne had confessed that at one time he had been arrogant enough to pity people who believed in such nonsense as ghosts, enchantments and sorceries. Now, however, (in disagreement with Scot) reason has taught him that 'to condemn anything so positively as false and impossible is to claim that our own brains have the privilege of knowing the bounds and limits of God's will, and of our Mother Nature's power'. Despite such piety, Montaigne nevertheless reserves the right to doubt stories of miracles and supernatural phenomena. It is only when miracles

have been personally observed and related by men of outstanding
virtue and learning, such as St Augustine, that Montaigne will
give his credence. For who, he asks, would be bold enough to
condemn Augustine of ignorance, simplicity, credulity, malice
and imposture? In such a case no further proof of a miracle is
necessary, Augustine's authority alone convinces Montaigne.[48]

This is the qualified sceptical attitude that Montaigne proceeds
to employ in his short essay on witchcraft published in 1588.
Regrettably he has to note that believers in the reality of
witchcraft are wont to threaten him with physical violence should
he persist in his scepticism. Stressing that no one's fists will
determine his opinion, Montaigne recommends the witch-hunters
rather to bully those who declare their opinion *false*, not people
like himself who accuses them only of holding a 'difficult and rash
opinion', not a false one.[49]

But why is the witchmongers' opinion difficult and rash?
Montaigne explains that despite a very great curiosity to witness
with his own eyes a supernatural phenomenon, he has to confess
that until now, 'all miracles and strange events have eluded me. I
have seen no monster nor more obvious miracle in the world than
myself!' How then does Montaigne explain that other people
have been privileged while he has not? The point is, declares
Montaigne, that men are prone to believe in the miraculous, they
love to exaggerate, and can rarely tell a remarkable story 'without
adding some interest and addition' of their own. Thus it
invariably comes about that the most remote witness is better
instructed about a highly unlikely event than the closest, and that
the last informed is more convinced of its reality than the first. In
the eyes of the storyteller, the sceptical listener has to be
convinced lest the storyteller's own credibility suffers; in such
circumstances, given the evident stupidity of the doubting
listener, a few embellishments, even lies, would seem to be quite
in order. 'How much more natural and plausible it seems to me',
Montaigne sums up, 'that two men are lying than that one man
should travel with the winds, and go from east to west in twelve
hours. How much more natural to believe that our understanding
was swept from its proper place by our volatile, untracked mind,
than to believe that one of us, in flesh and blood, should be
wafted up a chimney on a broomstick by a strange spirit.'[50]
Inconvenient though the point may be, Montaigne emphasizes
that the best test of truth is not the number of believers.

A suitably important criterion to consider before assenting to a
belief is the consequences of such assent. Since in the case of
witchcraft beliefs the consequences are extreme indeed—torture
and death to large numbers of people—Montaigne advises that

the utmost caution is necessary before assent be given. A conclusion follows that for Montaigne appears very reasonable indeed: 'Luminous, clear-cut evidence is needed in order to kill people; and our life is too real and essential to vouch for these supernatural and fantastic accidents.' It is therefore pardonable to disbelieve in supernatural phenomena, especially to try to substitute natural causes for the supernatural. Montaigne declares that he follows St Augustine in this, that 'it is better to be inclined to doubt than to have assurance in things that are difficult to prove and dangerous to believe'. And he concludes bitterly: 'All things considered, to have a man roasted alive because of our conjectures is to place a high value on them indeed.'[51]

But what about confessions freely made by witches who, moreover, bear the mark of their Satanic pacts? Montaigne explains how a prince attempted to convince him of his 'rash incredulity' by inviting him to question a dozen or so confessed witches. Among them was an old woman 'indeed a real witch in ugliness and deformity' against whom, it was alleged, were proofs, a confession freely made, and the witch's mark. Montaigne relates that although he conversed freely with the old woman and saw 'some barely perceptible mark' his scepticism remained unshaken: he would in all conscience have prescribed for the dozen convicted witches 'hellebore rather than hemlock', the physician rather than the executioner.[52]

In another of his later essays Montaigne confesses how he prefers to err—if err he must—on the side of generosity and not harshness. Indeed, his horror of the crime of murder makes him, as a lawyer, loath to commit more, hatred of the initial cruelty inspiring in him fear of any repetition. While of Charillus, King of Sparta, it was reported that he cannot be good since he is not hard on the wicked, Montaigne prefers Plutarch's alternative verdict, that he must certainly be good, since he is so even to the wicked.[53] Does not Montaigne fear as Bodin does the wrath of God should he not advocate severe punishment of the wicked? But how to identify the wicked? How can one be sure? And then is not God basically generous? Montaigne relates in an early essay how his father had brought him up with great tenderness and this was how he, Montaigne, was bringing up his sole surviving daughter: 'I believe', he wrote, 'that what cannot be accomplished by reason, and by wisdom and tact, can never be accomplished by force'.[54] Cruelty is the vice that Montaigne hates the most, and in his essay on the subject he makes his memorable remark that he is 'not so shocked by savages who roast and eat the bodies of their dead as by those who torture and persecute the living'. Furthemore, Montaigne's compassion, at least in theory, was not confined to human beings:

> [Y]et there is a certain consideration, and a general duty of humanity, that binds us not only to the animals, which have life and feeling, but even to the trees and plants. We owe justice to men, and kindness and benevolence to all other creatures who may be susceptible of it. There is some intercourse between them and us, and some mutual obligation.

And Montaigne relates approvingly how Plutarch would not send and sell to the slaughter-house 'for some trifling sum, an ox that had given him long service'.[55]

It is striking that Montaigne does not explicitly discuss in his essay on witchcraft the sabbat, Succubi, Incubi and sexual orgies. This is not because he is prudish for he discusses sexuality elsewhere, however not that imaginary sexuality between humans and demons but real sexuality between real men and real women. Given the witch-hunters' insistence on women's 'bestial cupidity' Montaigne comments are very relevant. Sadly but significantly Montaigne relates how women are more sexually capable and certainly more sexually ardent than men who in their old age are rendered not only miserable but, Montaigne believes, ridiculous too.[56] And not even Montaigne's legal skill can acquit his client, the penis, of wilfully disobedient behaviour on any number of embarrassing occasions, particularly on its always possible failure to rise to the occasion.[57] It is men, not women, who have the problematic sexuality! The fact of the matter, Montaigne acknowleges, is that since men, less ardent in love and above all less capable than women, make the rules without the consent of women, women are not to be blamed at all in rejecting them. But there is no suggestion in Montaigne that women seek satisfaction other than with human lovers. Despite the appearance in his writings of a few occasional grumbles about women, it is perhaps not very surprising that Marie de Gournay, one of the outstanding French writers and feminists of the period, not only initiated a close friendship with Montaigne but defended him after his death against his many critics and assumed responsibility as Montaigne's 'adopted daughter' for the 1595 and ten subsequent editions of his *Essays*.[58]

Such, then, were some of the principal arguments of two important opponents of witch hunting in the 1580s. On reflection, it would appear that Scot and Montaigne were not so different after all. To be sure, Scot categorically denied the possibility of effective witchcraft where Montaigne claimed only to doubt. But Montaigne's doubting appears to have been merely a tactical ploy disguising a basic disbelief in supernatural phenomena. Moreover, sincere or otherwise, since Montaigne publicly insisted that

one cannot be absolutely *certain,* this alone sufficed to ensure
that the verdict must go in favour of the accused. If a mistake is
thereby made, God—who is merciful and generous—will rectify
such mistakes; justice in such cases can be left to Him. We see
that what ultimately separated Scot and Montaigne from Bodin,
and probably from witch-hunters in general, was not only Scot
and Montaigne's reluctance to believe in the possibility of
supernatural phenomena but also their greater generosity and
their concomitant belief in a benevolent deity (if a deity existed at
all). In addition, might we not (simplistically?) conclude that Scot
and Montaigne did not accept the idea of a *cruel* God because
they were not cruel themselves? And whereas Bodin feared what
he believed to be women's excessive carnality, as had Kramer and
Sprenger before him, Montaigne calmly accepted what he saw as
men's sexual inferiority and recognised the unjust oppression of
women. Is it that Montaigne—unlike Bodin—had no psychological need to rationalize persecution of women? I will return to
these questions. But first I look at the credulity of the last of the
demonologists whose arguments I summarize in this chapter,
Montaigne's contemporary and a judge in Lorraine Nicolas
Remy. For these are the kinds of arguments that will prevail for
half a century more at least and will contribute to the horrendous
climax of witch hunting during the 1630s.

Witch hunting triumphant
In Judge Remy's work on witchcraft we are witness to the
thoughts of a man who wrote that over a span of fifteen years he
had personally investigated and executed over 800 people
accused of witchcraft, which is an execution on average of a
person a week. How, as Montaigne would surely have asked his
fellow countryman, could he have felt so *sure*? In his *Demonolatry*, published in 1595, Remy meets this question head on.
    He is not, he informs his readers, a 'retailer of marvellous
stories' of witches raising storms, flying through the air and
passing through the narrowest cracks, of their dancing and lying
with demons. He is a judge and *such stories are true*, they do not
derive from scattered rumours but from the independent and
concordant testimony of many witnesses. Indeed, although
everything that Remy argues is in the spirit of the Christian
religion, he states that from the facts alone 'it will be easy to
understand and be fully convinced that there are witches, unless
we deliberately intend to see and understand nothing'.[59] To set
his readers' minds at rest, Remy claims to be neither credulous
nor incredulous: witches cannot by their spells turn men into
beasts, neither can their souls separate from their bodies, nor can

they conceive from Incubi: but definite and terrible powers they do have.

These are some of the facts advanced by Remy. Most witches are women but 'it is not unreasonable that this scum of humanity should be drawn chiefly from the feminine sex'. That witches have demons as lovers is indisputable given the independent and concordant testimony of so many convicted witches. Remy stresses a fact he finds very relevant: '[A]ll female witches maintain that the so-called genital organs of their Demons are so huge and so excessively rigid that they cannot be admitted without the greatest pain.' Remy appears to sympathize with the claim of confessed witches that it is against their will that they are embraced and penetrated by demons.[60]

While all this (Remy believes) is not very controversial, there is much controversy over the vexed question of whether witches really do fly to sabbats or whether they merely dream that they do. However there can be no doubt, Remy asserts, that sabbats do actually occur. Most persuasive of all is the fact that conversations at sabbats 'have afterwards been reported in identical words by different persons who were present'. Remy gives three examples to settle all doubt. The first concerned a man who accidentally stumbled on a sabbat but lived to tell the tale. True or false? His story was 'in all respects' independently confirmed by one of the witches present except that the witch insisted that the officiating demon had attacked the trespasser not because of his intrusion but because he had tried to steal a gold cup from the demon's table. In the second example, Remy tells of a young man taken to a sabbat by his mother, who climbing a tree from which to play his flute was so astonished by what he saw that he called aloud the name of God, fell from his tree, and discovered that the sabbat had vanished. True or false? Soon afterwards a suspected witch related the same events, without knowing that the young man had already been spreading the story. The following year two more witches confirmed the young man's story. In the third example, a woman accidentally stumbled on a band of men and women dancing back to back together with other creatures whose feet had been deformed into those of goats and oxen. In fright she cried out the name of Jesus whereupon all the dancers immediately vanished, save one whom she recognized. Subsequently caught, the dancer was then 'with no great difficulty' induced to confess his crime and name his accomplices, who in turn all confirmed the woman's story. True or false? The 'final and incontrovertible proof of the truth of this occurrence', Remy relates, is that the day after the matter had been reported by the intruder the place of the witches' sabbat was found and it was observed that the ground had been trodden into a ring displaying among 'the other tracks . . . the recent marks of the hoofs of goats and oxen'.[61] Remy declares that if these three stories are not proof enough to convince anyone, there is no point in his giving more.

It is therefore established to Remy's satisfaction that witches can and do *really* fly. And in particular they usually leave their cottages through their chimneys. Should the objection be made that chimneys are too narrow to allow the passage of a human being, it should be remembered not only that supernatural phenomena are being investigated but that chimneys are square and wide in all peasant cottages, 'and that it is from this class that the vile rabble of sorcery is mostly derived'.[62]

Can witches cause storms in order to ruin crops? Remy confesses that there is 'no doubt that what follows will surpass all belief, and will appear very ridiculous to many'. Despite this admission, the fact of the matter is that he, Remy, has sentenced to capital punishment some two hundred people who freely confessed to this atrocious crime. It is striking, however, that despite the prevalence of the crime in Lorraine Remy does not give examples of eye witnesses from his own cases but relies upon stories from the *Malleus Maleficarum* which, he declares, 'being confident in the integrity of its authors, I have not hesitated to set out here'.[63]

In the closing chapters of his work Remy explains why he must reject Johann Weyer's pleas for leniency in the punishment of witches. For whereas Weyer believes that witches only imagine that they attend sabbats and commit their various crimes, this is clearly not the case as Remy has already demonstrated. He thus exhorts: 'Away then with those who would make Nature the standard and rule of all things, so that they think nothing can happen which does not conform to her methods and limits! For thus they constringe the hands and circumscribe the might of God . . .'[64]

But suppose Weyer is right (although he is not) that witches only wish to do evil but accomplish nothing themselves. Is he right in claiming that they should not be punished for their intentions? Remy is almost nonplussed at Weyer's reasoning: 'Now what more abominable thought or concept of an evil mind, what greater wickedness and depravity of the human heart can there be than not only to . . . plot and desire that which all other men regard with horror and apprehension—such as thunders and lightnings, the ruin and destruction of the crops, the violent agitation and even uprooting of trees, and the devastation and spoliation of wide and fertile tracts of land; but with might and main, by day and by night, to strive to bring these things about, and to wait upon, support, and as far as they can assist the Demons whom they believe to be the instigators of these upheavals. . . . ' Those who desire such effects and carry through all the actions they believe necessary are guilty indeed.[65]

Weyer, however, Remy continues, has another trick up his sleeve claiming that on account of the feebleness of the witches' age and sex, the heinousness of their crimes should be overlooked since it springs from a condition of mind for which nature alone is responsible. Remy cannot accept such reasoning for 'to argue in this way is to bring a very heavy charge against Nature, who is on the contrary wise in all she does'. Furthermore, although it is certainly the case that many women of extreme old age are accused and convicted of the crime of witchcraft, 'even in such cases the sin is one of long standing of which they have usually been guilty ever since the time of their youth'. In any case, everyone knows that the law cannot and does not allow age or sex to be an excuse for its infringement. Remy emphasizes how even the New Testament, generally 'more moderate and merciful' than the Old, commands that every branch that does not reside in Christ must be without exception cast out and thrown into the fire.[66]

Thus even if we grant Weyer his plea (which we should not) that 'through human weakness their foothold is so slippery that they cannot but fall', what madness it would be to condone in witches such a 'monstrous and deadly crime' with which they must always be contaminated. Should we keep alive mad dogs who, like witches, are incurable merely because their madness is not of their own making? The purpose of punishment is to deter, not to avenge, Remy continues (presumably rejecting the plea of madness). This being so, since the peace and safety of the public is the judge's first consideration, no sufficient argument can possibly be made to show 'that such scum who vow eternal allegiance to the Devil should not be put to death with every torment as soon as their guilt is known . . . '. Remy considers totally invalid the argument that there is never sufficient proof to warrant bringing women to trial on so grave a charge. As a judge Remy knows better: any person put to death for the crime of witchcraft has been 'manifestly proved guilty either by the clear evidence of witnesses or by her own persistent confession up to the time of her death'. Remy demolishes the last defence that those who are in Satan's clutches no longer have freedom of choice and therefore need not be punished for acts not freely executed. For how, asks Remy, did they get into Satan's clutches? They first turned their backs on God before God turned His on them. Such people deserve no mercy. Remy gives his final verdict:

Woe . . . to those who would palliate the odium of so horrible and execrable a crime, and would diminish its punishment on the plea of fear, age, sex, imprudence, and the like, which no sane man would dare to consider as grounds for mercy in even less abominable crimes! . . . This is to delay the coming of His Kingdom; for nothing can so firmly establish it as the routing, overthrow and destruction of all His enemies, together with Satan, who is their Captain . . . Such men act in the worst possible way for the security and peace of the human race; for . . . they who do not restrain the wicked wish to wrong the righteous [Montaigne is firmly reprimanded]. I shall . . . do all in my power to bring the very truth to light: namely, that their lives are so notoriously befouled and polluted by so many blasphemies, sorceries, prodigious lusts and flagrant crimes, that I have no hesitation in saying that they are justly to be subjected to every torture and put to death in the flames; both that they may expiate their crimes with a fitting punishment, and that its very awfulness may serve as an example and a warning to others.[67]

It was Remy's point of view that triumphed. In the next four decades the witchcraze increased in intensity until in the 1630s, the decade in which Galileo published his *Dialogue Concerning the Two Chief World Systems,* more witches were being burnt throughout Europe than at any time previously. The dissenters had failed. Had they failed to convince because their arguments were too inadequate or had they failed to convince because the social forces underwriting the witchcraze were too strong? Let me outline what some of these social forces might have been.

3   *The Social Basis of Witch Hunting*

It is a banal observation but probably still a true one that in a time of disaster and hideous death scapegoats will in general be sought. The chosen scapegoat in the two centuries after the publication of *Malleus Maleficarum* was the female sex, particularly those women living beyond the immediate control of men. Male hostility towards women was, of course, no new phenomenon in Europe, nor (for the record's sake) has it been a phenomenon confined to either Europe or Christianity. But Christianity did produce a particularly virulent form of male hostility to women. Accepting the Greek and Jewish belief that women are inferior to men, the early Church Fathers forbad women to speak in church, preach, or administer the sacraments. More sinisterly, women were held responsible for mankind's downfall through Eve's lamentable weakness and for having given birth to a race of demons after illicit intercourse with fallen angels. Women were considered sexual temptresses and since Christianity was (or attempted to be) an ascetic religion it was apparently impossible to forgive women their sexual desirability.

Tertullian told women that 'God's sentence hangs still over all your sex and His punishment weighs down upon you. You are the devil's gateway.' Origen castrated himself. Lactantius held that Eve had been the agent of the Devil. St John Chrysostom declared that 'woman taught once, and ruined all' and appealed to men to see through the beautiful female body to the 'white sepulchre' it truly is; while a rag covered in phlegm and spittle is repulsive to all, Chrysostom complained how men are nevertheless continually attracted to the 'store houses and depositories of these things'.[68] St Augustine identified the unbidden motion of the penis with original sin. It is indeed not an exaggeration when a male theologian concludes that the early Church Fathers promoted a view of women as essentially the 'devil's henchmen', plunging humanity into disorder, death, and damnation. (Henchmen?). A female historian concurs, soberly and accurately, that the early Christian Church created a 'tradition of misogyny unequalled before or since'.[69] Unfortunately, that tradition of misogyny characterized Europe into the Renaissance and early modern period. At most women were acceptable to the Church only as sexless or unattainable beings, the *Virgin* Mary being an impossible ideal for women to aspire to: virginity and celibacy were after all within human grasp unlike motherhood preceded by no carnal knowledge of men. Church hostility to women remained unabated. Three centuries before the witchcraze was under way the Abbot Conrad of Marchtal voiced a scarcely atypical sentiment:

We and our whole community of canons, recognizing that the wickedness of women is greater than all the other wickedness of the world, and that there is no anger like that of women, and that the poison of asps and dragons is more curable and less dangerous to men than the familiarity of women, have unanimously decreed for the safety of our souls, no less than for that of our bodies and goods, that we will on no account receive any more sisters to the increase of our perdition, but will avoid them like poisonous animals.[70]

Even granted such intense misogyny which initially the Protestant Reformation did little to abate, a problem remains. For no matter how widespread hatred of women and fear of female sexuality must have become in early modern Europe, it is still necessary to explain why such hatred and fear erupted in the brutal and amazing manner that we have been discussing. Even if we agree with an historian that women's overall influence and social position reached a peak towards the end of the late middle ages, so provoking by the sixteenth century 'a backlash affecting women of all ranks and in all regions for several centuries to come', the witchcraze still needs explanation.[71] For by and large it was a fearful upper-class response to a *non-existent* threat.

Erudite male magicians certainly existed, perhaps every village had its 'wise man' or 'wise woman', undoubtedly people here and there attempted Satanic witchcraft but it is extremely doubtful that throughout Europe women regularly gathered together for nocturnal orgies; and if the very occasional 'sabbat' did occur, it is certain that people attending were within walking—not flying —distance of their homes. Why, then, did the witchcraze develop and why were people suspected of being witches so hideously persecuted?

Many societies have believed in witchcraft and in the ability of 'witches' to fly at night to nocturnal gatherings, but Christianity, in adding the Devil to witchcraft beliefs, turned witches into heretics and apostates. Norman Cohn in *Europe's Inner Demons* has described how, inexorably, step by step, belief in Satanic magic and sabbats was developed in Europe from Biblical evidence, the writings of the misogynistic Church Fathers and the wisdom of the ages. When, by the fifteenth century the various pieces had been put together and, very importantly, *disseminated over all Europe by the new art of printing*, the witchcraze appeared to be an inevitable consequence. But the witchcraze needed a machinery of persecution. Why, we might ask, was such a machinery at hand?

Until the twelfth century or so heretical movements were virtually unknown in Europe. However, crusades were initiated in the twelfth and thirteenth centuries against the (revived) Catharist heresy that had upgraded the Devil to equal status with God, the Inquisition being founded by the Church in 1230 to help extirpate the new heresy by extirpating the new heretics. During the fourteenth century as Europe was decimated by the bubonic plague, social chaos inevitably followed and heretical movements multiplied. In particular the followers of the merchant Waldes, who had too literally taken note of Christ's teaching of the rich man and the eye of the needle, were not finally defeated until the 1488 crusade. It is, Cohn argues, from the persecution of the Waldensians that the persecution of 'witches' originates.

There is an important feature of these heretical movements that must not be overlooked, namely the 'disproportionate' role in them played by women. 'Almost all the medieval sects from the Manicheans to the Waldenses, the Donatists to the Cathars', Keith Thomas notes, 'received to a marked degree the support of women and welcomed them, sometimes as influential patronesses, but more often . . . as active members on a basis of practical equality'.[72] While the Catholic faithful saw this as nothing more than Satan acting in his unoriginal way, the women in the heretical sects gained by their membership, Thomas argues, greater self-experience, wider spheres of influence and an asceticism that could free them from family ties. A specialist on women in medieval Europe concurs in the claim that 'the prominent part which women played in heretical or near-heretical movements, such as Catharism, or the Order of the Béguines, was a manifestation of women's discontent with their lot in the world'.[73] Heretical movements, then, both led to the creation of a repressive apparatus and firmly established the connection between women and heresy. The witchcraze would engage that repressive apparatus which, at least in its initial phases, was directed principally at old peasant women living alone. We should note that a modern researcher, H.C.E. Midelfort, has quite properly emphasized that it is 'false to assume that this stereotype originated only in the modern age, as many scholars assert. The age of witch-hunts thought first in terms of old women, just as we do'.[74]

The repressive apparatus existed; the witchcraft belief system existed and was widely promulgated; misogyny was rampant; persecution of principally female 'witches' appeared the inevitable result. There is one striking phenomenon that, however, must not be overlooked. While many societies have persecuted 'witches' accused of maleficia, early modern Europe has been the only society that has attempted to persecute all witches, whether accused of maleficia or not (including, as we shall see, 'good witches'). In forcing witches to name 'accomplices' at sabbats, the repressive apparatus did not merely 'discover' witches, it *created* them. Even if such a comprehensive search for witches was a logical result of the belief that all witches were Satanical conspirators, an anthropologist has argued that this creation of witches also had an important social function.

Caught in the throes of traumatic social change, sixteenth-century Europe was ravaged (let us recall) by severe food shortages and price inflation, numerous peasant revolts (more properly called wars), violent millenarian movements and, of course, large scale witch-hunts. It is scarcely surprising that the worst years of famine were the years of greatest discontent. Thus the social historian Henry Kamen has noted that between '1550 and 1600 the worst food crisis experienced in Europe was in the years 1594–7, a time of great famine which caused severe hardships throughout the continent. Within this half century the peak period for popular rebellions was 1595–7'. The same social historian has noted another significant correlation: 'In every European country the most intensive outbreaks of witch persecution were in times of disaster.Taking the long view, the equation of crisis and witchcraft becomes even more striking. It was the very period of the greatest price rise—the late sixteenth and early seventeenth century—that saw the most numerous cases of accusation and persecution of witches.'[75] More specifically, the French social historian Emmanuel Le Roy Ladurie has observed that in the mountains of southern France between 1580 and 1600, especially in Vivarais and the Languedoc parts of the Pyrenees, witch-hunts and popular revolts occurred together. Indeed, 'the forces of order, tribunals and Parlements... led the hunt for witches and the repression of the uprisings with equal energy'. Claiming, controversially, that worship of the Devil was a real phenomenon, undertaken by a 'peasant consciousness... violated by war, haunted by poverty and death and often by sexual failure', Ladurie makes the point that between 'these fantastic revolts and the real popular uprisings... there were geographical, chronological, and sometimes even family coincidences'.[76] Male peasant rebellion and female peasant witchcraft thus sought a similar objective, Ladurie claims: to turn the world upside down.

However, one does not have to believe that the witch-hunters of Languedoc managed to identify peasant women who really attempted to practise witchcraft. Since the witch-hunters were simultaneously suppressing peasant rebellions, it was undoubtedly psychologically reinforcing for them to be able to seize the opportunity of identifying the *true* enemy of the peasantry—not the upper class and not its servants but an enemy from the ranks of the peasantry itself and from the traditional enemy of all *man*kind—*woman*kind. And, even more psychologically reinforcing, for the prosecution of such a remorseless enemy the men of the Parlements were themselves most necessary! Taking this argument a stage further, Marvin Harris controversially identifies what he believes to be the principal aspect of the witchcraze that helped to maintain its momentum throughout the turbulent decades of the sixteenth century. I let him speak for himself:

Military messianism brought the poor and the dispossessed together. It gave them a sense of collective mission, diminished social distance, made them feel like 'brother and sister'. It mobilized people over whole regions, focused their energies upon a particular time and place, and led to pitched battles between the propertyless and pauperized masses and the people who were at the top of the social pyramid. The witchcraft mania, on the other hand, dispersed and fragmented all the latent energies of protest. It demobilized the poor and the dispossessed, increased their social distance, filled them with mutual suspicions, pitted neighbour against neighbour, isolated everyone, made everyone fearful, heightened everyone's insecurity, made everyone feel helpless and dependent on the governing classes, gave everyone's anger and frustration a purely local focus. In so doing, it drew the poor further and further away from confronting the ecclesiastical and secular establishment with demands for the redistribution of wealth and the levelling of rank. The witch mania was radical military messianism in reverse. It was the magic bullet of society's privileged and powerful classes. That was its secret.[77]

It is difficult to believe, however, that the witchcraze was a cynical conspiracy on the part of the ruling classes of Europe. Neither does Harris claim it to be. It is sufficient for this argument that such a beneficial side-effect did not go unappreciated by the ruling classes. I have suggested that other beneficial side-effects were that the witchcraze deflected people's anger on to defenceless citizens and reassured rulers that they were not responsible for the sufferings of the masses, that on the contrary their existence was necessary if the well-being of the latter was to be restored. In the face of such powerful psychological reinforcement that the witchcraze gave the masters of western Europe, it is perhaps not surprising that sixteenth-century dissenters made little headway.

There were other social factors underwriting the persecution of witches. At a local community level witch beliefs presumably helped reassure the relatively wealthy whenever they refused to give charity to old women in need, the uncharitable act being vindicated when subsequent events proved the old woman to be a witch. It should be recognized, however, that while local accusations such as these supplied the authorities with the odd witch or two in each village, it was only the authorities' belief in a Satanic conspiracy that turned this otherwise English-type witch hunting into the Continental witchcraze.

In addition, as Weyer himself emphasized, witch beliefs helped excuse the ignorance and incompetence of physicians, for no physician could be expected to cure recalcitrant and therefore diabolically induced illness. The growing power of physicians was, however, threatened not just by witches but by the many people who practised medicine without university qualification. 'For in all times', Francis Bacon explained in his *Advancement of Learning* of 1605, ' . . . witches and old women and impostors have had a competition with physicians'—a competition, moreover, Bacon noted, in which 'empirics and old women are more happy many times in their cures than learned physicians.'[78] Of course, since it was all but impossible for female healers to enter university (reading for a degree being associated with training for priesthood), there was virtually no way in which women could gain professional respectability. Consequently, as physicians demanded the professionalization of medicine and petitioned kings and parliaments to make the unqualified practice of medicine illegal, women healers, especially the more successful of them, necessarily found themselves on the wrong side of the law. The famous trial of Jacqueline Felice springs to mind: found guilty in Paris in 1322 of the illegal practice of medicine, Jacqueline's defence was to no avail that she had cured patients given up as hopeless by qualified physicians, that she sampled all potients offered to patients, and charged no fee unless she was successful.[79] In the same century we find a London physician plagiarising a Continental treatise in order to complain that 'worthless and presumptuous women usurp this profession to themselves and abuse it; who, possessing neither natural ability nor professional knowledge, make the greatest possible mistakes (thanks to their stupidity) and very often kill their patients; for they work without wisdom and from no certain foundations, but in a casual fashion, nor are they thoroughly acquainted with the causes or even the names of the maladies which they claim that they are competent to cure'.[80] If charity requires one to refrain from comment on the 'certain foundations' available to male physicians at the time, the complaint that women did not know the names of the illnesses they treated invites reference to the famous work of the French physician and surgeon Guy de Chauliac who rather too honestly admitted that 'If the doctors have not learned geometry, astronomy, dialectics, nor any other good discipline, soon the leather workers, carpenters, and furriers will quit their own occupations and become doctors'![81] Professionalization of medicine intensified. In 1421 physicians in England petitioned Parliament to make the practice of medicine illegal for all men not trained by them and to proscribe medical practice for all women. The following century in 1511, an act of Parliament proscribed the practise of medicine to 'common artificers as smythes, weavers, and women', who were held to take upon themselves 'great cures and thinges of great difficultie in the whiche they partly use sorcerye and witchcrafte'. Not only had the literate urban healer been a threat to professional physicians, the village 'wise woman' had also become one. If she—an illiterate peasant woman—cured, then the presumption was strong that she must have enjoyed the Devil's aid.[82]

Devout men could not have been surprised to learn that Johann Weyer's teacher, the notorious master magician Agrippa von Nettesheim, author in 1505 of an impassioned indictment of men's so-called oppression of women, had not only in 1518 successfully defended an old woman accused of witchcraft (thereby provoking the wrath of witch-hunters) but had also criticized physicians for acquiring their knowledge from incorrect books, recommending them instead to learn from the 'old wife' who possessed great personal knowledge of the virtues of individual plants and who 'administers the surest remedy free of charge to everyone'.[83] But how could uneducated men and

women—especially women—heal if it were not by the Devil's
help (yet one more of his ruses to seduce people from God)? The
death penalty was therefore adjudged to be the proper punishment for 'good witches'. In England in 1608 the posthumously
published *Discourse of the Damned Art of Witchcraft* by William
Perkins declared that of the two kinds of witches, bad and good,
'the more horrible and detestable Monster is the good Witch',
proclaiming it to be 'a thousand times better for the land, if all
Witches, but especially the blessing Witch might suffer death'.
For in the event of serious illness the first thing a person does
is to 'inquire after some Wiseman or wise-woman, and thither he
sends and goes for helpe'. Unhappily, however, the sick person
who is thus cured 'cannot say with David: *The Lord is my helper*;
but the devill is my helper; for by him hee is cured'.[84]
Professionals against the unlicensed: male physicians against both
male and female healers; such rivalries all added fuel to the fires
of the witchcraze.

Such in outline were some of the various social tensions and
conflicts that helped maintain the momentum of the witchcraze;
the kinds of social forces that Scot and Montaigne indirectly
confronted in their negative attitudes to the reality of Satanic
witchcraft were clearly ones involving powerful interest groups
and indeed the very fabric of society. Even so, no matter how
strong the social forces, *if* ruling-class males could have been
dissuaded of their belief in the reality of Satanic witchcraft,
cynicism and corruption apart, the witchcraze must have come to
an end. Scot and Montaigne took on a cosmology and they
lost—at least for a further half century. Social forces notwithstanding, were their arguments sufficiently convincing?

4 *Demons and the Movement of the Earth*
In his classic work *Religion and the Decline of Magic* Keith
Thomas draws attention to the interesting point that 'Reginald
Scot had no difficulty in rejecting diabolical influence, before the
scientific revolution had scarcely begun'. However, Thomas
continues by making the following challenging observation:

But Scot and his imitators had . . . only been able to fill the gap left after the
elimination of religious or [demonic] magical explanations of natural phenomena by invoking spurious 'natural' causes, based on sympathy, antipathy and
occult influences. In admitting every kind of prodigy they were blocking the way
to a true conception of nature . . . the mechanical philosophy.[85]

Were, then, not only believers but also non-believers in the
reality of Satanic witchcraft too credulous with respect to the
phenomena of nature, however they were caused, demonically or

naturally? Thomas argues that this was certainly so:

It was because these men accepted so wide a range of supposed natural phenomena that they were able to dispense with witchcraft as an explanation of mysterious happenings. It was much easier for them to advance a 'natural' explanation of the witches' *maleficium* than it was for those who had been educated in the tradition of scholastic Aristotelianism. The sceptics thus explained away apparent mysteries, by proffering hypotheses about natural events which we should regard as entirely spurious.

Thomas continues that such schools of thought as natural magic

thus provided the vital intellectual scaffolding necessary to prop up the hypothesis that there was a natural cause for every event. When in the later seventeenth century this scaffolding collapsed under the onslaught of the mechanical philosophy it did not need to be replaced. The absurdity of witchcraft could henceforth be justified by reference to the achievements of the Royal Society and the new philosophy.[86]

It would appear to me that in these arguments Thomas is failing to do justice to Scot, and perhaps even to Weyer. While Scot certainly maintains that every event has a natural cause, he declares many phenomena to be totally spurious. In particular, since witches' flights are entirely fictitious no explanations are called for in terms of marvellous occult powers of unguents. Scot, of course, does not deny that storms occur, people and animals fall sick, men suffer from impotence, women do not conceive—and it is true that Scot offers explanations based on natural causes. But it cannot be convincingly argued that by accepting the reality of such marvellous phenomena as the reopening of the wound of a murdered man at the presence of the murderer and the galleon-stopping powers of the *echeneis* fish Scot and his imitators were thereby blocking the way to a 'true conception of nature' (which Thomas equates with the 'mechanical philosophy'). For the phenomenon of blood-running was widely accepted as real by mechanical philosophers; and even although the powers of the *echeneis* fish tended to be dismissed as impossible by mechanical philosophers, the latter were by no means alone in their scepticism. Moreover, the mechanical philosophy was itself problematic and on no account is it possible to argue successfully that an unproblematic conception of nature, let alone a 'true' one, had been established by the end of the seventeenth century (or, for that matter, today!). On the contrary, by 1700 the mechanical philosophers experienced the greatest difficulty, as we shall see in later chapters, in accounting for such a ubiquitous phenomenon as the *perpendicular* fall of heavy bodies to the earth's surface and they were forced to deny the hitherto widely subscribed-to belief in the reality of epigenetic development of foetuses, i.e. development in which true novelty emerges. In addition, mechanical philosophers opposed Newton's introduction of gravitational attraction on the grounds that such a force smacked far too much of occult qualities and the sympathies of natural magic! The 'scientific revolution' is a complex matter.

The basic questions dividing the witch-hunters from their opponents were such questions as: Is Satan active in the world? Do people, principally women, ally themselves to him? Do they worship him at sabbats? Are Satan and his demons able to give their human followers powers that enable them to fly to sabbats and perform maleficia (and occasionally, if always with ultimate evil intent, beneficia)? What was Scot's position?

Scot accepted (or believed it prudent to accept) the existence of a miracle-performing God. Scot agreed that nature is full of sympathies and antipathies. If Satan and demons exist, then Satanic witchcraft is a possibility. Since Scot denied such a possibility, confessions being the result either of self-deception or unbearable torture, it is clear that Scot either disbelieved in the existence of Satan and demons or took them to be purely spiritual entities able to interact only with the souls of people. I would maintain that he held the former position. Either way, however, neither old women nor erudite magicians can control the weather; that witches can summon storms by urinating in a puddle and stirring the contents while muttering an imprecation is a ludicrous supposition in the extreme. Scot was at a loss to know how to convince the witch-hunters of this. Burn all the witches—burn everyone—and there will still be storms; people deceive themselves in thinking that they have summoned demons (if he, Scot, cannot conjure demons, nobody can!); Bodin and company are sadistic fools in accepting confessions extracted under the cruellest torture. Scot was prepared to forgive even those women who genuinely wished to serve Satan provided they truly repented of such wickedness. Scot was, it seems safe to say, a generous and kind human being.

Bodin and the witch-hunters accepted the Bible literally. Since it is written that Satan transported Christ to a mountain top, the case for Satanic intervention in the world is proved. Sorcery is possible since the Bible relates how Pharaoh's magicians competed unsuccessfully against the powers granted Aaron by God. The Bible stipulates that a witch must not be allowed to live. So be it.

Is not Scot, from a contemporary's viewpoint, making a terrible mistake? Might it not be the case that Satan exists, that therefore Satanic witchcraft is possible and that innocent people are starving and dying because of the maleficia of witches? Scot did not consider this to be a possibility. Montaigne, however, did—at least in theory. If Satan does not or cannot intervene in nature's affairs, then Satanic witchcraft is impossible. But if Satanic intervention is a reality, then it still remains notoriously difficult to identify witches. Rather than persecute the innocent, rather than torture even the guilty, better to leave judgement in God's hands. But might not such 'idleness' bring down the wrath of God on all as Bodin and Remy fear? Scot and Montaigne are humane men. Montaigne is tender to his child and hates cruelty even to animals. In the face of hunger, famine, disease and war—in the face of widespread human suffering—Montaigne and Scot cannot believe that God—if He exists (for who knows their private thoughts?)—is not also a generous God. This would appear to be a basic and fundamental difference between Scot and Montaigne on the one hand and Bodin and Remy on the other. Montaigne, though he loves hunting, hates the moment of the kill; Bodin laments that vile female apostates cannot be kept alive for much longer than an hour in slowly roasting over a fire. Scot and Bodin have fundamentally different conceptions of the Deity. (In addition, it may not be unimportant that Scot and Montaigne expressed no hatred of women while Kramer, Sprenger and Bodin feared what they perceived to be the sexual and evil power of women.)

What might have brought an end to belief in the possibility of Satanic witchcraft? The disappearance of storms, famine, misfortune, disasters? Certainly, but the disappearance of human misfortune is not easily achieved! Increasing security of the ruling class together with growing belief in *potential* human autonomy and *potential* power over nature? Certainly, but how did this come about and, in particular, without casting doubt on the unique power of Christ's command over nature and thereby exacerbating the witchcraze? Rejection of the Christian religion? Certainly, but this did not happen. What did happen in the sixteenth and seventeenth centuries was, among other things, the widespread acceptance of a new and very bleak cosmology. In the next chapters we look at the arguments and changing social circumstances that underlay the adoption of the new cosmology —the 'mechanical philosophy'. But first it is necessary to take a detailed look at the prevailing Aristotelian-Thomistic cosmology.

This cosmology (still the predominant one during the sixteenth century) is both diabolicentric and geocentric, the earth occupying the unenviable position of the centre of the cosmos. In 1543, some fifty years before the writings on witchcraft by Bodin, Scot and Montaigne, Copernicus had published his provocative challenge to the entrenched Aristotelian-Thomistic cosmology.

Does the earth move? The demonologist Jean Bodin has often been accused of gross credulity. If credulous he was, there were nevertheless limits to his credulity. As he pointed out in his *Drama of Universal Nature,* if the Copernican world system be granted, 'then the very foundations of physics must fall into ruins'. But even more to the point, Bodin informs his readers that the Copernican theory is absurd:

No one in his senses, or imbued with the slightest knowledge of physics, will ever think that the earth, heavy and unwieldy from its own weight and mass, staggers up and down around its own centre and that of the sun; for at the slightest jar of the earth, we would see cities and fortresses, towns and mountains thrown down. . . . For if the earth were to be moved, neither an arrow shot straight up, nor a stone dropped from the top of a tower would fall perpendicularly, but either ahead or behind. . . . Lastly, all things on finding places suitable to their natures, remain there, as Aristotle writes. Since therefore the earth has been alloted a place fitting its nature, it cannot therefore be whirled around by other motion than its own.[87]

Demons, yes, but the motion of the earth, absurd!

Chapter 2

THE STATUS OF THE EARTH

> It is safe to say that even had there been no religious scruples against the
> Copernican astronomy, sensible men all over Europe, especially the most
> empirically minded, would have pronounced it a wild appeal to accept the
> premature fruits of an uncontrolled imagination, in preference to the solid
> inductions, built up gradually through the ages, of men's confirmed sense
> experience . . . . Contemporary empiricists, had they lived in the sixteenth
> century, would have been the first to scoff out of court the new philosophy
> of the universe
>
> E.A. Burtt, The Metaphysical Foundations of
Modern Physical Science, 1932
Andreas: Unhappy the land that has no heroes
Galileo: Unhappy the land that has need of heroes
>
> Bertolt Brecht, The Life of Galileo, 1937/8

IN 1611 the English poet and divine, John Donne, published a
satirical story *Ignatius His Conclave* in which Lucifer requests a
man knocking at the gates of hell to identify himself. The man
responds: 'I am he, which pitying thee who wert thrust into the
Center of the world, raysed both thee, and thy prison, the Earth
up into the Heavens.' Copernicus—for it is none other—thinks
he has an unanswerable case for admission: 'Shall these gates be
open to such as have innovated in small matters? and shall they
be shut against me, who have turned the whole frame of the
world, and am thereby almost a new Creator?'[1] The entire frame
of the world turned! Bodin—to say the least—was not alone in
thinking Copernicus' theory absurd, in believing that credulity
was running rampant. The earth obviously does not move. Five
decades after Bodin's condemnation of an absurd theory, none
other than Galileo himself conceded that 'the arguments against
the whirling of the earth . . . are very plausible'.[2] Neither did
Galileo express surprise that 'the Ptolemaics and Aristotelians
and all their disciples took them to be conclusive . . . '; Galileo's
surprise was rather that believers in the Copernican system were
to be found at all! Until, of course, Galileo had presented his
arguments and discussions! Interestingly enough, in the middle of
the nineteenth century the historian W.E.H. Lecky argued that
whereas the arrival of eighteenth-century disbelief in Satanic
witchcraft was not the result of a 'clear preponderance of
argument or fact' over the contrary beliefs of the sixteenth and

45

seventeenth centuries, the eventual triumph of the heliostatic over the geostatic world system was.[3] In this chapter I examine the validity of Lecky's claim with respect to the achievements of the major Copernican revolutionaries. Of course, since the views of particularly Aristotle and Ptolemy provided the foundations of the cosmos that Copernicus and Galileo set on its head, it is with an account of Aristotle's cosmos and Ptolemy's world system that I must begin.

1   *Aristotelian Cosmology and Male-Female Distinctions*

According to Aristotle there are four basic elements transmutable into each other: earth, water, air and fire. The natural position of the element earth is at the centre of the cosmos. Many reasons are adduced for this. Earthly matter, when picked up and released, moves of its own accord *perpendicularly* towards the earth's surface; hence it moves 'naturally' towards the centre of the (spherical) earth. But this does not necessarily mean that the centre of the earth coincides with the centre of the cosmos. Does, indeed, the cosmos have a centre? Experience shows that a force is required to move earthly matter in any direction that is not towards the earth's own centre; hence if the entire earth is being continually moved about some point, an external force is necessary. But where can such a force be found and if the earth is in constant motion, why is the movement not felt and why, for example, are the clouds not left behind? It is fairly clear the earth is at rest. But at rest where? If the cosmos is infinite in extent it is meaningless to ask this question since there are no *places* in an infinite universe. However, since it is in the nature of material bodies to occupy places appropriate to them, the cosmos is therefore undoubtedly finite. Observation supports this conclusion. The stars that never (seem to) change their positions *relative to each other*—the so-called 'fixed' stars—rotate daily about the earth in perfect circles. If the cosmos were infinite in extent, the parts an infinite distance from the earth would therefore have to travel with an infinite velocity (in order to traverse an infinite distance in a finite time). The idea is absurd. The cosmos is therefore finite. The question now arises as to the shape of the finite cosmos. Clearly the cosmos must always occupy the same space in its daily journey about its axis of rotation—for otherwise those parts of the cosmos 'jutting out' would have to be assumed to rotate continually into *what does not exist at all*. This is an impossibility. The cosmos is therefore 'rotationally invariant' about its axis of rotation. While admittedly this consideration fails to define the shape of the cosmos uniquely, there is every reason for assuming that the cosmos has the only perfect shape there is, namely that of a sphere. For if it is not a sphere but a lemon shape, why should it be a lemon shape and not a grapefruit shape? And vice versa. The conclusion is warranted that the cosmos is spherical and that the fixed stars are embedded in the outermost shell of this daily rotating sphere. What is the position of the earth? It is obvious that the earth lies on the axis of rotation of the cosmos for otherwise the angular separation between two adjacent stars when viewed from the earth would not remain the same. But where does the earth lie on this axis? It is difficult to imagine that the earth does not rest at the midpoint of this axis and therefore at the centre of the cosmos. For why should the earth be displaced from the centre just so far and not further? And why should earthly matter proceed naturally (without the application of an external force) to what would be such an arbitrary point? For these reasons alone, it is clear that the (stationary spherical) earth lies at the centre of the (rotating spherical) cosmos.[4]

Observation and reason together lead to more conclusions. Observation over the ages shows that there is never generation or corruption in the heavens and that all motion is in perfect circles (except, apparently, for the motion of the five wandering stars, Mercury, Venus, Mars, Jupiter and Saturn). On earth, on the other hand, generation and corruption follow each other regularly: the seasons come and go; people are born, mature, generate new human beings, and die; and so on. Hence it is clear that the cosmos is dichotomized into two qualitatively distinct regions, the celestial and terrestrial. The celestial region is eternal and immutable, consisting of a fifth pure element, the aether, which is neither 'heavy' nor 'light' and whose only natural movement is circular, unnatural, i.e. forced or violent movement of the aether being impossible. On the other hand, in the terrestrial region below the sphere of the moon there is no permanence of things—only permanence of change. Natural motion, no longer eternal, is in a straight line either towards the centre of the cosmos (in the case of the 'heavy' elements earth and water) or away from the centre (in the case of the 'light' elements air and fire), and has as its goal the attainment of rest either at the centre of the terrestrial sphere or at the circumference of this sphere. Circular motion at the earth's surface is clearly unnatural and requires the constant application of an external force. Were the heavens not in constant motion, the four transmutable elements would come to rest in such a way that a sphere of earthly matter would exist at the centre of the terrestrial region surrounded by a concentric sphere of water, then of air, and finally of the element fire. It is the constant movement of the heavens, generated in the first place by the unmoved mover, that causes the regular transmutation of the elements within the terrestrial sphere.

All this is very much as it should be. All men, whether barbarian or Greek, who believe in the existence of gods recognize the heavens as their abode, thus rightly associating the immortal with the immortal. Although reason and purpose are present throughout the entire cosmos, they reach perfection only in the heavens—the divine heavens, as Aristotle repeatedly insists. Moreover, Aristotle explains, in applying the terms 'male' and 'female' to the cosmos, men speak of the 'nature of the Earth as something female and call it "mother", while they give to the heaven and the sun and anything else of that kind the title of "generator" and "father"'.[5] Aristotle maintains further that whatever is superior should as far as possible be separate from what is inferior. Clearly that is why the heavens are separate from the lowly earth. In addition, Aristotle insists, that is why, 'wherever possible and so far as possible the male is separate from the female, since it is something *better* and more divine in that it is the principle of movement for generated things, while the female serves as their matter'.[6] But the male is not superior to the female merely because of the male's active generative powers; in the case of men and women the male is superior in the most important faculty of all, that of reason and deliberation. It follows that 'the relation of male to female is naturally that of the superior to the inferior—of the ruling to the ruled' (as also is that of the master to the slave). (Deficient as the female is in mental capacity, it is important Aristotle notes, to keep the minds of pregnant women 'free from exertion; for children evidently draw on the mother who carries them in her womb, just as plants draw on the soil'.)[7]

It is Aristotle's contention that in an important sense, female is to male as matter is to 'form'. According to Aristotle matter is inseparable from what he calls form, the latter being conveniently regarded as design embedded in matter, or, in Aristotle's words, 'that by reason of which the matter is some definite thing' or, alternatively, form is 'a kind of power immersed in matter'.[8] Thus the form of a marble statue is the shape of the statue, the form of an acorn is the oak tree which the matter of the acorn realizes in its development from potentiality to actuality (provided no external impediment interferes). Indeed nature itself can be considered as sculptor and material combined into one, or can be likened to a doctor treating himself. While a doctor, however, can make mistakes, as can nature, nevertheless 'in all things . . . Nature always strives after "the better"'.[9] Aristotle is careful to point out with respect to such striving that form cannot desire itself for it is not defective. What desires form is matter, just 'as the female desires the male and the ugly the beautiful . . . . '.[10] By this it should not be thought that nature *consciously* strives after 'the better', that matter consciously strives to realize the form embedded in it; all the processes occur without thought. Nevertheless purpose, albeit unconscious purpose, is characteristic of nature. Thus Aristotle insists that the 'local movement of each body into its own place must be regarded as similar to what happens in connection with other forms of generation and change' and therefore that 'the movement of each body to its own place is motion towards its own form'.[11] Hence the falling of a stone is given a teleological explanation by Aristotle: the 'final cause'—the goal—of the stone's motion is the centre of the cosmos. For this reason, let us remind ourselves, the earth as a whole must necessarily rest at the centre of the cosmos.

Life within the terrestrial sphere is defined by the possession of one or more of three souls. Plants possess only the vegetable soul which makes possible nourishment, growth and reproduction. The animal soul, however, possesses in addition to these three faculties, the faculties of local motion and sensation. At the summit of terrestrial life is the Greek male whose possession of a rational soul makes possible the greatest good of all, the *summum bonum* of reason and contemplation. From inanimate matter to animate beings, nature proceeds without making jumps. At the lower end of the ladder of life, spontaneous generation of living beings is possible (with putrefaction as the residue) but higher forms of life require generation from male and female principles. The male seed, Aristotle contends, supplies the active principle or form (and thus the sensitive or rational soul); the female, who is basically 'an infertile male', supplies merely the matter on which the active principle works.[12] All being well, a male offspring results from sexual union but if the active principle is defective and does not prevail over the resistance of the matter supplied by the female, then a female offspring results. Thus granular spermatic fluid produces male children while the thin and unclotted variety tends to produce female offspring.[13] Aristotle is emphatic over the nature of the female's imperfection:

Just as it sometimes happens that deformed offspring are produced by deformed parents, and sometimes not, so the offspring produced by a female are sometimes female, sometimes not, but male. The reason is that the female is as it were a deformed male; and the menstrual discharge is semen, though in an impure condition; i.e. it lacks one constituent, and one only, the principle of soul.[14]

The female's imperfection is manifested in an interesting although entirely predictable way among birds: for long and pointed eggs are female; 'those that are round, or more rounded at the narrow end, are male'.[15]

The four elements of the terrestrial sphere consist of primary matter with the addition of two qualities, one from the pair of contraries 'hot-cold' and one from the pair 'dry-wet'. Thus the element earth consists of the qualities 'cold' and 'dry' embedded in primary matter, water of the qualities 'cold' and 'wet', air 'hot' and 'wet', and finally fire 'hot' and 'dry'. By the interchange of the qualities 'dry' and 'wet', for example, earth becomes water and water earth. The natural motion of the two 'heavy' and two 'light' elements is towards and away from the centre of the earth respectively. The more resistant the medium through which a heavy element falls the slower its velocity; in a notation not used by Aristotle we can write that the velocity of motion v towards the centre of the earth of a heavy element of weight W in a medium offering resistance R is $v = W/R$. A similar proposition holds for unnatural, i.e. violent motion: if the constant, applied force is F and the medium offers a resistance R to the body then the velocity v of the body is $v = F/R$. If there is no medium then the resistance R is zero and the velocity of the body is infinite, which is an impossibility. Hence void is impossible and does not occur in nature; as everyone knows, nature abhors a vacuum. The cosmos thus consists everywhere of matter and, as we have seen, there is no 'outside' the finite cosmos; most certainly the cosmos is not 'suspended' in a void. Action at a distance is impossible since a body manifestly cannot act where it is not. If a body appears to act on another body separated from it, then this is possible only through the presence of an always-existing medium. In the case of projectiles after they have left the thrower's hand (or an arrow the string of the bow), it is the resultant movement of the air that pushes the projectile forward in its unnatural motion.

So much for the outlines of Aristotelian cosmology to which we shall be returning many times in this essay. Now let us consider Ptolemy's contribution to an explanation of the motions of the seven heavenly bodies which take place between the stationary terrestrial sphere and the sphere of the fixed stars. For it is their extraordinary behaviour that seems to violate at the outset Aristotle's belief, shared by Plato and other predecessors, that all heavenly motion is necessarily circular.

Ptolemaic astronomy
The fixed stars, the moon, the sun and the five wandering stars

(the planets Mercury, Venus, Mars, Jupiter and Saturn) all make a daily revolution around the earth from east to west. However, in addition to this daily motion, the moon, sun and five planets also move in their respective periods from west to east in the opposite direction, the moon in a month, the sun accompanied by Mercury and Venus in a year, Mars in approximately two years, Jupiter in twelve and Saturn in twenty nine, all orbits lying very nearly in the plane of the ecliptic (the name given to the sun's orbit). These contrary motions pose an obstacle not to the principle of circular motion of heavenly bodies but rather to the principle of circular motion with a constant velocity. In the case of the sun, for example, the Greeks postulated that its west to east motion with respect to the fixed stars is circular but that the centre *C* of the sun's orbit is displaced from the earth *E* which lies at the centre of the cosmos. This accounts for the observed fact—see Figure 2.1—that between the autumnal and spring (vernal) equinoxes *AE* and *SE* (the times when the sun rises exactly in the east), the sun spends more time in the northern hemisphere than it does in the southern. In the case of each planet, however, Ptolemy found it desirable to introduce the idea of an equant point *Q* slightly displaced both from the centre of the planet's orbit and from the earth's centre such that with respect to this point the planet moves on average with a constant angular velocity. For the five planets Ptolemy found it necessary

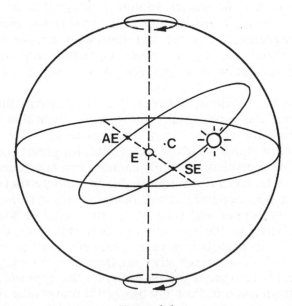

Figure 2.1

to introduce five different centres and five different equant points.

Now if all this were not complicated enough, the five planets have superimposed on their orbits around the earth a quite extraordinary behaviour. Every so often each planet slows up in its fairly regular west to east motion, eventually stops, retraces its steps in the opposite direction for a time, and then recommences its journey in the original direction! Such retrograde motion is shown in Figure 2.2 (i). Mars performs such a motion approximately once every orbit, Jupiter eleven times and Saturn twenty eight; in the case of Mercury and Venus the periods of their retrograde motions are 116 and 584 days respectively. As Geminus pointed out in disgust, such behaviour is more reminiscent of slaves at the beck and call of masters than of divine bodies who know their own minds! Despite its unseemly nature, the phenomenon of retrograde motion is easily accounted for by the addition of an epicycle to the main orbit of each planet. Since Mars, for example, shines somewhat more brightly at its point of maximum retrograde motion than elsewhere in its orbit, the observed retrograde motion of each planet may be conjectured to be similar to the motion described in Figure 2.2 (ii), and can thus be accounted for by epicyclic motion. The planet in question is considered to be attached to a point on an epicycle whose radius and period are chosen so as to reproduce the apparently anomalous behaviour of the planet. Such a saving of the phenomena for the planet Jupiter is illustrated in Figure 2.3 where the centre C' of the epicycle carrying the planet Jupiter orbits the centre C of the deferent with a constant angular velocity about the equant point Q, while Jupiter makes a complete revolution in its epicycle every year (as do Mars and Saturn).

Ptolemy has to admit, however, that while he can thus 'save the phenomena' the impression is unavoidably given that there is no great simplicity of motion in the heavens. Apart from the complexity of equants and epicycles (and, for greater accuracy, of epicycles on epicycles), Ptolemy cannot even give a unique order to the planets. Even if it is reasonable to suppose that because of its longest period Saturn is the planet furthest from the earth, followed by Jupiter and then Mars, the order of Mercury and Venus relative to the sun remains doubtful since the average period of both planets is a year. However, on the ground that Mercury and Venus never stray far from the sun whereas Mars, Jupiter and Saturn are regularly found on the opposite side of the heavens from the sun, Ptolemy thought it reasonable to conclude against Plato and Aristotle that Mercury and Venus lie between

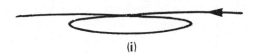

(i)

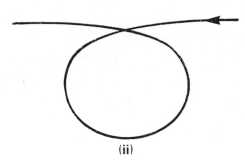

(ii)

Figure 2.2

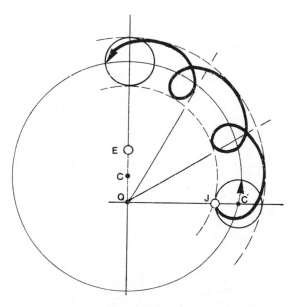

Figure 2.3

the earth and the sun while the other three planets lie beyond the
sun.

There is a further unsatisfactory feature of the Ptolemaic
system that needs emphasis. The centres of the epicycles of

Mercury and Venus have to be tied to the line joining the earth and the sun in order to ensure that Mercury and Venus remain roughly in line with the sun. On the other hand, the lines joining the centres of the epicycles of Mars, Jupiter and Saturn to their respective planets are required to remain parallel with the line joining the earth and the sun in order to ensure that when either Mars, Jupiter or Saturn is at its point of maximum retrograde motion the sun, as observed, is always diametrically opposite the planet in the heavens. These heavenly phenomena are illustrated in Figure 2.4 (in which Mars is shown at its point of maximum retrograde motion). Why such regularities should be thus and not otherwise remained a complete mystery to the Greeks. Obviously the sun exercised some sort of controlling influence over the behaviour of the planets but exactly why and how remained an enigma.

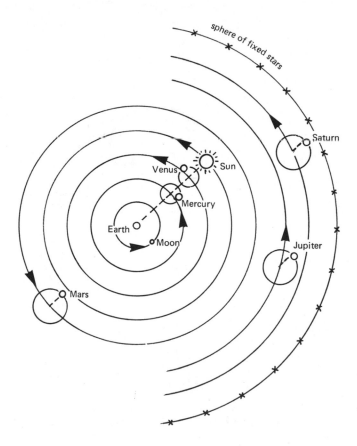

Figure 2.4

Aristotle did, however, attempt an explanation as to why Jupiter and Saturn make so many retrograde motions in their respective orbits around the earth while the nearer planets make so few. 'One thing then has and enjoys the ultimate good, other things attain to it . . .', Aristotle contends, 'while yet another does not even attempt to secure it . . .'. The required explanation follows: 'It is for this reason that the earth moves not at all and the bodies near to it with few movements. For they do not attain the final end, but only come as near to it as their share in the divine principle permits. But the first heaven finds it immediately with a single movement, and the bodies intermediate between the first and last heavens attain it indeed, but at the cost of a multiplicity of movements'.[16] Thus the earth, by its nature subject to generation and corruption, remains stationary at the centre of the cosmos; the divine principle being forever beyond its reach, any possible movement is rendered quite useless.

Whatever Ptolemy, as famed in antiquity for his astrology as for his astronomy, thought of this explanation, he found no cause for serious questioning of Aristotle's cosmology. He agrees that the fixed stars are always the same distance from the earth for otherwise the angular separation between any two stars would be variable. However, such parallax motion had never been observed. In addition, if the earth were not the centre of the cosmos then the point on the ecliptic corresponding to the spring equinox would not rise over the horizon exactly when the autumnal equinox is observed to be setting. Conversely, it also follows that the radius of the earth must be very much smaller than the radius of the cosmos for otherwise phenomena such as parallax motion would be detectable from different positions on the earth's surface.

Now, although the earth must lie at the centre of the cosmos, there remains the possibility that it is the earth which rotates daily from west to east and not the heavenly bodies from east to west. Ptolemy dismisses this Pythagorean idea as quite ridiculous. The natural motion of earthly matter is towards the centre of the cosmos and circular motion for earthly matter must be violent. How could such circular motion even begin, let alone be eternal? Furthermore, if the earth were rotating from west to east how could clouds ever be seen to move to the east, why is there not a perpetual wind from east to west? As Ptolemy concludes: 'in the light of what happens around us in the air, such a notion would seem altogether absurd'.[17] If, then, the idea of the earth's rotation about a north-south axis is absurd, of even greater absurdity is the idea proposed by Aristarchus in c.280 B.C. that the earth also orbits the sun once a year. Greek philosophers respectfully considered this idea but for very good reasons rejected it as quite false.

Aristotelian-Thomistic cosmology

My intention in this sketch has been to present essential features of Aristotelian-Ptolemaic cosmology, not to discuss debates in Greek society concerning the validity of particular features of this cosmology. Neither have I attempted to discuss alternative cosmologies, such as the atomistic cosmology of matter and void proposed by Democritus and Leucippus in the fifth century B.C. and developed by Epicurus in the third century B.C. Nor, for example, the important cosmology of Plato, Aristotle's teacher, who saw the (spherical) cosmos as a living, harmoniously proportioned whole, although also a material and therefore necessarily imperfect realization of a divine form or idea, animated throughout by a world soul responsible for the eternal, circular and divine motions of the heavens and heavenly bodies. It was in the hands of Plotinus and his successors that a 'neoplatonic' cosmology was articulated which would suggest the possibility of magical practices through contact with the hierarchy of Intelligences populating the heavens. Although condemned by Plotinus who advocated spiritual ascent to the Gods through the achievement of moral and ascetic purity, invocation of demons was to become a practice associated with neoplatonic cosmology. Alternative cosmologies, then, there certainly were to the Aristotelian which as late as the sixth century A.D. was being subjected to severe criticism. John Philoponus, for example, not only severely criticized Aristotle's two explanations of projectile motion, arguing that the projector necessarily imparts *some incorporeal motive force* to the projectile, but also pointed out against Aristotle that a heavy brick and a relatively light stone dropped simultaneously from a high cliff reach the bottom either together or with only an imperceptible time difference between their impacts.[18]

However, given that my subject is early modern Europe, I wish to bypass the thousand or so years of fluctuating fortune for Aristotelian cosmology to consider the views of the Dominican philosopher and theologian, St Thomas Aquinas (1225?–74) which were to make Aristotelian philosophy virtually unchallengeable. For after the Church's prohibitions of the study of Aristotle's natural philosophy in 1210, 1215 and 1231, it was above all Aquinas who in the second half of the thirteenth century rehabilitated and Christianized this heathen philosophy. Obviously Aristotle had to give way on certain issues: the cosmos was not eternal but had been created by God. Neither was

Aristotle correct in claiming that a void is impossible: it is obviously possible for God to create one. Nevertheless it remains true that voids do not exist in nature. With God's infinite power and creativity allowed for, Aristotle's cosmos in its broadest features was endorsed by Aquinas: namely, the earth's position at the centre of the cosmos and the terrestrial sphere's qualitative difference from the celestial sphere. Ptolemaic astronomy, however, was treated with caution as only hypothetical, Aquinas expressing the hope that eventually a simpler description of the planetary motions might be possible. The same point was made less diplomatically by Alphonso X the Wise of Castille who (legend has it) remarked after study of the Ptolemaic system that if the Lord God had consulted him before creating the cosmos he would have recommended something simpler! (One of Newton's disciples was to remember Alphonso's comment.)

With respect to the nature of woman and generation, Aquinas was once again in almost total agreement with Aristotle, except that a place must be found for God. Woman is naturally subject to man's control because in man the faculty of reason predominates. While it is true that woman had been created by God as a helpmate to man this is so only in the task of generation since in all other matters man is better helped by his fellow man. By delegating to woman this task of gestation, God in His wisdom left man free to pursue intellectual goals that are in any case beyond the capacity of woman. Although in gestation it is God who supplies the rational soul (Aristotle having to be corrected on this point), nevertheless Aristotle is correct in his claim that the mother supplies only formless matter for the baby's body, the formative power for the baby's development being transmitted by the father in his semen. 'And though this power cannot create the rational soul', Aquinas insists, 'yet it disposes the matter of the body to receive that form'. Again Aristotle is correct in believing that it is a defect in the active force of the semen that is responsible for the creation of a female. Aquinas' point of view would appear to be male: 'God is the principle of the whole universe', he sums up, 'so the first man, in likeness to God, was the principle of the whole human race'.[19] Let us also not forget, bearing in mind the subject matter of the first chapter, that Aquinas agrees with St Augustine that Satanic magic is possible, that demons exist and their conjuration possible, and that any magic involving signs and incantations is efficacious only through the agency of demons.

It is instructive to note that in the first decade of the fourteenth century, the Aristotelian-Thomistic cosmos was adopted by Dante as the stage for *The Divine Comedy*. In his epic journey

Dante descends to hell at the centre of the earth, ascends to purgatory on the other side and then, accompanied by his true love the virgin Beatrice, ascends to heaven through the spheres of the divine planets. At the start of his ascent to heaven, Dante, perplexed that he, a heavy earthly body, can be moving naturally away from the centre of the earth, away from hell, receives from Beatrice the explanation that having shed his earthly hindrance Dante is now a soul and the natural movement of a pure soul, like that of the element fire, is away from the centre. The Aristotelian cosmos and Aristotelian physics have become central to the drama of the Christian quest for spiritual salvation.

The following century, we recall, witnessed the start of the witchcraze and the subsequent publication of the *Malleus Maleficarum*. While the first chapter of this essay discussed some ineffective attacks made on the demonological aspects of Thomistic theology and its later developments, we are now in a position to outline devastatingly effective attacks made not on such a 'marginal area' as demonology but directed against the entire fabric of the cosmos. Let us proceed to turn the world upside down!

A precautionary note: in this chapter some pains have been taken to portray Aristotelian male-female dichotomization of the cosmos. In the remainder of this chapter no further extended reference will be made to the fate of male and female principles as the Aristotelian cosmos crumbles. In future chapters this important theme will necessarily be resumed.

2   The Copernican Transformation: Pro and Contra

If Nicolas Copernicus, educated at the Universities of Cracow, Bologna and Padua, is to be believed, then a draft version of *De Revolutionibus Orbium Coelestium (On the Revolutions of the Heavenly Spheres)* existed as early as 1506. But the worldly Canon at Frauenberg, who in 1526 at the request of the King of Poland had written a treatise on the problem of inflation,[20] was very reluctant to rush into print what he considered to be a potentially inflammable document. Thirty-six years later, however, encouraged by the Archbishop of Capua and by the success of the *Narratio Prima* of his student Rheticus, Copernicus undertook for publication a revision of the draft version, surviving just long enough to receive on his death bed a copy of his momentous book.

Why had Copernicus not accepted what everyone else accepted: 'the fact' that the earth lies stationary at the centre of the cosmos? The principal reason was because Copernicus not unreasonably believed God to be an architect of consummate skill and yet the Aristotelian-Ptolemaic world system was, let us not mince words, ugly. The pious conclusion necessarily follows that the Aristotelian-Ptolemaic world system has a basic flaw. This point deserves emphasis.

The Renaissance architect, Paladio, had attempted to define concisely the ideal of beauty. In the case of a temple, Paladio explained in 1560, beauty will result 'from the correspondence of the whole to the parts, of the parts among themselves, and of these again to the whole; so that the structure may appear an entire and complete body, wherein each member agrees with the other and all members are necessary for the accomplishment of the building'.[21] A specialist on Renaissance architecture describes in these ecstatic words Giulano da Sangallo's church, S. Maria dello Carceri at Prato, begun in 1485: 'Its majestic simplicity, the undisturbed impact of its geometry, the purity of its whiteness are designed to evoke in the congregation a consciousness of the presence of God—of a God who has ordered the universe according to immutable mathematical laws, who has created a uniform and beautifully proportioned world, the consonance and harmony of which is mirrored in His temple below.'[22] But this was exactly wherein lay Copernicus' problem. The church S. Maria dello Carceri may well have been a model of harmonious order; the cosmos of Aristotle and Ptolemy was not.

Copernicus made his aesthetic objection very clear in the Preface to *De Revolutionibus*. The Aristotelian-Ptolemaic astronomers have not been able 'to discern or deduce the principal thing—namely the shape of the Universe and the unchangeable symmetry of its parts'.[23] In their system, Copernicus complained, there was no way at all of ordering the planets. Rheticus exuberantly poses the principal problem: 'Moreover, ye immortal gods, what dispute, what strife there has been until now over the position of the spheres of Venus and Mercury, and their relation to the sun. But the case is still before the judge. Is there anyone who does not see that it is very difficult and even impossible ever to settle this question while the common hypotheses are accepted?' On Ptolemaic principles, why should not even Saturn be located between the earth and the sun?! But, Rheticus concludes modestly, accept his master's hypotheses and the resultant 'symmetry and interconnection of the motions and spheres' become 'not unworthy of God's workmanship and not unsuited to these divine bodies'.[24] God's handiwork is rehabilitated in the heliocentric system. In Copernicus' own words the cosmos becomes once again 'this most beautiful temple'.

Copernicus' first chapter is tactfully written. He is only too

aware that the 'authorities agree that Earth holds firm her place
at the centre of the Universe and they regard the contrary as
unthinkable, nay as absurd' (not just the authorities, recall Jean
Bodin's incredulity).[25] However, despite the difficulty of his views,
Copernicus believes they can be, God willing, made 'abundantly
clear at least to mathematicians'. Copernicus sensitively explains
that he has every confidence that the Pope will be able to
comprehend them and it is therefore to the 'Most Holy Lord,
Pope Paul III' that *De Revolutionibus* is dedicated.[26]

What, then, are the principal arguments that Copernicus
marshals in support of his revolutionary theory? He has, let us
note, no new 'facts' at his disposal. The old 'facts' must be made
to support a radically different theory! Let us see how Copernicus
proceeds.

Copernicus' arguments
If the earth is assumed to make a daily rotation from west to east,
then the daily east to west motion of all the heavenly bodies
becomes only apparent. This is the first stage of Copernicus'
argument and to make the idea of the earth's movement plausible
(be it only a daily rotation), he has to refute Aristotle's and
Ptolemy's objections.

To the objection that the earth would disintegrate under such
rapid circular motion about its own centre, Copernicus replies,
relying on Aristotelian categories of motion, that the earth's
motion is *natural* and not forced. It is true, he agrees, that things
'subjected to any force, gradual or sudden, must be disintegrated,
and cannot long exist. But natural processes being adapted to
their purpose work smoothly'. Thus Ptolemy need not fear for the
safety of the earth. 'Should he not fear', Copernicus counter-
attacks, 'even more for the Universe, whose motion must be as
much more rapid as the Heavens are greater than the Earth?'[27]

For Aristotelians this attempt to turn the tables on them fails
pathetically since the heavenly material is neither light nor heavy
and is therefore never in danger of disintegration under its only
possible motion, circular.

If the earth truly rotates, Copernicus has also to explain why
there is not a permanent wind from east to west, why clouds and
objects suspended in the air keep up with the earth. This is either,
Copernicus argues, because the air contains an admixture of
earthly or watery matter and so follows the earth's natural
motion, or because the air acquires such motion through its
continual contact with the earth and absence of resistance.

If, however, the earth has a natural circular motion, how is it
possible to explain the always perpendicular and apparently

natural fall of heavy objects towards the centre of the earth? Natural circular motion, Copernicus explains, occurs only if the moving body occupies its natural place and it is a motion that applies only to the body *as a whole*. If *a part* of that body is removed from its natural position by force, then, Copernicus argues, on release of that force the displaced part returns to its natural position by rectilinear motion. Thus a (part of a) body displaced from its natural position experiences a combination of rectilinear and circular motion; a body such as the earth constantly occupying its natural position enjoys only circular motion. In 1543 Aristotle must have been turning in his grave.

However, Copernicus does not make use of his hypothesis to try to upgrade the status of the earth. On the contrary, Copernicus explains that 'we conceive immobility to be nobler and more divine than change and inconstancy, which latter is thus more appropriate to Earth than to the Universe'.[28] In any case, is it not absurd to ascribe motion to that which contains rather than to that which is contained? Copernicus seems to have no idea that he is intent on opening a Pandora's box!

So far so good the argument? One must be generous because so far Copernicus is attempting only to soften up his readers for the main thrust of his argument. If we can agree that the earth has one motion, then perhaps we can proceed to agree that it has two! Perhaps it is a planet! If this is the case, then undoubtedly the Creator has bestowed on the parts of each planet, moon and sun a tendency to combine into a sphere, just as He has so bestowed on the parts of the earth. It is not surprising, then, that despite the various motions of the moon, planets and earth, each body maintains a spherical shape. And certainly the earth is a planet as the following arguments show.

If the earth is assumed to orbit the sun and not vice versa, then Copernicus can deduce 'the principal thing' which is the order of the planets. The fact that Mercury and Venus never stray far from the sun, whereas Mars, Jupiter and Saturn wander regularly to the opposite side of the heavens, means simply that Mercury and Venus lie between the earth and the sun, while Mars, Jupiter and Saturn lie further from the sun than the earth. In addition, Mercury's orbit is smaller than that of Venus. Indeed, it is easy for Copernicus to calculate the distances r_M and r_V of Mercury and Venus from the sun in terms of the earth's distance r_E, as is shown in Figure 2.5. When the angular separation between the sun and Venus is at a maximum α_V, then it follows that Venus subtends a right-angle at the earth and sun and hence $r_V = r_E \sin \alpha_V$. A similar argument holds for Mercury, and a slightly more complex argument gives the distances of Mars, Jupiter and Saturn

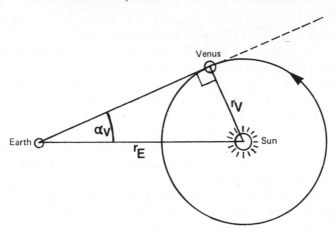

Figure 2.5

in term of r_E. The order of the planets is unambiguous: the sun at the centre, Mercury, Venus, the earth, Mars, Jupiter, Saturn. The moon, however, remains a satellite of the earth. Furthermore, the periods of the planets increase uniformly (but not proportionately) with distance from the sun. In Table 2.1 these periods are shown for convenience alongside the average distance of each planet from the sun as computed by Copernicus:[29]

Table 2.1

	Period	*Distance*
Mercury	88 days	0.38
Venus	225 days	0.72
Earth	1 year	1
Mars	1.88 years	1.52
Jupiter	11.87 years	5.22
Saturn	29.44 years	9.67

There is, however, a minor problem. If the earth orbits the sun then the stars should exhibit parallax motion which they do not. Copernicus is not held up for a moment by this potentially devastating fact. That there is no such motion for the fixed stars 'proves[!] their immeasurable distance, compared to which even the size of the Earth's orbit is negligible and the parallactic effect unnoticeable'. There is therefore a vast distance between the sphere of Saturn and the sphere of the fixed stars, 'so great is this divine work of the Great and Noble Creator'. Copernicus is rightly jubilant. According to his world system, 'the orders and magnitudes of all stars and spheres, nay the heavens themselves, become so bound together that nothing in any part thereof could be moved from its place without producing confusion of all the other parts and of the Universe as a whole'.[30] In his discussion of the 'wandering stars' in Chapter V of *De Revolutionibus,* Copernicus reemphasizes this fundamental achievement: 'the mobility of the Earth binds together the order and magnitude of their orbital circles in a wonderful harmony and sure commensurability'.[31]

There is a further central feature of the Copernican world system to be emphasized which is indeed one of its major triumphs: the retrograde motions of the five planets do not exist. They are apparent motions that result only from failure to take into account the earth's annual orbital motion. This phenomenon is shown for Mars in Figure 2.6 (i). Copernicus reasoned that every time the earth overtakes Mars in its orbit Mars necessarily appears to undergo retrograde motion. Thus when the earth is at position 1, Mars is at position 1 in its orbit but appears from the earth to be between the fixed stars *A* and *B*. At a later time when the earth is at position 2, and is slightly closer to Mars, Mars has moved on to position 2 in its orbit and appears from the earth to be between stars *E* and *F*, although still travelling in the 'forward' direction. As the earth begins to pass Mars, so Mars appears to stop and eventually to change direction, shining at its brightest at

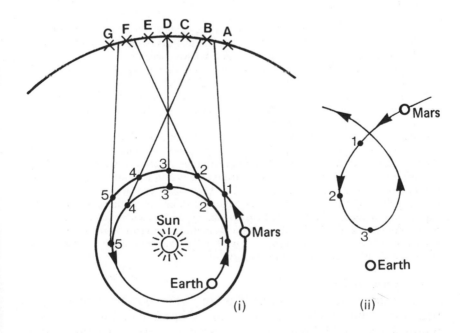

Figure 2.6

the time of maximum retrograde motion when it appears from position 3 of the earth to be in line with star *D*. Once the earth has overtaken Mars, the retrograde motion begins to slow down and by the time the earth is in position 5, Mars has once more resumed its forward course and appears to lie between stars *F* and *G*. Relative to the 'stationary' earth, the motion of Mars is as shown in Figure 2.6 (ii). Furthermore, it is now obvious why Mars and the sun must be diametrically opposite in the heavens at the point of maximum retrograde motion, and similarly with Jupiter and Saturn. Indeed it now becomes crystal clear why for the three 'superior' planets in the Ptolemaic system the line joining the centre of each epicycle to its respective planet is required to remain parallel to the line joining the earth and sun. All features of 'retrograde motion' for the three 'wandering stars', Mars, Jupiter and Saturn now become predictable. (In the case of Mercury and Venus it is, of course, when these planets overtake the earth that retrograde motion appears to occur.) There are no longer any problems—well almost no problems—in the heavenly motions.

   This is how Copernicus concludes with pride his introduction to *De Revolutionibus*:

In the middle of all sits Sun enthroned. In this most beautiful temple could we place this luminary in any better position from which he can illuminate the whole at once? He is rightly called the Lamp, the Monarch, the Ruler of the Universe; Hermes Trismegistus names him the Visible God. . . . So the Sun sits as upon a royal throne ruling his children, the planets, which circle round him. The Earth has the Moon at her service. As Aristotle says, in his *de Animalibus,* the Moon has the closest relationship with the Earth. Meanwhile the Earth conceives by the Sun, and becomes pregnant with an annual rebirth.
   So we find underlying this ordination an admirable symmetry in the Universe, and a clear bond of harmony in the motion and magnitude of the orbits such as can be discovered in no other wise. For here we may observe why the progression and retrogression appear greater for Jupiter than Saturn, and less for Mars, but again greater for Venus than for Mercury; and why such oscillation appears more frequently in Saturn than in Jupiter, but less frequently in Mars and Venus than in Mercury; moreover why Saturn, Jupiter and Mars are nearer to the Earth at opposition to the Sun than when they are lost in or emerge from the Sun's rays. Particularly Mars, when he shines all night, appears to rival Jupiter in magnitude, being only distinguishable by his ruddy colour; otherwise he is scarce equal to a star of the second magnitude, and can be recognised only when his movements are carefully followed. All these phenomena proceed from the same cause, namely Earth's motion.[32]

Arguments against
No new facts but new arguments and very powerful ones have been presented. Not only does the Copernican theory give a unique order to the planets but its explanatory power is greater than Ptolemy's, as the theory's supporters never ceased to

emphasize. The one assumption of the earth's yearly orbital motion around the sun uniquely orders the planets and explains a multiplicity of hitherto inexplicable phenomena connected with retrograde motion. If God is a good architect, then the world system is as described by Copernicus.

Why, then, was the Copernican system not immediately accepted? In the opinion of critics its obvious advantages were far outweighed by equally obvious and extremely serious disadvantages, outstanding among which were the following:

(a) The triple motion of the earth

The earth's axis of rotation cannot be assumed to be perpendicular to the plane of the earth's orbit around the sun for otherwise no reasons are possible, the sun always lying directly above the earth's equator. Accordingly the axis of rotation must be assumed to make an angle less than 90° with the plane of the earth's orbit, as shown in Figure 2.7, and to remain parallel with itself during the earth's journey round the sun (so that, for example, when the earth is at *A* the northern hemisphere is enjoying summer, at *B* the southern hemisphere). However, Copernicus assumed that a yearly conical motion of the axis—the infamous third motion—is necessary in order for the axis of rotation to remain parallel with itself. Very nearly but not quite a yearly motion. Since observation suggests that the north celestial pole itself undergoes circular motion with a period of 26,000 years—a phenomenon called the precession of the equinoxes and responsible for calendar difficulties over a long period—the axis of rotation must be assumed to perform a conical motion once every 26,000 years. Hence 13,000 years after the time of the orbit shown in Figure 2.7, the earth's axis of rotation will be as shown in Figure 2.8. The third yearly motion of the earth introduced by Copernicus is therefore needed to keep the earth's axis of rotation *almost* parallel with itself, 26,000 years having to elapse before the axis of rotation completes what would be without the third motion an

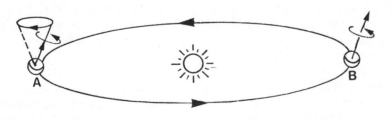

Figure 2.7

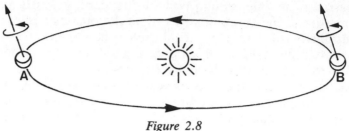

Figure 2.8

annual conical motion. From the point of view of Copernicus' critics, the earth cannot even have one natural motion. But Copernicus postulated three!

(b) The motion of the moon
According to Copernicus all the planets orbit the sun in their respective periods except the moon which orbits the earth. But why is the moon different? Does it not spoil the symmetry of the Copernican theory? How does the moon manage to keep up with the earth?

(c) The apparent size of Mars and Venus
If the orbits of Venus, the earth and Mars are as calculated by Copernicus, then sometimes the earth lies close to Venus and Mars, sometimes distant. Hence the apparent sizes of Venus and Mars should vary appreciably (by a factor of up to sixty). No such variation of apparent size had ever been observed. The conclusion is obvious that while the Copernican system saves certain of the planetary appearances, as does the Ptolemaic, it does not correspond to physical reality. Furthermore, if Venus orbits the sun as postulated by Copernicus, then observed from the earth Venus should exhibit phases exactly similar to the moon's. Again, no such phases had ever been observed.

(d) No parallax motion and large size of stars
If the earth undergoes a yearly orbital motion around the sun, then the stars should exhibit parallax motion. As we have seen, Copernicus explained the absence of such motion by offering the ad hoc explanation that the stars lie on a sphere at an immense distance from the earth. But if this is so then because the stars subtend a finite angle at the eye the actual diameter of many of them must be greater than the diameter of the earth's supposed orbit around the sun, even greater than the diameter of Saturn's orbit! The Copernican theory is ridiculous.

(e) Number of epicycles comparable with the number used by
    Ptolemy
Copernicus had objected to the use of the equant in Ptolemaic
astronomy and had replaced it by means of auxiliary circles. This
meant that in order to achieve accuracy comparable with
Ptolemaic planetary tables, Copernicus was forced to increase the
number of circles on circles until the actual number used became
comparable with the number used in the various Ptolemaic
systems. Hence from the point of view of circle counting,
Copernicus' system was not simpler than Ptolemaic varieties, and
not more accurate.

(c) Violation of Aristotelian physics
The Copernican system grossly violates Aristotelian principles of
motion and by locating the earth in the heavens destroys
Aristotle's dichotomization of the cosmos into celestial and
terrestrial regions. It was all very well for Copernicus to claim
that natural motion for the totality of earthly matter is circular (or
rather a combination of circular motions!), while for parts
displaced from the totality the motion is both rectilinear and
circular. To his critics this new physics—such as it was—seemed
a desperate and ad hoc affair to save a manifestly incorrect
theory.

(g) Violation of common sense and sense experience
No one has ever felt the motion of the earth and the eyes are
witness to the fact that the heavens revolve about the earth.
Apart from anything else, common sense underwrites the
Aristotelian cosmos.

(h) Biblical testimony
Apart from anything else? The Bible states in many passages that
the earth is stationary and that the sun and heavens revolve about
it. In Joshua 10 there is the famous passage: 'Thus spake Joshua
to the Lord, . . . and he said in the sight of Israel, Sun, stand thou
still upon Gibeon; and thou, Moon, in the valley of Ajalon. And
the sun stood still, and the moon stayed, until the people had
avenged themselves upon their enemies.' The Bible, common
sense, Aristotelian physics and the facts all prove Copernicus
wrong!
   Such must have been the conclusion of the overwhelming
majority of educated people in the second half of the sixteenth
century. Claiming that 'mathematics are for mathematicians',
Copernicus, after all, had not expected non-mathematicians to
accept his world system.[33] By and large they did not. And they

had an ace card to play. Was there not some way in which the manifest advantages of the Copernican system could be included in a new world system in harmony with theology, physics, common sense and the facts? The Danish nobleman and astronomer, Tycho Brahe, in concluding that there was, necessarily created great difficulties for those natural philosophers committed to proving the truth of the Copernican system.

The Tychonic compromise

'But are not earthly things being confused with celestial things? Is not the whole order of nature being turned upside down?'[34] Thus in 1589 Tycho Brahe, no slavish follower of Aristotle, saw where matters were heading. The new star of 1572, for which he could find no parallax motion, convinced Tycho that the heavens are not entirely immutable; the great comet of 1577 (shown to the young Kepler by his mother) convinced him that the heavens do not consist of crystalline spheres for no resistance is offered to the comet's passage. Nevertheless, although the advantages of the Copernican system were clear to Tycho, the Danish nobleman was adamant that 'the body of the Earth, large, sluggish and inapt for motion is not to be disturbed by movement (especially three movements) any more than the Aetherial Lights are to be shifted'. A compromise solution was necessary. 'I began to ponder', he tells his readers, ' . . . whether by any reasoning it was possible to discover an hypothesis, which in every respect would agree with both Mathematics and Physics, and avoid theological censure, and at the same time wholly accord with the celestial appearances.' Tycho's solution is shown in Figure 2.9: the earth occupies the central position of the cosmos, about which orbit the moon and sun, while the five planets have the moving sun—'their Leader and King'—as the centre of their respective orbits. 'Thus a manifest cause is provided', Tycho explains, 'why the single motion of the Sun is necessarily involved in the motions of all five planets, in a particular and certain manner'.[35] A compromise world system has been achieved: the Tychonic system has the advantages of the Copernican system; it does not have its revolutionary and absurd consequences. Above all, the earth retains its decadent position at the centre of the cosmos.

This is a good point at which to take stock. Copernicus' arguments are excellent but the consequences are too revolutionary—apart from 'empirical' refutation and violation of common sense!—to gain general acceptance. In any case, if it is granted that there are no crystalline spheres in the heavens, then Tycho's system maintains both Aristotle's dichotomization of the cosmos and the earth's central, decadent position. However, the non-

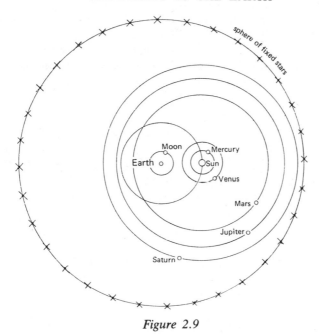

Figure 2.9

existence of crystalline spheres means that new causes of the motion of the solar satellites must be found. One thing has become clear: by 1600 there have been new arguments provided and new facts acknowledged. Nevertheless the Copernican theory has not been proved; if anything it has been disproved, although not conclusively. Are people who continued to support the Copernican theory guilty of gross credulity as Jean Bodin would have it? What were their motives in continuing their campaign in favour of a 'manifestly absurd' and dangerously revolutionary cosmology? 'Liberation'? Before we look at this possibility, it will be of future significance to note Michel de Montaigne's opinion of the Copernican system, the sceptic, we recall, whose down-to-earth and humane views we outlined in the first chapter. Is Montaigne in favour of the Copernican system and, if not, why not?

Liberation of the earth or of (some of) its inhabitants?
In his *Essays* Montaigne notes that Ptolemy and all the philosophers of antiquity believed that they knew the world's measure; yet Ptolemy had been totally wrong concerning the existence of land masses only recently discovered. '[I]f Ptolemy's reason deceived us in the past', Montaigne concludes, 'it would not be stupidity or obtuseness in me to mistrust what is being said

now, to believe that this great body that we call the world is something quite different from what we believe it to be'.[36] To make difficult matters worse, Montaigne wants to know how it is possible in principle to decide between the Ptolemaic and Copernican world systems? In a thousand years' time a third opinion might overthrow both! One thing, however, appears certain to Montaigne. It is that the motivation of the Copernicans is a combination of pride and arrogance; the Copernican system, Montaigne believes, is but a reflection of man's incorrigible desire to imagine himself lord of creation. Montaigne argues the case that all change—certainly all revolutionary change—is to be avoided, particularly in public affairs. For it is easy to criticize and no man ever fails who seeks to arouse discontent. 'But to establish a better state of things in place of what he has destroyed—many a man has failed in his endeavours to do that'.[37] It is then with foreboding—particularly for man's fellow creatures!—that Montaigne views the implications of the Copernican world system:

Presumption is our natural and original sickness. The frailest and most vulnerable creature is man, the vainest of all creatures. Man sees and feels himself lodged here in the filth and mire of the world, attached and nailed down to the worst, the deadest and most stagnant part of the world, the furthest removed from the celestial vault . . . and [yet] in his imagination he sees himself above the circle of the moon and watching the heavens move about beneath him. It is the vanity of this very imagination that makes man see himself as the equal of God, endowed with godlike qualities, cut off from all other creatures, the animals, his brothers in nature and his companions, to each of which he assigns its proper place and distributes among them such faculties and powers as he deems fit.[38]

How are Montaigne's scepticism and pessimism to be answered? Does the earth lie at the centre of the cosmos? If so, is that centre degenerate and corrupt compared with the divine immutability of the celestial sphere? If not, how can this be proved and what will be the consequences of liberating the earth—or European man—or rather, the male ruling classes of western Europe —from Aristotelian-Thomistic geocentric cosmology? The reader will recall that the discussion and analysis of Chapter 1 was basically restricted to the century preceding the year 1600 during which the revolutionary cosmology we have been discussing was almost silently undergoing gestation. In the early decades of the seventeenth century, however, this cosmology was thrust upon the consciousness of every educated person in Europe, as its two leading protagonists, Johannes Kepler and Galileo Galilei, made very clear their determination to push home (in Kepler's words to Galileo) 'this already moving carriage to its destination'.[39]

3 *Protagonists of the New Cosmology: Kepler and Galileo*

Kepler's astronomy

One of the major protagonists of the 'Copernican Revolution', Johannes Kepler, not only contained within himself the various contradictory, conflicting aspects of that revolution but experienced at first hand the terrible social conditions in which that revolution occurred. Peasant wars, the schism within the Church, the persecution of witches—all impinged forcefully on the life of Johannes Kepler. Although the major peasant war of 1594–7 did not directly affect Kepler's life, the peasant war of 1626, which was the largest uprising in central Europe since 1525, saw Kepler and the inhabitants of Linz besieged by peasant armies. Eventual defeat of the peasants by the Imperial armies left 12,000 of them dead and a larger number crippled and driven into exile. Kepler's own mother was accused of witchcraft. In his *Harmony of the World* the gentle Kepler beseeched God's help that His human servants might establish 'sanctity of life' on earth, that 'from the bringing of Thy people into concord the body of Thy church may be built up in the Earth, as Thou didst erect the heavens themselves out of harmonies'.[40] In the heavens above, the most beautiful harmonies; below on earth famine, disease, conflict, war, bloodshed and execution. Kepler never resolved that 'contradiction'. Indeed, Kepler's advocacy of the Copernican world system almost led to the execution of his mother.

According to Kepler, Tycho Brahe's world system could not be correct for many reasons. Since Tycho himself had shown that crystalline spheres do not exist, the issue had to be faced both in the Copernican and Tychonic systems as to the nature of the agency which moves the planets in their orbits round the sun. Calculating that the velocity of each planet decreases with its distance from the sun, Kepler reasoned that either the motive soul of each planet becomes weaker with increasing distance from the sun or that there are no motive souls at all in the planets. The motive soul, concluded Kepler, resides solely in the sun. But if the Tychonic system is correct what can account for the sun's motion? Is the earth responsible for the orbital motion not only of the moon and sun, but also that of the five planets carried around by the sun? Kepler argued that it is far simpler to assume, as Copernicus did, that the sun is the centre of the cosmos around which six planets revolve, each driven by the sun's motive soul, the earth being responsible for the motion only of the moon. Furthermore, the period of the earth's motion, one year, fits conveniently between the periods of Venus and Mars. Of supreme importance for Kepler is his discovery that by a certain ordering of the five perfect solids within a nest of concentric shells, the radii of the planetary orbits can be accurately predicted, except for the outermost and innermost planets Saturn and Mercury. In addition, since there are only five perfect bodies, there can be only six planets orbiting the sun. Kepler's conclusion is therefore that the Copernican theory is correct, not the Tychonic. He triumphantly explains to his former teacher, the astronomer Michael Maestlin, that 'the Sun which keeps its place, motionless, in the midst of the planets, and which is nevertheless the source of all motion, provides the image of God the Father, the Creator, for creation is to God, as motion is to the Sun'. In his *Mysterium Cosmographicum,* published in 1596 (from which the above arguments are taken), Kepler had written how 'it was absolutely necessary that the most perfect Creator should produce the most beautiful handiwork'.[41]

But how can the Copernican theory possibly be correct? Do not heavy objects such as stones fall perpendicularly to the earth's surface—in other words, in the direction of the earth's centre —thereby proving that this centre is also the centre of the cosmos? The intrepid Kepler totally rejects Aristotle's theory of gravity and, for good measure, Copernicus' as well, advancing in their place his own 'true theory of heaviness (or gravity)'. The all important point is that heaviness is a 'mutual corporeal disposition between related bodies toward union or conjunction (which, in the order of things, the magnetic faculty is also), so that it is much rather the case that the earth attracts a stone than that the stone seeks the earth'. Do, then, all objects have a mutual 'sympathy' or 'attraction' for each other? Kepler claims they do and argues that if two stones were placed near each other somewhere in the universe sufficiently far from all other bodies, then the two stones would move mutually towards each other. Were the earth and the moon not held in their respective orbits by some force, then they would also approach each other. It is, moreover, the attraction of the moon that produces the tides. To make matters crystal clear, Kepler adds: 'If the earth should cease to attract its oceans, the waters in all its seas would fly up and flow round the body of the moon.' Tycho Brahe's assistant has already proved himself a revolutionary thinker.[42]

All this, however, is only the preface to Kepler's *Astronomia Nova* of 1609. In the main text Kepler presents his arguments for taking the audacious and certainly revolutionary step of abandoning the time-hallowed belief in the necessity of the idea of perfect circular motion for the planets. Initially, by assuming the planes of the planets to intersect in the sun and by reintroducing equant points eliminated by Copernicus, Kepler had been able to ascribe to each planet just one circle. This in itself was a great triumph. But unfortunately—or fortunately for astronomy—the circle for Mars failed by eight minutes of arc to fit all of the relevant observations made by Tycho which Kepler knew were accurate to four minutes of arc (and which had passed into his possession following his collaboration with Tycho and Tycho's death). Accordingly Kepler decided that something had to go, namely the use of equant points, and by ingenious reasoning hypothesized that each planet in its circular orbit has a velocity such that the radius vector from the sun to the planet sweeps out equal areas in equal times. Confirming to his satisfaction that such an 'area law' holds also for the earth as for the planets Kepler turned his attention again to the troublesome orbit of Mars. But once again there remained a discrepancy of eight minutes of arc at certain positions in the orbit of Mars. At this point, rather than reject his now much-loved 'area law' Kepler made his momentous decision to consider the possibility that the planets and Mars in particular do not have exactly circular orbits. Subsequent calculations convinced him that this was indeed the case and that the area law could be retained. After much further computation and conjecture Kepler wrote in exultation to a friend and amateur astronomer: 'But I have the answer, my dear Fabricius: the orbit of the planet is a perfect ellipse, . . . or deviates therefrom by no more than an imperceptible amount.' This made Kepler increasingly suspicious of even the idea of a motive soul in the sun, pointing out in his *Epitome Astronomiae Copernicanae* of 1621 that 'the elliptical shape of the planetary orbits and the laws of motion by which such a figure is traced, reveal more of the nature of balance and material necessity than of the concept and determination of a mind'. The rotating sun with immaterial lines of force emanating from it sweeps the planets round it as if caught in a kind of 'very rapid whirlpool'. In the second edition of his *Mysterium Cosmographicum,* also published in 1621, Kepler summed up the direction of his thought: 'If we substitute for the word "soul" the word "force", then we get just the principle which underlies my physics of the skies in the *Astronomia Nova.*'[43] Despite such natural necessity the geometrical mind of God remains manifestly visible in the theory of the five perfect solids and in the relation Kepler had discovered—his famous 'third law'—between the average radius of each planetary orbit and its periodic time, namely that for *each* planet the square of the radius is equal to the cube of the periodic time multiplied by the same constant factor. A few years later Kepler published the so-called *Rudolphine Tables* of the planetary motions which were some 50 to 100 times more accurate than alternative tables. Game, set and match, one might naively imagine, to the Copernican system as developed by Johannes Kepler. Three years later in 1630 Johannes Kepler died penniless. Three years later again, Galileo was forced to make a public recantation of his almost life-long belief in the reality of the earth's annual orbital motion.

Kepler, too, very early in his adult life, had rejected geocentric cosmology and with it Aristotle's dichotomization of the cosmos. The earth's status, for Kepler, was no greater than *but also no less than* the status of the solar planets. In response to Galileo's telescopic discoveries of 1610 Kepler not only wrote that it was not improbable that the moon and the other planets were inhabited but looked forward to future space flight: 'Given ships or sails adapted to the breezes of heaven, there will be those', he rejoiced, 'who will not shrink from even that vast expanse'.[44] Galileo was called upon by Kepler to join him in the preparation of astronomical navigational tables for the future voyagers. The Aristotelian cosmos was for Kepler the relic of a bygone age!

It was also in 1610 that Kepler completed the manuscript of his famous *Dream* which he circulated to friends and which was to help produce such disastrous consequences. A description of a possible journey to the moon would have been provocative enough but Kepler included his 'mother' in the dream in a way seemingly calculated to invite disaster. The dreamer's mother, Fioxhilde of Iceland, recently deceased, had made her living by collecting herbs which she brewed with elaborate ceremonies and sold to sailors as charms. Her son Duracotus, after studying with a Danish astronomer called Tycho Brahe(!), learns from her that she can summon demons who can instantly transport her to foreign shores. A demon whom she conjures up describes a journey to the moon. This is easy for demons apparently but exceedingly difficult for men, particularly for fat Germans, although less so for the 'lean hard bodies' of Spaniards, while especially suited 'are dried-up old crones, who since childhood have ridden over great stretches of the earth at night in tattered cloaks on goats or pitchforks'.[45] The rest of the *Dream* need not be related; readers of Chapter 1 will understand that irreparable damage has been done.

The first copy of the manuscript passed outside Kepler's control, who believed to his disgust that it had reached John Donne, 'the author of that insolent satire' *Ignatius His Conclave*. It had reached, however, or reports of it had reached, his home duchy of Württemberg, whose inhabitants, Kepler learnt, associated Duracotus with himself and Fioxhilde with his mother

Katharina. In 1615 Katharina was accused of witchcraft. There followed for Katharina and Kepler six agonising years in which Kepler strove to defend his mother against the capital charge, arguing that all the maleficia she had supposedly inflicted on neighbours could be explained naturally. Bravely refusing to confess after being shown instruments of torture, Katharina was eventually released in 1621 but died a broken woman a year later. Bitterly Kepler wrote afterwards how his words 'had been taken up by dark minds which suspect everything else of being dark'. It was true he had referred to old crones: 'such a desire had I to jest and to argue jestingly!', he explained.[46] The accepted cosmology in which Johannes Kepler the astronomer, 'Platonic mystic', and would-be humorist had worked, and which he had sought to overturn, was geocentric and diabolicentric. But, as we noted in Chapter 1, the decade in which Kepler died saw both witch-burning at its most intense and the personal defeat of Galileo.

Galileo's struggle
In reply to Kepler's gift of his *Mysterium Cosmographicum* Galileo confided to Kepler that although for many years he had been a Copernican and that he had arguments in support of Copernicus he dared not publish them 'for such is the number of fools'.[47] To Kepler's anxious request for private communication of these arguments, Galileo made no reply. Thirteen years later Galileo constructed a telescope based on a design not his own and turned it to the heavens. New 'facts' in support of Copernicus were readily forthcoming and quickly published by Galileo in his sensational *The Starry Messenger* of 1610, followed by his *Letters on Sunspots* in 1613. In the publication of 1610 Galileo proclaimed for the first time in public his belief in the reality of the Copernican world system. But do the new 'facts' establish the truth of the heliocentric world system?

Many more stars are visible through the telescope than can be seen with the naked eye. This, of course, does not prove that the earth is not the centre of the cosmos. The stars that subtend a measurable angle at the eye are reduced to a point by the telescope. Strange for an instrument that normally magnifies! But if the telescope does give the true angular diameter of the stars, then an argument against the reality of the Copernican system conveniently disappears. The angular diameters of Venus and Mars when observed through the telescope are exactly as predicted in the Copernican and Tychonic world systems! Again the 'naked' eye deceives. Venus has phases similar to the moon's which is impossible in the Ptolemaic system but predicted in the Copernican and Tychonic systems. Venus therefore obviously orbits the sun. Jupiter has four moons. This shows the earth in the Copernican system is not unique in having a (single) satellite. But it does not prove the Copernican system to be correct. The moon's surface appears to have craters, valleys and mountains. Aristotle is therefore wrong in claiming that the moon's surface is perfectly spherical and that the moon consists of an immutable element qualitatively different from the four mutable terrestrial elements. Furthermore, since the moon, perhaps itself made of earthly matter, does indeed move (as proponents of all world systems agreed), then what is to stop the earth similarly moving? But to make this point is not to prove that the earth *does* move. Dark spots move across the surface of the sun. If the sun has spots, then not even this divine eternal body is free from mutation. The telescope has irretrievably destroyed Aristotle's dichotomization of the cosmos into the divine eternal superior matter of the heavens and the corruptible inferior matter of the terrestrial sphere. Galileo states a commitment of the greatest importance: 'We shall prove the earth to be a wandering body surpassing the moon in splendour, and not the sink of all dull refuse of the universe.' But he has not yet done so.[48]

There was an alternative and much safer interpretation of the recently observed celestial mutability and imperfections than that being developed by Galileo. We have already seen in Chapter 1 how European men and women believed themselves living in the last age before the Second Coming of Christ: man himself was believed to be growing old and the heavens likewise. Typical, for example, was the belief of the Puritan preacher John Dove who told his congregation in 1594 in *A Sermon . . . Intreating of the Second Comming of Christ and the Disclosing of Antichrist* that "Man himself . . . is of lower stature, lesse strength, shorter life than at the first he was, so that there is a general decay of nature, and in every leaf of that book it is written, that ye frame of that heavenly arche erected over our heads must very slowly lose and dissolve it selfe.' The end was proclaimed to be 'very neere' and it was noted, as King James also noted, that Satan, 'the neerer he is to his judgement the more he rageth'.[49] Six years after the publication of *The Starry Messenger* Godfrey Goodman, chaplain to the Queen of England, produced a massive array of evidence to substantiate his indictment of nature. There was, for example, the distressing fact that although 'males are the more noble' of the two sexes, 'nature being more and more defective, brings foorth the females in a farre greater number: whereas in the time of mans innocence, the number should have been equal'. But it was not only the earth and man that were in decay, so painfully demonstrated by the excessive number of females. Goodman dared to 'accuse the materiall heavens, as being guiltie, conspiring and ioyntly tending to corruption'. 'Scripture shall warrant me', he continued, *'the heavens shall waxe old as doth a garment,* Psalme 102, vers.26'.[50] Dove and Goodman were but two of a galaxy of preachers who proclaimed the general decay of nature and the last age of the world. But Galileo was not among these men. It was, he wrote, 'a very beautiful thing and most gratifying to the sight' to see the moon as if it were so close, to see its surface 'rough and uneven, covered everywhere, just like the earth's surface, with huge prominences, deep valleys, and chasms'. The telescope gave him a view of the heavens which filled him 'with wondering delight'.[51] The sunspots would be 'a parade of productions and destructions' that would endure 'through all future ages, allowing the human mind time to observe at pleasure'. Alteration does not mean annihilation, Galileo explained. If it did, the Aristotelian philosophers might have justifiable cause for concern; but it simply means mutation. Galileo therefore asks the Aristotelians: '[I]f "corruption" and "generation" are discovered in the moon, why deny them to the sky? If the earth's small mutations do not threaten its existence (if, indeed, they are ornaments rather than imperfections in it), why deprive the other planets of them? Why fear so much for the dissolution of the sky as a result of alterations no more inimical than these?'[52] The heavens were not, by Galileo, to be disparaged; it was rather the earth that was to be liberated. But what at the time were, or must have appeared to be, the implications of such 'liberation'?

Some of these implications can be understood by returning to the cast-iron case presented by Copernicus to gain him entry into hell. Unfortunately, the author of that 'insolent satire' has the Jesuit priest Ignatius dispute Copernicus' claims most effectively. 'Hath your raising up of the earth into heaven', Ignatius asks Copernicus disbelievingly, 'brought men to that confidence, that they . . . threaten God againe? Or do they out of this motion of the earth conclude, that there is no hell, or deny the punishment of sin?' Unhappily there is no danger for Christianity in Copernicus' publication: people believe just as before. Moreover, it is the opinion of Ignatius that the Devil's work is not done by telling the truth but by lying, and it is disapprovingly pointed out to Copernicus that 'those opinions of yours may very well be true'. The upshot of the matter is that Ignatius, remembering Copernicus' proud boast that he writes solely for mathematicians, appeals successfully to Lucifer: 'Let therefore this little Mathematician, dread Emperour, withdraw himselfe to his owne company.'[53] The gates of hell remained closed to Copernicus.

Although Donne leaves us no account of disputations at the gates of heaven, we can assume that Copernicus also met difficulties there since support for his world system had not always come from the most respectable quarters. Giordano Bruno, burnt at the stake in 1600 for advocacy of a return to an uncorrupted Egyptian magical religion, had interpreted the Copernican theory as a sign of the imminence of such a great change. The Dominican priest Tommaso Campanella, long imprisoned by the Holy Office on account of his advocacy of insurrection and adoption of heretical beliefs, had thrown his very doubtful weight behind Galileo in the growing confrontation of 1615. Campanella, like Bruno, believing great changes were imminent, interpreted the mutation of the heavens as an indication of 'the coming death of the world'.[54] The heathen Aristotle was proclaimed to be far more dangerous to the Christian faith than Copernicus and Galileo who in fact turn out to be not dangerous at all! This is because in postulating the eternity of the cosmos, Aristotle denied the existence of a Creator with the obvious conclusion that '[t]here is neither reward nor punishment after death'.[55] Campanella is of the opinion that if hell truly lies at the centre of the earth, then the earth must certainly move and be outside the centre of the universe. One can therefore understand Cardinal Bellarmine's insistence (in a letter to a Carmelite priest who had published a defence of Copernicus) that to speak hypothetically of the motion of the earth was acceptable to the Holy Office but to argue that the earth is in reality not the centre of the cosmos, as Copernicus had so argued, without 'true demonstration' but as a consequence merely of saving the appearances was necessarily 'a very dangerous thing, not only by irritating all the theologians and scholastic philosophers, but also by injuring our holy faith and making sacred Scripture false'.[56] The following year in 1616 the Holy Office accordingly declared belief in the *reality* of the Copernican system to be heretical and placed *De Revolutionibus* on the Index of Forbidden Books until all references to the earth as a planet could be removed. A question that must have seemed of great significance to the Holy Office, as well as to Protestant leaders, was whether the Copernican theory, if assumed true, would contribute to undermining belief in the physical existence of hell and eternal damnation of sinners? 'Ordinary people' might well ridicule Copernicus but belief in the immortality of the soul was a foundation stone not only of the Christian faith but of social stability as well. For example, Costantino Sacardino, hanged in 1619 in Bologna as an atheist and as leader of an unsuccessful lower-class conspiracy against the Papal government, was fond of saying, crudely but to the point: 'Only fools believe that hell does exist. Princes want us to believe it, because they want to do as they please. But now, at last, all the common people have opened their eyes.'[57] Since the heavenly hierarchy was mirrored in the social hierarchy it must have been feared that successful challenge to the Church in one sphere might lead to successful challenge in other and even more sensitive spheres. Unless they were intent on further destabilizing Christianity and the social order, the Copernican revolutionaries obviously needed to proceed with great caution. Indeed, perhaps no direct clash between the Papacy and Copernicans would have occurred if the latter had been content to bide their time, exercise tact in their confrontation with superior physical power, and allow the Church to beat a dignified retreat. But devout Catholic that he was, such a man was not Galileo: truth apparently demanded immediate recognition no matter what the social implications. Moreover, rubbing salt into the Church's wound, Galileo chose to publish in Italian, not in Latin, thereby making sure that his case would be heard well beyond a privileged Latin-reading minority. However, as would become dramatically clear, for the short-term successful prosecution of such a dangerous struggle Galileo lacked what above all else would be necessary, namely a 'true demonstration' of the heliocentric system as demanded by Cardinal Bellarmine.

Following the deaths of Paul V and Bellarmine in 1621, the new Pope, Urban VIII, assured Galileo that he was once again free to write on the respective merits of the competing world systems although not to pronounce in favour of one of them unless he had conclusive proof. In any case, the Pope assured Galileo, conclusive proof was impossible, since saving the appearances in one way could give no guarantee that God might not have 'saved the appearances' in a totally different way, an argument Galileo was accordingly told to insert in any future publication—clearly, a galling and totally unacceptable demand to a man who had proudly declared in 1613 that he sought 'to investigate the true constitution of the universe—the most important and most admirable problem that there is'. Emphasizing what he took to be obvious, Galileo had proclaimed that 'such a constitution exists; it is unique, true, real, and could not possibly be otherwise; and the greatness and nobility of this problem entitle it to be placed foremost among all questions capable of theoretical solution'! Galileo and the new Pope were to clash head-on.[58]

In February 1632 Galileo's *Dialogue Concerning the Two Chief World Systems* was published and, by August, when the Holy Office ordered the confiscation of Galileo's masterpiece, almost no copies remained unsold. The *Dialogue* relates a conversation that takes place over four days between three men, Salviati who speaks for Galileo, Sagredo, an intelligent friend, and Simplicio, an Aristotelian philosopher who—to put matters politely—never gets the better of any argument. Galileo's preface 'to the discerning reader' sets the tone for the whole book. 'Incensed' that foreigners impudently assert that the Holy Office acted unwisely and without understanding Copernican arguments when it passed the decree of 1615, Galileo will undertake to show that the Church fully understood the merits of the Copernican system, declaring it false only for those excellent reasons 'supplied by piety, religion, the knowledge of Divine Omnipotence, and a consciousness of the limitations of the human mind.'[59]

The first day's dialogue is devoted to undermining Aristotle's dichotomization of the cosmos into divine, immutable heavens and inferior mutable earth. The commitment announced in *The Starry Messenger* is here made good. The natural motion of *all* bodies whether celestial or not is circular (the less said about comets the better). To Simplicio's horrified protest that this 'way of philosophizing tends to subvert all natural philosophy, and to disorder and set in confusion heaven and earth and the whole universe', Salviati enthusiastically agrees. Simplicio is sarcastically told that since he holds the heavens to be unalterable and invariant he should not be concerned over their fate. As for the earth, Salviati tells Simplicio, 'we seek rather to ennoble and perfect it when we strive to make it like the celestial bodies, and, as it were, place it in heaven, from which your philosophers have banished it'. The Aristotelians believe that the divine lunar sphere contains at its centre the terrestrial sphere. What an amazing way, Salviati jeers (the following day), of separating 'the impure and sick from the sound—giving the infected a place in the heart of the city!' Salviati would have thought that 'the leper house would be removed from there as far as possible'.[60] Sagredo supports his friend asking Simplicio how he can possibly imagine that the celestial bodies serve the earth, 'that which you call', Sagredo scoffs contemptuously, 'the dregs of the universe, the sink of all uncleanness'. Sagredo gives Simplicio a lecture worth quoting at length:

I cannot without great astonishment—I might say without great insult to my intelligence—hear it attributed as a prime perfection and nobility of the natural and integral bodies of the universe that they are invariant, immutable, unalterable, etc., while on the other hand it is called a great imperfection to be alterable, generable, mutable, etc. For my part I consider the earth very noble and admirable precisely because of the diverse alterations, changes, generations, etc., that occur in it incessantly. If, not being subject to any changes, it were a vast desert of sand or a mountain of jasper, or if at the time of the flood the waters which covered it had frozen, and it had remained an enormous globe of ice where nothing was ever born or ever altered or changed, I should deem it a useless lump in the universe devoid of activity, and, in a word, superfluous and essentially non-existent . . . .

The deeper I go in considering the varieties of popular reasoning, the lighter and more foolish I find them. What greater stupidity can be imagined than that of calling jewels, silver, and gold 'precious', and earth and soil 'base'? People who do this ought to remember that if there were as great a scarcity of soil as of jewels or precious metals, there would not be a prince who would not spend a bushel of diamonds and rubies and a cartload of gold just to have enough to plant a jasmine in a little pot, or to sow an orange seed and watch it sprout, grow, and produce its handsome leaves, its fragrant flowers, and fine fruit. It is scarcity and plenty that make the vulgar take things to be precious or worthless; they call a diamond very beautiful because it is like pure water, and then would not exchange one for ten bowels of water.

Galileo adds the marginal note that the earth is 'nobler than gold and jewels'.[61] The matter is closed.

The second day's dialogue commences with Salviati's triumphant declaration that 'since in yesterday's argument the earth was lifted up out of darkness and exposed to the open sky', the time is opportune to refute objections that if the earth were daily to rotate from west to east, a stone dropped from a tower would not fall to the base of the tower but to the west of it, birds and clouds would always be left behind, and so on. Salviati argues that, on the contrary, it is the natural motion of all earthly objects to move in a circle and hence all earthly objects naturally follow the earth's daily rotation in addition to whatever motion is impressed upon them. Water, it should be noted, conserves any circular motion impressed upon it, while air close to the earth's rough surface has a circular motion constantly impressed upon it, at least to the level of the highest mountain. It is only over the oceans that the air fails to accompany the earth's rotation so that a permanent breeze from east to west results. For all other phenomena, however, no daily rotational motion of the earth can be detected. Galileo has already argued that Aristotle was quite wrong to believe that the velocity of a body in a vacuum is necessarily infinite (from which erroneous argument Aristotle had concluded that a vacuum cannot exist); Galileo's belief on the contrary is that the velocity of an earthly body falling freely to the earth's surface in a vacuum (could one be created) would be merely proportional to the time of descent. Moreover, Galileo goes on to argue, such a motion which would assuredly take the falling body to the base of a tower from which it is dropped is in reality, i.e. relative to a reference frame not rotating with the earth, a motion that is 'never accelerated at all, but is always equable and uniform'. Galileo's argument is as shown in Figure 2.10. The earth's centre is at C and the height of the tower is AB. The stone falling relative to the tower covers a larger distance in

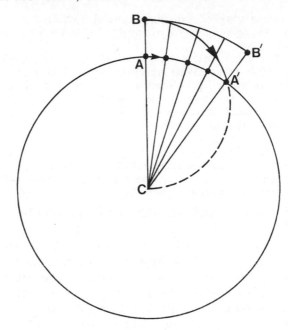

Figure 2.10

each successive equal interval of time so that by the time it hits
the base of the tower at A' it has traversed what Galileo
conjectures to be the arc BA' of a circle whose diameter is CB.
Thus one may understand, states Galileo, how such a motion
tends eventually to terminate at the centre of the earth. What a
triumphant conclusion! The 'true and real motion' of the stone is
circular, as it should be for the natural motion of an earthly body.
Salviati adds cautiously, however, which is just as well: 'But that
the descent of heavy bodies does take place in exactly this way, I
will not at present declare; I shall only say that if the line
described by a falling body is not exactly this, it is very near to
it.'[62]

The earth, then, has a diurnal motion but does it also have
an annual (circular, natural) motion about the sun? The third
day's dialogue is intended to establish that it does. Copernicus'
own arguments regarding retrograde motion are repeated and
admired, as are his other arguments regarding the advantages of
the heliocentric system. What were apparent refutations of the
Copernican system, moreover, turn in Galileo's hands into
confirmation. Copernicus had said nothing about the small
variation in size of Mars and Venus; 'I believe', said Galileo, 'this
was because he was unable to rescue to his own satisfaction an
appearance so contradictory to his view'. But the telescope gives

'to a hair' the required large variation in size, and thus turns the 'ferocious attack' launched by Mars and Venus against the Copernican system into victory for Copernicus—or rather for Galileo.[63] In addition, the infamous third motion of the earth is shown to be non-existent. By placing a large ball in a bowl of water and rotating the bowl round at arms' length Galileo is able to show that a line joining the centre of the ball to any point on the ball's surface does not change its direction relative to the floor, ceiling and walls of the containing room. The third motion attributed to the earth becomes, as Galileo puts it, a kind of steadiness. Cunningly, Galileo refrains from reminding readers at this point that the precession of the equinoxes requires a third conical motion every 26,000 years—small it is true but necessary just the same and Galileo now has no explanation for such a motion. Nevertheless, it is clear that arguments during a lifetime of long, laborious and difficult struggle have been impressively built up by Galileo in favour of Copernicus and against Aristotle and Ptolemy. When, however, Sagredo expresses surprise that not only have there been so few followers of Pythagoras and Aristarchus but that even today Copernicus is not faring very well, Salviati gives his deservedly famous reply:

No, Sagredo, my surprise is very different from yours. You wonder that there are so few followers of the Pythagorean opinion, whereas I am astonished that there have been any up to this day who have embraced and followed it. Nor can I ever sufficiently admire the outstanding acumen of those who have taken hold of this opinion and accepted it as true; they have through sheer force of intellect done such violence to their own senses as to prefer what reason told them over that which sensible experience plainly showed them to the contrary. For the arguments against the whirling of the earth which we have already examined are very plausible, as we have seen; and the fact that the Ptolemaics and Aristotelians and all their disciples took them to be conclusive is indeed a stronger argument of their effectiveness. But the experiences which overtly contradict the annual movement are indeed so much greater in their apparent force that, I repeat, there is no limit to my astonishment when I reflect that Aristarchus and Copernicus were able to make reason so conquer sense that, in defiance of the latter, the former became mistress of their belief.[64]

The arguments advanced by Galileo in the *Dialogue* are, I repeat, impressive. But they are not 'conclusive'. All celestial phenomena are saved equally well by the Tychonic system which, if beneath Galileo's contempt, nevertheless remained obstinately in existence. Furthermore, Galileo's own arguments mean that no phenomenon involving only *earthly* matter can be used to discriminate between the Copernican and Tychonic systems. Is there a way, Galileo asks—Pope Urban VIII notwithstanding —to prove the truth of the Copernican system, and by implication the falsity of the Tychonic? There is indeed, he believes.

Water and, we have seen, air do not have the same dynamical properties as earthly matter; while water, for example, does conserve circular motion initially impressed upon it, it does not respond instantaneously to the impressing force or to a different application of it; on the other hand, air is unable to conserve circular motion at all and responds only to the constant application of an impressing force. This being so, certain phenomena associated with water and air perhaps demonstrate the reality of the earth's motion. Galileo first considers the phenomenon of tides, the incomprehensibility of which—Galileo relates a well-known legend—supposedly provoked Aristotle to suicide! He, Galileo, can do that which no man has successfully done. He can explain the tides and in such a way that their occurrence proves the two-fold motion of the earth exactly as postulated by Copernicus!

The earth's annual circular motion imparts this annual motion to the oceans. The earth's daily circular motion imparts also this daily motion to the oceans—but not quite! The water is unable to follow exactly the combined circular motions of the earth, motions which together produce the result that relative to the sun and fixed stars any part of the earth's surface (except very near the poles) has a variable velocity. At noon, for example, Venice has a slower velocity than at midnight. Galileo's triumphant conclusion is that such a daily acceleration and retardation of each part of the earth's surface produce a high and low tide each day. Admittedly there are in general two high and two low tides a day but Galileo is not perturbed. 'Secondary causes' must be introduced, such as 'the greater or lesser length of the vessels [ocean beds] and the greater or lesser depth of the waters contained in them'.[65]

On the other hand, the air is so tenuous and fluid a body that it has the utmost difficulty in conserving a circular motion imparted to it. Consequently where the earth's surface is flat and reasonably smooth a permanent breeze from east to west is to be expected. And this, says Galileo again triumphantly, is exactly what we find in the open seas between the tropics. 'Now you see', Salviati concludes to Sagredo, 'how the actions of the water and the air show themselves to be remarkably in accord with celestial observations in confirming the mobility of our terrestrial globe'.[66]

Unfortunately for Galileo, the heights of the tides have monthly and annual periods, 'almost as though', Salviati broods, 'the moon and the sun were taking part in the production of such effects'. Salviati confides to Sagredo how after countless nights of racking his brains he had tried to console himself 'that that could not be true which had been nevertheless brought before my very eyes by the testimony of so many trustworthy men'. It seems that if Galileo could have denied the existence of lunar and solar periods he would have done! But his ingenuity eventually produced an explanation based on, in Galileo's opinion, the earth's inequitable motion about the sun arising from the motion of the moon. All this, however, required much further study and observation. Astronomy was after all only in its infancy, Salviati pointing out that '[W]e cannot yet determine surely the law of revolution and the structure of the orbit of each planet . . . ; witness to this fact is Mars, which has caused modern astronomers so much distress.'[67] Over twenty years earlier Kepler had published his treatise on Mars but his findings had apparently not been studied by Galileo!

This neglect by Galileo of Kepler's work is related to a very important feature of Galileo's theory of tides, namely that the theory is entirely 'mechanical' and assumes no mysterious 'sympathy' of the waters of the earth for the moon and sun. Indeed Galileo mocks the idea that the moon 'attracts' in some way the earth's oceans. For how can such an idea account for the fact that not only is there a daily high tide on the near side of the earth to the moon, but also on the far side? Does the moon attract the near waters and repel the far? (Now is not the time, then, for Galileo to remind his readers that his theory also predicts only one high tide a day!) Galileo will not even consider the possibility that the primary cause of tides is the moon's 'attraction' for the seas or other such 'occult qualities'. 'These are so far from being actual or possible causes of tides', he writes sarcastically, 'that the very contrary is true. The tides are the cause of them; that is, make them occur to mentalities better equipped for loquacity and ostentation than for reflection upon and investigations into the most hidden works of nature'. Kepler at last receives a mention but it is entirely unfavourable:

But among all the great men who have philosophized about this remarkable effect, I am more astonished at Kepler than at any other. Despite his open and acute mind, and though he has at his fingertips the motions attributed to the earth, he has nevertheless lent his ear and his assent to the moon's dominion over the waters, to occult properties; and to such puerilities'.[68]

'Natural magick' or 'mechanical philosophy'? The issue is joined and will be the central theme of the next chapter.

Our discussion of Galileo's quest to prove the earth moves is almost complete. The theory of tides was received with scepticism and disbelief. Even the faithful Campanella, though enthusiastic in his praise of the *Dialogue* and chuckling over the 'complete folly' of the 'laughing stock' Simplicio, wrote tactfully to Galileo 'About the movement of the sea, I am not altogether with you.'[69]

A spokesman for a group of French natural philosophers implored Galileo to explain to them 'how the parts of the earth, which always move in the same way relative to themselves and to the water, can impress varying motions to the water'.[70] Galileo's 'true demonstration'—in defiance of the Pope's advice—appeared to Galileo's contemporaries, to friend and foe alike, anything but a true demonstration.

Galileo did, however, remember the Pope's advice to insert his theory on the inability of human reason to lay bare God's design of the universe. Presented by Simplicio shortly after being called by Sagredo an 'ambling nag', Sagredo and Salviati are accordingly informed that it is a theory 'heard from a most eminent and learned person, and before which one must fall silent'. Salviati replies that it is an 'admirable and angelic doctrine' and falls silent. Sagredo recommends its acceptance as the 'final conclusion of our four days' arguments' and invites his two companions for a ride in a gondola.[71] Thus Galileo ends his *Dialogue*.

A year and four months after the publication of the *Dialogue* Galileo, on his knees, admitted defeat:

I, Galileo, . . . desiring to remove from the minds of Your Eminences, and of all faithful Christians, this vehement suspicion rightly conceived against me, with sincere heart and unpretended faith I abjure, curse, and detest the aforesaid errors and heresies and also every other error . . . contrary to the Holy Church, and I swear that in the future I will never again say or assert verbally or in writing, anything that might cause a similar suspicion toward me; . . . So help me God and these Holy Gospels which I touch with my hands.[72]

The Copernican System: an evaluation thus far
We have seen that only new arguments, no new 'facts', were advanced by Copernicus in support of his world system. While the new theory had far greater explanatory power than its rival in its account of *celestial* phenomena, the heliocentric theory violated both common sense and Aristotelian physics; moreover, the already known facts of lack of stellar parallax motion and the (approximately) constant angular sizes of Mars and Venus could be considered direct refutations of the new theory. 'Facts', however, are often open to theoretical re-interpretation. While the fact of no measurable stellar parallax was not reinterpreted, Copernicus postulated a very large earth-stellar distance to accommodate such an unwelcome fact. As to the facts of the constant angular sizes of Mars and Venus which were at variance with Copernicus' claims on behalf of the physical reality of his system, these 'facts' could be and were reinterpreted. It was claimed that the eye does not perceive shining objects in the same way as it perceives visible but non-luminous objects.

Natural philosophers and others were, we might say, as

dichotomized by the two world systems as the cosmos had originally been by Aristotle. Whereas astronomers impressed with the explanatory power of the Copernican system with respect to retrograde motions put less weight on counter-arguments and refuting facts, opponents of the Copernican system put far more weight on common sense, established physics, traditional cosmology and literal interpretation of the Bible than they did on the celestial niceties of Copernican theory.

Subsequent sighting of new lights in the sky, both stationary and moving, needed interpretation. When measurements of their possible parallax motion put the new phenomena—novae and comets—beyond the lunar sphere, new 'facts' for the first time were available in favour of Copernicus—and to be used against him. For the non-existence of crystalline spheres made possible the postulation by Tycho of a geocentric system possessing the celestial advantages of the Copernican system.

While Kepler's laws and his Rudolphine tables certainly pointed strongly to the reality of the heliocentric system, there was no 'conclusive' proof that the motions of the planets as hypothesized by Kepler were the physically real ones. Furthermore, Kepler's attempts to explain all motion in terms of the sun's magnetic power could by no means be considered conclusive. It is worth bearing in mind that more than half a century was to elapse after Kepler's death before a natural philosopher ventured to publish a theory expressly designed to separate relative from absolute motions.

True, Galileo's telescopic 'discoveries' of the moon's mountains and Jupiter's satellites served to make increasingly implausible the established belief in the (decadent) uniqueness of the earth in the cosmos. On the other hand, a counter-argument existed that the heavens themselves were in decay during the last age of the earth preceding the Second Coming of Christ. In any case the 'fact' that the moon's surface is rough and the 'fact' that Jupiter has moons do not establish that the earth moves!

4 An Ontology for the New Cosmology?

By 1640 the Copernicans had come so near, yet remained so far. The new arguments were theirs, the new facts were theirs (even if comets appeared to have embarrassingly non-circular trajectories). Yet they could not quite clinch matters. They sought to turn the world upside down, to liberate the earth from a depressing and dreadful and, as they increasingly believed, false cosmology. The English clergyman, John Wilkins, son of an Oxford goldsmith and ardent advocate of the Copernican system, summed up the traditional cosmology very accurately when in 1640 he argued that it depended upon the following assumptions:

1. That bodies must bee as farre distant in place as in Nobilitie.
2. That the Earth is a more ignoble substance than any of the other Planets, consisting of a more base and vile matter.
3. That the centre is the worst place . . . [having earlier stated that] Hell must needs be scituated in the centre of our earth.

'All which, are', declared Wilkins, '(if not evidently false) yet very uncertaine'. We can now, perhaps, in the 1640s, agree with Wilkins that Aristotelian cosmology, if not evidently false, is very uncertain and that the heliocentric theory, if not evidently true, is 'very probable'. So very probable, in fact, for Wilkins that he wrote enthusistically of a future voyage *to the moon*—impossible, of course, in an Aristotelian cosmos but one that in the new cosmos, Wilkins argued, a future Daedalus would make possible and a future Drake or Columbus would undertake. '[W]e have no just reason to bee discouraged in our hopes [of eventual success],' enthused the English clergyman. Wilkins and others like him clearly perceived the new cosmology as a liberation of 'man' from his dark and dreadful prison at the centre of the cosmos.[73]

A fundamental question, however, remained totally unresolved, and one which had been as passionately debated as the question of the earth's status in the cosmos. We return to the theme of Chapter 1. What kind of world is this? What kinds of things and entities populate it? Are there sympathies and antipathies between different material entities? Is all matter sentient and conscious to some extent? Or is all matter passive, inert and lifeless? What is the relationship between matter and life? Is control of the material world legitimate and, if so, how is it to be acquired? Is there a world soul? Is man's soul immortal? Do angels and demons exist? Is witchcraft possible? Does Satan exist? And finally (under our breath for we are still in early modern Europe), does God exist?

Chapter 3

THE BARRENNESS OF MATTER

> On occasion indeed, sixteenth-century natural magic was indistinguishable from true experimental science in its investigation of the effects of mysterious forces by means of observation and experiment. Natural magic and experimental science finally parted company when the latter was allied to that particular form of natural philosophy known as the mechanical which endeavoured to understand both the effects of such mysterious forces, and their cause, in truly rational terms.
>
> Marie Boas [Hall], *The Scientific Renaissance*, 1962

> The whole universe is harnessed to men's attempts to force one another into good citizenship.
>
> Mary Douglas, *Purity and Danger*, 1966

WE saw in the last chapter how Galileo Galilei, although not without reason known as the 'father of modern science', nevertheless respectfully rebuked his distinguished colleague Johannes Kepler for having lent his ear to such occult puerilities as the moon's attraction of the waters of the earth. Galileo's rebuke serves to draw our attention forcefully to the fact that modern science—whatever that might be!—did not automatically emerge victorious as a consequence of the triumph of the Copernican system. It was not a case of the Aristotelian cosmology crumbling and 'modern science' simply taking its place. It was a case of scholastic Aristotelianism crumbling and protagonists of very different and rival cosmologies engaging in a bitter and protracted struggle for supremacy, both with each other and against the entrenched proponents of Aristotelian-Thomistic cosmology. 'Modern science' emerged, at least in part, out of a three-cornered contest between proponents of the established view and adherents of newly prospering magical cosmologies, both to be opposed in the seventeenth century by advocates of revived mechanical world views. Scholastic Aristotelianism versus magic versus mechanical philosophies! My overall aim in this chapter is to give an account of and suggest reasons for the victory of the 'mechanical philosophy' over its magical rival. I shall argue that the victory of this extraordinary philosophy over its equally extraordinary rival cannot be understood in terms of the relative explanatory successes of each basic cosmology but rather in terms of the fortunes of the social forces identified with

89

each cosmology. That is the claim. I try in what follows to make it plausible.

There is, in addition, a further important distinction to be drawn with a corresponding debate to be analysed. Whereas Aristotelian philosophers did not seek power over the natural world, natural magicians and mechanical philosophers did. What, however, was the *method* to be used in the acquiring of power? Was the *primary* emphasis to be put on experience, observation and experimentation or on the unaided power of male reason? By and large all natural magicians and some mechanical philosophers subscribed to and advocated the 'experimental philosophy'. If by the end of the seventeenth century the cosmology of the natural magicians had been all but ousted by mechanical philosophers, the 'experimental philosophy' that they had done so much to promote survived their downfall and came to fruition in the eighteenth century.

Finally, it will be salutary to bear in mind that while the mechanical philosophy held sway among educated elites until the 1730s, the natural philosophy of Isaac Newton eventually undermined it by the success of its 'immaterial principles' or 'occult forces' or 'universal sympathy' in the predictions of both terrestrial and planetary phenomena. The scientific revolution of the seventeenth century is a thoroughly complex phenomenon. Our jumping-off point—but it is no more than that—will be the magicians' rejection of Aristotelian cosmology and the ensuing polemic between magicians and mechanical philosophers.

1 *Natural Magic and Demonic Magic*

William Gilbert's rejection of Aristotle
More than a hint that the 'cosmological' struggle was not a straightforward contest beween 'ancients and moderns' is suggested by the passage in Galileo's *Dialogue* in which Salviati can be found emphatically declaring his admiration for William Gilbert's *De Magnete* which had been published in 1600. Salviati jokes that very happily the book came into his possession as a gift from an Aristotelian philosopher who wished to protect his own library from its contagion. Gilbert's findings are very sound, the reader is informed, *all carefully established by much experimentation.* Yet, just as was necessary with Kepler, Salviati has to point out that Gilbert's own explanations of his findings are not acceptable. For it would appear that Gilbert, like Kepler, although having freed himself from Aristotelian contamination, had been contaminated in turn by the ubiquitous proponents of magical cosmologies.

Certainly *De Magnete* contains a severe criticism of Aristotle. Gilbert is horrified at Aristotle's dichotomization of the cosmos, in his maintaining the heavens as alive and divine but the earth as 'imperfect, dead, inanimate and subject to decay', made up of elements 'beggarly and despicable'. Gilbert totally rejects such a 'monstrous creation'. The earth is not to be 'condemned and driven into exile and cast out of all the fair order of the glorious universe, as being brute and soulless'. On the contrary, Gilbert proclaims his agreement with the master magicians of antiquity, Hermes, Zoroaster, and Orpheus, who in their wisdom all recognized the existence of a universal soul. 'As for us', Gilbert emphasizes, 'we deem the whole world animate, and all globes, all stars, and this glorious earth, too, we hold to be from the beginning by their own destinate souls governed and from them also to have the impulse of self-preservation'.[1]

The earth is alive and 'with her astral magnetic mind' rotates daily about a north-south axis. The opinion that the earth is stationary is 'superstition, a philosophic fable, now believed only by simpletons and the unlearned; it is beneath derision'.[2] If the earth is not alive Gilbert wants to know how soil taken from the bowels of the earth to the top of a tower can give rise to a miscellaneous herbage. The earth is alive. Aristotle is quite wrong to suppose that earthly matter removed from the surface of the earth returns to it when released because its natural resting place is the centre of the cosmos. Anything terrestrial falls to the earth's surface because all earthly matter is attracted to all other earthly matter just as all lunar things tend towards the moon, all solar things towards the sun. 'It is not a question of an appetite which brings the parts towards a certain place', explains Gilbert, ' . . . but of a propensity towards the body, towards a common source, towards the mother where they were begotten, towards their origin, in which all these parts will be united and preserved and in which they all remain at rest, safe from every peril'.[3]

It is true that Aristotle is being attacked, but Gilbert's ideas sound very strange indeed: the cosmos is alive; it is threaded throughout by a world soul; magnetic nature is proper to 'Earth, mother of all' and does not derive from the heavens. While it is false that the *echeneis* fish has remarkable powers (philosophers should not attempt to explain a phenomenon 'before ascertaining that the thing is so in fact'), it is true that the 'moon causes the movement of the waters and the tides of the ocean'. But not through compulsion, the thought of which is particularly abhorrent to Gilbert. He will not even use the term 'attraction' to describe interactions between a lodestone and iron 'for where attraction exists, there, force seems to be brought in and a tyrannical violence rules'. Gilbert prefers the term 'coition', remembering how Orpheus in his hymns relates 'that iron is drawn to the lodestone as the bride to the embraces of her spouse'.[4] One can begin to understand what Galileo might have had in mind when he complained of Gilbert's explanations! As he later complained of Kepler's. Yet both Gilbert and Kepler vigorously attempted to distinguish their own work from that of magicians. It is clearly necessary to look fairly closely at these two diametrically opposed visions of the cosmos, the magical and the mechanical, always bearing in mind that many philosophers such as Gilbert and Kepler, while they flirted with magical ideas, yet firmly rejected thoroughgoing magical philosophies.

I must stress that nearly all magicians wrote in a deliberately obscure way so that the secrets of nature could be understood only by the wise and morally pure who effortlessly comprehend each other's writings. I confess that after a laborious effort —although greatly aided by the work of D.P. Walker and Frances Yates—I still have only a very imperfect understanding of magical philosophies and practices. The wise and pure reader is referred to original sources.

Hermetic natural magic

In 1463 the first Renaissance magician Marsilio Ficino was commissioned by Cosimo de' Medici of Florence to translate a collection of Greek manuscripts that he had just acquired. The manuscripts were none other than the famous Hermetic texts, believed by Renaissance philosophers to have been written by the divinely inspired Hermes Trismegistus, Egyptian priest and contemporary of Moses. (Since the seventeenth century it is known that these texts were in fact written during the second to fourth centuries A.D.) The texts are religious and magical treatises. Exuding piety throughout, they describe practices by which, for example, statues can be animated by drawing into them celestial powers, together with various processes by which the magician's soul can be elevated into the divinity of the stars. The most humble aim of the Hermetic magician is to learn how to manipulate the natural and occult virtues of terrestrial things, *natural virtues* being the ordinary properties of elements and *occult virtues* the remarkable properties of objects such as possessed by the lodestone and the *echeneis* fish. Scholastic Aristotelians, too, distinguished between natural and occult qualities, natural qualities being explicable or apparently explicable in terms of the qualities of the constituent Aristotelian elements, while occult qualities were not so explicable and must have their origin, according to natural magicians, in the effluvia of influences emitted from the stars and planets. The magician Cornelius Agrippa von Nettesheim especially singled out the *echeneis* fish as the possessor of such an occult virtue: 'So that little fish . . . doth so curb the violence of the winds, and appease the rage of the sea, that, let the tempests be never so imperious and raging, the sails also bearing a full gale, it doth notwithstanding by its mere touch stay the ships and makes them stand still, that by no means they can be moved.' Agrippa cited countless other creatures possessing occult virtues, perhaps the most remarkable of all being the Phoenix as celebrated (Agrippa notes) by Ovid:

> All Birds from others do derive their birth,
> But yet one Fowle there is in all the Earth,
> Call'd by th' Assyrians Phoenix, who the wain
> Of age repairs, and sows her self again.

In addition, as experience showed, many terrestrial objects possessed the anti-Aristotelian occult qualities or virtues of *sympathy* and *antipathy* for each other, manifesting a pronounced attraction for certain objects and a pronounced repulsion for others. In Agrippa's view, such sympathies and antipathies in objects

are nothing else but certain inclinations of things of the one to the other, desiring such-and-such a thing if it be absent, and to move towards it unless it be hindered; and to acquiesce in it when it is obtained, shunning the contrary and dreading the approach of it, and not resting in or contented with it . . . [5]

A favourite example was the sympathy of the lodestone for iron but magicians invariably gave scores of other examples of sympathies and antipathies always uncritically drawn from folklore and ancient authorities. As magicians stressed, it was quite impossible for philosophers to discover the occult qualities of things by the use of *reason*; they were discoverable only through *experience*. Moreover, why things possessed whatever occult properties they had would always remain an unsolved mystery, the most humble aim of the natural magician being merely to identify the natural and occult properties of terrestrial objects and put them to use.

As well as seeking out and using both the natural and occult properties of things, natural magicians believed they could take their magic a stage higher by learning to tap and control the streams of influences continually emitted by stars and planets. Talismans, for example, can be made at the appropriate time by drawing the virtues of a particular planet into an object made of materials appropriate to the planet and inscribed with appropriate characters and images. In addition, appropriate Orphic songs can help to draw down the virtues of a particular planet either into the desired talisman or directly into the mind of the magician. Thus in various ways the magician learns how to marry the earth with heaven, a process which necessarily entails the continual drawing down of the virtues of stars and planets into terrestrial matter. With regard to the nature of this material world the Hermetic texts are ambivalent: some of the texts see the material world as wholly bad and corrupt, others as living and divine. However, the weight of the *Corpus Hermeticum,* Frances Yates comments, is towards an optimistic interpretation of the material world. According to one text, for example, 'this great body of the world is a soul, full of intellect and of God, who fills it within and without and vivifies the All', while another exhorts, 'Contemplate then the beautiful arrangement of the world and see that it is alive, and that all matter is full of life.'[6] In general, Yates writes, the (optimistic) magician could be said to participate in an erotic relationship with the world, and it was through entering with loving sympathy into the sympathies that bind earth to heaven that the magician derived his power. The translator of the Hermetic texts asks why Love is called a magician. And Ficino answers:

Because all the power of magic consists in love. The work of magic is the attraction of one thing by one another in virtue of their natural sympathy. The parts of this world, like the members of one animal, ... are united among themselves in the community of a single nature. ... From their communal relationship a common love is born and from this love a common attraction: and this is the true magic. ... Thus the lodestone attracts iron, amber straw, brimstone fire, the Sun draws flowers and leaves towards itself, the Moon the seas. ... [7]

Now while Ficino's very spiritual magic posed no great challenge to the Church, some claims advanced on behalf of natural magic were often very bold indeed. By understanding how to tap the virtues and influences of the planets and stars, some powerful magicians claimed that it was possible to perform marvellous, apparently miraculous, feats, especially if the mind of the practising magician was in an 'enhanced' state. Agrippa in particular had emphasized that there is 'a certain virtue in the minds of men', and that 'all things obey them when they are carried into a great excess of any passion or virtue, so as to exceed those things which they bind'. Such a *vis imaginativa* could therefore bring about truly marvellous effects. Agrippa claimed, for example, that the mind of the magician when 'strongly elevated, and inflamed with a strong imagination', is able to cause 'health or sickness, not only in its proper body, but also in other bodies'.[8] Not surprisingly, such claims were considered by the

Church to be very dangerous to the Christian faith since they implied that miracles supposedly performed by God and Christ had been either perfectly natural phenomena or marvellous phenomena brought about by the use of natural magic and not by divine intervention.[9]

The philosopher Pietro Pomponazzi (1462–1525) who taught at the University of Padua represented an extreme case of such a threat to Christianity. Rejecting scholastic Aristotelianism with its hierarchies of demons in favour of an Aristotelian naturalism devoid of demons—'It is ridiculous and foolish', claimed Pomponazzi in his *Treatise on Incantations,* 'to forsake what is observable, and what can be proved by natural reason, to seek what is unobservable, and cannot be proved with any verisimilitude'[10]—Pomponazzi argued that reason both denies the soul's immortality and the divine cause of so-called miracles. He is, he reassures his readers, not ignorant of the argument that belief in the soul's immortality has been and continues to be important for maintaining social order; for this reason, he writes provocatively, '[the lawgiver], intending the common good, has decreed that the soul is immortal, not caring for truth but only for righteousness, that he may lead men to virtue'. However, the 'socially irresponsible' Pomponazzi believes it better that people should be virtuous because they wish to be, not because they have hope of reward or fear of punishment, all of which suggests to Pomponazzi 'a certain servility'. If, at the end of his essay *On the Immortality of the Soul,* Pomponazzi has to concede to the Church that the soul is immortal for *faith* tells us that it is, which is a conclusion that properly serves to emphasize the fallibility of human reason, there remained for the Church the unwelcome possibility that Pomponazzi's readers might have come to a very different—and very heretical—conclusion, namely the one that Pomponazzi intended them to come to!

Reason is also unambiguous on the question of apparently supernatural events: 'All prophecy, whether vaticination, or divination, or excess, or speaking with tongues, or the invention of arts and sciences, in a word, all the effects in this lower world, whatever they be, have a natural cause.' Either the phenomena in question are mere fables or they are the results of the influences of particular conjunctions of the stars and planets: 'Nor is it strange', Pomponazzi explains, 'if such things [as, for example, apparitions] can be shadowed forth by the heavenly bodies, since they are animated by a most noble soul and generate and govern all things below.'[11] Once again, however, faith must not be contradicted by reason. While obviously God can be the supernatural cause of a 'miraculous' event, such an event can have a natural cause as well! The Holy Church will graciously inform any bewildered philosopher which is which. Of course, since the authority of the Church rests entirely on the reality of the miracles described in the Bible, Pomponazzi's overall argument, D. P. Walker points out, is totally subversive of Christian doctrine: if these 'miracles' could have been naturally caused, the edifice of the Church might well be constructed not even on sand, let alone rock. To make his position doubly clear, Pomponazzi describes how the course of religions is determined by the influence of the stars; their births and their deaths—all is the influence of the stars. One can perhaps share the amazement of the Jesuit demonologist Martin del Rio when in 1600 he wrote how he was totally at a loss to explain why only recently had Pomponazzi's *Treatise on Incantations* been placed on the Index of Forbidden Books. Del Rio complained bitterly that Pomponazzi showed himself neither a good philosopher nor, 'what is much worse, a good Christian when he ascribes all miracles to the influence of the stars and proposes that all religions and laws together with their proponents depend on them'. 'This is, indeed', Del Rio laments correctly, 'straightforward impiety'.[12]

The Christian response

Aristotelian naturalism combined with Hermetic natural magic implied acute trouble for the Church and the faithful. Their answer was obvious: natural magic is totally ineffective; all marvellous events are the work of demons, natural magicians are diabolical agents in disguise, miracles are the work of God. Even Johann Weyer and Jean Bodin found themselves in close agreement on this vital matter. While Weyer professed not to despise the 'profound contemplation of hidden natural things', how could one be sure that natural magic was not inextricably caught up in the 'temptations of sorcery and witchcraft, and ensnared in the tricks of evil spirits'? Horror and indignation were Weyer's response at the diabolical suggestion that Jesus Christ had performed his stupendous and incomparable miracles by means of demon-controlling (Cabalist) magic. Bodin, as we have seen, was not one to accept any nonsense in such matters: '[S]o many wonders which stupefy men, so many tricks and levitations of magicians, are accomplished', Bodin emphasized, 'not by nature but by the power of angels and demons outside of or contrary to nature'. Could there be any doubt that demons and Satan were continually intervening in the world? For nearly all Christians the constant and unwelcome attention of Satan and his demonic allies was conclusively demonstrated by the diabolical acts of witches. The claims of natural magicians could therefore at the very least be rendered suspect by the reality of the witch-trials.[13]

Moreover, no matter what Pomponazzi had argued, demons were known not only to exist but to be present everywhere. The English clergyman Richard Hooker's views on the ubiquity of the fallen angels were commonplace: 'For being dispersed, some in the air, some on the earth, some in the water, some among the minerals, dens, and caves that are under the earth; they have by all means laboured to effect a universal rebellion against the laws, and as far as in them lieth utter destruction of the works of God.'[14] One could therefore not be too careful in trying to avoid contact with demons. Even in the deepest mines, for example, demons were occasionally to be found and Agricola records how the Annaberg silver mine had to be closed after twelve workers were killed by demons. Good Christians took extra special precautions against encountering demons. What could one say about professed Christians who seemingly went out of their way to run the risk of contacting them?

Hermetic Cabalist magic

In the opinion of Ficino's contemporary, Pico della Mirandola (1463–94), Hermetic natural magic was insufficiently powerful. Although it could help the magician absorb into himself the power and virtues of the stars and thereby produce works of great benefit for humankind, nevertheless it is possible for men to possess God-like, divine powers and these are not obtainable through natural magic alone. It is only when Hermetic (Egyptian) magic is supplemented by Cabalist (Jewish) magic that the practising magician is able to command the powers of angelic and demonic forces, and even to reach to God Himself.

Cabalist magic derives from the belief that God created the cosmos by the spoken word and that the word therefore is powerful and creative.[15] The Jewish language is no mere convention by means of which objects are represented by signs and sounds quite arbitrarily chosen. On the contrary, since Hebrew was the language God used in speaking to Adam (a being, let us recall, made in the likeness of God Himself), it follows that Hebrew has the creative power entailed in God's Word. Marvellous effects are achieved by manipulation of the 22 letters of the Hebrew alphabet, and even more marvellous effects by manipulations of the numbers assigned to these 22 letters. Thus a word or sentence having a certain number is deemed to correspond with another word or sentence having the same number so enabling all kinds of interesting conclusions and predictions to be made. In addition, each planet has a number and letter assigned to it, the knowledge of which enables the Cabalist magician to construct very powerful talismans. Jupiter, for example, has the number 4 and corresponds to the letter Daleth, which also has the number 4. Thus a talisman to attract the virtues of Jupiter must have engraved on it a magic square consisting of 16 smaller squares, each of which is in turn numbered in a magical way, so that each row and each column and also each of the two diagonals adds up to 34. Even more powerfully, contact could be established with angels by manipulating the numbers corresponding to the names of the various angels. Obviously good magicians make contact only with angels, evil magicians with demons. It is therefore of the utmost importance for good magicians to make sure that their techniques do not become the property of all and thereby fall into bad hands. Truly man is a miracle. Although lodged in the 'excrementary and filthy parts of the lower world' (not, perhaps, the nicest possible view of the earth), Pico explains that man is nevertheless at the centre of the cosmos and from there it is possible to observe everything that is in the world.[16] And by the use of Cabalist magic man can become as God.

Now although Cabalist magic avoids the dangers that beset practitioners of natural magic (since it openly recognizes and makes contact with supernatural intelligent beings), its practitioners are continually confronted with other problems. Is it Christian to try to obtain such supernatural powers? The Church in general would not approve and the Protestants of the sixteenth century would most emphatically condemn all such magical practices. But even if such Cabalist magic were admissible, how could the magician be sure that he really had made contact with an angel and not with a deceiving demon leading him irrevocably to perdition? Cabalist magic was fraught with the most extreme dangers.

Diabolical magic

This is particularly clear in the case of the magician Agrippa von Nettesheim (1487–1535). Though of noble birth and a member of court circles, though a combatant against peasants in an uprising in Spain, almost suffering death at their hands, Agrippa was nevertheless regarded by Jean Bodin as the black magician par excellence, teacher of the diabolical arts and one of Satan's own. It was of no use that Agrippa protested in his *Three Books of Occult Magic* that his magic was good; it was enough that by its means Agrippa proclaimed that supernatural powers could be reached. And what powers! The truly pious magician who followed his methods would, Agrippa claimed, be able to 'attain power above nature, and perform operations so marvellous, so sudden, so difficult, by reason of which... the stars are disturbed, deities are compelled, the elements are made to serve'. 'Thus it is', Agrippa continued, '[that men] devoted to God, and lifted up by those theological virtues, command the elements, drive away fogs, call up winds, compel clouds to rain, cure diseases, and raise the dead'.[17] How could Agrippa justify the acquisition of such powers? Was he—the devoutly pious magician—compelling good demons to serve him or was such a magician the innocent victim of evil demons or worse still their malevolent manipulator? Agrippa had even discussed ways of summoning evil demons for magical operations! Well might Agrippa protest that his soul was pure and his intentions entirely good, that those magicians who failed to summon good demons and relied on natural magic alone were those who most exposed themselves to deception by evil demons! Agrippa's magic was openly demonic and that was sufficient for its condemnation. Such a man, it was thought, could have only diabolical intent.

The mystery—if ever mystery it was—is now explained as to why Johann Weyer had sought to protect witches. For, as Bodin argued, Weyer himself was a witch and, moreover, had as a young man in 1533 freely chosen to study with the 'master sorcerer' Agrippa von Nettesheim (who had likewise defended witches against prosecution). Indeed, Agrippa with his notorious black pet dog—which Weyer claimed to be *only* a black pet dog—came to be widely regarded as the prototype Johannes Faustus. Power on earth for the loss of his soul—that was the bargain Faustus had supposedly struck with Satan. The possibility of such a Faustian bargain fascinated the literate of Europe: the book published in 1587 describing the terrible end of Faustus at the hands of the Devil became an immediate success and was quickly translated and published in several European lanaguages. Diabolical magicians, by definition, sought power—power over nature, power over their fellow beings—and for this they would seek aid from demons, even from the Devil. In Christopher Marlowe's *The Tragical History of Doctor Faustus,* written before the sixteenth century ends, Faustus is observed meditating in his study:

> These necromantic books are heavenly,
> Lines, circles, scenes, letters and characters:
> Ay these are those that Faustus most desires.
> Oh, what a world of profit and delight
> Of power, of honour, of omnipotence
> Is promised to the studious artizan!

All things that move between the quiet poles
Shall be at my command.

The evil angel tempts him towards damnation:

Go forward, Faustus, in that famous art
Wherein all nature's treasure is contained.
Be thou on earth as Jove is in the sky,
Lord and commander of these elements.[18]

Perhaps the Cabalist magician did move in court circles. Perhaps
he did write a preface in English to a translation of Euclid's
Elements and help merchants with the problem of navigation (as
did the sixteenth-century English magician John Dee). Perhaps
he did protest his total benevolence. But, nevertheless, at best he
was widely feared as the possessor of forbidden powers, at worst
vilified and condemned as a Satanic agent.

Paracelsian natural magic

If Agrippa moved, or tried to move, in the best circles, the same
could not usually be said of his contemporary, Paracelsus
(1493–1541), alias Theophrastus Philippus Aureolus Bombastus
von Hohenheim. Whereas Copernicus had wanted to turn only
the cosmos upside down, Paracelsus attempted such subversion
not just in the world of learning but in the social world as well.
Whereas Agrippa had nearly been killed fighting rebellious
peasants, Paracelsus only just escaped death for actively supporting the peasants in their great uprising of 1525. A social outcast
(though not of a poor family), university educated, an attacker of
traditional medicine, influenced by the Hermetic-Cabalist tradition, Paracelsus added the very dangerous ingredient of social
dissent and protest to the magical tradition. It was an ingredient
that was to have significant consequences for the future development of natural philosophy.

The established Galenic tradition in medicine assumed that all
'diseases' were caused by an imbalance in the four humours of an
individual. Treatment aimed at restoring to the sick individual
that balance of humours appropriate to her or him by employing
such means as 'sweating, purging, bloodletting and inducing
vomiting'. Paracelsus, however, argued that disease was brought
about by an external agent, usually in the form of star-born
poisons that attacked a particular organ or organs of the body,
thus causing symptoms specific not to the individual but to the
external poison. Paracelsus therefore necessarily rejected Galenic medical practice, including the established principle that
'contraries cure'. In place of traditional practice, Paracelsus
sought cures for diseases based on the German folk principle that

'like cures like'. Since God's Word had created the cosmos all things in it, particularly plants and herbs, necessarily bore signs of God's Word that to the Hermetic physician indicated their efficacy in the treatment of various diseases. Paracelsus could therefore write:

Behold the *Satyrion* root, is it not formed like the male privy parts? No one can deny this. Accordingly magic discovered it and revealed that it can restore a man's virility and passion. And then we have the thistle; do not its leaves prickle like needles? Thanks to this sign, the art of magic discovered that there is no better herb against internal prickling. The *Siegwurz* root is wrapped in an envelope like armour, and this is a magic sign showing that like armour it gives protection against weapons. And the *Syderica* bears the image and form of a snake on each of its leaves, and thus, according to magic, it gives protection against any kind of poisoning.

These signs, however, are obvious. To see further into the secrets of plants and herbs the magician must make use of God's gift to all men of the light of nature. For as Paracelsus stressed, 'Magic has power to experience and fathom things which are inaccessible to human reason', adding how desirable and good it would be if doctors of theology were to learn the secret wisdom of magic and cease 'unjustly and unfoundedly to call it witchcraft'.[19] In particular, because men contain in themselves representations of all the substances and objects of the world (the famous microcosm-macrocosm analogy), Paracelsus held that it is possible to acquire by sympathetic seeing into substances and objects an awareness of their medicinal value. Indeed, for each disease a remedy exists and the physician must never despair. The light of nature is, however, not sufficient and the true magician must depend upon the light of grace, maintaining himself in a constant state of readiness to receive God's illumination concerning his mission on earth and how he can best accomplish it. For Paracelsus that mission meant, in part, capturing by alchemical means the heavenly gifts of God to man, so preparing by the fire metallic substances that could be used in the treatment of disease. Thus syphilis, which made its first virulent appearance in Europe at the close of the fifteenth century, could be successfully treated not by giving patients large doses of mercury but smaller doses carefully prepared by alchemical means. Likewise arsenic and iron could be so prepared as to produce therapeutic, not toxic, results. According to Paracelsus, such chemicals prepared by true alchemists were better for the treatment of disease than herbal medicines and, of course, infinitely better, proclaimed Paracelsus, than the totally useless Galenic humoural treatment. The iatrochemical ideas that Paracelsus thus developed were based on his postulation of three fundamental principles underlying all substances, 'mercury' an active, spiritual principle of volatility and fluidity, 'salt' a passive, corporeal principle of solidity, colour and taste and with 'sulphur' representing a mediatory principle of combustion and transformation. Each substance had its own 'mercury', 'sulphur' and 'salt' principles.

It must be stressed that like Agrippa Paracelsus believed that a magician's imagination was an essential force in his practice. Indeed, the *vis imaginativa* is a terrible force for either good or evil and it is for this reason that the magician—and all people—should live lives that are 'chaste, honest, and pure, in thought and desire'. While, for example, the pure magician could and did help bring about cures by the force of his imagination, in stark contrast not only were Incubi and Succubi continually being created as outgrowths of the 'intense and lewd imagination' of evil men and women but menstruating witches had even the power to dematerialize bodies by the power of their imagination.[20] Because of this power of imagination, idleness was always to be discouraged and women in particular, having a more powerful imagination than that of men, had always to be kept busy and, if possible, in an excellent humour.

Misogynist though he was, Paracelsus was a man of the people. He was opposed to capital punishment: 'How bad the thief ever be, that does not make the hangman honest.' The law aided only the rich, never the poor, sending the thief to the gallows but also, argued Paracelsus, 'the judge to eternal damnation'. Without charge, he cured the poor—or did his best to cure the poor. He investigated diseases specific to working-class occupations, such as silicosis in the case of miners. When he obtained his first university position at Basel, he not only flaunted academic tradition by lecturing in German but invited the lowly barber-surgeons to his lectures, anti-social actions that ultimately made it impossible for him to stay in Basel. He frequented 'low' taverns, taking much pleasure in challenging peasants to drinking competitions and then outdrinking them; Paracelsus' knowledge of wines was excellent. According to Paracelsus, the labourer has a divine mission as has the physician—all participate in attempting to bring to perfection the works of nature. The rich are parasites and Paracelsus cured their ailments only for large fees. 'There are not many rich people', observed Paracelsus, 'endowed by nature with blessed generosity'. Rich people, he stressed, men 'choking with vulgarity, cruelty, and avarice, and utterly lacking in understanding . . . stupid, arrogant, proud men who imagine that . . . they are the masters of heaven and earth'—such men should be taught generosity. 'For to be merry with the merry and to grieve with the aggrieved', only such a way of life is 'fair and just'. In brief, Paracelsus advocated reformation of religion and society, a redistribution of wealth and, above all, a transformation of nature and the social world achieved through participation in the Word of God, received and understood through divine illumination. Let us give to Paracelsus the last words: 'For those who have no generosity will be eternally damned.'[21]

In the closing decades of the sixteenth century the publication of Paracelsus' works reached a peak and by 1605 collected editions of his works were widely available. The growing Paracelsian movement was challenging not only established medical practice (a challenge which might have been and sometimes was grudgingly, even enthusiastically, accepted by the privileged) but also theology and the established framework of society—and this was in no way acceptable to the privileged.

Hermetic magicians: Bruno and Campanella

As was not the challenge of the Hermetic magician Giordano Bruno! However, where Paracelsus was at least a Christian, Bruno had no such pretensions. Christianity, Bruno believed, had destroyed the true Egyptian religion of Hermes Trismegistus, of the magi Orpheus and Pythagoras, and had put in its place a dead nature and worship of dead things. The magicians of antiquity were among the very greatest of men. Specifically they were, eulogised Bruno, 'moderate in their way of life, expert in medicine, judicious in thinking, outstanding [in] divinations, irreproachable in morality, divine in theology, heroic in all things'. All this was clearly demonstrated, Bruno pointed out, 'by their prolonged life, less infirm bodies, lofty inventions, verified prognostications, by the substances transformed through their efforts, by these people's peaceful way of life, unbroken oaths, most honest procedures, familiarity with the good and protective spirits, and the traces (if they still last) of their marvellous prowess'. As for their usurpers, Bruno states that he would rather leave them to be judged by others, although he drops a rather long hint of the direction such judgement might take. The opponents of the Egyptian magic, including mere 'logicians' and mathematicians, 'have found the way of disturbing the peace of others . . . by doubling the defects of man through commerce, by adding vice to vice from one generation to another, by propagating with violence new follies, and by planting unheard-of stupidities where none was, concluding in the end that the stronger is the wiser, by showing new studies, instruments, and skills to let people tyrannize and assassinate one another'—all of which folly and wickedness, Bruno concludes, will serve only to bring about the time when 'those who learned at their own expense, through the force of the vicissitudes of things, will have the know-how and will be able to produce similar and even worse fruits of such pernicious inventions'.[22]

Bruno believed a general reformation to be necessary, above all a restoration of the true Egyptian religion. The Copernican system of the world was a sign that the sunrise of a restored Egyptian religion was happily imminent. The argument that if the Copernican system were true Venus should undergo great changes in apparent size Bruno scoffed at, declaring it impossible to judge the distances of luminous bodies by their apparent size. Vulgar mathematicians could never determine by geometrization the non-regular orbits of the planets and such useless attempts should be abandoned. So much for Kepler's ambitions! The significance of the Copernican system was understood not by its creator but only by Bruno. The return of the Egyptian religion that it heralded would, Bruno believed, bring men once again into communication with divine, living nature. Hermetic magic would disclose the signs and images by which this would be achieved and the earth would consequently be restored to her full dignity. For it is most certainly not a body without soul and life, let alone—Bruno shudders at the Aristotelian scholastics—'the trash of all bodily substances'.[23] The cosmos itself is infinite, everywhere containing worlds like our own, populated with living and intelligent beings—all displaying the infinite creativity of divine nature.

Hermetic magic and Christianity again clashed head-on. In 1591 Giordano Bruno was betrayed to the Inquisition, kept in prison for nine years and in 1600 burnt at the stake in Rome as an unrepentant heretic.

In the same year as Bruno's execution the Hermetic magician Tommaso Campanella, whose support for Galileo we noted in Chapter 2, was undergoing torture by the Inquisition. This Dominican monk, born like Bruno in the Kingdom of Naples, had a year earlier attempted insurrection against Spanish rule in Naples in the hope of establishing an ideal Hermetic state. Only by feigning madness did Campanella escape execution but for the next 27 years he remained a prisoner of the Inquisition. It is understandable that Campanella in his sonnet 'To Jesus Christ' cries out in anguish to the Son of God:[24]

> If Thou return to earth, come armed; for lo,
> Thy foes prepare fresh crosses for Thee, Lord!
> Not Turks, not Jews, but they who call them Thine.

While in prison he wrote his famous Hermetic utopia *The City of the Sun* which provides a description of the universal republic he had intended his abortive uprising to help realize. Run by an autocratic Hermetic magician the City of the Sun is a state in which no private property exists, all goods are held in common, everyone works but for only a few hours each day, and sexual mating takes place at times decided by the state's astrologers, thus ensuring the birth of healthy children. There is no reason why crimes against the state should ever occur since the Hermetic ruler is 'never cruel nor wicked, nor a Tyrant, inasmuch as he possesses so much wisdom'.[25]

In despair, however, both because of the failure of his insurrection and because of what he reluctantly took to be the stupidity of the oppressed masses, Campanella wrote his bitter and remarkable sonnet 'The People':[26]

> The people is a beast of muddy brain,
>> That knows not its own force, and therefore stands
>> Loaded with wood and stone; the powerless hands
>> Of a mere child guide it with bit and rein:
> One kick would be enough to break the chain;
>> But the beast fears, and what the child demands,
>> It does; nor its own terror understands,
>> Confused and stupefied by bugbears vain.
> Most wonderful! with its own hand it ties
>> And gags itself—gives itself death and war
>> For pence doled out by kings from its own store.
> Its own are all things between earth and heaven;
>> But this it knows not; and if one arise
>> To tell this truth, it kills him unforgiven.

Like Bruno, Campanella believed all matter to be sentient and conscious to some extent, a belief that had earned him temporary imprisonment and torture even before his arrest for insurrection in 1599. 'It is an error', he argued, 'to think that the world does not feel just because it does not have legs, eyes and hands'. His arguments concerning the possibility of a void are particularly interesting. While it is true, as Aristotle writes, that 'nature abhors a vacuum', nevertheless a vacuum can be created by brute force as happens when the hole of a pair of bellows is blocked and the bellows then opened by force. Inside the bellows, Campanella argued, is a vacuum and Aristotle's claim that a void is impossible is thus refuted. However, when either the applied force is released or the aperture of the bellows unplugged, the bellows close instantly in the first case and in the second case air instantaneously rushes into the bellows. Why? Campanella answers:

'All bodies abhor the existence of a vacuum, and they rush, with natural impetus, to fill such a void in order to conserve the community alive. This is because all enjoy being together, and cherish their reciprocal contact with one another. . . . Moreover, if the air does not feel pain when it is not being touched by another body it would not rush so swiftly to the aid of the whole, which it does in order to bring itself into contact with other bodies.'[27]

Unfortunately, few people believed in the universal sentience of matter. Worse still, Campanella reasoned, the most rabid egotism ensured that men would not generally regard the earth and its elements as feeling beings. What follows logically from such egotism? Campanella answers in his sonnet 'Self-love':[28]

> Then all the tribes of earth except his own
>   Seem to him senseless, rude—God lets them be:
>   To kith and kin next shrinks his sympathy,
>   Till in the end loves only self each one.
> Learning he shuns that he may live at ease;
>   And since the world is little to his mind,
>   God and God's ruling Forethought he denies.
> Craft he calls wisdom; and, perversely blind,
>   Seeking to reign, erects new deities:
>   At last 'I make the Universe!' he cries.

Campanella's animism is not only explicit but once again a dangerous connection must have been drawn in the minds of ruling elites between animism, magic and political subversion.

The Rosicrucian Manifestos
Four years before the publication in 1623 of Campanella's *City of the Sun,* another Hermetic utopia was published entitled *Christianopolis.* The author, Valentin Andreae, strongly influenced by both Paracelsus and Campanella, prohibits private property in his ideal Christian community so enabling the inhabitants to devote their lives piously and joyfully to the alchemical study and use of nature for the benefit of all. Even more importantly, Andreae was also involved in the writing of the 'infamous' Rosicrucian manifestos of 1614 and 1615, the *Fama Fraternitatis* and the *Confessio.* Couched in a mystical, allegorical language, these two momentous manifestos proclaimed the imminence of a 'general reformation, both of divine and human things' and claimed that in these last days a group of learned men had formed a secret Fraternity of the Rosy Cross in order to help the world prepare for the new age. The authors lamented that though there was no lack of magicians, Cabalists, physicians, and philosophers in Germany, 'were there but more love and kindness among them, or that the most part of them would not keep their secrets close only to themselves'. The Brothers rejoiced, however, that in the convulsions of the preceding century great men had broken through the general darkness and barbarism, pointing the way that the members of the Fraternity would follow. Paracelsus had been such a great man although so hounded by the multitude of

'wise-seeming' men, the *Fama* deplored, 'that he was never able peacefully to confer with others of his knowledge and under-standing . . . of Nature'. The Brothers of the Rosy Cross intended to bring to fruition what Paracelsus had started. They were to observe six rules, the first of which was to pursue only the profession of curing the sick, 'and that *gratis*'. They were to adopt the customs of the countries in which they travelled and to meet once a year in order to report their progress to each other. Learned people throughout Europe were invited to collaborate with the Brothers of the Rosy Cross and to help spread the message that

God hath certainly and most assuredly concluded to send and grant to the world before her end, which presently thereupon shall ensue, such a truth, light, life, and glory, as the first man Adam had, which he lost in Paradise, after which his successors were put and driven, with him, to misery. Wherefore there shall cease all servitude, falsehood, lies and darkness . . . .[29]

The magical philosophy attacked
This obviously important message provoked an immediate response among the educated of Europe and within a decade several hundred tracts, both for and against the Rosicrucian manifestos, were being debated throughout Europe. Among the first to attack the mysterious Brothers of the Rosy Cross was the chemist Andreas Libavius who, in 1615, wanted to know how one was expected to discriminate between the multiplicity of divine inspirations flooding Europe:

Then in the face of so many contrary opinions and differing judgements, it must be asked whose light of nature and grace is true and whence does it come, since it is agreed that the devil can simulate the angel of light and cast out images of truth instead of truth itself, as may be the case in the similitudes, analogies and harmonies of Paracelsus.[30]

Libavius was answered by the English physician Robert Fludd (1574–1637) first in two brief tracts and then in his massive *History of the Macrocosm and Microcosm* replete with Hermetic, Cabalist and Paracelsian wisdom and dedicated to God and James I (a dedication that served Fludd in good stead when enemies at home informed the King that Fludd was a defender of the mysterious Rosicrucians).[31] In 1619 the English physician, still a fervent defender of a geocentric world system, was attacked by Johannes Kepler in the latter's attempt to distinguish his own use of mathematics from Fludd's Cabalist magic. Putting his case against Fludd in a nutshell Kepler unceremoniously proclaimed:

One sees that Fludd takes his chief pleasure in incomprehensible picture puzzles of the reality, whereas I go forth from there, precisely to move into the bright light of knowledge the facts of nature which are veiled in darkness. The former is the subject of the chemist, followers of Hermes and Paracelsus, the latter, on the contrary, the task of the mathematician.

Fludd could not agree, however, insisting as Bruno had done before him that the mere geometrizer will never understand nature: 'For it is for the vulgar mathematicians to concern themselves with quantitative shadows; the alchemists and Hermetic philosophers, however, comprehend the true core of the natural bodies.' Of what use is it, Fludd asked, to explain only the external movements of bodies, as the unambitious Kepler does? He, Fludd, contemplates the internal and essential impulses that issue from nature herself: '[Kepler] has hold of the tail', Fludd wrote, 'I grasp the head; I perceive the first cause, he its effects.' The man whom Galileo criticized for lending his ear to 'occult puerilities' did not totally disagree with Fludd's assessment of their respective activities. While it is true that Fludd grasps the inner impulses whereas he, Kepler, grasps only the visible movements, Kepler insisted on a devastating qualification: '*I hold the tail* but I hold it in my hand; *you may grasp the head mentally,* though only, I fear, in your dreams'![32] The indomitable Fludd found Kepler's qualification hard to accept. The following year in 1623, at the time of a supposed visit of Rosicrucians to Paris, a massive attempted refutation of Hermetic-Cabalist-Paracelsian philosophy was published by Marin Mersenne, devout Catholic and life-long friend of René Descartes. There were, Mersenne feared, as many as 50,000 atheists in Paris alone. Vilifying Giordano Bruno as 'one of the wickedest men whom the earth has ever supported . . . who seems to have invented a new manner of philosophizing only in order to make underhand attacks on the Christian religion', the devout father then proceeded to identify Robert Fludd as Bruno's vile successor and principal enemy of the Christian religion.[33] When the beleaguered Fludd bitterly answered his attacker, Mersenne requested help from his friend Pierre Gassendi who continued a more measured offensive against Fludd. Attacks there were in plenty against the dangerous magical philosophy. But attacks against a system are never enough to defeat it. What is needed is an *alternative* system. That alternative system—the mechanical philosophy—was provided by Gassendi himself and above all by René Descartes.

The magical philosophy: a review
Man in the magical world view is situated at the centre of an enchanted world. He is at the centre of a cosmos threaded throughout by a world soul, of a network of sympathies and antipathies, of stellar and planetary influences, of signs conveying

God's purpose, of angels and demons, of Satanic temptation, of divine retribution and divine redemption. He can sink to the basest depths. He can rise to the most elevated spiritual heights. He can seek diabolical aid for personal power (and ultimate perdition). Or he can learn to read God's message in the Work of Nature so that all of humankind can benefit from God's love.

Natural magic, despite the undoubted piety of (most) natural magicians, posed a threat to Christianity. If nature is occult and extraordinary phenomena have a natural (planetary-stellar, *vis imaginativa*) explanation, then the miracles of Christ may either have been natural phenomena or the work of an exceptional magician, not necessarily the Son of God. The response of orthodox Christians, it must be emphasized, was to declare natural magic inefficacious and all so-called magical feats either illusions or the work of demons. Natural magic therefore existed always under the cloud of Satanism. *And Satan's powers were daily proved by the necessity of witch-hunts.*

In the case of Paracelsian natural magic, suspicion of diabolical inspiration was reinforced by Paracelsus' social heterodoxy, by his obvious sympathy for the poor and dispossessed, and by his advocacy of a general spiritual and social reformation. At best, Paracelsus' effective treatments might be appropriated but with total rejection of the spiritual and social cosmology in which they were interpreted.

Although angelic magic in itself did not pose a threat to Christianity it was never clear to what extent such power was permitted Christians by God. Worst of all, the Cabalist magician could never be sure that the angels he had contacted were not deceiving demons. Indeed he might be a diabolical magician merely pretending to make contact with angels. The safest path for a Christian was not to become involved in any way with magic, natural or angelic—except, of course, that magic inherent in Christianity, particularly Catholicism, of the power of sacred relics, of many Church rituals and especially transubstantiation. Since God had agreed to transform bread and wine into the body and blood of Christ during the celebration of the Eucharist, the significance could not be doubted of the magical words uttered by the priest 'Hoc est corpus meum' and 'Hic est calix sanguinis mei'. It is not surprising that in the developing confrontation between magic and Christianity, Christians and particularly Catholics found it very difficult to prune their religion of all traces of magic. As D.P. Walker has rightly emphasized: 'The task of taking all the magic out of Christianity was an impossible one; it was there right from the beginning.'[34]

Be this as it may, the extreme heterodoxy of Giordano Bruno's magic brought home to the Church the dangers inherent in the natural magical and Hermetic tradition. By the time the Rosicrucian manifestos had appeared in print naming the Pope as the Antichrist and calling on all Christians to prepare for the coming Spiritual and Social Restoration, a Christian counter-attack on all aspects of magical thought and practice was well under way.

The thrust of this attack was the familiar one of declaring terrestrial matter to be devoid of all occult properties peculiar to natural magic, the stars and planets to be natural bodies that in no way emitted influences that could be tapped by natural magicians, that God alone knew the names of the objects, that Hebrew was the language of Adam not of God, and that therefore use of the Hebrew language gave the Cabalist magician no magical power over objects of the natural world. If incantations were efficacious in any way, this was through the agency of demons and not through the power of words over things or through the force of the magician's *vis imaginativa*. Christians in general did not wish to deny the reality of marvellous phenomena, only to deny them non-demonic natural magical explanations based on the ascription to matter of very remarkable properties. For the denial of the reality of demonic phenomena meant the effective denial of the reality of spirits, both good and bad, a position tantamount to atheism, as we have seen in the case of both Pietro Pomponazzi and Reginald Scot. In Scot's case non-demonic occult phenomena—such as the powers of the lodestone and *echeneis* fish, the running of the blood of a murdered man upon the approach of the murderer—could be and were accounted for by Scot in natural magical terms. Christians needed exactly the opposite approach: belief in the reality of most kinds of occult phenomena, denial of the efficacy of natural magic, acceptance of the efficacy of demonic magic (although with its practice proscribed for all true Christians), above all the successful articulation of a cosmology incorporating these requirements. In the confused intellectual atmosphere of the seventeenth century the mechanical philosophy (with Aristotelian cosmology under considerable strain) seemed to many not only to meet the requirements of a threatened Christianity but to meet them with a requirement to spare and a bonus: the attack on natural magic no longer demanded belief in the efficacy of demonic magic; the bonus was that human domination of the natural world became in principle achievable and entirely legitimate.

2 The Mechanical Philosophy in France

The mechanical philosophers of the seventeenth century took the audacious step of declaring matter to be totally inert, completely devoid of any interesting property. Thus René Descartes (1596–1650) spoke for all mechanical philosophers when he declared categorically that 'there exist no occult forces in stones or plants, no amazing and marvellous sympathies and antipathies, in fact there exists nothing in the whole of nature which cannot be explained in terms of purely corporeal causes, totally devoid of mind and thought'.[35] For Descartes all natural phenomena were explicable solely in terms of the sizes and shapes and velocities of particles, the latter characterized solely by the property of extension. The consequences of such a viewpoint are dramatic.

At a stroke the claims of natural magicians are demolished. Occult phenomena are either not real or they have mechanical explanations. The subversive connotations of natural magic therefore take, by association, a battering as well. The mechanical philosophy, however, does not have the atheistic implications of natural magic for the miracles described in the Bible can in no way be explained in mechanical terms. Moreover, since matter, according to the mechanical philosophers, is entirely devoid of sentience and consciousness, the reasoning powers of the human mind can likewise in no way be interpreted as a property of matter. Hence it follows that the mind must be immaterial, undoubtedly a gift from God, and is immortal. Certainly, orthodox theologians, still looking to Aristotle, would reject such a philosophy but less conservative Catholics would recognize these and, indeed, further advantages.

Demons may or may not exist but they are no longer necessary to underwrite the truth of Christianity and may thus be dispensed with. Likewise demonic witchcraft is no longer necessary as a prop for religion and (many of) the phenomena associated with it may safely be declared illusory. The claim of the mechanical philosophers that all natural phenomena are explicable in mechanical terms (and hence that there are no marvellous phenomena needing diabolical explanation) appeared sufficient to guarantee both the immateriality and immortality of the human soul.

Finally, if matter is characterized solely by the property of extension then it necessarily becomes mere stuff. Its mechanical appropriation by men is not merely legitimate, it is the only sensible course of action. While one might stand in wonder at the matter apprehended by natural magic, try to command it

mentally, or revere nature as a goddess or 'mother earth', one
can hardly stand in wonder at or revere the inert, barren matter
of the mechanical philosophy. 'Know that by nature I do not
understand some goddess or some other sort of imaginary
power', wrote Descartes. 'I employ this word to signify matter
itself.'[36] It follows logically that Descartes could write—the
Descartes whose only child died of scarlet fever—that he was
developing a philosophy that would enable mankind to become,
in his famous words, 'masters and possessors of nature'.[37] And,
after all, why not?

Perhaps, however, a distinction should be drawn. For while it is
necessary to attempt to free oneself—and humankind—from the
many tyrannies of nature that exist, so enabling all people to
enjoy lives free from hunger, disease, brute labour and exposure
to the elements, it is quite another thing to attempt to become
tyrant over nature in turn, recklessly appropriating the natural
world in a continual demonstration of human—let us be more
precise—male ruling-class power. The former goal of 'peace and
plenty' may in any case require not so much achievement of
greatly increased power over nature as achievement of the proper
kind of social organization combined with a sensibility that is
appreciative of the aesthetic qualities of the natural world and the
rights of all other living beings (human health permitting); the
latter goal would seem to entail the trampling underfoot of other
life forms and perhaps of a majority of people. 'After all, why
not?' It all depends on what is meant by 'mastery of nature' and
what are the underlying motivations. We shall return to this
theme.

The Cartesian cosmology
Descartes, the giant of the mechanical philosophy in the first half
of the seventeenth century, was born into the lesser nobility and
lived off his private income throughout his life. He was opposed
to social change: 'For public affairs are on a large scale, and large
edifices are too difficult to set up once they have been thrown
down . . . and their fall is necessarily catastrophic.' In any case,
'present institutions are practically always more tolerable than
would be a change in them'. That is why, Descartes explains, he
cannot at all approve of 'those mischievous spirits who, not being
called either by birth or by attainments to a position of political
power, are nevertheless constantly proposing some new reform'.
But how is it possible that people dare to live a sinful life and to
rebel against divinely appointed rulers? Descartes proposes that
there is no error 'which is so apt to make weak characters stray
from the path of virtue as the idea that the souls of animals are of

the same nature as our own, and that in consequence we have no more to fear or to hope for after this life than have the flies or ants'.[38] The prime necessity, therefore, is to prove the immateriality and immortality of the human soul and a first step is to prove the uniqueness of human beings in comparison with animals.

Now human beings think and reason and Descartes insists that soul is synonymous with mind. This means, however, Descartes argues, that if Montaigne is correct in attributing understanding and thought to animals then human beings are not unique; for if humans have immortal souls, i.e. minds—as humans certainly do have—then animals have likewise. Descartes' counter-argument is to declare that there is no reason to believe that some animals have souls and not all. But since it is absurd to believe that oysters and sponges possess immortal souls, Descartes draws the conclusion that no animals at all possess immortal souls. Therefore it cannot be the case that animals reason and think. Only humans do. Descartes' intention is therefore to prove that animals are mere automata and so establish the human claim to uniqueness and to the sole possession of an immortal soul.

Descartes can establish both the automaton-like nature of animals and the immaterial nature of the human mind if he can establish that all phenomena of nature (not involving the human mind which is immaterial and of supernatural origin) are explicable in terms of the behaviour of matter that is totally inert and angels no longer intervene in the mechanical world, the human body is a machine and the human mind is immaterial and Descartes will be able to demolish the competing views of natural magicians whose 'impostures' and 'disreputable doctrines' he claims to have seen through.[39] If he is to be successful in this disenchantment of the world, he must either convincingly deny the reality of occult phenomena or account for them in terms of matter stripped of all interesting properties. Descartes basically made the second choice. According to Cartesian philosophy, God and angels no longer intervene in the mechanical world, the human body is a machine and the human mind is immaterial and unextended. The latter has therefore at least good claims to being immortal.

There is a feature of Descartes' cosmology, of great importance to Descartes himself, and which on no account must be overlooked. The philosophies against which Descartes contends are anything but clear. Even if they are clear to their proponents, their public exposition is made deliberately obscure so that, as we have remarked, only the wise and morally pure are able to understand. Descartes is incensed by such obscurity and claims that it is 'the chief cause of the heresies and dissensions now at work in the world'. In the preface to the 1647 French translation of his *Principles of Philosophy* (published first in Latin in 1644), Descartes emphasizes that it is essential to construct a cosmology based on first principles that are 'so clear and evident that the human mind cannot doubt their truth when it attentively considers the matter'. Descartes assures his French readers that the first principles of his cosmology meet this essential requirement.[40]

Above all Descartes claims to possess—he certainly wants to possess—a methodology which leads infallibly to truth about the natural world. Thus he writes to Mersenne: 'I should believe myself to know nothing . . . if I were able to say only how things may be without demonstrating that they cannot be otherwise.'[41] A brilliant man proceeding at breakneck speed without the correct method will arrive anywhere but at truth; on the other hand, an ordinary mortal proceeding slowly and surely according to the correct methodology—Descartes'—will always increase his certain knowledge of the natural world. What in essence is that method? In tackling a problem precipitancy and prejudice are to be avoided; only clear and distinct ideas are to be accepted as true (God, who does not deceive, would not permit clear and distinct ideas to be false); each problem is to be divided into as many separate parts as possible; there should be a gradual ascent from simple to complex problems; finally an exhaustive review must be made to ensure that nothing essential has been omitted. Descartes subsequently explains that having obtained the first principles of his cosmology he was able to deduce from these principles the existence of 'skies, stars, and earth, and even on the earth, water, air, fire, minerals, and several other things which are the commonest of all and the most simple, and in consequence the easiest to understand'.[42] No comment! Descartes does emphasize, however, that not all the true causes of phenomena can be identified using his explanatory principles alone since alternative mechanisms each compatible with his explanatory principles are in many cases conceivable and thus only careful experimentation will enable the actual mechanism to be identified. But this is to beg the all-important question: Are Descartes' *general* explanatory principles, from which all else follows, true? In his *Principles of Philosophy* Descartes reassures his readers:

They who observe how many things regarding the magnet, fire, and the fabric of the whole world, are here deduced from a very small number of principles, although they considered that I had taken up these principles at random and without good grounds, they will yet acknowledge that it could hardly happen that so much should be coherent if they were false.[43]

Now the only *clear and distinct* idea of matter that Descartes is able to conceive is the following: 'The nature of matter or of body in its universal aspect', Descartes explains, 'does not consist in its being hard or heavy, or coloured, or one that affects our senses in some other way, but solely in the fact that it is a substance extended in length, breadth and depth'.[44] Matter therefore cannot give rise to *living beings,* it has no goal-seeking behaviour, it is not sentient or conscious in any way, no sympathies or antipathies exist between matter, matter has no hardness, no taste, no colour. Matter, Descartes affirms, is characterized only by extension, by the size, shape and velocity of its various parts, and only these (primary) properties are available for accounting for the phenomena of nature.

The phenomena of taste, colour and sound are easily explained. These result when particles of the appropriate size, shape and velocity strike the sense organs of the human observer and produce in her or his consciousness the sensations of taste, colour and sound. As Galileo agreed, take all living observers away and taste, colour and sound would vanish from the world. These (secondary) qualities are not properties of matter.

The existence of a void in nature is quite impossible, Descartes further argues. Matter is characterized by extension and, conversely, where there is extension there is matter. If quite literally there is nothing—a void—between the walls of a container, then the walls must be in contact! Descartes can now dispense—as he must—with the sympathies and antipathies of the natural magicians since he has everywhere at his disposal a material medium that in some way must be the carrier of interactions between bodies.

Descartes also argues that God had only to create matter in any shape at all, and impose motion on it, for ensuing collisions to eventually generate the three different kinds of matter now found in the world, the first kind consisting of (Descartes claims) extremely fine shavings filling all nooks and crannies and moving always at extremely high velocities, the second kind consisting of very small spherical (aether) particles usually moving at relatively high velocities, and finally lumps of gross matter usually moving relatively slowly with respect to each other. The earth and planets necessarily consist mainly of gross matter (Descartes argues), the sun and stars entirely of fine matter, while celestial matter consists mainly of aether particles with fine matter filling up all gaps. In addition, Descartes postulates that could a body be free from contact with any other body (which admittedly is an impossibility) it would travel always in a straight line with constant speed—a quite remarkable and very important claim. However, since the cosmos is everywhere full of matter, any motion of a body necessarily means a rearrangement of bodies, the net result of any initial displacement being a continual circular motion. Indeed, the cosmos is asserted to consist of an infinite system of vortices or whirlpools with suns or stars at their centres, surrounded by systems of planets 'floating' in their respective vortices. In the case of the solar vortex, the aether particles move quickly at the surface of the rotating sun (being swept round by it), then slowly decrease in speed until a minimum is reached (at the distance of Saturn from the sun), then once again increase in speed. Since the planets have different densities, i.e. different volumes of gross matter contained within their respective boundaries, their equilibrium orbits have different distances from the sun, the least dense planet lying nearest the sun, the densest and therefore slowest planet (Saturn) lying furthest from the sun. The stability of each orbit results from the fact that if a particular planet, say the earth, descends towards the sun it encounters more rapidly moving aether particles, hence its speed increases and the radius of its orbit increases. If it ascends away from the sun, its speed decreases and it falls back to its original orbit. A minor vortex circulates about the earth, thus causing the rotation of the earth and at the same time 'supporting' the motion of the moon. Descartes thought he could agree with both Copernicus and the Church. For Copernicus is correct in stating that the earth orbits the sun while the Church is correct in stating that the earth is stationary—stationary that is, Descartes explains, with respect to the aetherial vortex!

After explaining to his satisfaction all terrestrial and celestial phenomena—more of this later—Descartes turned his attention to 'living' beings. All non-human beings are mere automata, as totally mechanical as the other phenomena of nature. Building on the work of the English physician William Harvey, Descartes argued that the heart of an animal acts merely as a pump, constantly circulating the animal's blood but without 'rejuvenating' it as Harvey had supposed. Similarly all organs of animals are conceived by Descartes to be machines having purely mechanistic functions. The human body likewise is a machine. The human mind, which alone is immaterial and does not possess extension, Descartes conceives as 'interacting' with the body via the pineal gland. There is really not very much to be puzzled by in the construction of animal machines and the machine that is the human body. Consequently the spontaneous generation of 'life', i.e. mere machines, presents no problems for Descartes: 'Since so little is necessary to make an animal, it is certainly not surprising that so many animals, so many worms and insects, are formed spontaneously under our very eyes in all kinds of putrefying matter.'[45] If for William Gilbert the spontaneous generation of living beings had also presented no problems this was because Gilbert, contaminated with natural magical ideas, conceived all matter to be to some extent alive. For Gilbert, what is *alive* spontaneously produces *living* things. For Descartes, what is *dead* spontaneously produces *mechanical* things. The contrast between natural magicians and mechanical philosophers is starkly drawn. For the mechanical philosopher there is never any good reason to wonder at anything in nature. True to his philosophy we find Descartes expressing the fervent hope 'that those who have understood all that has been said in this treatise will, in future, see nothing . . . whose cause they cannot easily understand, nor anything which gives them any reason to marvel'.[46]

Nothing at all to marvel at? Have all apparently occult phenomena been accounted for in mechanistic terms? The answer is in the affirmative. The cohesion of bodies is accounted for by Descartes merely in terms of the mutual relative rest of the matter comprising each 'cohesive' body. Because of the distinctive shapes of various particles, large distances may be travelled by particles of a particular kind before they meet bodies with which they can suitably interact. In this way it is possible to suggest mechanistic explanations for phenomena that natural magicians can account for only by invoking sympathies and antipathies. Even the 'fact' that the blood of a murdered man runs at the approach of the murderer is explained mechanistically. The phenomenon of magnetism is a test-case for the mechanical philosophy and Descartes rises to the occasion: magnets have, he insists, 'no qualities so occult nor effects of sympathy or antipathy so marvellous or strange' that their properties cannot be explained in terms of the 'size, shape, situation and motion of different particles of matter'.[47] Descartes' explanation is ingenious in the extreme. The earth itself is a magnet which means that running through the earth in a north-south direction are grooved tunnels that allow the passage in one direction of grooved particles with a right-hand screw and in the other direction of grooved particles with a left-hand screw. Magnets have similar, grooved tunnels and hence when free to move on the earth's surface align themselves with the earth's streams of screw-like particles. Moreover, each magnet itself possesses two streams of screw-like particles, as shown in Figure 3.1(i): at one end (the south pole) the right-hand screws leave and the left-hand screws enter, at the other end the situation is

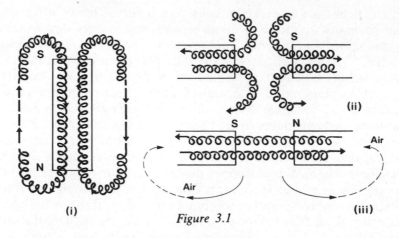

Figure 3.1

obviously reversed. If the ends of two magnets are placed side by side—see Figure 3.1 (ii)—then if the two ends are similar, say both south poles, then the right-hand screws leaving each end cannot enter the adjacent end and the two colliding streams push the two ends apart: thus there only *seems* to be an antipathy between the two similar ends. On the other hand, if two opposite poles are placed side by side, as shown in Figure 3.1 (iii), then since right-hand screws leaving one pole readily enter the end adjacent to it, air is necessarily displaced between the two adjacent ends which moving round towards the two far ends propels the two magnets towards each other: thus there only *seems* to be a sympathy between the two opposite poles. Iron, on the other hand, unlike a magnet, possesses its appropriately grooved tunnels running in all directions. However, when a piece of iron is placed sufficiently near a magnet the screw-like particles leaving the magnet are able to enter some of the iron's tunnels, consequently aligning them with those of the magnet, with the result that the magnet and the iron are pushed towards each other by the displaced air. 'In truth', Descartes writes, 'there is no attraction; for as soon as the iron is in the magnet's sphere of virtue, that virtue is communicated to it, and the screw-like particles which pass from the magnet to the iron expel the air between them and thus force them together'.[48] What a triumph for the mechanical philosophy!

The baffling phenomenon which reputedly drove Aristotle to suicide and brought Kepler his rebuke from Galileo likewise offers no difficulty for Descartes. But whereas Galileo's explanation could only account for one tide per day, Descartes' explanation gives the observed two tides per day. The earth has its own slightly non-spherical vortex of fine celestial matter in which the moon makes its monthly journey about the earth.

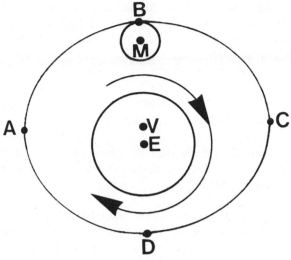

Figure 3.2

However, the centre E of the earth is not at the centre V of the earth's vortex $ABCD$—see Figure 3.2—since the movement of the celestial matter between the moon and the earth pushes the earth away from the moon until the pressure in the vortex between the moon and the earth is equal to that between the earth and the near boundary D of the earth's vortex. Despite this equalization of pressure on the two sides of the earth, the celestial matter between BE and ED has less space to flow in than elsewhere, with the result that the pressure on the earth's oceans is always greatest directly underneath the moon and on the side of the earth opposite the moon. Thus two low tides are produced at the equator, one always directly underneath the continually moving moon and the other always on the far side of the earth to the moon. Moreover, Descartes explains, the tides are greatest when the moon is new and full at positions B and D since the distance BD is the least distance across the vortex (which is a very convenient assumption indeed!) and hence at new and full moons the pressure on the earth's oceans is greatest.[49] Obviously the extent of the non-sphericity to the earth's vortex (shown, of course, somewhat exaggerated in Figure 3.2) can in principle be chosen to reproduce average differences between full and neap tides.

Without doubt, Descartes has provided an alternative explanation of phenomena to that proposed by natural magicians. The question is, however, which philosophy is correct or, should one say, which is on fruitful lines? Of course, Descartes' version of the mechanical philosophy was not the only one developed at this time. In particular, the atomistic theories of Democritus and

Epicurus were also revived, these theories presupposing the existence of indestructible atoms moving through the void both Aristotle and Descartes agreed could not exist. Despite such fundamental differences, the Cartesian and atomistic mechanical philosophies nevertheless shared the claim that nature is in no way animate and possesses no occult properties; hence it is totally erroneous to claim that nature abhors a vacuum (as the Aristotelians claimed) or that there exist sympathies and anti-pathies between particles (as natural magicians claimed). A striking experiment performed in 1647 totally demolishes the Aristotelian position. But, we must ask, does it also demolish the natural magical position?

Natural magic versus the mechanical philosophy

It had been known for some time that it is not possible to suck water up a tube to a height of more than about 30 feet. Is it nature's horror of a vacuum that draws the water up so far and no further? What is the nature of the space above the water? Is that space a vacuum? Is nature's horror of a vacuum of only finite extent so that sufficient brute force can succeed in overcoming it? Blaise Pascal was in no doubt about the matter writing in 1647 to his brother-in-law Florin Périer:

[T]o tell you frankly what I think, it is hard for me to believe that nature, which is not animate or sensitive, is capable of horror, since the passions presuppose a soul capable of feeling them, and I incline much more to impute all those effects to the weight and pressure of the air.

Pascal also found it difficult to understand how natural magicians could claim that 'the sympathy and antipathy of natural bodies are efficient causes, responsible for many effects as if inanimate bodies were capable of sympathy and antipathy'. Wrong such ideas might be but—Pascal's problem—how were they to be refuted? Substitution of water with mercury showed that the height of liquid drawn up in a tube was inversely proportional to the density of the liquid, the maximum height of a mercury column being some 76 cms or 29 inches. Pascal hit upon an ingenious idea. If his idea was correct that it is the weight of the earth's atmosphere which is responsible for the rise of the mercury in the sealed tube, then if such a tube is taken up a mountain top the mercury column should drop somewhat since it is certain that the weight of the earth's air is less at the top of a mountain than at the bottom. The experiment was done; while the column being taken up the mountain dropped steadily a column at the foot of the mountain stayed the same height. Pascal was jubilant. The supporters of Aristotle, he affirmed, could hardly claim that nature abhorred a vacuum more at the foot of a mountain than at its summit! Let them recognize, he concluded in triumph,

that experiments are the true masters to follow in physics, that the experiment made on the mountains overturned the universal belief everywhere held that nature abhors a vacuum and opened up this knowledge which can nevermore be foregotten, that nature has no horror of the vacuum, that she does nothing to avoid it, and that the weight of the mass of air is the true cause of all the effects hitherto attributed to that imaginary cause.[50]

The question now is, what is the cause of weight? Is the cause mechanical or is it occult? Aristotle is apparently out of the running. The two contestants are the mechanical philosophy and natural magic.

The cause of weight was to prove a permanent stumbling block to the proponents of mechanical philosophies. Descrates assumed that faster moving celestial matter would by its greater 'centrifugal force' push earthly bodies downwards. But why always towards the centre of the earth? This would certainly happen, Descartes argued, if the celestial matter moved radially outwards. But in this case there would be no circular vortex motion of celestial matter around the earth. The Cartesian theory of weight was extremely unsatisfactory. Nevertheless for Descartes and his followers a natural magical explanation of gravity could on no account be admitted. When the philosopher Gilles Roberval cautiously proposed (in the same year as the publication of Descartes' *Principles of Philosophy*) that particles of the same kind have an 'attraction' for each other, Descartes' response was as emphatic as Galileo's had been to Kepler's suggestion of a universal 'attraction'. Believing Roberval to be making such a proposal, Descartes wrote scathingly to Mersenne that 'nothing is more absurd than the assumption...that a certain property is inherent in each of the parts of the world's matter and that, by the force of this property, the parts are carried towards one another and attract each other'. The absurdity is obvious:

In order to understand this, we must not only assume that each material particle is animated, and even animated by a large number of diverse souls that do not disturb each other, but also that these souls of material particles are endowed with knowledge of a truly divine sort, so that they may know without any medium what takes place at very great distances and act accordingly.[51]

Roberval was not perturbed and after Descartes' death continued his attack on the mechanical philosophers' banishment of 'occult forces'. Accordingly, at several meetings in 1669 of the recently constituted Paris Academy of Sciences, Roberval again proposed the 'most probable' hypothesis, namely that gravity was a mutual attraction. In defence of Descartes' explanation of weight the

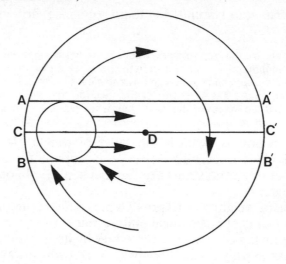

Figure 3.3

Dutch philosopher Christiaan Huygens offered a mechanistic example, improved and published in 1690 in his *Discourse on the Cause of Gravity*. On the bottom of a cylindrical vessel filled with water Huygens placed a small ball constrained to move between three horizontal strings, two of them *AA'* and *BB'* each side of the ball and the third *CC'* immediately above the ball, as shown in Figure 3.3. After rotating the vessel until the water shared the vessel's circular motion, it was observed that on suddenly bringing the vessel to rest the water continued to rotate but the ball, constrained by the strings, moved to the centre of the cylinder. The difficulty with this demonstration, of course, is that without the strings the ball would be swept around with the water and even with the strings the ball is swept to the axis of rotation. Where are the strings surrounding the earth and how are they placed so that all bodies are pushed downwards *perpendicularly* to the earth's surface, that is, towards the centre of the earth, not towards its axis of rotation?[52] One is almost led to believe that if the Cartesians could have denied the reality of the phenomena of weight and the fall of bodies at right angles to the earth's surface, then they most certainly would have done! As we shall see later, the reality of some rather important but very exasperating phenomena was to be denied. But the phenomenon of falling bodies could not be so easily wished out of existence! Huygens's response was to suggest that fluid matter surrounding the earth rotates 'in part' in circular motions *in all directions* so that the *net* movement of a gross body is downwards towards the centre of the earth. The audacity of the mechanical philosophers was nothing short of impressive.

The triumph of Cartesian philosophy

Cartesian philosophy steadily gained ground. By the end of the 1650s Jacques Rohault (1620–72), the son of a rich wine merchant, was holding highly successful lectures each week at his home in Paris during which he performed experiments and expounded Cartesian physics to a large audience, with women as well as men, and many foreigners, making a point of attending these famous Wednesday meetings. Church authorities and the Sorbonne, however, attempting to remain faithful to the dying doctrines of Aristotle, became increasingly hostile to the mechanical philosophy as its popularity grew. During his lifetime Descartes himself had been criticized principally for the supposed failure of his theory of matter to account for Catholic doctrine on transubstantiation. If during the celebration of the Eucharist the sensible qualities of the bread and wine—their taste, colour and odour—remained the same, then how could the bread and wine become *in reality* the body and blood of Christ? Descartes' reply was that Christ's body and blood occupied the same spaces as originally defined by the bread and wine and therefore produced the same sensations in the human observer as the original bread and wine. This explanation proved unacceptable to the Church which subsequently in 1663 placed most of Descartes' writings on the Index of Forbidden Books and also to the Sorbonne's theologians and philosophers who persuaded Louis XIV in 1671 to prohibit the teaching of Cartesian philosophy in French universities. In that year of prohibition, however, Rohault's classic work, the *Traité de physique,* was published to acclaim both in the *Philosophical Transactions of the Royal Society* and the *Journal des Savants* (whose first numbers had both appeared a few years earlier in 1665). Three years later a Latin translation of Rohault's work appeared and indeed within five years of its publication in 1671 three new editions were published in Paris and two in Amsterdam. Following his success with the *Traité de physique,* the intrepid Rohault also published in 1671 a defence of Descartes' explanation of transubstantiation and attempted to rebut charges of materialism against Descartes. It is apparent that despite rearguard religious opposition, Cartesian philosophy and physics continued to thrive. The Archbishop of Paris himself became an enthusiastic student of Rohault's successor in Paris Pierre Sylvain Régis (1632–1707), while Nicolas Malebranche (1638–1715) of the Congregation of the Oratory devoted his life to a reconciliation of Cartesian philosophy with Catholicism, publishing in 1674–75 his influential work *Recherche de la Vérité*. Cartesianism obviously had devout Christian supporters.

Moreover, given Descartes' emphasis on the importance of clear, logical thinking and disregard for classical erudition, it is not surprising that the upper-class 'feminist' movement in France, associated with the (female-run) *salons,* found Cartesian philosophy particularly appealing, the letters of Mme de Sévigné amply demonstrating the interest of upper-class women in the propagation of Cartesian ideas. The radical French priest Poulain de la Barre (later a convert to Protestantism) also used the Cartesian method to argue the cause of women's emancipation in his remarkable 1673 publication *De l'Egalité des deux sexes,* having two years earlier included Descartes' *Discourse on Method* and Rohault's Cartesian physics in his *Education des dames.* Poulain, however, was no admirer of Cartesian metaphysics nor of the *salons,* which he regarded as too socially conservative. Nevertheless, Cartesian ideas were being well absorbed by many upper-class women as they attempted to increase their influence on French social life and respond to growing social mobility.[53] The acceptability—and controversiality—of Cartesian ideas are poignantly illustrated both by the notoriety of a certain Mlle Dupré, called 'la Cartesienne', 'whose glory was to consider herself incapable of tenderness' and in the response of the 'militant' Cartesian, Mme de Grignan (daughter of Mme de Sévigné), to the sadly misguided offer of a pet dog for her daughter Pauline. 'Please do not bring a dog for Pauline', she wrote (in 1690) to her daughter's would-be benefactor, explaining that 'we want only rational creatures here, and belonging to the sect we belong to we refuse to burden ourselves with these machines: if they were constructed so as not to have dirty business to perform, well and good, but what one has to put up with makes them unbearable'![54]

This perhaps is the appropriate time, with Cartesian physics, despite its manifest difficulties, steadily gaining ground outside the universites in both France and the Low Countries, to take up the vicissitudes of the mechanical philosophy in England, the country in which prominent natural philosophers first accepted the mechanical philosophy and then rather indecently hurried to reject it.

3 The Mechanical Philosophy in England

Natural magic at the turn of the century
Christopher Hill and Keith Thomas relate how at the turn of the seventeenth century nobility, property owners and clergy ex-

pressed little confidence in the religious convictions of the lower classes. It was, for example, reported in 1573 that a group of sectaries in the diocese of Ely persisted in denying the physical reality of hell. Five years later a Norfolk ploughwright, Mathew Hamont, was burnt at Norwich for declaring the New Testament to be 'mere foolishness, a story of men, or rather a mere fable'. In 1589 Bishop Cooper began his *Admonition to the People of England* by referring to 'the loathsome contempt, hatred and disdain that *the most part of men* in these days bear . . . towards the ministers of the church of God'. In the year 1600 the Bishop of Exeter complained that in his diocese it was 'a matter very common to dispute whether there be a God or not', while in Essex a husbandman of Bradwell-near-the-Sea was said to 'hold his opinion that all things cometh by nature and does affirm this as an atheist'. William Perkins, Puritan preacher and witch-hunter, complained that the so-called Familists, members of the Family of Love and followers of Henry Niclaes, born in Münster in 1502, dared to teach that heaven and hell were of this world, interpreted the Bible allegorically, held their property in common and maintained that all phenomena are naturally caused.[55]

Although natural magic had not acquired in England at this time the socially subversive connections Paracelsus in particular had won for it on the Continent, nevertheless it was apparently still seen as a threat to religion and consequently the feats claimed by natural magicians tended to be either dismissed as illusions or condemned as diabolically caused. A few examples will suffice to illustrate the nature of the accusations that magicians either faced or perceived themselves to face. Thus in his 'Mathematical Preface' to the English translation of Euclid, published in 1570, the controversial Elizabethan magician John Dee praised the pious philosopher (namely, himself!) who sought 'in the Creatures Properties, and wonderful vertues, to finde iuste cause, to glorifie the Aeternall, the Almightie Creator by'. Dee continued, however, indignantly and incredulously:

Shall that man, be (in hugger mugger) condemned, as a Companion of the Helhoundes, and a Caller, and Coniurer of wicked and damned Spirites? . . . I have not learned to make so brutish and so wicked a Bargaine . . . What a Land: what a People: what Maners: what Times are these? Are they become Deuils, them selues: and, by false witnesse bearing against their Neighbour, would they also, become Murderers?'

Ten years later, it is true, Dee made his first attempts to contact spirits—good spirits of course.[56] On the other hand, Thomas Hariot, who compounded Epicurean atomism with his magic, found himself denounced in 1591 as that 'Magus' and 'Epicurus' from whom, apparently, could shortly be expected a proclamation in which 'the immortality of every soul, and the expectation of another life, are distinctly, clearly, briefly and without circumlocution denied'. At the trial of Hariot's fellow magician, Walter Raleigh, we find Chief Justice Popham therefore advising, '[L]et not Heriott nor any such Doctor, persuade you there is no eternity in Heaven, lest you find an eternity of hell-torments.'[57] Satanist or atheist but in no way a good Christian: this was the predicament of the natural magician. In 1585 an English Paracelsian appropriately noted that Erastus finds 'great falte with the celestiall medicine of Paracelsus, saiying that they have their strenthe and power of the devilles and evell spirites'.[58] But the truth of the matter, he insisted, albeit anonymously, is that Paracelsus excluded 'from the true, pure, and aunciente Magike, and from his coelestiall medicine, all Nigromancie, Sorcery, Ceremonies, Coniurations, and all manner of invocations of devilles, *Demones* and evill spirites'. Would that that were true! The Hermetic philosopher Robert Fludd, roundly denounced as a diabolical magician by Mersenne, received similar treatment in England at the hands of the clergyman Willam Foster, who expressed surprise that such a man as Fludd should be allowed to live and write in England. Foster also had no doubts over the primary allegiance of Fludd's intellectual master, Paracelsus. After describing a reputedly magical cure by Paracelsus for impotency, Foster comments: 'Now then Paracelsus being a Witch, and this experiment being placed amongst his Diabolicall and magicall conclusions, it cannot choose but be Witchcraft, and come from the grandmaster of Witches, the Divell.'[59] The search for knowledge of the secrets of nature was an activity fraught with considerable danger. As William Perkins argued with great conviction, it all stemmed from a discontentment of the mind, from that state of Satanic curiosity 'when a man resteth not satisfied with the measure of inward gifts received, as of knowledge, wit, understanding . . . but aspires to search out such things as God would have kept secret'. The tragedy of such a man, lamented Perkins, is that 'he is mooved to attempt the cursed art of Magick and witchcraft, as a way to get further knowledge in matters secret and not reveiled, that by working wonders, he may purchase fame in the world'.[60] In every magician William Perkins saw a Doctor Faustus.

Purified natural magic, the 'experimental philosophy' of Francis Bacon and 'the masculine birth of time'
It is in the context of this suspicion towards natural magic, not to say intense fear, that we must interpret the endeavours of Francis Bacon, one-time Lord Chancellor of England, to legitimize the

goal of man's domination over the natural world. Bacon needed to do two things: (1) to show that there was no prohibition by God of men's quest to control nature *by lawful means* and (2) to identify a means which arrives at results that can be put to use and which is lawful, i.e. which manifestly makes no contact with demons. Bacon employs the following arguments.

Adam fell from grace not because he sought power over nature—he had been granted that by God from the outset—but because he sought knowledge with a view to following his own moral laws, not those imposed by God. Although Adam's fall resulted in his and his descendants' loss of power over nature, by God's mercy this power could be restored by following a necessarily long and arduous procedure. For as the Lord God had commanded, 'In the sweat of thy brow shalt thou eat thy bread'! Some men, however, believe it immoral and unchristian to seek power over nature. This is because they erroneously believe that the world is made in the image of God, whereas, Bacon affirms, only man is made in God's image. There is nothing in God's commandments to forbid the acquisition of power over nature, Bacon constantly emphasizes, provided only the means is lawful and the ends just, namely for 'the benefit and use of life'.[61]

Bacon unreservedly condemns the use of *vis imaginativa* to gain power over nature, especially since Paracelsus and 'the disciples of pretended Natural Magic' have claimed that by the power of the imagination miracles can be performed. It is this feature of natural magic that makes it so dangerous to Christians: 'For it may be pretended that Ceremonies, Characters, and Charms do work, not by any tacit or sacramental contract with evil spirits, but serve only to strengthen the imagination of him that useth it.' Bacon emphasizes, however, that even if imagination has power, and that ceremonies fortify it, and that Paracelsians and natural magicians sincerely use ceremonies only for that purpose, nevertheless he would still hold such ceremonies to be unlawful. For such magicians seek noble effects by a 'few easy and slothful observances' whereas God's commandment is clear that such effects must be won at the price of prolonged labour. It is only, Bacon writes, 'if we labour in thy works with the sweat of our brows, thou wilt make us partakers of thy vision and thy sabbath'.[62]

This still leaves the method unidentified. It has been established only that it must be arduous. In the first place it is clear, Bacon argues, that if power over nature is sought, it is useless to look for the ends of phenomena: 'For the inquisition of Final Causes is barren', he comments, 'and like a virgin consecrated to God produces nothing'. Just as the *echeneis* fish prevents the ship from sailing, so the search for final causes produces the same effect on natural philosophy. What instead must be sought are efficient causes of phenomena, knowledge of which enables the knower to produce the required effects at will. No ceremonies are to be used, no incantations, no force of imagination (witchcraft and demonic effects may lawfully be studied but only to understand better the *natural* properties of matter). Mark well what Bacon writes for it is deceptively simple: 'Toward the effecting of works, all that man can do is to put together or put as-under natural bodies. The rest is done by nature working within.' Such a natural magician need fear no accusation of diabolical sorcery and Bacon can therefore insist that magic, 'which has long been used in a bad sense, be again restored to its ancient and honourable meaning'. While vigorously condemning the 'idle and most slothful conjectures' of natural magicians who have ascribed wonderful virtues to substances and condemning especially the secretive magician's quest for personal aggrandizement, Bacon nevertheless approvingly points out that 'natural magic preten-deth to call and reduce natural philosophy from variety of speculations to the magnitude of works'. And there is nothing more important than the magnitude of works.[63]

Bacon's method—the experimental philosophy—is to be long and laborious but it is to be certain. There is to be no need for individual brilliance or special illumination. The method is one that 'goes far to level men's wits' for the simple reason that 'it performs everything by surest rules and demonstrations'. Men's wits are to be supplied not with wings but with weights. Whereas in the past men have guessed at comprehensive systems of nature or claimed special illumination in so doing and from very general principles have worked out particular consequences—always wrong—the correct method is exactly the reverse of this. It is to start with careful observation of particular phenomena and by cautious hypotheses and the use of experiments to construct 'by successive steps not interrupted or broken' systems of ever greater generality which are at all times correct. Experiment is of crucial importance in Bacon's methodology since 'nature exhibits herself more clearly under the trials and vexations of art than when left to herself'; more precisely, nature is compelled to answer questions when under experimentation. Error is thereby con-tinually identified and eliminated. It is in principle a simple method and a certain one; and it is lawful because it means a long and laborious toil—there are to be no short cuts to success.[64]

But success there will be, such success that will enable men—virile men—not merely to exert a 'gentle guidance over nature's course' but to 'conquer and subdue her, to shake her to her foundations'. Bacon's method is one that will enable such men to voyage to 'remote and hidden regions of nature', there to discover the 'secrets still locked in Nature's bosom'—it is therefore a method that will inaugurate the 'truly *masculine* birth of time' (italics added). It is a method that will lead men to 'Nature with all her children to bind her to your service and make her your slave'.[65] Bacon's method is an invitation to those 'true sons of knowledge' who aspire 'to penetrate further' to pass beyond the 'outer courts of nature' and 'find a way at length into her inner chambers'. Bacon's method is a trumpet that calls on men to make peace among themselves in order to turn 'with united forces against the Nature of Things, to storm and occupy her castles and strongholds, and extend the bounds of human empire, as far as God Almighty in his goodness may permit'. Bacon's method is intended to establish the 'Dominion of Man over the Universe.'[66]

Perhaps it is appropriate to leave this very male apostle of works by quoting a striking passage in which Bacon seeks to mollify those who claim the pursuit of knowledge is the pursuit of truth, not power. The point is that truth is measured by power, that is Bacon's claim.

But if to any one given to the love and worship of contemplation, this frequent and honourable mention of works sounds somewhat harsh and offensive, let him be assured that he thwarts his own wishes. For in nature works are not only benefits to life, but pledges of truth. The rule of religion that a man should justify his faith by works applies also in natural philosophy; knowledge should be proved by its works. For truth is rather revealed and established by the evidence of works rather than by disputation, or even sense. Hence the human intellect and social conditions are enriched by one and the same means'.

The measurement of truth is power.

When Bacon died in 1626, Charles I had been king just one year. At the start of his reign, it would have been difficult to predict how the purified, collaborative natural magic that the former Lord Chancellor had advocated would fare against the mechanical philosophies soon to be developed on the mainland of Europe. Charles' policies, however, influenced the course of natural magic in a dramatic fashion.[67]

The English Civil War
The Irish rebellion of 1641 necessitated an English army for its suppression. Parliament refused to grant a Royal nominee control of any such army; the king withdrew from London to Oxford; the English Civil War began. Briefly, the king sought absolute control over the affairs of the country, while Parliament representing the new men of property and commerce wanted at least an effective sharing of control. Crudely speaking, the

economically developed south-east fought the economically underdeveloped north and south-west. It was far from clear to the contending parties which of them would emerge victorious; and not without reason a fear existed that the war might encourage all kinds of ultra-subversive actions. Indeed, Christopher Hill reports how Charles himself had warned Parliament in 1642 that the 'common people' may 'destroy all rights and properties, all distinctions of families and merit'. Similarly, Hill notes, the Scottish poet William Drummond had asked fearfully whether 'peasants, clowns, farmers, base people all in arms, may not swallow the nobles and gentry, invest their possessions, adhere together by a new Covenant, and follow our example'.[68] If they did not in the end do this, they did enough to scare very thoroughly the men who were disputing over the ownership of England. I give below merely some highlights of the subversive religious and political writings that flourished in England at this time.

In 1643 Richard Overton, a founder of the Leveller party that advocated popular franchise for all free men, i.e. non-wage earners, published a book *Mans Mortallitie* in which he claimed the soul to be material and mortal and indeed to perish with the body until Resurrection at the Day of Judgement. In the following year when it was reprinted in a new edition, Parliament responded by ordering an investigation into publishers of tracts preaching the mortality of the soul. The damage, however, had been done and in any case censorship was now impossible. The less exalted people of England could have their say and have it they did. In a pamphlet entitled 'Truth Lifting up its Head', the 'True Leveller' Gerrard Winstanley wrote: I am made to change the name from God to Reason; because I have been held under darknesse by that word, as I see many people are.' It is not surprising to find a contemporary reporting that many of his acquaintances 'did say in their hearts and tongues both, that there is no God but nature only.'[69] Atheism was seen to be a very real threat by the disunited English ruling class.

Not only atheism but also social subversion. A pamphlet distributed in 1649 is worthy of extensive quotation. The pamphlet begins:

We ... do in the name of all the poor oppressed people in *England,* declare unto you, that call your selves Lords of Manors, and Lords of the Land, ... That the earth was not made purposely for you, to be Lords of it, and we to be your Slaves, Servants, and Beggers; but it was made to be a common Livelihood to all, without respect of persons; And that your buying and selling of Land, and the Fruits of it, one to another, is *The cursed thing,* and was brought in by War; which hath, and still does establish murder, and theft, in the hands of some branches of Mankinde over others, which is the greatest outward burden, and unrighteous power, that Creation groans under. . . . It is that which makes some Lords, others Beggers, some Rulers, others to be ruled; and makes great Murderers and Theeves to be imprisoners, and hangers of little ones, or of sincere-hearted men. . . .

The pamphlet concludes:

And thus in love we have declared the purpose of our hearts plainly, without flatterie . . . intending no other matter herein, but to observe the Law of righteous action, endeavouring to shut out of the Creation, the cursed thing, called Particular Propriety, which is the cause of all wars, bloud-shed, theft, and enslaving Laws, that hold the people under miserie.

Significantly, the pamphlet is signed 'for and in behalf of all the poor oppressed people of *England,* and the whole world'.[70]

Of great importance for the future development of natural philosophy in England was the perceived spread of atheistic ideas. Members of the ruling class appeared to be caught in a pincer movement. For at the other extreme to atheism, radical sects of all kinds espoused the ideas of Paracelsus, claiming divine inspiration for their subversive social objectives. Specialists of this period have noted how in England 'democratization' of the magical tradition came about during the Civil War years of the 1640s and the turbulent decade that followed. Not only in that decade were more Paracelsian and alchemical works translated into English than in the preceding 100 years but great interest was also shown in the Rosicrucian movement. The radical sects, recruiting their membership chiefly from the lower classes, believed that the fall of the Antichrist was imminent, to be followed by the Second Coming of Christ. Cromwell may have defeated mutinous Leveller troops at Burford in 1649 but he had not extirpated the heretical and politically subversive ideas that now swamped the country. The Parliament of men of property had just executed the King of England in the name of the people of England. The people of England—or at least too many of them for the liking of Parliament—now wished to see the construction of a 'truly' Christian society, each sect according to its own special divine illuminations.

If that were not enough for a disunited and warring ruling class to contend with, a man of Royalist sympathies published in 1651 a book that undercut Cartesian dualism, arguing that thought is nothing but the complicated motion of matter in the brain and that spirits—if they exist at all—are not immaterial, but have extension and are very much made of matter. From this material-ist philosophy Thomas Hobbes argued in his *Leviathan* that all men—who are as basically equal as the atoms of matter—must renounce their liberty in favour of unconditional allegiance to an absolute ruler. Failure to do so ensures that the life of each man in competing with the objectives of every other man becomes life in the state of nature, namely, solitary, poor, nasty, brutish and short. The victors who had just executed Charles I and who looked towards religion to help them unify the country did not welcome these arguments.

What were the consequences for natural philosophy that stemmed from the uniquely promising yet extremely difficult situation in which men of property found themselves in mid-seventeenth-century England?

Conversions to the mechanical philosophy
At first sight it appeared to several philosophers that any variant of the mechanical philosophy would help undercut the double danger facing both established religion and the precarious *status quo* of Cromwellian England. For the atheistic implications of Aristotelian naturalism augmented with star-induced occult qualities (Pomponazzi's writings had become well-known during this period) were totally undermined by the stark dualism of Descartes' cosmology: on the one hand, inert matter devoid of all interesting properties, on the other, unextended, immaterial mind. At the same time the clarity of Descartes' thought undermined, or at least vividly contrasted with, the obscurity of Paracelsus' writings and provided a weapon with which the social, philosophical and religious pretensions of Paracelsian-Rosicrucian sects could be fought. But was Cartesian cosmology correct? That is another question which in the heat of battle must be temporarily deferred! Let us for the time being look at some examples of how the mechanical philosophy secured a bridgehead in the strife-riven England of the 1650s.

The man on whom the mantle of Robert Fludd had fallen, Thomas Vaughan, published in 1650 a collection of writings steeped in Hermetic-Paracelsian philosophy reinforced by the addition of Pico's and Agrippa's Cabalism and in which non-magical writers were given short shrift. Aristotle, in particular, was held responsible for having given rise to an all-pervasive 'spirit of Errour'. Laying aside Aristotle's 'Vain Babling', Vaughan publicly acknowledged his immense debt to Agrippa to whom 'next to God', he declared, he owed everything. In *Anthroposophia Theomagica* Vaughan approvingly quoted the master magician that 'there is no work in this whole world so admirable, so excellent, so wonderfull, which the soul of man . . . cannot accomplish by its own power without any externall help'. What incredible blasphemy! (This power of the soul was, however, possessed only by the soul's masculine part, Vaughan explaining that the 'Soul of man consists chiefly of two Portions ... the *superior* Masculine and *Eternall,* the *inferior Foeminine* and *Mortall'*.) Indeed, Vaughan was so confident that with Agrippa's aid he had shown how nature might be pierced to her innermost centre that he feared he could hear nature cry out that he had 'all most broken her Seale, and exposed her naked to the World'.[72] In 1652, having survived a vitriolic debate with Henry More, Vaughan published the first English translation of the Rosicrucian manifestos under the title *The Fame and Confession of the Fraternity of RC, commonly of the Rosie Cross.*

Against Vaughan's belief that the world soul was rational, particularly against his all-pervasive Paracelsian enthusiasms, the influential Cambridge philosopher Henry More sought to defend a strict neoplatonism of a cosmos of inert matter threaded throughout by a non-material, non-rational world soul. While recognizing that Vaughan himself was not a member of a religious, subversive sect, More nevertheless believed it necessary to demolish Vaughan's ideas in order to help others perceive the folly and sinfulness of allowing themselves to be 'driven by heedlesse intoxicating imaginations under pretense of higher strains of Religion and supernaturall light'. For once a man has rejected 'sober reason and a purified mind', he inevitably becomes 'first fanaticall; and then Atheisticall and sensuall'. One has only to look, More thought, at the sorry figure of Vaughan himself who so openly boasts of being a 'very knowing Disciple of *Agrippa,* and puts in as far for the name of a Magician, as honesty will permit, and safety from... the Witch-finder'. In addition, feeling particularly aggrieved that Descartes had been contemptuously slighted by Vaughan, More was led to suggest that Vaughan had either not read or had not understood the 'most admirable philosophy, that ever yet appeared in these *European* parts since *Noahs* floud'. Certainly Vaughan should not be concerned, More wrote consolingly, that he had violated nature's innermost secrets: such a 'chast and discreet Lady' was not to be 'lewdly prostituted' by 'immodest hands'. 'I warrant thee', More mocked the presumptuous magician, 'Thou has not laid Madam Nature so naked as thou supposest, only thou hast, I am afraid, dream't uncleanly, and so hast polluted so many sheets of paper with thy Nocturnall Canundrums. . . . '.[73]

Against fanatical enthusiasms, the neoplatonic More turned to the Cartesian mechanical philosophy for proof that matter is totally inert and that the 'enlivened Universe' described by Vaughan is only the wildest fiction.[74] With the best will in the world Vaughan could only express amazement at such ignorance and in a public response he informed More that Descartes was merely a 'fellow that invented ridiculous *principles* of his own, but hath cast them into such a *method,* that they have a *seeming dependency,* and thou doest mistake his *Knavery* for his *Reason*'.[75] Once again More could not let such 'rash and unworthy abuse of DesCartes' go unanswered for only fools could fail to appreciate that Cartesian philosophy was 'an Hypothesis accurately and continuedly agreeing with the *Phaenomena* of Nature'. In increasingly vitriolic language More told Vaughan that his understanding of such natural phenomena as the tides and the loadstone was that of an imbecile: 'I tell thee thou wilt never be able to answer sense to them, unlesse thou turn Cartesian, and explain them out of that Philosophy'.[76] Enthusiasm and atheism: both were perceived to represent a threat to the precarious stability of English society. More had surely made an appropriate and telling response: against both enthusiasm and atheism the mechanical philosophy could—and would—be called upon to render service to the state.

We can also see the perceived social menace of enthusiasm informing a debate over the curricula at the universities of Oxford and Cambridge. When in 1654 John Webster published his *Examination of the Academies,* advocating that the teaching of Aristotle and Ptolemy be dropped by the two universities and the natural magic of Paracelsus, Bacon and Fludd taught in their place (having carefully dissociated himself from that 'impious and execrable Magick' that makes contact with demons), he was angrily attacked by Thomas Hall as having the 'Familisticall-Levelling-Magical temper' and for advocating a way—and a quick one at that—of bringing 'men to the Devill or the Devill to them'.[77] A longer, more measured response was given by the Oxford astronomer, Seth Ward, who argued that while Agrippa and the rest of them were certainly despised at Oxford, this was not because of the name Magick, and even less because of any conjuring of demons they might do, but because of their 'cheat and imposture' in claiming the existence of occult celestial signatures and the like. It was all very well for Webster to ask for the training of 'true natural Magicians, that walk . . . in the center of natures hidden secrets'. But the only true natural magic, Ward explained, is the experimental discovery of the rules of applying agent and material causes to produce effects, thus following the path mapped out by Bacon and by Bacon only. That Webster could mention Bacon and that 'villainous man' Fludd in the same breath only went to show, the appalled Ward continued, that Webster has no idea of the differences between their two ways, the former founded upon experiment, the other upon the Cabala, and the 'windy impostures of Magick and Astrology'.[78] Although Webster has thus laid himself open to the accusation of witchcraft, Ward generously writes that Webster's ignorance makes it plain that he is no witch and that he is therefore free from persecution.

In 1650 the Royalist physician Walter Charleton had published three books within the alchemical-magical tradition, including a translation of a work on the weapon salve by Jean Baptiste van Helmont. As a good natural magician van Helmont had claimed that the phenomenon of curing a wound by applying ointment to the offending weapon rather than to the wound itself was, of course, a natural process and in no way diabolical but had then earned himself harassment from the Inquisition for the remainder of his life by suggesting that 'the miracles wrought by the relics of saints could be similarly explained'.[79] By 1654 Charleton was publicly dissociating himself from the 'hairbrain'd and contentious' van Helmont, insisting that it was impossible to believe in the efficacy of such a cure. In place of alchemical-magical doctrines, Charleton now advocated Cartesian philosophy or, even better, the corpuscular mechanical philosophy developed by Gassendi. The running of the blood of a murdered man at the approach of the murderer receives a mechanistic explanation. On the other hand, Charleton admits that gravity is a perplexing phenomenon 'which, though most obvious to the observation of sense, hath much of obscurity in its Nature', and he concedes that no explanation is satisfactory. There is, however, no occult influence of the moon on the waters of the earth, Descartes' mechanistic explanation of tides receiving Charleton's approval in this case. The *echeneis* fish has no powers at all and undersurface contrary currents are responsible for the sudden stopping of a ship when under full sail. Witchcraft is impossible. The mechanical philosophy is Charleton's new cosmology: apparent attraction is caused by 'Hooks, Lines or some such intermediate Instrument continued from the Attrahent to the Attracted', while every apparent repulsion is caused by 'some Pole, Lever, or other Organ intercedent, or somewhat exploded or discharged from the Impellent to the Impulsed'.[80]

What could have given rise to such a dramatic conversion? In 1652 Charleton published a book *The Darknes of Atheism Dispelled by the Light of Nature* which dwelt upon the twin threats of atheism and sectarian enthusiasm that had followed 'our Fatall Civill Warre'. Charleton lamented how atheists plotted to 'undermine the received belief of an omnipotent *eternal Being,* to murder *the immortality of the Soul* (the basis of all religion) and to deride the *Compensation of good and evil actions after death'.*

The mechanical philosophy was the answer to both atheism and sectarian enthusiasm, even if, as Charleton recognized, it was not the answer to many of the most important phenomena of nature, particularly the generation of living beings. Despite this recognition and despite many remaining vestiges of the concepts he had until recently held so dear, Paracelsus and his disciples were unmercifully ridiculed by Charleton for 'Hermetical Follies', especially all ideas connected with the microcosm-macrocosm analogy (which had been rejected as well by van Helmont): such 'absolute Chimaeras', Charleton mocks, are 'conceived in the luxuriant womb of a perturbed or deluded Imagination'; they are a 'fantastique Hobgoblin . . . hatched in the adled brains of mad men, Poets and idolatrous Pagans and so below our laughter, much more our serious confutation'.[81] That he had only very recently subscribed to such ideas was embarrassing but Charleton was pleased to have the opportunity to refute conclusively all those unsound and spurious ideas whose growth and authority he might unfortunately have aided. The opinion of an historian who has looked carefully at Charleton's reversal of thought is that it was brought about not by any one clinching argument or experiment but because Charleton 'wanted' to change his official position. Quite so! It seems very plausible that Charleton wanted and needed to change his position because of his growing perception that the ideas of natural magic had such embarrassing social connections. The mechanical philosophy seductively beckoned.[82]

The development of the ideas of Robert Boyle is also particularly revealing. Between 1645 and 1652 Boyle had expressed great interest in Hermeticism, particularly in Hermetic chemistry, and was in close touch with refugees from the Continent who had Hermetic-Rosicrucian backgrounds (such as the influential Samuel Hartlib). Again, like Charleton, Boyle was to renounce not the 'experimental philosophy' but the conceptual framework that Paracelsian Hermeticism provided and in its place deliberately chose the mechanical philosophy. Again we ask why. Was it merely the rejection by an older man of some 'romantic' ideas of youth?

Boyle's father, let us note, had been an 'impecunious adventurer' who after travelling to Ireland in 1588 quickly made himself a fortune by corruption, fraud and marriage, ending up a Privy Councillor, Earl of Cork, Lord High Treasurer of Ireland and one of the wealthiest men in England. On the death of his father, Robert Boyle inherited a manor in Dorset and lands in Ireland only to find himself financially hard-pressed after the rebellion in Ireland had relieved the Boyle family of most of its wealth. Thus

when Cromwell offered his brother Roger, of Royalist sympathies, a choice between imprisonment in the Tower of London
or service in Ireland against the rebels, both Roger and Robert
saw where their primary duty lay. Indeed, after the family had
regained its property from the rebels, Robert went three times to
Ireland to see to his share.[83] Boyle had now a sizeable stake in the
Republic and it is understandable that, as a devout man, he saw
the necessity of defending established Christianity against the
twin threat we have had occasion to refer to so much: on the one
hand, atheism and denial of divine punishment for rebellion, on
the other, sectarian enthusiasm and divine sanction for social
subversion. Once again it is the (corpuscular) mechanical
philosophy that is called upon to help deflect and refute these
threats.

As Boyle argued in his *Certain Physiological Essays* of 1661,
for the purposes of opposing Aristotelian and Paracelsian
doctrines the mechanical philosophies of Gassendi and Descartes
can be looked upon 'by a person of a reconciling disposition' as
but one philosophy.[84] For both deduce all the phenomena of
nature from matter and local motion and both, in opposition to
Epicurean atheistic philosophy, see God's providence behind the
laws of nature. The fact that brute matter, devoid of understanding, can be fashioned into so intricate and vast a machine as is
this cosmos displays in its greatest majesty the infinite wisdom of
God. In his 1674 essay on *The Excellency and Grounds of the
Corpuscular or Mechanical Philosophy* Boyle spells out the
principal conceptual advantage his preferred philosophy offers
over Aristotelian and Paracelsian-Hermetic competitors. It is the
'intelligibleness or clearness of mechanical principles and explanations'. Boyle finds the first principles of neither the Aristotelians nor Paracelsians intelligible and finds it hardly surprising
that from obscure principles ever more obscure explanations
should be deduced. 'But [as] to the corpuscular philosophy, men
do so easily understand one another's meaning'. Matter interacts
with other matter only on contact and all the phenomena of
nature result from 'the effects and consequences of local motion'.
A mechanical philosopher could never be satisfied with, for
example, the explanation of witchcraft or demonic intervention
as the cause of a disease; furthermore, even if there are heavenly
intelligences, they too must work their effects by matter and
motion alone. Boyle's conclusion is that 'if the proposed agent be
not intelligible and physical, it can never physically explain the
phenomena; so if it be intelligible and physical, it will be
reducible to matter and some or other of those only catholick
affections of matter'. The way to uncover exactly how matter and

its local motions generate the phenomena of nature is, of course, through painstaking Baconian experimentation, following therefore the method of 'one of the first and greatest experimental philosphers of our age, Sir Francis Bacon'. With the sectaries' claim of divine sanction for social change in mind, Boyle confesses in his *Usefulness of experimental natural philosphy*: 'I dare not affirm, with some of the Helmontians and Paracelsians, that God discloses to men the great Mystery of chymistry by good angels, or by nocturnal visions'.[85]

As an example of the intelligibility of mechanical principles —which he hopes are underwritten by the experimental philosophy—Boyle offers the following explanation as to why liquid rises in a tube when one end is immersed in the liquid and the other end is sucked. It is because of the pressure of the air on the liquid and not because of nature's abhorrence of a vacuum as Peripatetics claim. In addition, if the liquid can so 'intelligently' act in order to prevent a vacuum and has no immortal soul, does this not imply that human beings likewise have no immortal soul? Boyle therefore recognizes that the mechanical philosophy, by depriving matter of any semblance of self-activation helps safeguard the uniqueness of man and the immortality of his soul. Likewise, Boyle argues in *The Christian Virtuoso,* since no explanation of miracles is possible within the principles of the mechanical philosophy, mechanical philosophers will 'frankly acknowledge, and heartily believe, divers effects to be truly miraculous, that may be plausibly ascribed to other causes in the vulgar philosophy'. For Boyle regrets that in the vulgar conception of nature 'men are taught and wont to attribute stupendous unaccountable effects to sympathy, antipathy, *fuga vacui*, substantial forms, and especially to a certain being... which they call nature: for this is represented as a kind of goddess, whose power may be little less than boundless'. Thus once again the mechanical philosophers prove themselves friends to Christianity. Such friendship needs emphasis. For this is in stark contrast, Boyle had explained elsewhere, to 'those enemies to Christianity... that granting the truth of the historical part of the New Testament, (which relates to miracles) have gone about to give an account of it by coelestial influences, or natural... complexions, or such conceits, which have quite lost them, in my thoughts, the title of knowing naturalists'.[86]

Despite Boyle's opposition to such paracelsians, he had, as I stated earlier, been greatly influenced by natural magical ideas and, like Descartes, had accepted a great many occult phenomena as real. However, such phenomena could all be accounted for within the mechanical philosophy by postulating the existence of flows of invisibly small particles passing from body to body. In this way—as Lynn Thorndike has observed—Boyle could explain how the air in fields through which wounded wild animals have passed become poisoned for up to a year or two afterwards, how wearing the tooth of a hippopotamus or a ring made from the hoof of an elk serves to relieve cramp, and how haemorrhoids can be cured by wearing a ring made from an appropriate metal.[87] In the minds of its leading protagonists the mechanical philosophy had great explanatory powers.

It must not be forgotten that in addition to combatting Aristotelian naturalism and Hermetic Paracelsian alchemy, the mechanical philosophy served yet another social function, one that both Descartes and Boyle regarded as extremely valuable. For while the experimental philosophy promised future control and appropriation of the natural world, the mechanical philosophy served to *legitimize* such control and appropriation. Certainly it is true that this great machine of the world compels our admiration, but Boyle insists that it must be admiration for the Maker, not for the machine. There can be no admiration for a de-mothered nature of brute, inert matter, only for the wisdom of God the Father in the laws He imposed on this unknowing, unfeeling, above all inert, barren matter. Man can clearly make use of such matter as he pleases; such matter has no rights. Thus in his *Inquiry into the Vulgarly Received Notion of Nature,* Boyle took pains to emphasize that 'the veneration, wherewith men are imbued for what they call nature, has been a discouraging impediment to the empire of man over the inferior creatures of God' and that while men 'look upon her as such a venerable thing, some make a kind of scruple of conscience to endeavour so to emulate any of her works, as to excel them'.[88] Such inhibition is clearly not called for within the mechanical philosophy.

Boyle's concern to legitimate the appropriation of nature was obviously far from 'academic'. We have many times noted how such appropriation of nature had been feared in Christian countries as achievable only with demonic aid. But there were more than Christian countries to worry about; there were also recently colonized lands where non-Christian peoples, imbued with strange views of the world, were offering resistance to the civilizing and exploitative mission of white settlers. Boyle was able to help in an official capacity. As Governor of the New England Company, the Christian mechanical philosopher hoped to eliminate from the minds of the Indians of New England 'their ridiculous Notions about the workings of Nature' and, as he wrote, the 'fond and superstitious practices those Errors ingag'd them to'.[89] Overall, progress was to be far less rapid than Boyle had hoped. Some 200 years after Boyle had proclaimed the truth and virtues of the mechanical philosophy, at a time when the official policy of the United States government was to force all Indians to become farmers, Smohalla, leader of the Columbia Basin Indian tribes, advocated resistance to government policy on the following grounds:

You ask me to plough the ground; shall I take a knife and tear my mother's bosom? Then when I die she will not take me to her bosom to rest. You ask me to dig for stones; shall I dig under her skin for her bones? Then when I die I cannot enter her body to be born again. You ask me to cut grass and make hay and sell it and be rich like white men; but how dare I cut off my mother's hair?

Smohalla's religion led in 1877 in Idaho to the revolt by Nez Percé Indians, crushed by United States troops with the killing of Indians of both sexes, adults and children.[90]

The 'confirmation' of (male) ruling-class superiority
The advantages of the mechanical philosophy rested on the distinction its proponents drew between matter and mind: between matter possessing no value at all and the reasoning mind of man, indivisible, immaterial and immortal, and the locus of all that is valuable. Religion is thereby underwritten, atheism and natural magic undermined and enthusiasm discredited. In addition, man's superiority over and legitimate appropriation of the material world (including the animal world) are inherent features of Cartesian cosmology.

Of course, the term 'man' in the last sentence stands for the ruling-class males of the emerging capitalist societies of western Europe whose rule over other men and all women itself needed legitimation: clearly, not all men could therefore be granted the possession of *acute* minds and certainly very few women. Indeed, according to the experimental and mechanical philosopher Henry Power, the multitude of men should rather be likened to Descartes' automata since they have almost zero reasoning power and it is (he claimed in 1664) only by the favour of a metaphor that they are called men. It was his opinion that understanding the divine management of 'this great Machine of the World'—a world which now includes the overwhelming majority of men and women—'must needs be the proper Office of onely the Experimental and Mechanical Philosopher'.[91] As for women, the Catholic priest and mechanical philosopher Nicolas Malebranche stressed in his *Recherche de la Vérité* that they were intellectually inferior to men since the female 'cerebral fibre' is 'soft' and 'delicate', altogether lacking the hardness, solidity, strength and consistency of male cerebral fibre. This being so not only are abstract matters quite incomprehensible to women, but in general they are able to consider only the surface aspects of problems, their imagination totally lacking the 'vigor and reach necessary to penetrate to the core of things'.[92] Thus, just as it is intellectual capacity that legitimates the ruling male's privileged economic and social position vis-à-vis other men, so it is superior intellectual capacity—capacity to 'penetrate'—that legitimates men's rule over women (Aristotle for once standing in no need of revision). When in 1708, a reader inquired of *The British Apollo* whether women might be able to receive the same education as men, he was accordingly told that 'they are cast in too soft a mould, one made of too fine, too delicate a composure to endure the severity of study, the drudgery of contemplation, the fatigue of profound speculation'. In France, two historians concur that by the end of the seventeenth century women with philosophical ambition had so withered under heavy male sarcasm that they no longer regarded intellectual curiosity as a means of liberation or of successful entry into a male world but as providing only personal satisfaction carefully concealed beneath a genuine modesty. 'The myth of the inequality of the two sexes' was, it would appear, the one which even 'the most enlightened minds [found] the most difficult to denounce'.[92]

Now this was all very well but perhaps a nagging worry yet remained for the mechanical philosopher. For could he take a demonstration of 'superior' mental capacity over 'inferior' males and all women to be a sufficient demonstration of his masculinity? Would not the mechanical philosopher—as a non-fighting male—have felt a need for a more visible display of *virility* in the face of potentially sexually demanding women and the possibly superior body of the 'mentally inferior' male? (Even the 'progressive' Pierre Bayle, normally so anxious to combat 'myth' and 'superstition', had argued in 1683 that 'if women could satisfy their desires without risking their reputations, they would take debauchery much further than men do'. Moreover, perhaps it is not inappropriate to recall how great had been the public humiliation of the Marquis de Langey and the Comte de la Suze who, when accused of impotency by their wives, had failed in 'that most dreadful of legal dramas' to 'penetrate' their accusers to the satisfaction of expert judges.[93]) If, then, the thinking, reasoning mechanical philosopher did share in what appears to be a rather universal male need to display virility—and if at the same time his rejection of the body entailed a rejection of sexuality (or vice versa)—then nevertheless a means to display masculinity was available to him that had not been previously available to men devoted to a life of the mind. His masculinity and virility could be demonstrated to 'inferior' males—and to all women —by application of the mechanical philosophy in the achievement of an always developing technological appropriation of a demothered and passive natural world. It is surely not a coincidence that Descartes—sexual ascetic and articulator of mind-matter dualism—stressed that the mechanical philosophy would enable man to become 'masters and possessors of nature'.

The validity of the mechanical philosophy

There comes a point perhaps when we ought seriously to question whether certain propositions are true. Earlier in this chapter we did raise the tactless question as to the overall truth of the mechanical philosophy but since at the time we were in the middle of the English Civil War this question was postponed. Now that we are in Restoration England—albeit with a Court sympathetic to (respectable) Helmontian physicians—we might —indeed we must—look at perhaps the most difficult aspect of Cartesian cosmology to swallow, which is the insistence by Descartes (although sometimes a wavering insistence) that animals are no different in principle from the various kinds of mechanical machines constructed by men.

Descartes, we recall, had accepted the reality of the phenomenon of spontaneous generation of simple (mechanical) organisms from putrefying matter. However, if these simple organisms feel or think or do both, no matter to how small a degree, then the mechanical philosophy is sunk without trace. For either matter itself must be assumed to some extent sentient and conscious or the matter must be assumed colonized by a 'vital force'. Both alternatives are in total conflict with the principles of the mechanical philosophy. Furthermore, the first materialist alternative has atheistic implications; the second undermines the promise of total (male) ruling-class control of the material world. For how is the 'vital force' to be commanded? A similar argument applies in the case of the development of the animal foetus. If the development proceeds by 'epigenesis' from a homogeneous egg (consisting of nothing but matter), and the fully developed foetus is to some extent sentient and conscious, then either the original matter of the egg must have been (to some extent) sentient and conscious or a 'vital force' was responsible for the development. Again, either way, the mechanical philosophy is in desperate trouble.

Even if we can assume that non-human 'living' beings are mere automata, the mechanical philosophers still need to give a convincing account of the development of such beings via either spontaneous generation or epigenesis. Failure to do so means once again either that matter has more interesting properties than the sole one of extension ascribed to it by Descartes or that 'vital forces' and 'formative virtues' are everywhere creatively present. *In the mechanical philosophy the very existence of living beings posed what appeared to be an insuperable challenge to the ingenuity of its exponents. To say the very least, life became a conceptual embarrassment.* I conclude this chapter by tracing the development of mechanical philosophy to its highest point: a resolution of the difficulties just described and a sure demonstration of God's existence.

4 *Occult Forces, Living Beings and the Problem of Generation*

The problem of life

The dilemma facing the mechanical philosophers is clear: if the claim that animals are mere automata cannot be successfully defended, then the uniqueness of man over animals has to be argued in a way that does not depend on the mind-matter dichotomy. In addition, if the mechanical philosophy cannot account for spontaneous generation and epigenesis, then the reality of both phenomena must be denied. Let us look at what happened.

Even at the time of Henry More's greatest commitment to Descartes' philosophy, there is a central feature of this philosophy that More cannot stomach, as he eloquently explains to Descartes in a letter on 11 December, 1648:

For the rest, my spirit, through sensitivity and tenderness, turns not with abhorrence from any of your opinions so much as from that deadly and murderous sentiment which you professed in your *Method,* whereby you snatch away, or rather withhold, life and sense from all animals, for you would never concede that they really live. Here, the gleaming rapier-edge of your genius arouses in me not so much mistrust as dread when, solicitous as to the fate of living creatures, I recognize in you not only subtle keenness, but also, as it were, the sharp and cruel blade which in one blow, so to speak, dared to despoil of life and sense practically the whole race of animals, metamorphosing them into marble statues and machines.[94]

More understands why Descartes has been forced to take such a drastic step; that wherever there is mind there is an immortal soul and since Descartes wishes to deny the possession by animals of immortal souls the only way he can achieve this in his philosophy is by turning them into machines. But More insists that common sense tells us that animals are alive, that dogs plead to go for a walk, that birds sing in part because they enjoy it, that foxes develop sly tricks, the examples are endless. The conclusion More draws is that animals have immortal souls but they are of an inferior kind to human souls.

Descartes will have none of this nonsense. There is no prejudice greater than the one we imbibe from childhood that animals think. The shrewdness and cunning of dogs and foxes, any other deed animals perform for food, sex or fear, all such behaviour, Descartes writes to More, he can explain 'as arising from the sole configuration of the parts of the body'. It is, he writes ironically, somewhat preferable to believe that worms, gnats and caterpillars move about after the fashion of machines than endow them with immortal souls. More is being sentimental. 'And thus', concludes Descartes, 'my opinion is not so much cruel to wild beasts as favourable to men, whom it absolves . . . of any suspicion of crime, however often they may eat or kill animals'.[95]

And so the Cartesians believed. Following Descartes' death his principal follower (and innovator) Nicolas Malebranche maintained that animals 'eat without pleasure, they cry without pain, they grow without knowing it; they desire nothing, they fear nothing, they know nothing'.[96] Accused of cruelty in their many vivisection experiments, Cartesians replied that their calumniators had not yet shaken off childhood prejudice and centuries of superstition.

In England Henry More remained unconvinced. Also at Cambridge, the man who was to teach mathematics to Isaac Newton, reflecting on his own interest in botany and dissection, wondered if there had ever been a time when such 'a murderous curiosity' had wrought more 'death and dismemberment against so many dogs, fishes, and birds'. 'A most innocent cruelty! An easily excusable ferocity!' was the self-justificatory if uneasy verdict of Isaac Barrow. His fellow student, the future naturalist John Ray, was later to express an unambiguous verdict concerning his own opposition both to Descartes' philosophy and to the practice of vivisection. In Ray's opinion, if animals were automata, then how was it possible to explain their undoubted suffering and the disgust any decent person feels at cruelty to them. 'If it is argued that this is a mere prejudice unworthy of a philosopher', Ray addressed the Cartesians, 'then I shall stand by that prejudice: put it down to my stupidity or the weakness of your arguments as you like: the torture of animals is no part of philosophy'. The Cartesians were forced to ascribe Ray's opinions to his stupidity.[97]

It was in the face of such strongly expressed scepticism and open disbelief that Cartesian philosophers continued to argue that animals were nothing but automata, that theirs was a true belief and entirely defensible. Could, however, the Cartesians make good their grandiose claim to be able to account for *all* animal behaviour in terms of only the size, shape and velocity of constituent particles (as More challenged Descartes in his reply)? Could they even hope to explain the phenomena of spontaneous generation and epigenesis within the mechanical philosophy? Descartes in several letters claimed to have accomplished this latter task and in 1664 his work *On the Formation of the Foetus* was posthumously published.

One can sympathize with Descartes in his necessary task. He undoubtedly convinced himself of the plausibility of his description—and it was at least an (anti-Aristotelian) account that gave equal status to both male and female contributions in conception. But Descartes did not convince his successors. Aghast they read his account that the matter of the male and female seminal fluids might be so mixed and separated that an organism, indeed a perfectly formed human body, easily results. 'We see how wretchedly Des Cartes came off', exclaimed the Scottish divine George Garden in his paper of 1691 on the 'modern theory' of generation.[98] Henry More, turning increasingly against Cartesian philosophy, maintained that no amount of twisting and turning would enable mechanical philosophers to explain how a highly differentiated living being is made from mere matter in motion. According to More a 'vital force' must be present; his neoplatonic colleague Ralph Cudworth and sympathizer Joseph Glanvill agreed. Eventually convinced that matter and motion are not in themselves sufficient to account for spontaneous generation and epigenesis, the mechanical philosophers took the only possible way out—they denied the reality of such embarrassing phenomena!

The denial of spontaneous generation:
the barrenness of matter
Until the second half of the seventeenth century, it was common knowledge that spontaneous generation either occurs in putrefying matter or leaves such matter as a residue. Aristotle had believed the latter, Paracelsus, Gilbert, Fludd, van Helmont and Descartes the former, to name but a few. However, in 1668 in a series of classic experiments the Italian natural philosopher Francesco Redi showed that in all cases investigated dead organic matter does not spontaneously produce maggots but that, on the contrary, maggots result from the eggs of flies. Covered and uncovered jars of meat were left for several days: the covered meat contained no maggots, the uncovered meat not protected from flies was eventually full of maggots. In response to criticism that he had excluded life-supporting air from the covered meat, Redi covered jars of meat with a gauze, finding that the eggs laid by flies on the gauze later hatched into maggots but that no

maggots appeared in the meat. Redi's conclusion was that *dead* organic matter produces no living organism, unlike the case with living organic matter, both vegetable and animal: '[I]f the thing is alive', he affirmed, 'it may produce a worm or so, as in the case of cherries, pears and plums'. 'In this manner', he continued, 'I am inclined to believe, tapeworms and other worms arise, which are found in the intestines and other parts of the human body'.[99] 'Living organic' matter produces worms; 'dead organic' matter cannot produce worms but only infusorians (microscopically small living organisms).

Greatly aided by Redi's experiments, mechanical philosophers needed to postulate the impossibility of such spontanous generation. The generation of infusorians could be denied without too great a fear of experimental disproof. Thus, throwing caution to the winds, the Dutch naturalist Jan Swammerdam declared that 'nothing is produced by putrefaction' and that the opposite opinion is contrary to experiment, observation and 'sound reason', and, moreover, 'savours rankly of atheism'. But how to explain the presence of worms in the intestines and especially in the organs of the body with no obvious entrances and exits? 'It is certainly very difficult to explain what manner Worms are bred in living animals', Swammerdam reluctantly admitted.[100] While it was clearly necessary to claim that eggs entered the host organism either from the air or from food and water or from the parent organism through copulation or lactation, it was a very difficult matter to substantiate such a claim. Undoubtedly, therefore, the presence of parasitic worms proved a serious stumbling block in the research programme of the mechanical philosophers to demonstrate that suspected spontaneous generation is always generation from eggs. The phenomenon of internal parasites remained a problem even after the successful development of the other half of the research programme: the 'demonstration' that epigenesis does not occur.

The denial of epigenesis: preformation
and emboîtement
After a careful examination of the chrysalis of a butterfly, Swammerdam reported the discovery of a perfectly formed butterfly waiting, as it were, to be hatched. With the use of a microscope Marcelo Malphigi was able to observe the existence of a chick's heart on only the second day after the egg's appearance, whereas William Harvey without a microscope had observed the heart's existence on only the fourth day. Even more dramatically, Malphigi emphasized that while 'we are studying attentively the genesis of animals from the egg, lo! in the egg

itself we behold the animal already almost formed', and he cautiously declared it 'proper to acknowledge that the first filaments of the chick pre-exist in the egg and have a deeper origin. . . .'.[101] The mechanical philosophers had experimental pointers to what they desired to establish. In 1667 Swammerdam made the first public statement of the theory of preformation: within the caterpillar there exists the preformed 'nymph', and within the nymph the butterfly already exists, also preformed. Thus there is no true metamorphosis. Eggs are not transformed into chicks, declared Swammerdam, 'but grow to be such by the expansion of parts already formed'. Similarly, a tadpole is not changed into a frog but becomes a frog by an 'unfolding and increasing of some of its parts'.[102] The mechanical philosophy can cope with the growth or disappearance of parts existing in a preformed state; what it cannot cope with is the (ordered and interconnected) appearance of parts where none had existed before. In asserting that within each egg there existed a miniature organism needing in order to become the adult organism only the quantitative growth of preformed parts (and possibly the disappearance of other parts), the theory of preformation had transformed defeat of the mechanical philosophy into glorious victory.

Had, however, the fundamental difficulty facing the mechanical philosophy only been pushed back a stage? How, after all, does the preformed organism get into the female ovum? Put another way, as the preformed female animal slowly develops into an adult animal and produces her own eggs, how can the generation of such remarkable eggs, each containing a preformed animal in miniature, be accounted for? If one remembers that a principal aim, if not the principal aim, of the mechanical philosophers was to save God's creativity from the threat of natural magic, the solution again is obvious: it is that at the time of the Creation, God created all life that would ever exist, the first female of each kind containing within her eggs perfectly preformed beings, which in turn if female contained within their eggs more perfectly preformed beings, and so either *ad infinitum* or to the number of generations that God had decided on. *Ad infinitum*? Since according to Descartes matter is in principle infinitely divisible, there can be no theoretical objection on this ground to such a possibly infinite series of 'Russian dolls' or 'Chinese boxes'. The theory of preformationist *emboîtement* steadily gained adherents. In 1673 Nicolas Malebranche declared his belief that as soon as philosophers possessed the necessary experimental skill they would be able to uncover animals within their 'germs'. However, he went on, since 'the vision of the mind has a far greater reach

than that of the body', the mind should not stop at the limits of
the eye's vision (an echo of Galileo's famous assertion that
Copernicus had made reason triumph over sense experience).
This awareness led Malebranche to suggest that 'all the bodies of
men and animals, which will be born until the end of time, were
perhaps made at the world's creation; I mean to say', he clarified,
'that the females of the first animals were perhaps created
together with all those of the same kind which have been
begotten, or will be begotten, during the continuation of time'.[103]
George Garden agreed: it seemed 'most probable' to him that the
'*stamina* of all the Plants and Animals that have been or ever shall
be in the World, have been formed *ab Origine Mundi* by the
Almighty Creator within the first of each respective kind'.[104]
Some seventy years later and with the benefit of considerable
hindsight, the French natural philosopher Charles Bonnet claimed
the theory of *emboîtement* to be 'one of the most beautiful
victories of pure reason over the senses'. The existence of organic
beings decisively proved the existence and creative power of God
the Creator Father. As Bonnet remarked: 'A sound philosopher
has eyes that discover in every organized body the ineffaceable
imprint of a work done at a single stroke, and which is the
expression of that Adorable Will that said "Let organic bodies
be" and they were'.[105]

Ovism or animalculism?
But which theory of *emboîtement*? In 1677 the Dutch microscop-
ist Antony Leeuwenhoek published his discovery that in the
semen of male animals, including men, there existed an extremely large number of incredibly tiny worm-like creatures very
similar to tadpoles. Now an important drawback to the 'ovist'
theory of *emboîtement* had been the transferring of all fecundity
to the female. Even if it was true that the male semen initiated
some kind of triggering action, nevertheless each woman contained within her womb a (possibly infinite) series of future
human beings. Leeuwenhoek was therefore not slow to restore
the male claim to supremacy in reproduction, 'that it is
exclusively the male semen that forms the foetus, and that all that
the woman may contribute only serves to receive the semen and
feed it'. Among the natural philosophers who supported
Leeuwenhoek might be mentioned his Dutch colleague Niklaas
Hartsoeker (who sketched a picture of how a small human being
might appear folded up inside an animalcule), the Frenchman
Nicolas Andry, the Scottish divine George Garden, the London
physician George Cheyne, the German philosopher Wilhelm
Leibniz and his disciple G.F. Meier. The latter put the

animalculist version of *emboîtement* very succinctly: 'Adam carried all men in his seed including the spermatozoon from which Abraham issued. And when Abraham engendered Isaac, Isaac came forth from the belly of his father carrying within him the whole of his posterity'.[106] Happily, as one can see, it is no longer necessary to refer to any women.

However aesthetically annoying it was to animalculists to contemplate that men begin life enclosed in tadpole-like creatures, there was in addition a major difficulty facing the animalculist version of *emboîtement* from which the ovist version was free. If it was true that each animalcule of a man contained a microscopic human being, which, if male, contained hundreds of millions of further animalcules, containing in turn hundreds of millions of further animalcules and so on, then since *at most* only a few animalcules could grow into foetuses within the womb, the wastage of animalcules (and therefore of potential human beings) was scarcely fathomable. Not all mechanical philosophers could therefore accept animalculism as correct and, however battered perhaps their male egos, remained ovists. Among the more prominent were Swammerdam, Malebranche, Malphigi and his pupil Antonio Vallisneri.

The question then arose for the ovists as to why animalcules existed in the semen at all. Were they parasites? It was established that boys of 13 or so at first had no animalcules in their semen and old men either none or few. It was therefore conjectured that semen that possesses a fertilizing potential is a suitable host medium for the existence of such parasites. The English physician Martin Lister thought that the function of the animalcules was to excite males to coition, while Vallisneri expressed the opinion that animalcules prevented fertile semen from clotting. Whatever the function of the animalcules, their presence in the semen served to remind mechanical philosophers that the existence of worms in the organs of the body was a source of deep embarrassment for their philosophy.

Both Hartsoeker and Vallisneri, unhappy with the theory that worms somehow or other entered the host body from the outside, proposed a double *emboîtement* theory according to which God created worms in the bodies of Adam and Eve who then passed their worms on to their descendants. This, of course, created theological problems since it was not clear why either Adam or Eve in a state of grace would have needed worms in their intestines. To the proposal that before the Fall the worms did their hosts a kindness in consuming unwanted food but that after the Fall they turned rebellious and vicious, the objection was made that Adam and Eve in a state of grace would not have needed the assistance of worms for digestion. As one specialist in the matter has commented, while proponents of the theory that worms entered externally in eggs predominated over proponents of double *emboîtement*, all mechanical philosophers remained uneasily aware that parasites presented for their philosophy a somewhat indigestible problem.[107] Accurately enough, the 1710 edition of John Harris's *Dictionary of Arts and Sciences* stated in a summary on spontaneous (equivocal) generation that although the hypothesis of the external origin of parasitic worms was generally favoured, nevertheless 'scarce any thing seems more to countenance Equivocal Generation, than the Production of Worms...in the Bodies of Animals'.

The mechanical philosophy in retrospect
It is difficult to overestimate the importance of the mechanical philosophy or the audacity and ingenuity of its proponents. To maintain, as Descartes did, that the entire universe is crystal clear to reason and, apart from God and the human mind, is completely explicable in terms of size, shape and velocity of divisible particles of matter is to make a proposal of such breath-taking audacity and implausibility that it cries out for explanation. A (non-human) world stripped of all immanent creativity and purpose, all sentience and consciousness, all sympathies and antipathies, all heat and cold, all beauty and ugliness, all colour, taste and odour: a world of mere matter in motion and the most uninteresting matter imaginable at that —this was the totally mechanical, unmysterious, lifeless, barren world that mechanical philosophers persuaded so many of their educated contemporaries to accept that they were living in. It was a revolution in male thought of the most momentous significance.

In their struggle with natural magicians mechanical philosphers possessed several advantages. They could offer clarity of thought and, in principle, a visualizable mechanism underlying each phenomenon. The mind-matter dualism inherent in the mechanical philosophy helped underwrite the Christian conception of the human soul. The miracles performed by Christ could in no way be accounted for in terms of the mechanical philosophy. Experimentation in the mechanical philosophy made no use of ceremonies, signs or incantations and was therefore in no way demonic. Demonic magic itself seemed of little importance since demons (if they existed at all, which was extremely doubtful) had at their disposal only matter and motion. Witch hunting was unnecessary. Finally a mechanical world existed to be appropriated, not contemplated or sensuously appreciated, and moreover appropriated by mechanical means: there is really nothing else that one can do with it. If demons do not exist, verbal appropriation is impossible; if matter is devoid of sentience and consciousness—which it is—mental appropriation utilizing the *vis imaginativa* is useless; the message of the mechanical philosophy is that nature can be commanded only through either the juxtaposition or separation of matter.

While the mechanical philosophy was not entirely free from religious problems, natural magic was saturated with them. But not only did natural magic have atheistic connotations, it had socially subversive ones as well, a dual threat to the privileged that gave the mechanical philosophy its eventual cutting edge over those traditions and practices too closely associated with the beliefs of 'the people'.

There were, however, two major difficulties confronting the mechanical philosophy. First, mechanical philosophers came to grief in their attempted explanations of the most common daily phenomena. Second, it was not clear—even if the mechanical philosophy turned out to be true—how it would enable Descartes' disciples to become 'masters and possessors of nature'. Leibniz's ruminations in the draft of a letter to Malebranche, dated 1679, are particularly revealing:

The value and even the mark of a true science consists in my opinion [he writes] in the useful inventions which can be derived from it. But I have not yet seen that any Cartesian has found anything useful by means of the philosophy of his master . . . It seems that the harvest of Descartes' philosophy is finished, or else that the promise of it was destroyed while it was still growing by the death of its author. For the majority of Cartesians are but commentators . . . What is more, even if all Descartes' physics were granted, this would not take us very far. For, after all, the first and second elements are difficult things to handle . . .[108]

This, then, was a problem: even if Cartesian philosophy were true how would it help philosophers and emerging manufacturers achieve control over the matter of the world? But, as we have seen, it was not true. At the very least, it could not account for the creation of life at conception and the subsequent (epigenetic) growth of the foetus. Accordingly, all hope of the manipulation of foetuses was abandoned and development of the theory of preformationist *emboîtement* saw all creative power transferred to God the Father at the time of the Creation. Power over nature was not to come via the mechanical philosophy—it was to come through the Baconian experimental tradition when that tradition reached maturity towards the end of the eighteenth century.

Before I leave the mechanical philosophy, there is an aspect of its preformationist *emboîtement* version which needs emphasis. From Aristotle to Aquinas women had been looked upon not only as inferior in intellect to men but had been ascribed the passive role in reproduction, mere suppliers of matter for the foetus's physical growth; in direct contrast, Aquinas had proclaimed, the human father and God the Father enjoyed the creative privileges of supplying the foetus with its animal and rational soul respectively. In the theory of *emboîtement* woman's creative role in procreation was reduced to zero, and woman became in theory only a glorified container and, as it were, mobile canteen for the succession of foetuses. It was apparently God the Father's plan to leave the male sex free from gestational cares so that thereby men could better appropriate the world, a masculine task that the mechanical philosophy legitimated and underwrote so convincingly: the mechanical philosophy informed the rising male bourgeois that he was not tied in any way to the earth, that it was even a mistake to believe that Western ruling-class males had at last achieved independence from 'mother earth' in the same way as a boy achieves independence from his mother; for according to the *emboîtement* mechanical philosophy the earth had never been the 'mother' of mankind but 'merely' the mechanical product and artifact of God the Creator *Father*. As Robert Boyle explained, God had created the world 'as He pleased and thought fit, at the beginning of things, when there was no substance but Himself, and consequently no creature, to which He could be obliged or by which He could be limited'.[109] The *emboîtement* mechanical philosophy described therefore an almost totally masculine world: God the Creator Father had created a mechanical universe and all life with no feminine help whatsoever; man had been made by God in His likeness and commanded to appropriate the mechanical world, not merely, it would seem, for the purpose of liberating all humans from whatever tyrannies of nature existed after the Fall; while woman's sole non-creative role—if essential one—was to contain and nourish life (the animalculist version of *emboîtement* denying her even the former role). The *emboîtement* mechanical philosophy was clearly a sternly masculine one. It may not have been, after all, a statement of no moment when in 1664 Henry Oldenburg, the Royal Society's Secretary, asserted that its business was to raise 'a Masculine Philosophy'.[110]

In summary we see that the theory of *emboîtement* was a logical necessity if the mechanical philosophy was to be saved. Given its proponents' evident inability to account for the phenomena of spontaneous generation and epigenesis, the only course of action open to mechanical philosophers was either to abandon the philosophy or deny the phenomena. The theory of *emboîtement* was, therefore, the ingenious though flawed culmination of a philosophy developed half a century earlier whose proponents sought to combat atheism, 'enthusiasm' and social subversion and to praise, legitimate and make possible male ruling-class appropriation of the matter of the world.

Recognition of the difficulties that continually confronted the mechanical philosophy makes its success equally impressive and problematic. Not even Descartes could satisfactorily account for the perpendicular fall of a stone to the ground (as Charleton ruefully acknowledged). In the domain of embryology the difficulties it could not resolve ought, one feels, to have undermined the theory of *emboîtement*, ovist or animalculist, from the outset. For how could either theory explain that 'monsters' were occasionally born (for example, a child with a single body but two heads), or that the product of a cross between two close species resulted in a hybrid having characteristics in between those of both species, or that children sometimes resembled their mother, father, grandparents or even next-door neighbour. These well-known biological phenomena were a source of deep embarrassment to theorists of *emboîtement* but, fundamental as these phenomena were, preformationists remained committed to their mechanical philosophy. In 1712 the French natural philosopher R.A.F. de Réaumur was unkind enough to publish an account of the phenomenon well-known to fishermen that if the leg of a crayfish is cut off, the crayfish grows another. This phenomenon of 'regeneration'—so obviously linked to that of generation —was discussed at length by natural philosophers and set on one side. There was, after all, no 'rational' alternative to the theory of *emboîtement*. But the phenomenon was sufficient to cause the defection of one formerly prominent proponent of *emboîtement*, Niklaas Hartsoeker, who promptly rejected what he now realized was 'such an absurd and bizarre idea', which, he claimed, he had expounded in his youth only because he had fallen under the influence of 'Cartesian ideas'. The phenomenon of the crayfish's regenerative powers showed that it was necessary to hypothesize the existence of 'an Intelligence, whatever its nature might be, which resides in the animal and replaces its missing leg', in fact the very same Intelligence which had originally made the entire animal 'within the body of the Male which begot it'.[111]

The foundations of the mechanical philosophy were threatened with collapse. In the next chapter I attempt to show how in a small corner off the mainland of Europe a foundation stone of the mechanical philosophy had already been undermined in quite another direction and entirely replaced. But I must begin this discussion with an account of the political and religious context in which this remarkable development occurred.

Chapter **4**

GRAVITATIONAL ATTRACTION

> But all the different schemes of nature that have been drawn of old, or of late, by Plato, Aristotle, Epicurus, Des Cartes, Hobbes, or any other that I know of, seems to agree but in one thing, which is, the want of demonstration or satisfaction, to any thinking or unpossessed man; and seem more or less probable one than another, according to the wit and eloquence of the authors and advocates that raise or defend them...; whereas perhaps, if we were capable of knowing truth and nature, these fine schemes would prove like rover shots, some nearer and some further off, but all at great distance from the mark; it may be, none in sight.
>
> Sir William Temple, 'Upon the Gardens of Epicurus;
> Or, of Gardening, in the Year 1685'.

> These are Things which have no Dependence upon the Opinions of Men for their Truth; they will admit of fixed and undisputed *Mediums* of Comparison and Judgment: So that, though it may be always debated, who have been the best Orators, or who the best Poets; yet it cannot be a Matter of Controversie, who have been the greatest *Geometers, Arithmeticians, Astronomers, Musicians, Anatomists, Chymists, Botanists,* or the like . . .
>
> William Wotton, F.R.S., *Reflections upon Ancient and Modern
> Learning,* 1690

1 *From Mechanistic Theism to Materialistic Atheism*

In 1651, two years after the execution of Charles I, a momentous book was published entitled *Leviathan or The Matter, Forme, and Power of a Common-Wealth Ecclesiasticall and Civill.* Thomas Hobbes, a friend of Francis Bacon, later of Mersenne and Gassendi, a man whom Galileo had received warmly in Florence, pleased no one with this book and knew that he would please no one. In the eyes of Christians it represented the dangers now recognized to be implicit in the 'mechanistic theism' of Descartes, namely that it could all too easily be transformed into a materialistic atheism. For in abandoning the mind-matter dualism of Descartes, Hobbes had postulated that everything that exists in the universe—spirits as well, even God—is corporeal; conversely, that anything which is not corporeal has no existence whatever. It is beside the point that Hobbes declared angels to be made of an extremely fine substance; it is a material substance all the same for that. And the thrust of Hobbes' argument implied that both natural philosophy and the stability of society would be better off without the existence of angels and God.

For Hobbes' principal aim was to legitimate sovereign power on purely naturalistic grounds, making no appeal to divine law. In

154

this way he intended to undermine the arguments of both atheists and sectaries that sovereign power could safely be challenged, in the former case because no divine retribution was to be feared, in the latter case because divine permission supposedly santioned rebellion. Reason alone, argued Hobbes, made it plain that any challenge to sovereign power, be it to Royal power or parliamentary power, was an act that could in no way achieve a more secure life for the nation's citizens.

Hobbes' argument was predicated on the denial of the Aristotelian claim that contemplation is the greatest good, that the felicity of life consists 'in the repose of a mind satisfied'. There is no such *finis ultimus* (utmost aim), he tells readers, nor *summum bonum* (greatest good). Instead there is a continual progress of desire, from one object to another, competition being inevitable since men in general desire the same object. Noting that competition is won by the more powerful against the less powerful, Hobbes arrives at his fundamental explanatory principle: 'So that in the first place, I put for a general inclination of all mankind, a perpetual and restless striving of power after power, that ceaseth only in death'.[1] From this basic principle Hobbes deduces conclusions which have, he believes, the same certainty as theorems in Euclidean geometry. For if men were simply to follow their natural impulses, then death would very quickly be the outcome for nearly every man, life in the state of nature being, Hobbes decides, 'solitary, poore, nasty, brutish and short'.[2] This being so, there is only one course of action that guarantees for all men inhabiting a particular region of the earth the possibility of living a life that is not so extremely undesirable and short as life in the natural state: it is the course of action of renouncing their natural individual freedoms in favour of absolute obedience to a sovereign power, be it one person or an assembly. Obviously, unconditional obedience to a sovereign power brings hardships but they are small in comparison with the hardships of the state of nature, hardships of anarchy and of civil war—the unhappy experience of which obsessed not merely the person of Thomas Hobbes.

Religion, and in particular belief in the existence of God, undermine Hobbes' arguments as he himself clearly recognized. 'It is impossible a Common-wealth should stand', he believed, 'where any other than the Soveraign, hath a power of giving greater rewards than Life; and of inflicting greater punishments than Death'. But since God can reward with *eternal* life or punish with *eternal* damnation, according to the usual interpretation of the Bible, it is 'manifest enough' that if there be conflict between the commands of the Sovereign and of God, a man ought to obey

God's command and God's command only.[3] Hobbes laments that the most frequent pretext for sedition and civil war in Christian countries has been the supposed divergence between the commands of the lawful Sovereign and of the one and only God.

Sectaries in particular continually claim to receive personal illumination from God which happens in many cases to be in direct conflict with the commands of the Sovereign. Yet, argues Hobbes, no man should give his assent to a person who claims divine illumination, for there is no way of assessing the truth of the claim. It is not enough for a man to declare that God spoke to him in a dream since, according to Hobbes, this means no more than that the man dreamed God spoke to him—which is not at all the same thing; moreover, such dreams often result from self-conceit, foolish arrogance, and a man's false opinion of his own godliness which convinces him that he has merited the favour of extraordinary revelations. Hobbes' considered opinion is 'that though God Almighty can speak to a man, by Dreams, Visions, Voice, and Inspiration; yet he obliges no man to beleeve he hath so done to him that pretends it, who (being a man), and (which is more) may lie'. Although the occurrence of a miracle might command assent that a man is speaking the truth when he claims to have had personal contact with God, the age of miracles is past and thus there is no way but to reject all Prophecy and to rely on the Holy Scriptures; and from which, Hobbes asserts, 'by wise and learned interpretation, a carefull ratiocination, all rules and precepts necessary to the knowledge of our duty both to God and man, without Enthusiasme, or supernaturall Inspiration, may easily be deduced'.[4] God Hobbes cannot jettison but witches he can! Indeed, if belief in the active intervention of spirits, good or bad, could be totally eradicated, 'men would be much more fitted than they are for civill Obedience'.[5]

Having thus dismissed the claims of sectaries and eliminated the power, if not the reality, of the spirit world, Hobbes undertakes to show that conflict can never arise between the Sovereign's commands and the dictates of the Holy Bible when the Scriptures are interpreted wisely, learnedly and carefully. After pointing out (and making himself no friends at all in doing so) that Christians do not know but only believe the Scriptures to be the Word of God, Hobbes claims that the Christian can be confident of salvation provided he always has faith in Christ and obeys God's Laws. Now since God's Laws, Hobbes claims, are the Laws of Nature, 'where of the principall is... a commandment to obey our Civill Soveraigns, which were constituted over us, by mutuall pact one with another', there cannot be conflict between obedience to the Sovereign and obedience to God.[6] The

Sovereign interprets the Scriptures and the lawful citizen's duty is to obey, no matter what the latter's private interpretation. Even in the case of the Infidel Sovereign, absolute obedience to him is still necessary for a Christian. Although it is true that the Christian has made a promise to Christ to obey Him as King, this is to take effect only at Christ's Second Coming; in the meantime a Christian's duty is to obey the Infidel Sovereign. And no Sovereign, no matter how Infidel, would be so unreasonable, Hobbes declares, as to persecute such a Christian citizen whose loyalty to him is to end only at Christ's Second Coming.

Hobbes believes he has made an intellectual breakthrough of the greatest importance. Although for a long time, he explains, people built only unstable, impermanent homes unaware of the principles by which stable, permanent homes could be constructed, nevertheless these principles were eventually discovered. Similarly for a long time men have constituted imperfect Commonwealths which have always relapsed into disorder. Nevertheless, Hobbes contends, the 'Principles of Reason' by which everlasting Commonwealths can be constituted are discoverable by industrious meditation. And he adds modestly: 'And such are those which I have in this discourse set forth'.[7]

As to the supposed difficulty that though the principles might be correct the common people have insufficient 'capacity' to understand them, Hobbes replies that the difficulty lies elsewhere. Men of power and men of learning will be the ones who experience the most difficulty in accepting the principles explained in *Leviathan*. This is not because of the difficulty of the subject matter but 'from the interest of them that are to learn'.[8] For 'Potent men' find it almost impossible to digest anything that might curtail their power; while 'Learned men' can never admit to making errors and thereby undermine their own authority. However, the minds of the common people, Hobbes asserts, unless they are under the control of powerful men or have already been indoctrinated by learned men are like clean paper on which the public authority can write whatever it pleases. Moreover, since millions of men have been made to acquiesce in the great mysteries of the Christian religion which are 'above Reason' and even 'against Reason', then surely, Hobbes unkindly concludes, teachers and preachers, protected by the law, can instil into the minds of the masses principles that are so 'consonant to Reason' that any unprejudiced man has only to hear them to accept them.

There can be little cause for surprise that Hobbes found himself attacked from all sides. Kings could hardly be expected to be grateful for Hobbes' removal of their divine right, or bourgeois men of property for Hobbes' undermining of traditional Christian principles (and his insistence that the sovereign power be self-renewing instead of elected). Sectaries would hardly claim Hobbes to be one of their own. Vilified by just about all, it was even proposed in the House of Lords at the time of the Great Fire of London in 1666 that Hobbes be burnt as a heretic. What Hobbes had unforgivably done in a time of great social upheaval was to expose the possibility of, and seemingly embrace, atheistic developments out of a mechanistic theistic cosmology.

2 The Rejection of Descartes in England

Henry More's criticism

The attack on Hobbes that for our purposes is most relevant came from that admirer of Descartes introduced in Chapter 3. There we saw Henry More combatting the twin threat of sectarian enthusiasm on the one hand and materialistic atheism on the other. Before *Leviathan* More had seen Descartes as a valuable ally against both threats. After *Leviathan* More was to become increasingly disillusioned with Cartesian philosophy, seeing it at best as inadequate to counter the threat of materialism, at worst as a permanent source of inspiration for materialistic subversion. The promulgation of More's own cosmology was necessary.

In earlier works but particularly in his *Enthusiasmus Triumphatus* of 1656, More passionately affirms that reason remains the most adequate defence against the enthusiasms of sectaries. Their so-called philosophies will nearly always fail to meet the test of reason which consists solely of a settled, cautious, composed examination made in the light of, More problematically writes, 'the Common notions that all men in their wits agree upon, or the *Evidence of Outward Sense,* or else a *clear* and *distinct Deduction from these*'. In any case, reason is hardly necessary, More adds, to reject the 'Conceits and Fancies' of many of the 'Chymists': 'That they are but Counterfeits, that is, *Enthusiasts,* no infallible illuminated men, the gross fopperies they let drop in their writings will sufficiently demonstrate to all that are not smitten in some measure with the like Lunacy with themselves'.[9] Paracelsus in particular is singled out by More for severe criticism. Well-meaning Paracelsus might have been, but in ascribing great powers to the stars and the imagination, More argues that he unintentionally strengthened the arguments of atheists that so-called miracles have a natural explanation. The ravings of enthusiasts are without doubt a terrible menace to the Christian religion.

Although the sectaries—or many of them—are at least well intentioned for they do not intend to undermine Christianity, unfortunately the same cannot be said of the intentions of Thomas Hobbes, 'that confident Exploder of *Immaterial Substances* out of the world'.[10] After an opening sally in 1652 with his *Antidote against Atheism,* More published in 1659 his major work *The Immortality of the Soul,* the aim of which was at least to make plausible the idea that immaterial spirits are possible. Even this modest aim, More explains, was worthy of the very considerable effort he had put into the book. For the consequences of denying the possiblity of a spirit or an immaterial substance are horrendous indeed (it is instructive to quote More at length on these consequences):

> That it is impossible that there should be any God, or Soule, or Angel, Good or Bad; or any Immortality or Life to come. That there is no Religion, no Piety nor Impiety, no Vertue nor Vice, Justice nor Injustice, but what it pleases him that has the longest Sword to call so. That there is no Freedome of Will, nor consequently any Rational remorse of Conscience in any Being whatsoever, but that all that is, is nothing but *Matter* and *corporeal Motion*; and that therefore every trace of mans life is as *necessary* as the tracts of Lightning and the fallings of Thunder; the blind *impetus* of the *Matter* breaking through or being stopt everywhere, with as certain and determinate *necessity,* as the course of a Torrent after mighty stormes and showers of Rain.[11]

Against these horrendous consequences it is the duty of a Christian man to do battle by undermining the fundamental premise from which they flow—the denial of the possiblity of spirit or immaterial substance. More will attempt to do this by proving (1) the existence of an immaterial non-rational guiding principle or 'plastic nature' existing throughout the cosmos and (2) the reality of witchcraft and hence of, at least, evil spirits. But if there are evil spirits, it follows that there are spirits and the truth of the Bible is to this extent established.

I remarked earlier how if mechanical philosophers could have convincingly denied the phenomenon of falling bodies, it would have been in their best interests to do so. For no mechanical philosopher was able to suggest a plausible interpretation of this universal phenomenon, Hobbes' account leading him to the conclusion that even heavy bodies would fail to fall at the north and south poles which he wisely qualified by the comment 'whether it be true or false, experience must determine'. Not that the ever confident Hobbes was unconvinced by his own 'mechanical philosophy'. 'For as for those that say anything may be moved or produced by *itself*, he scoffed, 'by *its own power,* by *substantial forms,* by *incorporeal substances,* by *instinct* . . . by *antipathy, sympathy, occult quality,* and other empty words of schoolmen, their saying so is to no purpose'. And that is that.[12]

Hobbes apart, however, a philosophy that has great difficulty in accounting for such an apparently simple and certainly rather common phenomenon—and what is more a phenomenon central to its concerns—ought to be a philosophy always in the most serious trouble. That the Cartesian philosophy was not ousted in France until the 1730s is—or ought to be—a matter of great interest for sociologists of knowledge. But at least in Cambridge that very religious man, Henry More, now deeply troubled by the materialistic atheism he read into Hobbes' *Leviathan,* brought the problem of falling bodies encountered by the mechanical philosophy to the attention of all who would deign to read his book. For not only was Descartes' solution to the problem of falling bodies totally inadequate, More claimed, but experience demonstrated the similar total inadequacy of the solution proposed by Hobbes. Indeed, if Hobbes' solution was correct, then even in England heavy bodies ought not to descend perpendicularly to the earth, so that, More pointed out in excellent humour, 'Mr *Hobbs* need not send us so farre off as to the Poles to make the experiment.' Now a natural philosophy that cannot account for the motion of a falling stone is, More insisted, no philosophy at all. And if it cannot account for 'so simple' a phenomenon as this, how can we even begin to entertain the hope that it can account for the formation of plants and animals?[13] (More's colleague Ralph Cudworth firmly rejected the account offered by Descartes, noting among other things that Descartes offered no explanation as to why the seed of one kind of animal should not grow into an animal of a quite different kind.[14]) More was, however, careful to point out that although the Cartesian mechanical philosophy is so woefully inadequate in its explanation of basic phenomena, Descartes had nevertheless been totally correct in maintaining that mind is immaterial and can in no way be accounted for in terms of the properties of matter. Atheistic mechanical philosophers are quite wrong in believing that mind is in some way a consequence of a special 'organization' of matter and disappears when that organization disintegrates or decays. Mind can in no sense be a property of inert matter, More insists, any more than a living watch can be constructed out of totally inert parts. Where Descartes erred was in his assumption that mind—because it is immaterial—has no extension; it is this assumption which makes it difficult to believe that mind and spirits really exist in the world. But mind has extension just as space—which is also immaterial—has extension. Furthermore, Descartes is totally wrong in having believed and argued that inert matter is responsible for all natural phenomena. It is not and cannot be. Throughout the cosmos there exists an immaterial '*Spirit of Nature*', which More interestingly calls 'the great

Quarter-master General of divine Providence'.[15]

If matter is totally inert, then More believes he can convincingly argue that an immaterial 'spirit of nature' is everywhere present. He knows, however, that there are certain materialists —and he includes Hobbes among the dismal company of such 'hylozoic atheists'—who claim that matter is far from inert and that all material objects to some degree possess sense and have the capacity of perception.[16] This being so, such materialists are able to claim that all natural phenomena are explicable in terms of the properties of matter and, as a consequence, the concept of God to be totally redundant. The baffled More finds it difficult to credit that such men can seriously maintain that, for example, a ringing bell is a sensitive creature, a 'thing so foolish and frivolous', he writes, 'that the mere recitall of the opinion may well be thought confutation enough with the sober'.[17] But even if such nonsense be granted the 'hylozoic atheists', nevertheless such sentient, perceptive matter would still be completely unable to form the marvellous bodies of plants and animals without the guidance of an immaterial principle. More's conclusion is that materialism of any kind is a totally inadequate philosophy; an immaterial spirit of nature is everywhere present.

As for the charge that members of the recently constituted Royal Society were promoting atheism by their adoption of the mechanical philosophy More was quick to point out that the philosophy of the Society was not Cartesian but experimental —and this was a philosophy which had his unreserved support. Writing to his friend Joseph Glanvill More explained that members of the Royal Society aimed at a 'more *perfect Philosophy,* as yet to be raised out of faithful and skilful *Experiments* in Nature, which is so far from tending to *Atheism,* that I am confident, it will utterly rout it and the *Mechanical Philosophy* at once . . . '.[18]

Perhaps so, but it was best to make absolutely certain by turning to the phenomenon of witchcraft in the reality of which More totally believed. Unfortunately, the one stumbling block here is that Paracelsian natural magic offers non-demonic explanations of the powers and maleficia of witches. However, if Paracelsus and his followers are raving fools—and More has done his best to convince his readers they are—then the phenomenon of witchcraft demonstrates the existence of God. In his *Antidote to Atheism* of 1653 More had included a long section on the activities of witches, their powers, their flights, their carnal intercourse with demons, their maleficia. With materialists like Hobbes very much on his mind, More wrote a quarter of a century later an emphatic declaration to his friend Glanvill. The year is 1678 and for 14 years both writer and recipient have been Fellows of the Royal Society of London:

I look upon it as a special Piece of Providence [More rejoiced], that there are ever and anon such fresh Examples of Apparitions and Witchcrafts as may rub up and awaken their benummbed and lethargick Mindes into a Suspicion at least, if not assurance that there are other intelligent Beings besides those that are clad in heavy Earth or Clay: In this, I say, methinks the Divine Providence does plainly outwit the Powers of the Dark Kingdom, in permitting wicked men and women and vagrant Spirits of that Kingdom to make Leagues or Convenants one with another, the Confession of Witches against their own Lives being so palpable an Evidence, (besides the miraculous feats they play) that there are bad Spirits, which will necessarily open a Door to the belief that there are good ones, and lastly that there is a God.[19]

More's friend was in total agreement.

At Cambridge University, then, Cartesian philosophy was in serious trouble, at least with the neoplatonists. Matter was for More as inert as it had been for Descartes but the Cartesians' bluff had been called. A cosmology that fails to account for the most basic, ubiquitous phenomena is a cosmology either wrong in one or more of its basic principles or is lacking a basic principle. To the inertness of Cartesian matter More added a vital principle, a 'spirit of nature', that can in no way be used for magical purposes but which is responsible for bringing about the phenomena that the Cartesians claim to explain but do not. How, then, according to More's (neoplatonic) philosophy, is matter to be controlled and manipulated? As early as 1649 More had emphasized the very firm opinion that the worth of a philosophy is not to be measured by 'what it can procure for ye back, bed and bord'.[20] Finally, though the existence of a spirit of nature testifies to the existence of non-material entities, the reality of witchcraft testifies to the existence of *intelligent* if evil spirits and hence points even more directly to the existence of a Deity.

Descartes' authority has thus been undermined and the way cleared for new approaches. The all-important breakthrough is to be made by a Cambridge philosopher, probably greatly influenced by Henry More, but unlike More having great mathematical expertise. Whereas Descartes entitled his major work *Principles of Philosophy,* Isaac Newton will counter with *Mathematical Principles of Natural Philosophy (Principia Mathematica).* Copernicus, we remember, had written that 'mathematics are for mathematicians', Kepler proclaimed God to be a geometer, Galileo expressed the belief that the language of nature is written in the language of mathematics. In Newton's work we are able to reintroduce this missing mathematical component into the controversies we have been discussing. Let us, however, begin with some anti-Cartesian views expressed by Newton's teacher, Isaac Barrow.

Barrow's critique of prevailing cosmologies

In a fascinating oration which he delivered in Latin in 1652 Isaac Barrow referred approvingly to Descartes, that 'ingenious and important philosopher', who despite a magnificent attempt had nevertheless developed a philosophy which had come seriously to grief in attempting to explain key phenomena. 'Nature', declared Barrow, 'does not at all proceed according to this mechanical way'. How was it possible to explain, for example, the formation of plants, the attainment of 'such beautiful shapes, qualities so pleasing to every sense'?[21] Neither were animals unfeeling, unthinking machines. Descartes was simply wrong. Moreover, in Barrow's view, the illustrious philosopher had thought unworthily of God in supposing him to have made just one homogeneous material extended throughout all space. God would never have created such a boring universe! It was clear, finally, that Descartes had violated the rules of sound methodology in refusing to learn from things and in attempting to impose on particular phenomena his own *a priori* general principles—principles which, Barrow emphasized with some exasperation, he had framed without so much as consulting nature.

Against the Cartesians, Barrow considered the views of Plato and Aristotle, Democritus and Epicurus, and especially natural magicians, 'those who profess to understand natural sympathies and antipathies'. The magicians' philosophy was considerably more interesting than that of the Cartesians since, in Barrow's understanding of them, they supposed each body to be a mixture of two distinct parts, just as men are composed of soul and body, the former consisting of a spirit 'subtle, pure, most potent' and the latter being a material body 'dark, foul, impure, and feeble'.[22] Interesting as this philosophy was, however, Barrow had to note that it stood as condemned as the Cartesian on the charge of being constructed on totally premature hypotheses. Natural philosophy must aim at certainty and it can achieve this only by considering the phenomena that really do exist and by slowly building up valid general principles in the experimental manner explained and advocated by Bacon. Bacon, however, had not understood the importance of mathematics. Barrow would not make this mistake. The Lucasian professor of mathematics at Cambridge University had a high opinion of mathematicians. Mathematicians, he declared in his 'Mathematical Lectures' of 1665–6, 'only meddle with such things as are certain, passing by those that are doubtful and unknown. They profess not to know all Things, neither do they affect to speak all Things. What they know to be true, and can make good by invincible Arguments, that they publish'. In these lectures Barrow severely criticized Cartesian philosophy and other premature syntheses in which, he lamented, a new and distinct hypothesis is offered for every new phenomenon encountered. However ingenious such hypotheses may be, Barrow claimed, only a very simple or credulous person would accept them as true or even to any degree probable. 'Divine Archimedes' is to be Barrow's guide and vulgar disputation will be eradicated by weighing 'the Reason of Things in the Balance of Experience'. And this is the task of the mathematician![23] It would appear that Newton who had entered Trinity College in 1661 at the age of 19 took his professor's ideas very much to heart—but not totally to heart.

3 *Newtonian Synthesis and Occult Forces*

Centripetal acceleration and gravitational attraction
We recall that Galileo had conjectured, and had attempted to demonstrate, that a heavy body falls towards the earth with an acceleration such that its velocity increases from rest 'in simple proportionality to the time, which is the same as saying', Galileo clarified, 'that in equal time-intervals the body receives equal increments of velocity'.[24] Galileo had further *conjectured* (much to the derision of Descartes) that in a vacuum all bodies, including 'light' bodies such as feathers, would fall with an identical constant acceleration—let us call its magnitude g. This is certainly interesting, obviously totally anti-Aristotelian, but it is not clear what the conjecture implies. Galileo reasoned further (although not, as follows, algebraically): if a body falls from rest, its starting velocity is $v = 0$; at time t its velocity is $v = gt$. Its average velocity $\bar{v}$ is therefore $\bar{v} = gt/2$ and therefore the distance $s = \bar{v}t$ fallen in this time is

$$s = \tfrac{1}{2}gt^2. \tag{4.1}$$

By measuring the distance s a heavy body falls from rest in a measured time t we can therefore calculate g. However, while it is certainly remarkable that the fall of bodies is expressible in a simple mathematical way, what is one to do with the result? Bypassing Galileo's important investigations into projectile motion, let us turn to Newton and the heavens.

According to Kepler, dabbler in 'occult puerilities', planetary bodies orbit the sun in ellipses with the sun at a common focus. Now since the planetary ellipses are very nearly circles but not quite, we may for simplicity consider a planet moving with constant speed v in a circle of radius r having, as shown in Figure 4.1, the sun at its centre. At time $t = 0$ when the planet is at position A the velocity has a magnitude v which, if the planet

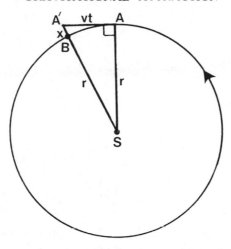

Figure 4.1

were not moving round the sun in a circle, would take it to position A' at a time t later. However, at time t (where we are assuming that vt is very small compared with r) the planet is actually at position B and can therefore be considered as having 'fallen' a distance $A'B$ towards the sun with a centripetal acceleration a which we wish to determine. If we call $A'B = x$ as shown in Figure 4.1, we have from Equation 4.1

$$x = \tfrac{1}{2}at^2. \tag{4.2}$$

To determine a we therefore need to determine x.

By the theorem of Pythagoras we have

$$(A'S)^2 = (A'A)^2 + (AS)^2$$

or

$$(x + r)^2 = (vt)^2 + r^2.$$

Dividing through by r^2 we have

$$\frac{1}{r^2}(x + r)^2 = 1 + \left(\frac{vt}{r}\right)^2. \tag{4.3}$$

Now

$$\left(1 + \frac{1}{2}\left(\frac{vt}{r}\right)^2\right)\left(1 + \frac{1}{2}\left(\frac{vt}{r}\right)^2\right) = 1 + \left(\frac{vt}{r}\right)^2 + \frac{1}{4}\left(\frac{vt}{r}\right)^4. \tag{4.4}$$

But since we are assuming a time t so small that vt/r is very much less than unity, we can neglect the last term of Equation 4.4 in which case Equation 4.3 becomes

$$\frac{1}{r^2}(x+r)^2 = \left(1 + \frac{1}{2}\left(\frac{vt}{r}\right)^2\right)^2.$$

Now we can take the square root of each side giving

$$\frac{1}{r}(x+r) = 1 + \frac{1}{2}\frac{v^2 t^2}{r^2}$$

or

$$x + r = r + \frac{1}{2}\frac{v^2 t^2}{r}$$

so that

$$x = \frac{1}{2}\frac{v^2 t^2}{r}.$$

Hence from Equation 4.2 we have the result that the acceleration which a planet (or body) experiences when travelling always in a circle of radius r with constant velocity v is directed towards the centre and is given by

$$a = \frac{v^2}{r}. \tag{4.5}$$

At each instant, therefore, the planet may be regarded as falling towards the sun with an instantaneous acceleration $a = v^2/r$ such that its trajectory is a circle of radius r around the sun.

This result for the centripetal acceleration was obtained by both Huygens and Newton (although Huygens probably some ten years after Newton) but it was Newton who made the most extraordinary use of the result. For according to Kepler's third law, which Newton as a student had carefully noted, the periodic time T for each individual planet is related to the (average) radius R of its orbit by the equation

$$R^3/T^2 = k \tag{4.6}$$

where k is the same constant for all the planets. If we denote the average velocity of the planet in its orbit by V, then since $T = 2\pi R/V$ we have

$$V^2 R = K \tag{4.7}$$

where K is a new constant ($=4\pi^2 k$) for each planet. But we have shown that the acceleration a of each planet (Equation 4.5) is V^2/R. Hence we have immediately that the acceleration of each planet is directed towards the sun with a magnitude given by

$$a = \frac{K}{R^2}. \tag{4.8}$$

Now Newton sees what to do with the claim that a stone (or the proverbial apple!) falls with a constant acceleration g towards the centre of the earth. For likewise the moon constantly falls towards the earth with an acceleration $a = v^2/d$ (where v is the moon's average velocity and d the distance of the centre of the moon from the centre of the earth). Newton makes the daring conjecture that if the stone and moon are accelerating towards the earth *according to the same laws as the planets are accelerating towards the sun,* then denoting the radius of the earth by r we should have $g = K'/r^2$ and $a = K'/d^2$ (where K' is a constant characteristic of the earth) so that

$$\frac{g}{a} = \frac{1/r^2}{1/d^2}. \qquad (4.9)$$

In his early twenties (while taking refuge in his Wiltshire birthplace from the plague of 1665) Newton checked the two numbers g/a and $1/r^2/1/d^2$ and found them to agree 'pretty nearly'.[25] Unfortunately the estimated radius of the earth that Newton had used was inaccurate and if a more accurate estimate had been available Newton would have found the two numbers agreeing 'very nearly'.

To this extent, then, Newton had confirmed his daring conjecture that falling stones and the moon are constantly accelerating towards the centre of the earth in the same way that each planet (including the earth) is constantly accelerating towards the sun. For in each case the acceleration is inversely proportional to the square of the distance between the accelerating body and the centre of the body towards which it is accelerating.

At the same time, however, Newton has made a revolutionary leap of the imagination. Newton supposes that the sun constantly *attracts* the planets (including the earth) towards itself while the earth constantly *attracts* falling stones and the moon. But not content with this step Newton makes the additional revolutionary conjecture that *all* bodies have an attraction for each other, the sun attracting Mars just as Mars attracts the sun, the earth attracting the stone just as the stone attracts the earth.

Immediately there are problems. If this generalization is true, why does Mars revolve about the sun rather than the sun about Mars? Newton supposes that this is because the sun is a much more massive body than Mars and hence it is Mars that undergoes much more acceleration than the sun does (which acceleration is non-zero, but negligible). If we write that the sun and Mars, of mass M and m respectively, attract each other with a 'force' F ('coition' is the term Gilbert asked us to use) given by

$$F = G\frac{Mm}{R^2}$$

where R is the (average) distance of Mars from the sun and G is a universal constant, then Newton has the result he wants in supposing that *the acceleration of a body caused by a force is in the direction of that force and is equal to the magnitude of the force divided by the mass of the body.* Hence the acceleration of the sun according to this hypothesis is

$$a_{\text{sun}} = \frac{F}{M} = G\frac{m}{R^2} \tag{4.10}$$

which is a small amount relative to the acceleration experienced by Mars which is

$$a_{\text{Mars}} = \frac{F}{m} = G\frac{M}{R^2} \tag{4.11}$$

The implications of these revolutionary conjectures by Newton are breathtaking. Before we examine them, however, let us pause to look briefly at Newton's philosophical development. Of course, this development, and indeed the nature of Newton's 'real' thoughts about the cosmos and its secrets, have been controversial ever since Newton published the *Principia* in 1687. Clearly there is no possibility here of examining these controversies in any detail. All I want to do is to indicate reasons for the controversies that exist over Newton's cosmology and presumably will always exist.

Newton as an alchemist
As a student at Cambridge Newton had imbibed Aristotle, had studied the writings of the mechanical philosophers, had read Henry More, and no doubt had taken to heart the advice of his teacher Barrow. In the next two years after getting his degree at Cambridge in 1665 Newton had made the revolutionary conjectures that have just been discussed. If these conjectures are true, then the (Copernican) heliocentric system is true but the mechanical philosophy is in desperate trouble. Newton has ambitions to become a natural philosopher yet he is, and he knows he is, subverting the explanatory principles adopted by a majority of his colleagues.

In an unpublished draft paper on gravity written in about 1670 Descartes is severely criticized by Newton for several reasons. 'If we say with Descartes that extension is body', complains Newton, 'do we not manifestly offer a path to Atheism, both because extension is not created but has existed eternally, and because we have an absolute idea of it without any relationship to God . . . ?'

Moreover, in Descartes' cosmology there is no absolute motion of bodies with respect to a space which exists independently of them, but only motion of bodies relative to other bodies. All motions are therefore relative, there being no motion which can be said to be 'true, absolute and proper' in preference to other motions—a starting point, Newton writes, 'than which nothing more absurd can be imagined'. In addition, Newton continues, if extension is necessarily the property of and only of a material body, then mind which is immaterial cannot be extended—as Descartes insisted—but this seems to Newton to be the same as denying the existence of mind, at the very least of rendering its union with the body totally unintelligible, not to say impossible. A necessary step towards solving these difficulties, Newton believes, is to postulate the existence of an absolute space with respect to which bodies have position and motion; such a space, argues Newton, is 'eternal in duration and immutable in nature, and this because it is the emanent effect of an eternal and immutable being', namely God. Newton then argues that it is by His endowing a certain region of space with properties such as impenetrability that God, by an act of His Will, creates what we perceive as a 'material' body—a body which, Newton writes, would equally 'operate upon our minds and in turn be operated upon, because it is nothing more than the product of the divine will realized in a definite quantity of space.' As for the ideas of Henry More, Newton states that while some prefer to suppose that 'God imposes on the soul of the world, created by him, the task of endowing definite spaces with the properties of bodies', he, Newton, prefers to believe that 'this function is directly discharged by God'.[26] Newton will even write in the *Principia* that space is the 'sensorium' of God.

Now these ideas are obviously in conflict with the ideas of Descartes but not necessarily with the ideas of the atomists who together with Gassendi assumed that space exists independently of the existence of bodies. But if Newton is to make good a public claim to be a mechanical philosopher (and hence to be respectable), a mechanical explanation has to be provided of the gravitational attraction that he has postulated between the material bodies of the solar system. In the middle 1670s Newton attempted to do this by supposing the solar system to be undergoing a constant bombardment of aether particles. At about this time, however, he was also developing an intense interest in alchemy and the Hermetic philosophy, as is made evident by a letter he wrote in April 1676 to the Secretary of the Royal Society concerning a request from Robert Boyle.

Boyle had been performing experiments with mercury and had

found a preparation that grew hot when mixed with gold. Since alchemists claimed that such a property is characteristic of a much sought after 'philosophical mercury' having very special powers, Boyle believed that his new mercurial substance might prove, among other things, very beneficial in the treatment of disease. Well aware, however, as he wrote in his paper, of the 'political inconveniences' that might result if the preparation should fall into 'ill hands', Boyle requested advice from the 'wise and skilful' concerning the wisdom of possible publication, reassuring his readers that until he received such advice he considered himself 'obliged to silence'.[27]

Newton's cautious and guarded reply—remember he is writing to the Secretary of the Royal Society—is extremely revealing. Believing that the 'fingers of many will itch to be at ye knowledge of ye preparation of such a [Mercury]', Newton advised against publication on the following ground:

> . . . because ye way by wch [Mercury] may be so impregnated, has been thought fit to be concealed by others that have known it, and therefore may possibly be an inlet to something more noble, not to be communicated *without immense damage to ye world* if there should be any verity in ye Hermetick writers, therefore I question not but that ye great wisdom of ye noble Authour will sway him to high silence till he shall be resolved of what consequence ye thing may be either by his own experience, or ye judgmt of some other that throughly understands what he speakes about, that is of a true Hermetic Philosopher, whose judgmt (if there be any such) would be more to be regarded in this point then that of all ye world beside to ye contrary, there being other things besides ye transmutation of metalls (if those great pretenders bragg not) wch none but they understand[28] [emphasis added].

Was Newton aware that in 1609 the Paracelsian Hermetic philosopher Oswald Croll had advised the 'compleat Phylosopher' to endure a 'hundred most cruell deaths' rather than publish information about the 'greatest and richest Terrene Treasure' to the 'wicked enemies of the Children of Art and Science' and so cause the 'ruine of the whole world'?[29] Aware or not, the private Newton appeared to be in far less doubt than the public Newton over the worth and reliability of 'ye Hermetick writers', for he was at this time deeply committed to making a philosophical mercury for himself. Believing that antimony, when it is prepared so that it crystallizes in the shape of a star, has the power of drawing out philosophical mercury from other metals, Newton undertook to prepare by such means a philosophical mercury—a feat which he believed he had accomplished, apparently some time in the middle 1670s. For his preparation, Newton records in his alchemical notes, 'makes gold to swell, to be swollen, and to putrefy, and also to spring forth into sprouts and branches, changing colours daily, the appearances of which fascinate me every day'.[30] Whatever significance we give to Newton's alchemical-Hermetic researches there can be little doubt that by the end of the 1670s, as a principal student of Newton's alchemical researches argues, the universe everywhere exhibited a living presence for the private Newton. Forces and active principles, themselves the direct manifestations of divine agency in nature, existed everywhere throughout the cosmos.[31] Another student of Newton's alchemy notes how less than five years after the publication of the *Principia*, Newton undertook a 'monumental' study of the entire alchemical tradition. R.S. Westfall appropriately concludes: 'One cannot avoid the question: Have we perhaps mistaken the thrust of Newton's career? To us, the *Principia* inevitably appears as a climax. In Newton's perspective, it may have seemed more like an interruption of his primary labour'.[32] When in 1696 Newton finally abandoned his Cambridge activities to become Warden of the Mint at London, he packed into a chest the incriminating evidence of disreputable intellectual interests. *Very* disreputable interests: when the chest was opened after his death, an executor of his will wrote on one of the manuscripts that it was 'loose and foul' and 'not fit to be printed'. In what follows we shall be chiefly concerned with the public Newton—the author of the *Principia*—and with the reaction of mechanical philosophers to a work they regarded with the gravest suspicion. But the private Newton—who remains an enigma—will never be far from our minds, the enigma that in 1946 made John Maynard Keynes, after a study of Newton's alchemical researches, declare that 'Cambridge's greatest son' was 'not the first of the age of reason' but 'the last of the magicians'![33]

The power of Newtonian theory
It is well known how in 1684 Edmond Halley, Fellow of the Royal Society and son of a rich London landowner and manufacturer, visited Newton in Cambridge to ask him what path a planet would follow under an inverse square law. After an exchange of letters with Robert Hooke in 1679–80 Newton had worked out that a closed orbit would be an ellipse and it was with this reply that Newton amazed and delighted Halley. From then until 1687 Halley was the financial and emotional driving force behind Newton and Newton's *Principia Mathematica*. This book was made deliberately abstruse by Newton (as reported by his friend the Rev Dr Derham) so that Newton could avoid 'being baited by little smatterers in mathematics'. However, Newton did include, at Halley's insistence, his famous third book which Halley hoped Newton would make accessible to those 'that will call themselves

philosophers without mathematics, which are by far the greater number'.[34] But third book or no, Newton's great work is an exposition of the *mathematical* principles of natural philosophy, as he emphasizes in the Preface to the first edition of 1687.

In this Preface, he explains how, by invoking the force of gravity, and 'by other propositions which are also mathematical, I deduce the motions of the planets, the comets, the moon, and the sea'. There follows a declaration of hope, of intent, of commitment to an ongoing research programme:

I wish we could derive the rest of the phenomena of Nature by the same kind of reasoning from mechanical [!] principles, for I am induced by many reasons to suspect that they may all depend upon certain forces by which the particles of bodies, by some causes hitherto unknown, are either mutually impelled towards one another, and cohere in regular figures, or are repelled and recede from one another. These forces being unknown, philosophers have hitherto attempted the search of Nature in vain; but I hope the principles here laid down will afford some light either to this or some truer method of philosophy.[35]

Newton begins the *Principia* by defining the framework of space and time in which phenomena take place. Absolute space, the reader is assured, remains always similar and immovable, and it is not to be defined with respect to anything external. Similarly, absolute, true and mathematical time, of its own nature, flows equally without relation to anything external. The problem is to determine the true motions of bodies from their apparent motions—which is 'a matter of great difficulty', Newton comments, since it is impossible to bring absolute space under the observation of our senses. 'Yet the thing is not altogether desperate'—the reader is to take heart—because the philosopher can observe and measure the apparent motions which are the differences of the true motions and he 'knows' that forces are the causes of these true motions. Just how the true motions are thereby to be determined is to be explained in the *Principia*. 'For to this end it was that I composed it', affirms Newton proudly.[36]

Newton begins the task of making good his proud claim by postulating three laws of motion. The first which he takes over from Descartes states that a body not acted on by forces continues in its state of rest or constant rectilinear motion as the case may be; the second states that any acceleration of a body is caused by an impressed force and takes place in the direction of the force and that (not in Newton's words) the magnitude of the acceleration is equal to the magnitude of the force divided by the mass of the body; the third law states that the force one body exerts on a second is equal and opposite to the force that the second exerts on the first. The law of gravitation states that any two particles of mass m_1 and m_2 separated by a distance r attract each other with a force F given by

$$F = \frac{Gm_1 m_2}{r^2}$$ (4.12)

where G is the universal constant referred to previously. Clearly Newton's third law is satisfied since m_2 attracts m_1 with a force F in the direction of m_2 from m_1 while m_1 attracts m_2 with an equal force F in the opposite direction (from m_2 to m_1). Using these four laws Newton accomplishes a breathtaking analysis of phenomena.

If a single planet is orbiting the sun, and if the only force acting on the planet is that from the sun of mass M, Newton demonstrates that the line from the planet to the sun will necessarily sweep out equal areas in equal times. This is Kepler's first law. Newton also shows that if the force decreases inversely as the square of the distance (the universal law of gravitation), then a closed planetary orbit about the sun is necessarily an ellipse with the sun at one focus. This is Kepler's second law. Finally if the semi-major axis of the ellipse is denoted by a and the periodic time denoted by T, then it follows that

$$\frac{a^3}{T^2} = \frac{GM}{4\pi^2}$$ (4.13)

from which Kepler's third law immediately results. Of great consequence is the fact, as Newton points out and investigates, that Kepler's three laws cannot be exact if Newton's laws are true. For the above results follow only if the mass of each planet is totally negligible with respect to the mass of the sun and if the attractions between the masses of the planets themselves are ignored.

At the same time Newton shows that Galileo's hypothesis that in a vacuum all bodies at the earth's surface fall with the same constant acceleration is only approximately true. First Newton demonstrates that the attraction of a stone of mass m by each particle of a perfectly spherical earth of uniform density is equal to the attraction of the stone by a mass M equal to the mass of the earth and situated at the earth's centre.[37] Let us call this attractive force F. Then the acceleration of a stone attracted by a non-rotating earth when allowed to fall freely towards the earth's centre is independent of the mass of the stone and given by

$$a_s = \frac{F}{m} = \frac{GM}{d^2}$$ (4.14)

where d is the distance of the stone from the centre of the earth. The weight W of the stone (which is defined as the magnitude of

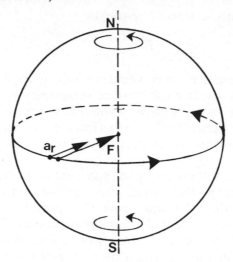

Figure 4.2

the upward force necessary to hold the stone at rest relative to the earth) is therefore given by

$$W = F = \frac{GMm}{d^2}. \tag{4.15}$$

The point is that the acceleration a_s clearly depends on the height of the stone above the earth's surface. Because, moreover, the earth is spinning about a north-south axis—see Figure 4.2—part of the gravitational attraction F maintains the centripetal acceleration a_r which the stone undergoes in rotating with the earth, while only the remainder of this attractive force gives rise to the weight of the stone. In other words

$$F = ma_r + W. \tag{4.16}$$

From this effect alone, therefore, the weight of a stone at the equator must be less than the weight of the same stone at the poles. Newton thus supplies a solution to the problem that so vexed Galileo as to why bodies are not flung off the surface of the rotating earth. It is because the gravitational attraction of the earth is more than sufficient to maintain the centripetal acceleration which the stone undergoes in rotating with the earth (and thus the stone possesses weight and remains stationary with respect to an observer on the earth's surface).

There is a further effect to consider. If we assume that the spinning earth originally existed as molten matter, then the weight of fluid matter at the poles must have pressed out the rotating and therefore lighter fluid matter at the equator. Consequently the earth cannot be spherical but must bulge slightly at the equator. This means that a stone is less distant from the centre of the earth when at one of the poles than when at the equator and correspondingly from this effect as well weighs less at the equator than at either of the poles. Clearly, however, the calculation of the acceleration of a falling stone depends upon the latitude of the stone in a rather complex manner.

Newton also shows that because the earth bulges at the equator the combined attractions of the moon and the sun cause the phenomenon of the precession of the equinoxes. This is schematically illustrated in Figure 4.3 where the departure of the earth from sphericity is shown by the shaded region and where, for reasons of simplicity, only the sun's influence on the earth is considered. As shown in Figure 4.3 (when the northern hemisphere is enjoying summer) we see that the gravitational pull at B from the sun is greater than the sun's gravitational pull at A, since B is marginally nearer the sun than is A. Now if the earth were not spinning about its (north-south) axis, then the excess

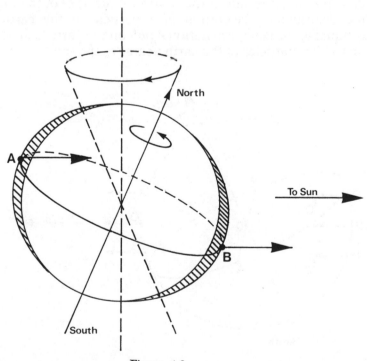

Figure 4.3

gravitational pull at B would begin to tilt the earth, causing the plane AB of the earth's equator to become closer to the plane of the ecliptic. However, because the earth is spinning once a day about its north-south axis, Newton is able to show that this axis must precess very slowly about an axis perpendicular to the ecliptic as illustrated in Figure 4.3. The phenomenon that Galileo thought it best not to dwell on in his *Dialogue* now receives a dynamical explanation. (The reader may like to refer back to the discussion in sections 2 and 3 of Chapter 2.)

In addition, Newton accounts for the phenomenon of two tides a day in a way that would have warmed Kepler's heart, although perhaps not Galileo's. The account is by no means simple and I merely indicate schematically the approach developed by Newton and as corrected and improved by his followers. Once again the phenomenon is more easily explained with reference to the sun's attraction rather than to the moon's although the principle is the same for each. Let us consider, then, the earth orbiting the sun once a year with the centre of the earth at a distance d from the centre of the sun. Now the essential feature to grasp of a Newtonian explanation of tides is that while all the particles of the earth have the same orbital centripetal acceleration with respect to the sun, it is only at the centre (of mass) O of the earth that the centripetal acceleration of a particle of the earth is exactly equal to the sun's gravitational pull on the particle divided by its mass. For particles of the earth nearer to the sun than is the

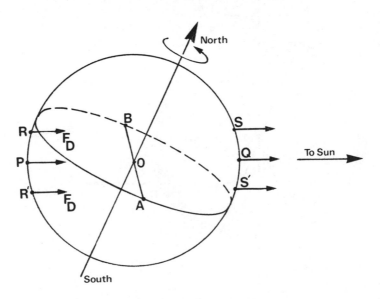

Figure 4.4

centre O of the earth, the sun's gravitational pull is in excess relative to the centripetal acceleration; for particles further than O it is deficient.

Thus in Figure 4.4 the sun's attraction at Q is greater than at O and therefore the sun exerts an 'excess' attraction at Q in a direction opposite to the earth's gravitational attraction at Q. Consequently, a unit mass of matter weighs less at Q than, for example, at two points A and B on the equator a distance d from the sun. Conversely, at P the sun's attraction is less than at O (and than at A and B) and therefore there is a deficiency of attraction from the sun made up for by part of the earth's attraction which therefore no longer produces weight. Hence once again a unit mass of matter at P weighs less than at A and B. However, no tides are directly caused as a result of this lessening of weight at P and Q.

To get an additional insight into the *tide-producing* forces it is sufficient to consider the situation at two points S and S' on either side of Q. At each point there is an excess attraction from the sun as at Q but this excess now has a component parallel to the earth's surface (see Figures 4.4 and 4.5). Hence at S and S' water experiences a pull towards Q and, therefore, as the earth rotates daily underneath the bulge of water, a high tide at Q is produced at noon each day (according to this simple model which was only

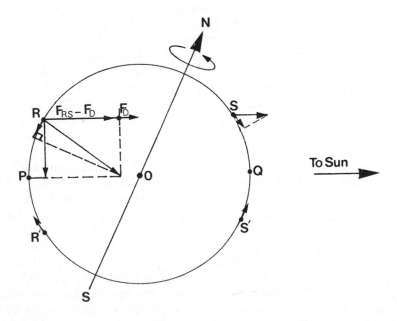

Figure 4.5

partially elaborated by Newton). At R (and R'), on the other hand, there is a deficiency, say F_D, in attraction towards the sun which is made up for by a part F_D of that component of the earth's attraction F_{RS} acting in the direction RS as shown in Figure 4.5. Hence at R, there is only a weight-producing force of magnitude $F_{RS}-F_D$ in the direction RS. However, since in a direction perpendicular to RS all the earth's gravitational attraction at R produces weight, the earth's *overall* weight-producing attraction at R has a direction no longer towards the centre of the earth at O but towards a point between P and the centre O. Since this weight-producing force has a component parallel to the earth's surface at R, and since a similar argument holds for R', water at R and R' 'falls' towards P so creating a high tide each midnight.

A similar argument holds for the moon's attraction whose tide-producing is twice that of the sun. Clearly when the moon and the sun are in line with each other, i.e. at new moon and full moon, the daily tides are highest. The 'explanatory embrace' of Newtonian theory is evident. Although the above analysis is highly schematic and many other factors must be taken into account if predictions of the times of tides and of tide heights are to be made, nevertheless Newtonian theory is in principle quantitative and its predictions can be compared against observations of tides.[38]

These are all tremendous achievements and which in addition offer the prospect of much pleasing work for the astronomer. Newton is, it would seem, justifiably scathing with respect to Descartes' theory of vortices which cannot account even for Kepler's three laws, let alone all the phenomena Newton can account for. With respect to Kepler's first two laws Newton writes that 'the parts of a vortex can never revolve with such a motion'; as for Kepler's third law Newton challenges: 'Let philosophers then see how that phenomenon of the 3/2th power can be accounted for by vortices'.[39]

Even worse was to befall Descartes as Newton continued his investigations into the motions of comets. Originally Newton had believed that the great comet observed from November 1680 to March 1681 had been two comets moving in opposite directions but eventually the astronomer John Flamsteed convinced him that there had only been one comet which had turned about the sun. While Newton worked out in the first edition of the *Principia* a parabolic orbit for the comets, Halley postulated in 1695 that the comet was actually orbiting the sun in a highly elongated ellipse and he and Newton worked at the details. As Newton wrote in the 1713 second edition of the *Principia*:

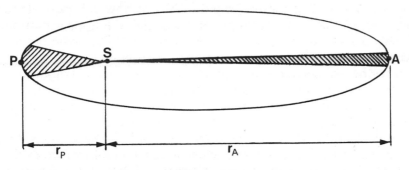

Figure 4.6

The motions of the comets are exceedingly regular, are governed by the same laws with the motions of the planets, and can by no means be accounted for by the hypothesis of vortices; for comets are carried with very eccentric motions through all parts of the heavens differently, with a freedom that is incompatible with the motion of a vortex.[40]

Clearly the highly elliptical motion of comets presents no difficulty to Newton's theory. Indeed, it is easy to see from Kepler's second law that the inverse square law certainly accounts for the motion of the comet both at its nearest approach to the sun, the perihelion *P*, and at its furthest distance from the sun, the aphelion *A*. If we call the distances *PS* and *SA* r_P and r_A respectively—see Figure 4.6—then all we have to show is that

$$\frac{a_P}{a_R} = \frac{r_A^2}{r_P^2} \qquad (4.17)$$

where a_P and a_R are the respective centripetal accelerations of the comet at *P* and *A* respectively. Now at both *P* and *A* (because of the symmetry of the ellipse) the comet is instantaneously proceeding in a circle of, let us say, radius *R* so that if v_P and v_A are the velocities of the comet at *P* and *A* we have

$$a_P = v_P^2/R \qquad (4.18)$$

and

$$a_A = v_A^2/R \qquad (4.19)$$

so that

$$\frac{a_P}{a_A} = \frac{v_P^2}{v_A^2}. \qquad (4.20)$$

But from Kepler's second law we have at *P* and *A*

$$v_P r_P = v_A r_A \qquad (4.21)$$

which substituted into Equation 4.20 gives the required inverse square law 4.17 at these two points.[41] But how is it possible for Descartes' theory to account for such highly elliptical motion? Newton sums up in a few trenchant words: 'The hypothesis of vortices is utterly irreconcilable with astronomical phenomena, and rather serves to perplex than explain the heavenly motions.'[42]

In addition Newton claimed his method to be diametrically opposed to Descartes'. Whereas Descartes sought general explanatory principles that are clear and distinct—and believed thereby that he had discovered true principles—Newton claimed to proceed from the phenomena towards general principles that explain these phenomena—and others! 'I frame [or feign] no hypotheses' is Newton's famous if misleading dismissal of his principal rival's methodology.[43] There is much, however, to be debated on this matter, Leibniz making a telling point when he commented: 'I am strongly in favour of experimental philosophy, but M. Newton is departing very far from it when he claims that all matter is heavy (or that every part of matter attracts every other part) which is certainly not proved by experiment.'[44] Newton, however, as he later clarified, did not believe that the universal principles he claimed to derive from the phenomena were necessarily true, pointing out in the 1726 third edition of the *Principia* that in 'experimental philosophy we are to look upon propositions collected by general induction from phenomena as accurately or very nearly true, notwithstanding any contrary hypothesis that may be imagined, till such time as other phenomena occur by which this may either be made more accurate, or liable to exceptions'.[45] Perhaps it was not Newton's fault if his disciples later accepted the theory of universal gravitation as an absolutely true theory, never to be successfully challenged. But this is looking ahead—at the moment Newtonian theory is very much the underdog.

Occult forces and mechanical philosophers

During the 1680s and indeed until the 1730s the mechanical philosophy remained the touchstone of the more prominent of the new philosophers. In 1690, for example, a book was published by Rohault's successor, Pierre Régis, in which he attempted to give a mechanical explanation of the phenomenon of falling bodies, that tantalizing yet so common phenomenon. The explanation was by no means satisfactory. Indeed, having to assume that a heavy body falls towards the axis of rotation of the earth rather than towards its centre, Régis hypothesized the earth to be a prolate spheroid and that bodies weigh nothing at the poles (the conclusion that Hobbes had also come to). Would, therefore, the mechanical philosophers accept the mathematical philosophy offered by Newton, putting on one side the vexed question of the cause of gravitational attraction and proceeding to work out the many implications of Newtonian theory? The foremost mechanical philosopher in Europe at this time, Christiaan Huygens, was in any case not in agreement with Descartes that extension alone constitutes the essence of a body, but agreed with atomists that a void must be postulated if motion is to be satisfactorily explained and was prepared even to ascribe the quality of perfect hardness to atoms. However, not even Huygens was prepared to accept as a foundation stone for a cosmology a principle which to him appeared quite ridiculous. In a letter which he sent to Leibniz on 18 November 1690 Huygens declared categorically:

Concerning the cause of the flux [tides] given by M. Newton, I am by no means satisfied, nor by all the other theories that he builds upon his Principle of Attraction, which to me seems absurd. . . . And I have often wondered how he could have given himself all the trouble of making such a number of investigations and difficult calculations that have no other foundation than this very principle.[46]

In his *Treatise on Light* published in the same year Huygens insisted that philosophers must either remain committed to the explanatory principles of the mechanical philosophy or else 'renounce all hopes of ever comprehending anything in Physics'.[47]

This seemed to be the general view of mechanical philosophers. Newton's *Principia* created no very great stir. It was, of course, clear that Newton was a good mathematician but he was no philosopher. A reviewer in the *Journal des Savants* summed up the typical view by praising Newton's ingenuity while declaring his mechanics devoid of physical value because 'they do not fulfil the necessary requirement of rendering the universe intelligible'.[48] Indeed, like Johannes Kepler before him, Newton was accused of dabbling in occult qualities but whereas Kepler could be excused on the grounds that the mechanical philosophy was then only in its barest infancy Newton could not be thus excused. Newton was clearly making a retrograde step in natural philosophy by attempting to base a cosmology on such an absurd principle.

The public Newton was extremely sensitive to possible insight into the beliefs of the private Newton. Thus Newton gladly consented when Richard Bentley, chosen to give the first of the lectures that Robert Boyle had provided for in his will, appealed to Newton to assist him in his understanding of the ideas of the *Principia.* Bentley hoped to use the *Principia* to refute atheism, particularly the obnoxious ideas of Hobbes, who seemed not to understand that society could only be maintained 'upon the basis of religion'.[49] Newton, who a year later wished John Locke dead on the erroneous suspicion that Locke was a 'Hobbist' (and a 'Hobbist', moreover, Newton believed, who was so reprehensively attempting to 'embroil' him with women)[50] began his first letter to Bentley with the now well-known affirmation: 'When I wrote my treatise about our system I had an eye upon such principles as might work with considering men for the belief of a Deity; and nothing can rejoice me more than to find it useful for that purpose.'[51] There was particularly one point that Bentley would have to understand well. Gravity is not an innate property of matter but has a cause about whose nature, however, Newton will not be drawn into debate, other than to claim that there is no proof that such a cause is material. Newton thus tells Bentley:

It is inconceivable that inanimate brute matter should, without the mediation of something else which is not material, operate upon, and affect other matter without mutual contact; as it must do if gravitation, in the sense of Epicurus, be essential and inherent in it. And this is one reason why I desired you would not ascribe innate gravity to me. That gravity should be innate, inherent and essential to matter, so that one body may act upon another at a distance through a vacuum without the mediation of anything else, by and through which their action and force may be conveyed from one to another, is to me so great an absurdity that I believe no man who has in philosophical matters a competent faculty of thinking can ever fall into it.[52]

Bentley reached a conclusion greatly to Newton's liking and in his sermon on 5 December 1692 told his congregation that there were very good grounds for affirming that universal gravitation which certainly does exist in nature is the result of a 'Divine energy', a manifestation of God's active presence in the world. Not only had Newton produced an excellent account of terrestrial and celestial phenomena but that account could be used and most certainly was used by Newtonian theologians to argue the existence of God and thus to underwrite social stability and thereby the established social stratification.

Mechanical philosophers, however, were entirely unconvinced of the wisdom of Newton's approach, as were philosophers at least sympathetic in part to the ideas of the mechanical philosophers. Certainly in the 1706 edition of his *Opticks* the beleaguered Newton expressed his total agreement with the view that merely to state that 'every Species of Things is endow'd with an occult specifick Quality by which it acts and produces manifest Effects' is to say nothing of value at all. But, Newton went on in defence of his programme of inquiry, 'to derive two or three general Principles of Motion from Phaenomena, and afterwards to tell us how the Properties and Actions of all corporeal Things follow from those manifest Principles, would be a very great step in Philosophy, though the Causes of those Principles were not yet discover'd'. Not all philosophers felt able to agree! Indeed, just before the publication of the second edition of the *Principia* in 1713 Roger Cotes, the professor of astronomy and experimental philosophy at Cambridge, brought to Newton's attention a letter from Leibniz to Hartsoeker, published in a London weekly, claiming that if Newton's gravitational attraction is produced by a law of God 'without using any intelligible means', then gravitational attraction must be assumed such a 'senseless occult quality . . . that it can never be cleared up, even though a Spirit, not to say God himself, were endeavouring to explain it'.[53] In a preface approved by the exasperated Newton for the second edition of the *Principia*, Cotes launched a vigorous counter-offensive. The gauntlet is thrown down to Newton's opponents. Whatever the cause of gravity, effects prove its existence as Newton has amply demonstrated; to throw gravity out because its cause is not known is an absurdity that overturns the foundations of all philosophy. It cannot be helped that Newtonian physics contradicts the opinions of Descartes since the business of true philosophy is to discover the principles on which God actually chose to found 'this most beautiful Frame of the World', not those which He might have used had He been so inclined. Those philosophers must be peculiarly attached to chimeras who spend their time attempting to patch up the 'ridiculous figment' of vortices, disproved by so many phenomena, that of comets being merely an obvious one. Cotes eulogises the work of Newton and remembers in doing so the advice that Alphonso the Wise would have imparted to the Creator had God consulted him before embarking on the construction of the world:

The gates are now set open, and by the passage he has revealed we may freely enter into the knowledge of the hidden secrets and wonders of natural things. He has so clearly laid open and set before our eyes the most beautiful frame of the System of the World, that if King Alphonso were now alive, he would not complain for want of the graces either of simplicity or of harmony in it. Therefore we may now more nearly behold the beauties of Nature, and entertain ourselves with the delightful contemplation.[54]

Leibniz was by no means satisfied and during 1715–16 exchanged letters with one of Newton's most talented disciples, Samuel Clarke. In 1694 Clarke had presented at Cambridge University a thesis defending Newtonian natural philosophy, while three years later in 1697 at the age of only 22 he had brought Rohault's classic work up to date with a new Latin translation, thereafter producing successive editions in which he systematically refuted the Cartesian text with Newtonian footnotes! But Clarke was primarily a theologian. In his Boyle lectures of 1704 and 1705 he had won for himself a great reputation by using Newtonian cosmology to demolish the 'atheistic' views of Hobbes and the deistic views of Clarke's contemporary John Toland. Strongly influenced by Giordano Bruno, Toland subscribed to what Margaret Jacob denotes as a pantheistic materialism in which gravity became an innate property of atoms and upon which basis Toland called for a utopian republic, 'free from clerical influence and religious intolerance, where intellectual political freedom amounted to a loosely defined social equality'.[55] In Toland's cosmology the downgrading of the immaterial principle ruling the behaviour of supposedly inert atoms corresponded to the downgrading, indeed the removal, of king and clergy. Clarke's lectures were designed to counter such a threat. Just as God continually ensures an harmonious order in nature, so all men have the responsibility of ensuring an harmonious social order. For this to be possible the individual must always respect and obey his superiors. Moreover, just as 'brute and stupid' matter is controlled by God's spiritual presence, so people in lower walks of life must submit to the judgement of their superiors. By way of explanation Clarke expressed his firm conviction that the individual must consequently

attend the duties of that particular station or condition of life, whatsoever it be, wherein providence has at present placed him; . . . without being either uneasy and discontented, that others are placed by providence in different and superior stations in the world; or so extremely and unreasonably solicitous to change his state for the future, as thereby to neglect his present duty.[56]

Newton, greatly pleased with Clarke, commissioned him in 1706 to translate his *Opticks* into Latin and thereby reach a wider audience. In this work Newton had implied that God would periodically adjust the world system He had created in order to prevent planetary irregularities from becoming too great, an idea ridiculed by Leibniz with the suggestion that such men as Newton 'must needs have a very mean notion of the wisdom and power of God'. Taking up cudgels on behalf of Newton, Clarke countered Leibniz by arguing that those men who claim a kingdom functions perfectly without the periodic intervention of the king 'may reasonably be suspected that they would like very well to set the king aside'. Responding that Clarke's analogy was inappropriate since God sustains everything in being and nothing can exist without him, Leibniz nevertheless maintained that it was necessary to draw a clear distinction between what is natural and supernatural on the grounds that that which is supernatural 'exceeds all the powers of creatures'. It follows—Leibniz makes the complaint that must have been driving Newton mad—that the attraction of bodies 'is a miraculous thing, since it cannot be explained by the nature of bodies'.[57] In defence of Newton's conception of space (namely that it necessarily exists and does not depend on the existence of bodies) Clarke replied that by void is not meant space empty of everything but merely empty of bodies, i.e. of anything that might be an object of the senses. Moreover, Clarke explained, gravity cannot be considered miraculous merely because it does not arise from, or is not explicable by, the natural powers of bodies. For otherwise, all animal motion would have to be considered miraculous since it is likewise inexplicable in terms of the natural powers of bodies as is also the generation of plants and animals. Clarke attempts to turn the tables on his and Newton's adversary. To believe, as does Leibniz, that the soul does not operate on the body is ridiculous enough but to maintain that God causes the body's mechanical movements to conform to the will of the soul as in Leibniz's doctrine of pre-established harmony is to believe in a perpetual miracle. However, gravity, no matter what its ultimate cause, is not a miracle. Certainly there is an intermediate means responsible for the attraction between bodies but, Clarke claims, this means may well be invisible and intangible and of an entirely different nature from that of a mechanism. It is therefore totally misguided to insist that gravitation must have a mechanical cause.

In a last (fifth) critique written shortly before his death Leibniz maintained his position. There can be no such thing as a void; and the gravity of bodies towards the centre of the earth must be explicable by the motion of fluids as must also the gravity of planets towards the sun and towards each other. Noting that Clarke has at least admitted that the means of gravity is invisible and intangible, Leibniz mocks that Clarke might as well have added 'inexplicable, unintelligible, precarious, groundless and unexampled'. We are told that space is not void. 'What is it then full of?', Leibniz mockingly continues. Perhaps it is full of extended spirits or immaterial substances which can extend and contract themselves and mutually interpenetrate without inconvenience. Leibniz thinks he sees here the 'odd imaginations' of that otherwise learned and well-meaning man, Dr Henry More. However all this, Leibniz laments, is to take us back into the kingdom of darkness and certainly far from the time of Mr Boyle who so properly inculcated the belief that everything must be explained mechanically. But now, Leibniz's lamentation continues, chimeras are once again appearing: 'What has happened in poetry, happens also in the philosophical world. People are grown weary of rational romances . . . and they are become fond again of the tales of fairies'. In addition, Clarke errs horribly in claiming the correspondence Leibniz ascribes between soul and body to be a perpetual miracle; it is only the effect of an 'original miracle, worked at the creation of things'. Likewise there is nothing remotely miraculous about the motions of the celestial bodies or even about the generation of plants and animals. Only their beginning is a miracle: 'The organism of animals is a mechanism', Leibniz explains, 'which supposes a divine preformation. What follows upon it is purely natural, and entirely mechanical'.[58] Although Leibniz does not agree with Descartes that matter is characterized only by extension and indeed believes all matter is characterized by perception, nevertheless from the point of view of his disagreement with Clarke and Newton this is irrelevant. The mechanical philosophy, he maintains, can account for all the phenomena of the world *except for their origins*.

Clarke's final reply re-emphasizes that since God is omnipotent it is incorrect to state that one phenomenon is more miraculous than another. The ordinary generation of animals we call natural only because it is a daily phenomenon, the resurrection of a dead body we call miraculous only because it is uncommon; but to God each phenomenon is a simple consequence of His Will. By attraction is meant the phenomenon, not the cause, be it mechanical or not mechanical. To call a phenomenon occult because its cause is not known is bad enough; to suggest that therefore the phenomenon itself is non-existent is, Clarke writes laconically, 'very singular arguing indeed'. As to why Leibniz wants so desperately to prove that immaterial substances cannot act on matter, Clarke confesses himself baffled: 'But is not God an immaterial substance? And does not he act upon matter?'[59] Clarke claims to be able only to stand and wonder at the doctrine of the pre-established harmony. The absurdity of the commitment apart, it is up to Leibniz and his colleagues to explain mechanically the movements of the planets, the generation of plants and animals, and the multiple movements of animals, none of which they have been able to do (or will ever be able to do). Why is there this desperate desire to remove God from the world after His first stupendous creative act and to turn the world into a Great Machine, despite the absurdity and impossibility of the task? Clarke appeals to Leibniz for explanation. But two weeks later Leibniz was dead.

Leibniz's death allowed Newton as the anonymous author of a report supposedly written by members of the Royal Society to vent his anger on Leibniz (the two had been also embattled over priority for the invention of the calculus): 'And must Experimental Philosophy be exploded as *miraculous* and *absurd*', Newton asked, 'because it asserts nothing more than can be proved by Experiments, and we cannot yet prove by Experiments that all the Phaenomena in Nature can be solved by meer Mechanical Causes?' Newton's verdict was unambiguous: 'Certainly these things deserve to be better considered.'[60]

But Newton was not so easily to convince his contemporaries. Even that apostate from the mechanical philosophy Niklaas Hartsoeker claimed in 1722 that 'we take chimeras for the truth' in believing in mutual attraction between particles, backing up his claim by reporting the fact that steel cubes suspended side by side in a vacuum do not approach each other.[61] (Anticipating such an objection, Newton had claimed in the *Principia* that the gravitational attraction was too weak to detect in this way.) A year after Newton's death in 1727 a disciple of Malebranche, Joseph Molières, explained to the Newtonians that they should not hope 'that their opinions will be received other than by those who would speak and write on physics without understanding it'. In his review of Molières' work in 1728 the Permanent Secretary of the Paris Academy of Sciences, Bernard de Fontenelle, took, however, a more 'balanced' view of the conflict: there was nothing more interesting for philosophers to know, Fontenelle declared, 'than whether the ingenious system of vortices of Descartes, which appears so agreeable to the intellect, will fall overwhelmed by the difficulties which oppose it, and whether we shall be reduced to taking another which has difficulties as great, and more striking, although it has some very advantageous aspects'.[62] In his generous and graceful eulogy of Newton for the Paris Academy Fontenelle nevertheless made his preferences clear: 'Attraction and Vacuum banished from Physiks by DesCartes, and in all appearance for ever, are now brought back again by Sir Isaac Newton, armed with a power entirely new, of which they were thought incapable, and only perhaps a little disguised.'[63] It was to no avail, however, that in 1752 the 95-year-old Fontenelle rallied once more to the defence of Descartes' mechanical philosophy with his *Theory of Cartesian Vortices and Thoughts on Attraction*. By this time the war between the two research programmes had been decisively lost by the Cartesians.

4 The Newtonian Maupertuis and 'Hylozoic Atheism'

Occult powers and foetal development
In 1728 the French natural philosopher Pierre Louis Maupertuis, who had been elected a member of the Paris Academy of Sciences at the age of 25, visited London and became converted to Newton's theory of dynamics and universal gravitation.

Subsequently, in 1732, Maupertuis courageously brought out the first book to be published in France in support of Newtonian theory. In his *Discourse on the Various Shapes of the Stars* Maupertuis explained that he had been attracted to the project of explaining all physics in terms of matter and motion but that he had become disillusioned when he realized that for each phenomenon a different set of matters and motions became necessary. Where was the much vaunted explanatory power of Cartesian theory? On the other hand, Newtonian theory referred only to gravitational attraction between particles in order to explain *all* planetary motions. And, added Maupertuis, 'we cannot see without admiration that the comets are found at the points of their orbits thus determined; almost with as much precision as the planets are found at the points of the orbits determined by the ordinary tables'.[64] Although mechanical philosophers rejected the concept of a gravitational attraction as absurd, Maupertuis argued that they were incorrect to do so. According to Malebranche, bodies do not even interact with one another on contact, a collision between bodies merely supplying God with the 'occasion' to change the motion of the colliding bodies according to His Divine Will. This being so, 'is it more difficult for God to make two separated bodies endeavour the one towards the other', inquired Maupertuis gently, 'than to delay moving a body until it has been struck by another?'[65] The answer is clearly in the negative. If God is the agent, then He can carry out one way of moving bodies as readily as He can another. Three years later Maupertuis went as the head of an expedition to northern Sweden to measure the length of a degree of latitude while another expedition made a journey to Peru; the results corroborated Newton's theory that the earth is an oblate spheroid bulging at the equator. Five years later four French philosophers shared the honours in a prize competition organized by the Paris Academy on the nature of tides. Significantly, three of the essays were Newtonian and each one made an important contribution to tidal theory. It is interesting that the prize-sharing Newtonian contestant Daniel Bernoulli referred to the mutual gravitation between bodies as 'this incomprehensible and incontestable principle, that the great Newton has so well established and that we can no longer hold in doubt'.[66] Bernoulli in particular could no longer hold it in doubt. He had managed to achieve good agreement between his calculations and the phenomena in question without previously knowing the results he wanted—he had consulted data only *after* making the calculations. Could any Cartesian ever claim such a success? As Maupertuis had earlier emphasized, Newtonian theory allows predictions to be made but

Cartesian theory only works backward from each phenomenon or set of observations. From now on the Newtonian theory of gravitation will displace the Cartesian theory of vortices.

Are now the gates open wide to the return of occult qualities, of sympathies and antipathies inherent to matter, of a materialism inimical to Christian belief? What will become of God the Father Creator in a philosophy that accepts the existence of a gravitational attraction between all particles? One can to some extent answer these questions by noting the development of the ideas of the first man who had the courage to defend Newtonian ideas in France.

In 1746 Maupertuis published anonymously a new account of generation, a very new account! In this short and popular essay entitled *The Earthly Venus* Maupertuis first summarized the ovist theory of *emboîtement*: 'All fecundity then fell to the females.' And then the animalculist theory of preformation: 'Now here was fecundity, formerly attributed to the females, given back to the males!' Male honour restored. However, Maupertuis immediately apologizes to his fellow natural philosophers for his refusal to accept either theory. For he is, he explains, unable to accept a theory, no matter how ingenious, that is incompatible with certain basic phenomena; and both preformationist theories, ovist and animalculist, are incompatible with the well-known facts that a child resembles sometimes the father, sometimes the mother, and that hybrid animals are born from two different species. Descartes is therefore surely correct when he argues that offspring result from contributions from each parent. But as to the soundness of Descartes' own explanation Maupertuis is emphatic: 'Although I have the deepest respect for Descartes and believe, as he does, that the foetus is formed from the mixture of the two seminal fluids, I cannot believe that anyone is satisfied with the explanation which he gives.' What is to be done? The reintroduction of 'occult qualities'! Maupertuis explains that bolder philosophers are not frightened to assume the existence of attractive forces and it is only by assuming the existence of special attractive powers that the formation of a foetus can be explained. Maupertuis thus asserts:

If there are, in each of the seminal seeds, particles predetermined to form the heart, the head, the entrails, the arms and the legs, if these particular particles had a special attraction for those which are to be their immediate neighbours in the animal body, this would lead to the formation of the foetus. Even though the foetus were a thousand times more complex, if the process above were exact, it would still be formed.[67]

The flood gates are opened wide and the mechanical philosophy is threatened with inundation. Unless the preformationist theories can be developed to account for the difficulties they are in (a 'research programme' undertaken by Charles Bonnet and Albrecht von Haller), either vitalist or hylozoistic theories will overtake biology. Neither did the discovery in 1740 of the regenerative powers of the polyp help the mechanical philosophers: a small acquatic animal (the hydra) which when cut up into several parts has the power to regenerate itself *from each part* seemed to indicate that at least living matter (if indeed there is any dead matter) has rather more interesting properties than the sole one of extension! Not without reason R.A.F. de Réaumur explained excitedly a year later: 'The story of the Phoenix that is reborn from its ashes, wholly fabulous as it is, offers nothing more marvellous than the discovery of which we are about to speak.' He still could not believe his eyes after witnessing the hydra's rebirth 'hundreds and hundreds of times'.[68] How ecstatic a Cornelius Agrippa would have been to observe such an acquatic Phoenix before his very eyes. No occult qualities indeed! But Newtonian-influenced natural philosophers would need to invoke more than a finite number of 'occult' attractive powers if they were to account successfully for that so common, yet most baffling of natural phenomena—the development of the foetus. For if the foetus is not preformed and if there is development that is not a mere growth or contraction of parts, then attractive powers alone are not sufficient to do the job. The most distinguished member of the Paris Academy of Sciences who in 1712 had reported the regenerative powers of the crayfish pointed out to Maupertuis what he would need in addition to attractive powers. It is worth quoting Réaumur in full:

Everything has its fashions nor is philosophy itself an exception to it: those occult qualities, those sympathies and antipathies which nobody would have dared to name in physicks fifty years ago, have, since that time, showed themselves again with splendour under the name of attraction: although we never were taught what this attraction consisted in, very noble uses have been made of it with regard to the motions of the celestial bodies; great efforts have been made likewise, to make it serve in general to explain all the phenomena in nature. People thought it . . . capable of operating the miracle of the formation of the foetus; in order to which people judged it sufficient to suppose that the similar parts of one and the same kind had the property of mutually attracting one another, and that there were different laws of attraction for similar parts of different kinds: by virtue of these laws, all the similar parts fit to make a heart, all these fit to make a stomach, a brain, etc. will seek for their own kind, draw near and unite with them. . . . We are nevertheless as yet very far from seeing anything that resembles any of the organisations which are to concur towards the formation of our great work: how will attractions be able to give to such and such a mass the form and structure of the heart, to another that of the stomach, to a third one that of the eye, and to another that of the ear? How will they frame other masses into vessels, valves, etc. All their tendency will amount barely to the reunion of the similar parts into solid masses. What law of attraction shall one imagine for the making of that small bone of the ear, whose figure makes it to be called the stirrup? How shall so many different organs be placed and assembled in their proper order? We see with the most glaring evidence, that in order to arrive at the formation of so complicated a piece of work, it is not enough to have multiplied and varied the laws of attraction at pleasure, and that one must besides attribute the most compleat stock of knowledge to that attraction.[69]

Maupertuis was not discouraged. In his *System of Nature,* published in 1751 under the pseudonym of Dr Baumann, Maupertuis now added adapted components of Leibniz's natural philosophy to his Newtonian heterodoxy. Matter can think! Extension is not incompatible with thought any more than it is incompatible with mobility. If we regard with repugnance the idea that thought and extension exist in one and the same subject it is only because, unlike the case of mobility and extension, we cannot directly perceive the two together but must rely, Maupertuis claims, upon inference and induction. All matter, therefore, has the properties of perception, sentience and consciousness if only to an infinitesimal extent, different forms of organization of matter giving rise to different levels of sentience, consciousness and, indeed, self-consciousness. Where Réaumur sadly points out that Maupertuis' theory of foetal development needs not just attractive powers but *memory* in the particles comprising the foetus, Maupertuis happily agrees: 'The elements suitable for forming the foetus swim in the semens of the father and mother animals; but each, extracted from the part like that which it is to form, retains a sort of recollection of its old situation; and will resume it whenever it can, to form in the foetus the same part.'[70] The hypothesis of God is now unnecessary in the theory of foetal development.

But how did the first highly adapted organisms of a particular type arise? Is God's direct action necessary here? Apparently not. Maupertuis suggests that by chance a very large number of organisms may have been produced but only those organisms which possessed a certain degree of adaptation to a particular environment survived to reproduce themselves. All the rest necessarily perished. 'Thus', Maupertuis concludes, 'the species which we see today are but a small part of all those that a blind destiny has produced'.[71]

This, then, is the kind of 'hylozoic atheism' that the Cambridge neoplatonists had been so intent on refuting. The implications are many, one of which—and not the least by any means—being the problem of legitimating social stratification and privilege in a Godless society. Hobbes, of course, had suggested a way. Not, however, that Maupertuis was an atheist. The 'Doctor Baumann' of *The System of Nature* (although immediately recognized as

Maupertuis) had argued that man's religious awareness, and in particular his awareness of God, distinguishes him from animals and mere rational beings. On one thing Maupertuis claims to be clear and this statement, he tells readers, must suffice: 'we have an indivisible, immortal soul entirely distinct from the body, and able to earn eternal pains or eternal compensations'.[72]

There is an additional matter that must be mentioned, one that had preoccupied, among others, Montaigne, Campanella, More, Barrow and Ray. Maupertuis obviously rejects the Cartesian claim that animals are automata and even if animals do not possess immortal souls they nevertheless possess the capacity to feel. The question then arises as to how human beings ought to treat animals (by-passing for the moment the question as to how human beings ought to treat each other!). In his letter 'On Duty towards Animals' Maupertuis is vehement that although animals are different from humans the fact that they are sentient creatures is sufficient to make infliction of unnecessary suffering on them totally inexcusable. 'Must a soul be precisely similar to the soul of this or that man', Maupertuis asks, ' . . . in order not to inflict pain on it? Might not those who think like that proceed by degrees to kill or torture, without scruple, all who are not relatives or friends?[73] But we are back to the question of how people ought to treat each other. Perhaps as Maupertuis suggests (and as Campanella in his sonnet 'Self-Love' had insisted), the two questions are not independent of each other.

The mechanical philosophy: the briefest look ahead
It is with extreme reluctance that I break off here this account of the collapse of consensus over preformationist theories. For the next half century is a fascinating one of conflict and changing allegiances between preformationists and epigenesists resulting by the close of the eighteenth century in a triumph of vitalist cosmology, eventually to be stemmed, although not eradicated, by Darwin's theory of evolution in the mid-nineteenth century. The mechanical philosophy in its original form was always a non-starter. I have attempted to explain in this and the preceding chapter how nevertheless the mechanical philosophy met the social needs of particular groups of people and thus became a predominant cosmology in France, England, and the Low Countries. It was Newton who destroyed the mechanical philosophy in its original pristine form. If Pope in 1730 could proclaim:[74]

> Nature, and Nature's Laws lay hid in Night
> God said *Let Newton be*! and All was *Light*

the Scottish philosopher David Hume was a few years later to give a different and, I think, more accurate verdict: 'While Newton seemed to draw off the veil from some of the mysteries of nature, he showed at the same time the imperfections of the mechanical philosophy; and thereby restored her ultimate secrets to that obscurity in which they ever did and ever will remain.'[75]

But there is more to be said on the matter than this. For in a fundamental sense the mechanical philosophy still provides the ontology against which advances in both the natural and human sciences are measured. Any departure from the mechanical philosophy is by and large a heresy that must be fought over bitterly before its adherents can claim victory (as in the case of the Newtonians) or are forced to concede defeat. In any case, although modern physics is now inundated with all kinds of (precisely mathematically articulated) 'sympathies' and 'antipathies'—and although matter according to quantum theory is a rather 'occult' substance to say the least—the mechanical philosophy has not been forced to concede any major defeat: sentience and consciousness are still not considered to be immanent properties of matter: neither are beauty and ugliness, taste, colour and odour; above all, the natural world is still held to lack creative powers and telos. A dissenting contemporary scientist is, I think, correct when he writes: 'Deeply ingrained in science is a view of the natural order as being passive and inert and having no initiating powers of its own. This I believe is a greatly mistaken image of reality—an image which pervades non-scientific as well as scientific thinking'.[76]

Lest it be thought that Darwin's theory of evolution completed the breach that Newtonian theory first made in the mechanical philosophy—for, it would seem, matter must have *very* interesting properties indeed if it can evolve, given the right conditions, into sentient, self-conscious, purposeful creatures as are human beings—the answer leading spokesmen for biology give is in the negative. Variations in living forms are said to occur 'at random'; natural selection allows only the better adapted (no thanks to themselves) to survive and produce offspring. Nobel prize winners in molecular biology even see variations or changes in genetic 'material' as 'mistakes', maintaining (as a matter of faith and without justification) that evolution is a result of such 'mistakes' and 'errors of replication'; for example, Jacques Monod writes (and the emphasis is his): 'for modern theory *evolution is not a property of living beings,* since it stems from the very *imperfections* of the conserving mechanism which indeed constitutes their unique privilege.'[77] Here nature is conceived to have a telos but, incredibly, that telos is the *non-production and non-evolution of life,* continually undermined, however, by the constant occurrence of *mistakes*. Aristotle is here being placed firmly on his head. Nature, as it were, had no 'unconscious wish' to become 'Mother Nature'; it is just that 'her' contraceptive system was not and is not foolproof and mistakes continually happen!

Life, then, continues to be a challenge to the contemporary biologist just as it was to her or his seventeenth-century predecessors but it is now to be explained (away) in terms of modern physics and chemistry. The irrepressible Monod goes even further: after declaring what he has termed the 'Postulate of Objectivity' to be 'essential for the development of science', he continues that 'the essence of living beings (that is to say, of living beings which in their structure and their functions must be recognized as showing every evidence of some sort of project) is a constant challenge and a menace to the postulate of objectivity'.[78] The deduction automatically follows that the existence of living beings is a 'constant challenge and a menace' to the development of science—which is by no means an uninteresting conclusion! Returning to Darwin's theory of evolution, Michael Morgan has summarized the perplexing situation very succinctly indeed: 'The strange consequence of Darwinism for psychology has been', he explains, 'not what would seem to follow most naturally from the demonstration of continuity, to see in animals the variety of our own mental life; but first to degrade animals to object status in order to pursue the anti-pathetic fallacy up the evolutionary tree to human beings themselves'.[79]

There is much to be analysed and explained here. But that is not my task in this essay. My purpose in jumping so abruptly to a contemporary and widely-prevalent ontology of nature is to emphasize that the mechanical philosophy of the seventeenth century is still a living force—if that is the right expression for it—and must in no sense be regarded as an important philosophy of nature that had its fling in the seventeenth century and was later discarded as matter was ascribed increasingly interesting properties. Modified the mechanical philosophy had to be—but its principal descendant, physicalism, remains—for better or worse—the dominant philosophy underlying the natural and, controversially, even the human sciences.

But let us return to the seventeenth century. At the end of Chapter 2 we asked a series of questions only some of which had been answered by the 1640s. Certainly, by the end of the seventeenth century it was widely appreciated that Copernicus had been basically right; and that the laws of motion apply equally to the earth and earthly phenomena as to Mars—indeed that they apply universally. However, as both Descartes and

Leibniz had lamented, the mechanical philosophy, even if correct, did not seem to offer the prospect of new and striking powers over nature. Newtonian gravitational theory likewise scarcely seemed to herald a major advance in this respect. Power over nature was in fact not to come via the Descartes of the *Principles of Philosophy* nor directly via the Newton of the *Principia Mathematica*. It was to come through the gradual development of the Baconian (non-mathematical) experimental philosophy, institutionalized in the 1660s in the Royal Society and in the following century in provincial philosophical societies, reaching maturation in the decades around 1800 and in some fields achieving synthesis with the mathematical tradition of Copernicus, Kepler, Galileo and the Newton of the *Principia*. It was the experimental tradition of Gilbert, Bacon, Boyle and the Newton of the *Opticks* that was to give birth to the new sciences of heat, electricity and magnetism and chemistry, and these were the sciences that were to make an impact on the industrial revolution.[80] The fortunes of the experimental philosophy in the eighteenth century are, however, beyond the scope of my essay. In the concluding chapter I necessarily focus on questions central to the seventeenth-century scientific revolution. How is power over nature to be achieved? Does Satan exist? And (still under our breath) does God the Father exist? Above all, and related to these three questions, what is the nature of a just society and how is it to be achieved?

Chapter 5

THE APPROPRIATION OF NATURE

> We cannot any longer endure injuries so great and cruel; nor can we without
> being moved by it, behold the insolence of the nobility and gentry: we will
> sooner betake ourselves to arms, and mix heaven and earth in confusion,
> than submit to such atrocities. . . . Look at them and look at us: have we not
> all the same form? And are we not all born in the same way? Why, then,
> should their mode of life . . . be so vastly different from ours? We see plainly
> that matters are come to an extremity, and extremities we are determined to
> try. We will throw down hedges, fill up ditches, lay open the commons, and
> level to the ground whatever enclosures they have put up, no less shamefully
> than meanly.
>
> Robert Ket, 1549, according to Alexander Nevylle,
> *The Commotion in Norfolk*, 1750.

> Inequality of conditions is not to be counted among evils, and M. Jacquelot
> rightly asks those who would have all things equally perfect, why rocks are
> not crowned with leaves or why ants are not peacocks. If equality were
> everywhere requisite, the poor man would set up his claim to it against the
> rich man, the valet against his master.
>
> Leibniz, *Theodicy*, 1710.

1 *The End of Witch Hunting*

By the middle of the eighteenth century we have reached a
period when, generally speaking, men of the upper classes can
look back on many of the beliefs and practices of their immediate
ancestors and congratulate themselves not only on their deliver-
ance but on the part they and their illustrious predecessors had
played in their disappearance. The elimination of witch beliefs
and witch hunting deservedly ranked high on their congratulatory
list. A central question remains, however, to be answered:
Exactly what had brought witch hunting to an end and eliminated
educated belief in the possibility of Satanic witchcraft? Had
'reason' at last triumphed? Were educated men now confident
that nature was, or soon would be, at their command?

Keith Thomas, we recall, claims in his remarkable *Religion and
the Decline of Magic* that it was not the development of
technology in Europe that brought with it a disappearance of
belief in magic and witchcraft but rather the reverse: it was the
prior disappearance of belief in occult and demonic powers that
made possible the technological appropriation of the natural
world that Europe would dramatically accomplish after the
seventeenth century. And, according to Thomas, one of the

principal factors relevant to the disappearance of belief in both magic and witchcraft was the success of the mechanical philosophy. On the one hand, natural magic is held to have collapsed under the onslaught of the mechanical philosophy while, on the other, Thomas claims, the 'absurdity of witchcraft could henceforth be justified by reference to the achievements of the Royal Society and the new philosophy'. Although Thomas warns that some of the early converts to the mechanical philosophy were indecisive on the question of witchcraft, nevertheless in the long run the mechanical philosophy offered a comprehensive explanation for natural phenomena 'which needed no external assistance'. He points out that one of the three members of parliament who initiated the repeal of the witchcraft act in 1736 was John Conduitt, a great admirer of Sir Isaac Newton (who also married Newton's niece) and he cites Richard Bentley, who in an attack on 'Free-thinkers' challenged them: 'What then has lessen'd in England your stories of sorceries? Not the growing sect [of free-thinkers], but the growth of Philosophy and Medicine. No thanks to atheists, but to the Royal Society and College of Physicians; to the Boyles and Newtons, the Sydenhams and Ratcliffs.'[1]

These claims, however, are problematic. While it is true that natural magic and the mechanical philosophy each offered (or attempted to offer) a comprehensive explanation of natural phenomena and in the process either incorporated supposedly supernatural phenomena within the domain of the natural or denied their reality, it is by no means clear which cosmology offered the more cognitively compelling account of the world and its entities. Indeed, I have argued that to the extent the mechanical philosophy triumphed over natural magic it did so, at least in part, not solely because it was an ingenious philosophy (admittedly faced with recalcitrant phenomena), but also because it was regarded as an 'establishment' philosophy that upheld religion and the social order against the perceived threat from natural magic and 'enthusiasts' while at the same time it legitimated and suggested the feasibility of mechanical appropriation of the natural world without impugning the miraculous nature of Christ's works. Given, then, that the mechanical philosophy upheld belief in a Divine Creator and the immortality of minds without presupposing the existence of evil spirits, belief in Satanic magic and the powers of witches became socially unnecessary: Descartes did not believe, Boyle (perhaps a more devout Christian) did. Furthermore, since the *emboîtement* version of the mechanical philosophy relegated God Himself to the position of Divine Creator and Retired Engineer, the Devil

appropriately and necessarily all but dropped out of sight.
Conversely, attempts to transform the mechanistic theism of
Descartes into materialistic atheism tended to be met by
reversions to defence of the reality of Satanic witchcraft and thus
of the existence of God. Although I am therefore to this extent in
agreement with the argument of Thomas (and of Trevor-Roper
presented in Chapter 1) that it was the mechanical philosophy
that helped undermine belief in the reality of witchcraft, I
emphatically depart from Thomas in his tendency to accept the
mechanical philosophy as an unproblematic, indeed 'true', cosmology. The various mechanical philosophies need as much critical
examination as do the acceptance and ultimate rejection of
witchcraft beliefs in early modern Europe. But my immediate
problem is with witchcraft.

The disappearance of the witchcraze

As outlined in Chapter 1, neither the half-way arguments of
Johann Weyer nor the more emphatic and radical arguments of
Michel de Montaigne and Reginald Scot prevailed against the
counter-arguments of Jean Bodin, Nicolas Remy, Martin del Rio
and a host of other writers who believed in the reality of Satanic
intervention, Sabbats and witches' maleficia. The first decades of
the seventeenth century saw an escalation of witch hunting
culminating in those terrible periods in which unrestrained use of
torture invariably turned a handful of initial accusations into
chain reactions of denunciations, followed by mass executions. In
the very decade in which Galileo published his *Dialogue*—in the
support, let us remember, of a most anti-commonsensical
claim—witch hunting reached a ferocious climax. What arguments could opponents of witch hunting give that had not already
been given? What could—indeed, what did—stop the terrible
slaughter?

One work published anonymously in 1631 stands out as an
eloquent condemnation of gross legal abuses in witch trials. The
author was a Catholic priest, Friedrich Spee, who had acted as
father confessor during the height of the witchcraze in Würzburg
and whose experiences convinced him that the overwhelming
majority of convicted people, indeed perhaps all of them, had
been wrongly convicted. There is in this work no argument
against the possibility of diabolical witchcraft as is to be found in
Scot, the reader finding instead a passionate condemnation of
judicial processes, particularly the unrestricted use of torture.
The basic thesis Spee emphasizes is that whether guilty or
innocent, the accused cannot escape: no matter how she reacts,
no matter what she says, in the eyes of her inquisitors she only

thereby further demonstrates her guilt. There can therefore be no possibility of justice. Spee summarizes his long argument as follows: A misfortune happens in a community and immediately, Spee explains, 'malign and idle rumour' points to some poor and helpless 'Gaia'. But Gaia is not at once arrested for it is necessary to investigate her past life. The authorities are then accused by Spee of making the following circular considerations:

Either Gaia has led a bad and improper life, or she has led a good proper one. If a bad one, then, say they, the proof is cogent against her; for from malice to malice the presumption is strong. If, however, she has led a good one, this also is none the less a proof; for thus, they say, are witches wont to cloak themselves and try to seem especially proper.

Upon Gaia's arrest, Spee explains how officers of the law are immediately able to produce further evidence of her guilt:

Either she then shows fear or she does not show it. If she does show it (hearing forsooth of the grievous tortures wont to be used in this matter), this is of itself a proof; for conscience, they say, accuses her. If she does not show it (trusting forsooth in her innocence), this too is a proof; for it is most characteristic of witches, they say, to pretend themselves peculiarly innocent and wear a bold front.

So Spee continues to indict the judicial process: Gaia is tortured; either she confesses the first time or she does not. If she confesses, she is executed; if she does not, she is tortured again, 'For in an excepted crime there is no limit of duration or severity or repetition of the tortures.' Eventually Gaia either confesses, as did nearly all people in Würzburg accused of witchcraft, or she dies under the torture, in which case her accusers claim that she died obstinate and impenitent, preferring to keep faith with her paramour. 'Now, in Heaven's name, I would like to know', Spee cries out in anguish, 'since both she who confesses and she who does not perish alike, what way of escape is there for any, however innocent?'[2]

Of course, all opponents of witch hunting had denounced the use of torture in trials, yet their denunciations had not proved effective. Furthermore, it must be recognized that Spee was denouncing procedures that were excessive even with respect to the horrendous procedures normally used; for example, between 1607 and 1683 in Fribourg, 24 out of 45 men tortured on accusation of witchcraft managed to survive the torture while 51 out of 79 women sucessfully withstood it.[3] But where torture was used almost without legal restraint, then the witchcraze itself led to a situation where the prosecutors themselves called a halt to the chain reaction—indeed, were forced to call a halt. For as long as the stereotype of the witch—an old woman living a solitary and eccentric existence—did not seriously break down, no compelling reason appeared to exist why other citizens should have paid special attention to the plight of old women who, they were assured, were a menace to public security. But where the stereotype did seriously break down in the crazes, where age and sex barriers completely crumbled, where respectable citizens, even magistrates themselves, fell under suspicion and were even executed, in such cases a totally different situation prevailed. H.C.E. Midelfort, who has made a detailed study of witch hunting in southwestern Germany, relates how the city of Rottenburg, where older women had been unproblematically hunted for 30 years, experienced its first crisis of confidence only after the first decades of the seventeenth century in which men and high officials found themselves accused and convicted of witchcraft. Midelfort emphatically summed up his findings by citing the case of the iron Bishop of Würzburg (who had had one of his own nephews executed after conviction of witchcraft):

Even Würzburg, where trials had raged until 1630, produced a solemn reconsideration when Bishop Philip Adolf von Ahrenberg found both his chancellor and himself accused of witchcraft. In an about-face that symbolizes the whole process throughout southwestern Germany, the bishop prohibited further trials and established regular memorial services for the innocent victims of justice.[4]

Men—ruling-class men—still believed in the reality of the Devil and witches, but they had lost confidence in their ability to identify the latter. Thereafter they would take Friedrich Spee's arguments very seriously. Sporadic trials involving the stereotype witch would still occur but the *crazes* would not.

Midelfort's findings apply with less force, however, to those regions where legal excesses of the magnitude found in southwestern Germany occurred less often or less severely. Moreover in regions where respectable citizens faced quite different degrees of danger, during the second half of the seventeenth century even sporadic witch trials were brought or came to an end—in France by the royal edict of 1682, in England in the 1680s with the reluctance of judges to allow conviction. Another puzzling feature of the end of witch hunting is that the about turn, when it came, was sudden—so much so that in his essay *Witchcraft in France and Switzerland* E. William Monter suggests that the 'rapid collapse of witch-hunting in the second half of the seventeenth century is as difficult to explain as its general acceptance until then'.[5]

It is at this point that it would be convenient to be able to invoke the help of the Cartesian mechanical philosophy and later of *emboîtement* theories. But even if acceptance of the Cartesian mechanical image of nature logically demanded the rejection of belief in Satanic witchcraft—which it did not—the acceptance of the mechanical philosophy itself needs sociological explanation, as does the rejection of belief in witchcraft. One suspects that those educated people who both accepted the mechanical philosophy and at the very least declared their opposition to witch hunting did so for the same set of reasons: what one has to explain is rather the (rapid) acceptance of an *anti-demonological* mechanical philosophy or, more generally, an *anti-demonological* natural philosophy.

Keith Thomas puts the emphasis on the blossoming self-confidence of educated male Europeans, stressing that the decisive change which occurred in the seventeenth century was not so much technological as mental. Educated men intended to appropriate the world and they convinced themselves that they would be able to do so (1) because God permitted it, (2) because He had created a mechanical world totally *regular* and *uniform* in behaviour thus making (mechanical) appropriation entirely possible, and (3) because even if Satan and demons do exist they either cannot or do not interfere in the otherwise regular and uniform workings of the mechanical world. A favourable, if not necessary, mental climate was thereby established for the European industrial revolutions of the following centuries.

Plausible, however, as such an explanation in this direction might initially appear, such a dramatic transformation in Western educated man's view of himself and his powers itself needs explanation. Thomas, however, reluctantly declares that the 'ultimate origins of this faith in unaided human capacity remain mysterious'.[6]

2 The New Confidence and the Appropriation of Nature

Qualified optimism: Joseph Glanvill and belief
in Satanic witchcraft
I wish to illustrate this dramatic upsurge in self-confidence of Western ruling classes, especially in England and France, by first looking at a particularly prominent *rearguard* action undertaken by a Fellow of the Royal Society who, while he believed in the possibility, and advocated the necessity, of progress (taking such practical steps as sending to the Society accounts of mining processes and technical advances in Devon), yet at the same time believed in the reality of witchcraft and did his best to convince his sceptical or scoffing colleagues and countrymen of the reality of this phenomenon. First his support for the new philosophy.

Joseph Glanvill (1636–80), born in Devon the son of a

merchant, wrote while studying at Oxford University such a lively defence of the 'New Philosophy' that it was to involve him in prolonged controversy.[7] Published in 1661, *The Vanity of Dogmatising* called for the rejection of claims to certainty of knowledge in favour of useful (mechanical) hypotheses and experimentation. It is significant, for example, that Glanvill, despite an undiluted admiration for Descartes, exposed what he saw as weaknesses of the Cartesian mechanical philosophy: for he pointed out that we cannot understand how the mind is united with and moves the body, neither do we understand the nature of sensation and memory, nor how plants and animals are formed; we do not even understand the cohesion of material bodies which can scarcely be accounted for, as Descartes supposed, by the mutual rest of the parts: '[I]f the *Union* of the *Parts* consist only in *Rest*; it would seem that a bagg of *dust* would be as firm a consistence as that of *Marble* or *Adamant*: A Bar of *Iron* will be as easily broken as a *Tobacco-pipe*; and *Bajazets* Cage had been but a sorry *Prison*.'[8] When despite such protestation Glanvill's work was nevertheless attacked by a Catholic Aristotelian as an endorsement of the mechanical philosophy, and in particular of Hobbesian atheism, Glanvill replied with a revised version which this time included a long preface addressed specifically to the newly constituted Royal Society and which was so fulsome in its praise that it gained Glanvill immediate membership. In this revised work Glanvill took the opportunity of stressing at greater length the primacy of experimentation over premature theorizing: Descartes, Glanvill dubiously asserted, 'intends his principles but for *Hypotheses,* and never pretends that things are really or necessarily as he hath supposed them: but that they may be admitted pertinently to solve the *Phaenomena,* and are convenient supposals for the *use of life*'[9]

But the problem stubbornly remained: how to defend the truth of Christianity given that certain knowledge is impossible and recognizing that Hobbes had committed the unforgivable crime of transforming the mechanistic theism of Cartesian duality into a materialistic atheism. There seemed to be at least one apparently sure defence of both Christianity and the established social hierarchy that Glanvill would not be alone in resorting to. As his friend Henry More had emphasized: 'For assuredly that Saying is not more true in Politick, *No Bishop, no King*; than this in Metaphysick, *No Spirit, no God*.'[10] Mechanical philosophers, and particularly the notorious Hobbes, scoffed at belief in the reality of Satanic witchcraft. Christianity would therefore be defended by proving the reality of witchcraft. In 1666 Glanvill published *A Philosophical Endeavour towards the Defence of the*

Being of Witches and Apparitions, the first blow of a life-long struggle to undermine the arguments of, for Glanvill's liking, far too many of his contemporaries.[11]

The consequence of failure in this essential task would, Glanvill knew, be sobering indeed:

If the Notion of a Spirit be absurd, as is pretended; that of a God, and a Soul distinct from Matter, and Immortal, are likewise Absurdities. And then, That the World was jumbled into this elegant and orderly Fabrick by chance; and that our Souls are only parts of Matter, that come together we know not whence, nor how; and shall again shortly be dissolv'd into those loose Atoms that compound them; That all our Conceptions are but the thrusting of one part of Matter against another; and the Idea's of our Mind meer blind and casual Motions.

What a horrendous outcome! Yet while there are few philosophers, Glanvill believes, who would dare assert such outrageous propositions openly, there are many who would like to. They craftily attack in stages; in particular, 'those that dare not bluntly say, *There is no God,* content themselves, for a fair step and Introduction, to deny there are *Spirits,* or *Witches'.* Small as is this step towards the achievement of their ultimate atheistic goal, the would-be atheists are not entitled to take it: for such a step denies both 'the plain Evidence of the Senses of Mankind' and the excellent arguments that demonstrate the reality of witchcraft. Glanvill sadly recognizes, however, that

those that deny the being of Witches, do it not out of ignorance of those Heads of Argument, of which probably they have heard a thousand times; But from an apprehension that such a belief is absurd, and the things impossible. And upon these presumptions they contemn all Demonstrations of this nature, and are hardned against Conviction.

What, therefore, has Glanvill to combat? He tells us that it is a 'mighty Confidence grounded upon nothing, that *swaggers,* and *Huffs,* and *swears* there are no *Witches'.* But such men cannot be combatted. Glanvill will therefore leave them to wallow in their own dogmatic convictions and address himself only to reasonable but misguided men.[12]

Now such reasonable men, Glanvill maintains, disbelieve in the existence of the spirit world because they cannot believe that poor miserable spirits can do such marvellous things as transport witches through the air or enable witches to raise storms and tempests; hence they come to the conclusion that 'the whole mystery of Witchcraft is but an illusion of crasie Imagination'.[13] Glanvill therefore sets himself the modest task of demonstrating only the *possibility* of the marvellous phenomena in question. For this will be *sufficient* to undermine all but the most dogmatic incredulity.

Glanvill tells the reader that in the first place the 'more absurd and unaccountable' the witchcraft phenomena the more he is disposed to believe in the veracity of the witnesses.[14] For men, he protests, do not usually seek to tell stories of plainly impossible happenings but on the contrary of plainly possible ones. That throughout the ages witnesses have testified to the most incredible events is therefore testimony, Glanvill claims, to the possiblity and reality of such events. That some of the witnesses may have been fools, knaves or madmen can in no way mean that all of them have so been. Glanvill is forced to the conclusion that at least some of the witchcraft phenomena really happened. (Montaigne, we might note, would have been turning in his grave as Glanvill produced this argument!)

Yet how can 'mere' spirits be adjudged capable of transporting witches and of giving witches the power to raise storms? Glanvill reminds the reader that we do not know, for example, how our minds move our bodies, nor how foetuses are formed. This being so—that we are ignorant of how the most obvious things about us are caused or come into being—there can be no cause for wonder that we are ignorant of the powers of spirits, which are beings so very far removed from us in nature. Whether therefore the question is that of the power of mind over body, the formation of a foetus, the transportation of witches, or the raising of storms, Glanvill argues that 'Matters of Fact well proved ought not to be denied, because we cannot conceive how they can be performed'. (Is it fair play to point out here that *emboîtement* mechanical philosophers would later deny not only the possibility of witchcraft but also and perhaps with even more conviction the possibility of embryonic transformation and development?!) But Glanvill *can* conceive how the various witchcraft phenomena might be brought about—or, rather, he claims that he can. There is no difficulty, he writes, in conceiving how a spirit may transport a witch through the air. And that is that! There is even less difficulty if it is supposed that the witch's soul may leave her body to be guided by the spirit to the place of general rendezvous. 'On which *Hypothesis*', Glanvill suggests, 'the witch's annointing her self before she takes her flight, may perhaps serve to keep the Body tenantable, and in fit disposition to receive the Spirit at its return'. As for the witches' raising of storms, it is all the work of the evil spirits, the various ceremonies commonly employed serving either to entertain the witches or to deceive them into thinking that they have such power by themselves. But despite the demons' deception in the raising of storms, witches truly have the power of the 'evil eye' by means of which they are able to cause disease in people of frail temperament. Such power, Glanvill suggests, is perhaps given to the witch by her Familiar who when sucking her simultaneously 'infuseth some poisonous ferment into her'. But whatever the nature of her evil power 'this kind of Agency', Glanvill asserts, 'is as conceivable as any of those Qualities, which our Ignorance hath called *Sympathy* and *Antipathy*; the reality of which we doubt not, though the manner of Action be unknown'.[15] As for Reginald Scot, whose *Discoverie of Witchcraft* had just been republished, Glanvill informs the reader that 'His Reasonings are Trifling and Childish; and when He ventures at Philosophy, He is little better than absurd.' In particular, Glanvill argues, if we are allowed to take such liberties with Biblical texts as Scot takes, then the Bible may be interpreted to mean whatever we wish it to mean. Glanvill continues with a long series of arguments. What is of more than passing interest, I think, is his conclusion to these arguments, especially the sad remark that 'there is nothing can render the thoughts of this odd Life tollerable, but the expectation of another' and his confession that this is the principal reason why he is 'much concerned for the justification of the belief in *Witches*, Because it suggests palpable and current Evidence of our *Immortality*'.[16]

Admittedly, Glanvill is optimistic that mankind can learn through the experimental philosophy to control and appropriate the natural world even if certain knowledge of nature is forever denied humans. 'To them, that come after us', he comments, 'it may be as ordinary to buy a *pair of wings* to fly into remotest *Regions*, as now a *pair* of *Boots* to ride a *Journey*'.[17] Also there is little fear in Glanvill's writings: the world is not in decay but is entering its prime with the best yet to come as the experimental philosophy proceeds. Nevertheless, this life, which is not worth living in itself, is made tolerable for Glanvill only by the promise of a future immortality. It is therefore not basically in order to instil fear into his readers' hearts that this Fellow of the Royal Society writes of witches (although the souls of the wicked after death will certainly suffer terrible torment). It is rather to reassure himself—and his readers—that this miserable earthly life is not all there is. It is worth bearing in mind that only a few months before the publication of Glanvill's *Philosophical Endeavour* some 70,000 Londoners died of the plague and in the year of publication two-thirds of London was destroyed by fire. Life was harsh and not only for the unprivileged masses.

Let us now note that when John Webster attacked Glanvill's belief in the reality of witchcraft with his *Displaying of Supposed Witchcraft*, published in 1677, not only Henry More sprang to Glanvill's defence but Robert Boyle as well. Glanvill was especially upset because Webster's book, after receiving an at least not unfavourable report by three Royal Society members, had been accorded the imprimatur of Jonas Moore, vice-president of the Society in 1676. In his book the Hermeticist chemist and parson (who, like Glanvill, was interested in mining techniques and had published *Metallographia* in 1671) attempted to deny the reality of witchcraft by turning Glanvill's own arguments against their author. If the powers of nature are as yet totally unknown, then it 'must needs be folly, madness, and derogative against Gods power in Nature' to attribute the effects supposedly due to witchcraft to 'wicked, fallen and degenerate Demons'. No powers beyond those found in nature need be supposed by the rational philosopher. Moreover, the learned understand what 'great abstruse things may be lawfully done by Natural Magick' and what 'great Feats may be performed by the Mathematicks and Mechanical Arts'. Indeed, Webster argued, the many 'continued discoveries of these learned and indefatigable persons that are of the Royal Society' conclusively demonstrate our previous ignorance of almost all the true causes of things, and it is only through our blindness that we have attributed certain phenomena to the operation of demons that were truly wrought by nature and 'thereby not smally augmented and advanced this gross and absurd opinion of the power of witches'. Not, however, that Webster wishes to deny the reality of the spirit world and in particular of the existence of Satan and evil angels. What it is here important to bear in mind is that 'when the Almighty maketh use of Satan or his Angels, they are only so let loose that he hath a hook in their Nostrils, and their Necks in a chain, that they can act no more nor no further than he ordereth and gives them leave to accomplish. . . . .' While Robert Boyle, Fellow of the Royal Society, hastened to reassure Glanvill that there was no truth in the rumour, put about by Webster, that he no longer believed in the account of a famous demonic happening, Henry More, Fellow of the Royal Society, wrote to Glanvill an impassioned letter of support, strongly criticizing Webster's arguments. 'But what', asked More, 'will this profane Shuffler stick to do in a dear regard to his beloved Hags, of whom he is a sworn Advocate and resolved Patron, right or wrong?'[18]

It might seem that there is a paradox here. Glanvill is a champion of the Royal Society whose appeal to him led to the writing and publication in 1688 of Glanvill's *Plus Ultra: or, the progress and advancement of knowledge since the days of Aristotle.* More, too, was a Fellow of the Royal Society while Boyle was its most illustrious Fellow and practising experimental philosopher. Yet these three philosophers and Fellows subscribed to belief in the reality of witchcraft. Clearly, therefore, membership of the Society is no guarantee of disbelief in witchcraft.[19] But Fellows there were who certainly did not believe. Let me now turn to a work that displays such an excessive degree of confidence that belief in witchcraft is effectively banished.

Unqualified confidence: Thomas Sprat, control of nature and the 'experimental philosophy' of the Royal Society

In 1663 John Wilkins proposed a young Oxford graduate for membership of the Royal Society on the understanding that he would write a history of the Society in its defence. Duly elected, Thomas Sprat included in his now famous 'history' a (premature) celebration of the disappearance of belief in evil spirits from which a quotation was given in Chapter 1—albeit with the comment that Sprat offered no evidence to back up his affirmations. What, however, Sprat certainly did offer was an impassioned defence of the Society in everything it publicly stood for and everything it publicly stood against.

The origin of the Royal Society can be traced to regular meetings of natural philosophers in London from the end of 1644 onwards, leading members of the so-called Philosophical College being John Wilkins, John Wallis and William Petty. Having agreed to promote 'the *New Philosophy* or *Experimental Philosophy*', the members of the Philosophical College were, Wallis relates, required to pay a weekly contribution towards the cost of experiments.[20] The 'Philosophical College' was no mere talking shop! Wilkins, we remember, had already done much to promote the Copernican world system; now in 1648 he published *Mathematical Magic,* a treatise on the mechanical principles of machines from which, he wrote, 'there is also much *real Benefit* to be learned; particularly for such Gentlemen as employ their Estates in those chargeable Adventures of Draining Mines, Coalpits, etc, who may from hence learn the chief Grounds and Nature of Engines'.[21] After the defeat of Charles in the Civil War and the subsequent purge of Oxford, Wallis and Petty left London for Oxford to become professors of geometry and anatomy respectively while Wilkins was appointed Warden of Wadham College where he was able to form the successful Oxford 'Philosophical Society' (which lasted until 1690). With the restoration, however, of Charles II in 1660 these men returned to London, though not to remain inactive. At a meeting in Gresham College the following November they and others formally proposed the creation of a 'College for the promoting of Physico-Mathematical Experimental Learning' with Wilkins elected chairman and a list of 41 potential members drawn up most of whom were, for rather obvious reasons, Royalist. The

King approved of the College and two years later confirmed the charter of 'The Royal Society for the Improvement of Natural Knowledge'. A courtier was made president, Wilkins and Henry Oldenburg joint Secretaries, and Robert Hooke, Boyle's former assistant, Curator of Experiments. The following year in 1663 Hooke observed that the 'business and design of the Royal Society is: To improve the knowledge of naturall things, and all useful Arts, Manufactures, Mechanick practises, Engines and Inventions by Experiments—(not meddling with Divinity, Metaphysics, Moralls, Politicks, Grammar, Rhetoric or Logick)'.[22] With an eye on the opening theme of the chapter let us note that Meric Casaubon, Churchman and vigorous opponent of the Royal Society, expressed in 1669 what would become a typical complaint against the Society and its 'experimental philosophers': 'Men that are much fixed upon matter and secondary causes and sensual objects . . . may in time . . . forget that there be such things in the world as *Spirtis*, . . . and at last that there is a God, and that their souls are immortal.'[23] It would be Sprat's task to defend the Society against such detractors and detractions.

Sprat's *History* is a remarkable document and affords its readers an insight into the beliefs and aspirations of some of the more prominent of the Society's founding members, especially Wilkins. Or, rather more accurately, into the beliefs and aspirations that these founding members thought it was in their interests to have publicly proclaimed through the considerable writing talents of Thomas Sprat. In what follows I shall not go sequentially through the arguments and examples given by Sprat but will highlight those of his arguments that appear to me to shed most light on the social function of the new philosophy as advanced and advocated by Sprat and the Fellows supervising his work.

The principal purpose of the new philosophy, Sprat candidly admits, is to acquire power over nature, an ambition whose eventual realization is guaranteed by the Society's practice of the experimental philosophy as described and promulgated by Francis Bacon. The Society, Sprat writes, will therefore not accumulate a 'confus'd heap of vain and useless particulars', nor will its endeavours be too closely circumscribed by prematurely drawn general principles. On the contrary, it will be by a 'painful digging and toiling in *Nature*' guided by an 'inviable correspond-ence between the hand, and the brain' that the Society will ensure that knowledge of nature always and steadily advances, depend-ing neither on chance fortune nor the skills of a particular individual. Correct method is therefore all important. To this end, the experimental philosophers of the Royal Society will shun all rhetoric and impassioned speech and strive to achieve a 'Mathematical plainness', a 'close, naked, natural way of speaking', which Sprat sees as similar to that found among artisans, countrymen and merchants.[24] Indeed, the Royal Society will not need to make propaganda either by ostentation of ceremonies or by pomp of words because it will be known by the best propaganda of all, the 'unanswerable Arguments of real Productions'. For even if at first sight the activities of experimental philosophers do not always appear relevant to the concerns of practical men, nevertheless both groups of men have interest in the same thing, namely matter: 'It is *matter,* a viable and sensible *matter,* which is the object of their *labours*', informs Sprat. It follows that it can only be a question of time before the experimental philosophy and technical works mutually support each other: 'This likeness of their Imployments', Sprat exclaims, 'will soon make the one excel in the other'. Eventually, by means of experimental philosophy and works, man will gain a total command over the things of this world and thus 'make them all serviceable to the quiet and peace and plenty of Man's life'. What greater happiness could be asked for than this? It can only be, Sprat replies, to take advantage of such high ground to look the nearer into heaven.[25]

Herein lies, as we have seen, one of the fundamental criticisms of the Royal Society, which Sprat and its members must conclusively answer. For while there can be no objection to seeking mastery over nature by that lawful and sure method advocated by Bacon, involving as it does a necessarily difficult and tedious labour, will not such concentration on the material world and its successful appropriation inevitably make men forgetful of religion? Will experimental philosophers be able to detect the presence of God amidst all that matter to which they devote their lives? Sprat's reply is that it is absurd to consider the experimental philosophy an enemy of religion. On the contrary, the experimental philosophy is its friend.

''Tis true his *employment* is about material things', Sprat unashamedly admits of the experimental philosopher. But the experimental study of material things, far from making the philosopher disbelieve in the existence of invisible beings, reinforces his belief in them. For in every work of nature that is studied the experimental philosopher knows that not only is there a gross substance which presents itself to all men's senses but that there is also an infinite subtlety of parts which cannot be detected by the sharpest sense. Hence, Sprat concludes, 'what the *Scripture* relates of the Purity of *God,* of the Spirituality of his *Nature,* and that of *Angels,* and the *Souls* of men, cannot seem incredible to him'.[26] Confirmation that the experimental study of nature convinces its proponents of the existence of God lies in the fact, Sprat argues, that God seldom or never chooses to perform miracles in times when natural knowledge prevails but only in dark and ignorant ages: for the experimental philosopher is clearly in no need of miracles since he cannot fail to see the impressions of God's footsteps in His creatures. Likewise the experimental philosopher cannot fail to believe in the Divinity of Christ since the truth of the Gospels has been proved to him 'his own way'; Sprat excuses his boldness but what he means by this is that the miracles in which God chose to reveal the Divine Message may be regarded as being *'Divine Experiments* of his *Godhead'*. Moreover, since recognition of what is supernatural depends on prior understanding of what is according to nature, no person is more competent to identify a miracle than an experimental philosopher. Reason, however, has its limits. Since not even the experimental philosopher can grasp such unfathomable depths as *'Gods Decrees,* his *Immateriality,* his *Eternity,* and the Holy Mystery of the *Trinity'*, Sprat readily concedes that 'a plain *Believing* is at last acknowledged by all to be our only Refuge'. The point has been made, however, that experimental philosophers are at least as devout as other men, and probably much more so. The truths of Christianity are therefore not only safe but strengthened in the hands of the practitioners of the new philosophy.[27]

Sprat's claim that God does not perform miracles in an age of natural knowledge—which above all defines the age of the Royal Society—allows him to attempt to demolish the pretensions and impostures of those enemies of both King and men of property, the sects and enthusiasts who claim direct communion with God and who are always invoking the occurrence of miracles to underwrite their fraudulent claims. How contemptible are these men, Sprat protests. By claiming that miracles are but everyday occurrences, the enthusiasts debase the Authority of the True and Primitive Miracles. On the other hand, how different are the true believers, the men of the Royal Society. The experimental philosopher, witnessing the presence of God in all His works, holds it sufficient that God guides His creation in its course of causes and effects and is not forever having to intervene in order to adjust His Creation. How much superior, after all, is the Prince who rules his subjects peaceably by his known and standing laws than the Prince who is often forced to make use of extraordinary justice to punish or reward. The true philosopher must therefore, Sprat argues, be most unwilling to grant that anything exceeds the force of nature except where a full evidence convinces him to the contrary. Although this correct and devout attitude is misguidedly called by the ignorant a blindness of mind, or hardness of heart, there can be no doubt that the experimental philosopher is totally superior to the enthusiast who 'pollutes his *Religion* with his own passions'. The men of the Royal Society, Sprat continually emphasizes, have at all times attempted to free experimental philosophy *'from the Artifice, and Humors, and Passions of Sects'*.[28]

Experimental philosophers, then, are enemies of religious enthusiasts. But this does not necessarily mean that experimental philosophers are automatically loyal and obedient to the King and civil government. Is it conceivable that by supporting the Royal Society and its experimental philosophers the King might be inadvertently undermining his own ruling position? Sprat hastens to reassure any Prince that, in backing experimental philosophy, he would never at the same time be backing subversion. It is sufficient to note that violent desires, malicious envies and indeed all the griefs by which men make their own lives miserable have as their principal cause idleness—but experimental philosophers are never idle. It is also obvious that their acquired soberness of thought and inquiry, and their refusal to allow wings to their understanding, will likewise be characteristic features of their attitudes to civil matters. Experimental philosophers know that the best way to aid mankind is through the advancement of knowledge and certainly not through civil strife 'in which both the Conquerors and the Conquer'd have always reason to repent of their success'. Above all, Sprat continues, experimental philosophers are not proud and haughty men—and therefore potentially rebellious men—but are constantly made humble by nature that all too often makes them painfully aware of their fallibility. Furthermore, if it is such a difficult undertaking to order the motions of senseless things, experimental philosophers realize how much more difficult it must be 'to rule the restless minds of men'. Knowing that it is a full-time task to command nature, they necessarily respect and admire the Prince who has on his hands an altogether more difficult task. The Prince has nothing—absolutely nothing—to fear from experimental philosophers. For last but not least, they realize that their programme of work is so vast that it cannot be performed without the assistance of the Prince: the experimental philosophy 'will not therefore undermine his *Authority* whose aid it implores'. The experimental philosopher has only one objective which is control of the natural world.[29]

Sprat's *History* is characterized throughout by the conviction that given sufficient time experimental philosophers will achieve total command over nature. Since God Himself no longer intervenes in its course, the way is clear for experimental philosophers to learn nature's inviolable laws and thus achieve in time a total control over things. But are there not evil spirits and such like, outside the control of men, that make men's total control of the things of this world in principle impossible? Sprat is contemptuous: not only is experimental philosophy manifestly possible but experimental philosophy itself, not scholastic philosophy, has already rid the world of whole armies of invisible spirits. This is Sprat's long statement of optimism:

And as for the *terrors* and *misapprehensions* which commonly confound weaker minds, and make mens hearts to fail and boggle at Trifles; there is so little hope of having them remov'd by *Speculation* alone, that it is evident they were first produc'd by the most *contemplative* men among the *Ancients*; and chiefly prevail'd of late years, when that way of *Learning* florish'd. The *Poets* began of old to impose the deceit. They to make all things look more venerable than they were, devis'd a thousand false *Chimaeras*; on every *Field, River, Grove,* and *Cave* they bestow'd a *Fantasm* of their own making: with these they amaz'd the world; these they cloath'd with what shapes they pleas'd; by these they pretended, that all Wars, and Counsails, and Actions of men were administred. And in the modern *Ages* these *Fantastical Forms* were reviv'd, and possess'd *Christendom*, in the very height of the *Scholemens* time: An infinit number of *Fairies* haunted every house; all Churches were fill'd with *Apparitions*; men began to be frighted from their *Cradles*, which fright continu'd to their *Graves*, and their Names also were made the causes of scaring others. All which abuses if those acute *Philosophers* did not promote, yet they were never able to overcome; nay, even not so much as King *Oberon* and his invisible *Army*.

But from the time in which the *Real Philosophy* has appear'd, there is scarce any whisper remaining of such *horrors*: Every man is unshaken at those Tales, at which his *Ancestors* trembled: the cours of things goes quietly along, in its own true channel of *Natural Causes* and *Effects*. For this we are beholden to *Experiments*; which though they have not yet completed the discovery of the true world, yet they have already vanquish'd those wild inhabitants of the false worlds, that us'd to astonish the minds of men. A Blessing for which we ought to be thankful, if we remember, that it is one of the greatest Curses that God pronounces on the wicked, *That they shall fear where no fear is.*[30]

This is an impressive statement of faith: God exists and keeps the universe in being but no longer intervenes; the only way for men to command nature is through the experimental philosophy; angels, good or evil, play no part in this process; the overwhelming majority of phantoms, ghosts and such like are mere chimera. Sprat intends to have his cake and eat it: the experimental philosophy convinces men of the reality of invisible beings; yet the experimental philosophy has dismissed whole armies of phantom shapes!

How can Sprat and those Fellows of the Royal Society supervising his work be so optimistic? Sprat's *History* appeared in

1667, only a year or so after the devastating plague of London which we should not forget claimed some 70,000 victims, followed immediately by the Great Fire of London, which destroyed two-thirds of the city. Enthusiasts and millenarians pointed to these two catastrophic events as a sign of God's displeasure with the King and as a sign of the long expected Second Coming. The year, after all, was 1666, the *annus mirabilis*. In opposition to the enthusiasts and millenarians Sprat offers his countrymen not the Second Coming but the experimental philosophy, not Christ's return to earth but the 'new philosophy' and the institutionalization of the 'new philosophy': just 'as this *terrible Disease* and *Conflagration* were not able to darken the honour of our Princes Armes', he announces, 'from the sad effects of these disasters, there may a new, and a powerful *Argument* be rais'd, to move us to double our labours, about the *Secrets of Nature*'.[31] Sprat acknowledges that although the terrible evil of the plague has hitherto defeated all former remedies, he insists that there is no reason to think it will continue so for ever. Why should we not believe that in the vast compass of nature an antidote is available? If when the plague strikes, men only accuse the anger of God or the cruelty of nature then they lay the blame where it is not justly to be laid. The truth is that men have only themselves to blame that such difficult cures are still outside their powers.

Men must aim high, Sprat insists, and never give up trying. If they realize that the cures for the mildest diseases were discovered only after prolonged inquiry, then each such cure, each battle won, should raise still higher our expectations of further conquests, even over this greatest terror of mankind. 'Distrust, and despair of our own indeavours', Sprat exhorts, 'is as great a hindrance in the progress of the *True Philosophy* as it is wont to be in the rise of men's private fortunes'. One must recognize, Wilkins' protegé emphasizes, that nature, just like a mistress, yields sooner to the forward and the bold; thus if men are to succeed in their 'Courtship to Nature' (Bacon's metaphor of rape of nature is, we note, changed by Sprat to one of courtship), then it is impossible that experimental philosophers can enterprise or attempt too much. Eventually nature will yield and the rewards will be great: 'The Beautiful Bosom of *Nature* will be Expos'd to our view', Sprat rejoices, 'we shall enter into its *Garden*, and tast of its *Fruits*, and satisfy ourselves with its *plenty*'.[32]

The 'masculine philosophy' of the Royal Society
Perhaps we ought to note here (I return to the theme later) that

not only were members of the Royal Society *men* but, as the Secretary Henry Oldenburg had stated in a preface to a book by Boyle, they were men whose business it was 'to raise a Masculine Philosophy', one 'whereby the Mind of Man may be ennobled with the knowledge of the solid Truths'.[33] *What is feminine had necessarily to be excluded from the Society's true philosophy'.* While it was, of course, Eve who had first succumbed to the wiles of the serpent, Glanvill lamented and reminded his readers that 'our *masculine powers* are deeply sharers of the consequential mischiefs'; and that in so far as men allow their passions to hold sway over their reason, the '*Women* in us', Glanvill warned, 'still prosecutes a deceit'.[34] Then again, as Oldenburg confided to Boyle in a letter of 1659: 'ye French naturalists are more discursive than active or experimental. In the meantime the Italian proverb is true: *Le parole sono femine, li fattj maschij*' (Words are feminine, facts—or, rather, deeds—are masculine)![35] The members of the Royal Society consequently intended to prune their speech of all unnecessary eloquence; Glanvill tells the Society that he too is 'more gratified with *manly sense*, flowing in a *natural* and *unaffected Eloquence*, than in the *musick* and *curiosity* of *fine Metaphors* and *dancing periods*'.[36] It is obvious why the Society should want to establish a specifically masculine philosophy: for, as Sprat explains, 'The *Wit* that is founded on the *Arts* of men's hands is masculine and durable.'[37] God's 'great... pregnant automaton'—as Boyle called nature—will thereby come under men's control;[38] and there can be no greater male triumph than this, 'to know the wayes of *captivating Nature*, and making her *subserve* our *purposes*' for the benefit of mankind. How much more glorious are such successes, Glanvill rejoices, than 'such *ruinous ones* as are dyed in *humane blood*, and *cloathed* in the *livery* of *Cruelty* and *Slaughter*'.[39]

A basic difference between Glanvill and Sprat is that Glanvill believes religion is under a greater threat from materialistic atheism than does Sprat. Hence Glanvill reverts to attempts to prove the reality of witchcraft as a first step to making belief in the existence of a spirit world credible. But Glanvill is not afraid that the Devil is about to take over Christendom; as we have seen, he merely wants to reassure himself of his own immortality. Since Sprat, on the other hand, believes that Christianity is secure, he has no need to invoke fear of the Devil. On the contrary, he has—or displays—supreme confidence in the powers of ruling-class men to manage their own affairs, and, with the aid of the experimental (masculine) philosophy, to dominate the world of matter. 'For they shall fear where no fear is'! That is God's curse on the wicked. Sprat and members of the Royal

Society are not wicked and they do not fear. They and their successors believe they will inherit the earth.

Ruling-class confidence: Colbert and the Paris Academy

Above all this applies to Jean Baptiste Colbert (1619–83), statesman, ruler, and founder of the Paris Academy of Sciences. As the powerful Minister of Finance under Louis XIV, Colbert illustrates perfectly the rising confidence of the ruling calss and its concomitant dismissal of supernatural interference in both the course of nature and in that class's attempt to gain control of the 'material' of the world.

Colbert's intention was to make France under his leadership and control the greatest economic power in Europe, indeed in the world. But manufactured, not agricultural, products were to be the source of France's wealth. For manufactures, Colbert explained, are under men's control—'they depend on the art, industry and application of men'—whereas agricultural products are liable 'to a thousand accidents before arriving at maturity'.[40] Colbert, together with Louis XIV, intended to make France also the greatest military power, possessing both a large standing army able to suppress any peasant revolt and a military fleet able to control the high seas in defence of French shipping. Accordingly, Colbert in 1665 initiated a scheme for the development of the French armament industry incorporating a programme to manufacture iron guns, iron being less expensive than bronze and France having large supplies of iron ore.[41] The following year in 1666 Colbert founded the Paris Academy of Sciences which held its first meeting in the private library of the King. Unlike the members of the Royal Society, the members of the Paris Academy enjoyed a salary from the King and thus were not plagued by financial problems that so beset the Royal Society. In the same year Colbert also created a commission which was assigned the task of examining the work methods of artisans and technicians and of studying defects of their instruments. The members of the Paris Academy had had their mandate drawn up for them by Huygens (invited to Paris by Colbert) and which Colbert had approved. In a word, the members of the Paris Academy, unlike those of the stillborn General Academy, were to be 'technocrats': 'The company will be composed', wrote Huygens, 'of the most learned persons available in all the true sciences, such as geometry, mechanics, optics, astronomy, geography, etc., in physics, medicine, chemistry, anatomy, etc., or in the practice of the arts such as architecture, fortification, sculpture, painting, drawing, the channelling and raising of water, metallurgy, agriculture, navigation, etc.' In the meetings, reassured Huygens, 'there will never be a discussion of the mysteries of religion or the affairs of state; and if there is at times talk of metaphysics, morals, history, or grammar, it will only be in passing and in relation to physics or to exchanges among men'. The academy was to have two sections, a mathematical one including all the 'exact sciences' and a physical one with more 'experimental sciences', such as physics, chemistry, anatomy, and botany.[42] In Huygens' proposal to Colbert in 1666 there is (from our point of view) the interesting declaration of intent to examine 'the explosive force of gunpowder enclosed (in small amounts) in an iron or very thick copper box'.[43]

Colbert, as it turned out, was to experience great difficulty in establishing a satisfactory armaments industry based on iron rather than bronze. Indeed in 1670 most of the guns made blew up on being tested but Colbert persisted. In 1671 he felt completely discouraged.[44] Nevertheless, during the years 1670–72 Colbert advised the King to commute the death penalty passed on convicted witches by the Parlements of Pau, Rouen, and Bordeaux to perpetual banishment. In response to the anguished request by the Parlement of Rouen to allow the executions to take place and future trials to proceed, the King confirmed his decision and, as Colbert had recommended, ordered the immediate suspension of all prosecutions.[45] Witchcraft trials were an administrative inconvenience and anachronism to this chief minister intent on the appropriation of the material world, no matter what the difficulties. In the middle of the 1670s Colbert requested the members of the Academy to prepare a report on the existing state of the technical arts.[46] By 1680 the factories Colbert had established at Périgord and Angoumois gave satisfactory results producing guns 'lighter and better than those of Sweden', but the manufactures established in Nivernais and Burgundy were total failures.[47] Why the cannon cast in one place remained brittle and the cannon cast in another proved reliable remained an insoluble mystery for the technicians of Colbert's time. Nature might be obstreperous but this was not due to witchcraft or diabolical interference: in 1682 Louis XIV promulgated a Royal Decree which made sorcerers indictable as charlatans, subject to the death penalty only if they added either poisoning or sacrilege to their essentially harmless although always thoroughly deceitful practices.[48]

The confidence of the new philosophers
The new philosophy has restored autonomy to man in his confrontation with nature and man will triumph (the term 'man' I

use as a shorthand for men of the ruling and privileged classes in western Europe). Whether he will triumph as a mechanic over an engine, a man-midwife over a woman in labour, a seducer over a mistress, or as a rapist over his female victim, he will triumph. The unbounded confidence of natural philosophers is quite astonishing. They see themselves as men of a new age, who will make a new age, and they begin by forging a cosmology in which God is effectively relegated to a spectator's seat while the Devil drops from view altogether. It is not that they do not have reason for confidence. Printing, the compass and gunpowder define a new age. The ships of western Europe have discovered new lands and have shown Ptolemy the cartographer to be wrong. Western territorial expansion overseas has begun. The slave trade is thriving. Copernicus has successfuly challenged a 2000 year-old cosmology. Ancient authority is not always right; indeed it is usually wrong. Undoubtedly an 'unknown *Peru* of Nature' awaits discovery.[49] After 150 years of political and social upheaval, something like stability has returned to western Europe and confidence is returning to the ruling classes. While Reginald Scot could say in 1584 that 'truth must not be measured by time: for everie old opinion is not sound',[50] some 100 years later Pierre Bayle could say with far more evidence to back him up than was available to Scot: 'I have said it before, and I say it again; it is the purest delusion to suppose that because an idea has been handed down from time immemorial to succeeding generations, it may not be entirely false'.[51] Only a few years before the apocalyptic year of 1666, Henry Power was convinced that the world was neither in decay nor at its end, the belief in which, he noted, though it had been a pervasive belief of all past ages, had now risen to a crescendo. But in place of Christ's Second Coming Power looked forward to the establishment of the 'new philosophy': 'Me-thinks, I see how all the old Rubbish must be thrown away, and the rotten Buildings be overthrown, and carried away with so powerful an Inundation. These are the days that must lay a new Foundation of a more magnificent Philosophy, never to be overthrown . . . a true and permanent Philosophy.'[52] Fontenelle thanked the ancients for exhausting all the false philosophies that were possible. He, like Power, supported the mechanical philosophy. In his famous 1699 'hymn to science' that commemorated the rejuvenation of the Paris Academy of Sciences Fontenelle joined Kepler and Wilkins before him in a declaration of confidence in the powers of the new philosophy: 'The application of science to nature will constantly grow in scope and intensity and we shall go on from one marvel to another; the day will come when man will be able to fly by fitting on wings to keep him in the air; the art will increase more and more till one day we shall be able to fly to the moon.' What confidence![53]

Christian mechanical philosophers against witch hunting

It is exactly this kind of confidence, Keith Thomas has suggested, that had as a welcome consequence the disappearance of witch hunting and the decline of belief in the Devil's powers. Of course, sincere Christians, no matter how personally optimistic they were, found it difficult to deny at least the *possibility* of Satanic witchcraft. As Voltaire reasonably mocked in the eighteenth century: 'A divine may write against Belzebub as much as he pleases, but he must of necessity admit his existence; he may then explain the difficult texts if he can.'[54] Nicolas Malebranche therefore had no alternative but to admit that it is 'indubitable that real Witches deserve death'. But otherwise Malebranche attempted to explain witchcraft away as a good mechanical philosopher might: 'When men talk to us, they engrave in our brain traces similar to those which they possess.' Thus a shepherd who really believes he has been to the sabbat easily convinces his wife and children by his 'natural eloquence' of the reality of the night's strange events, thereby leaving definite traces in their brains. If as is usually the case the shepherd's dependents eventually decide to go to the sabbat to see for themselves, they rub themselves with a certain drug, and upon falling fast asleep 'the traces the Shepherd had formed in their brains open up' so that they consequently experience the sensation of being at the sabbat. It is not surprising that after a few mutual discussions their stories of nocturnal, orgiastic events soon concur. Perhaps such people, Malebranche grumbles, should not be treated as completely innocent since they do desire to attend a sabbat, but nevertheless sabbats are completely fictitious events. The Devil has no power over Christians who should tremble before God alone. Malebranche admonishes: 'But when men talk to us about the power of the devil, it is a ridiculous weakness to be frightened and troubled.'[55]

Likewise the Protestant pastor Balthasar Bekker had to admit that the Devil exists. However in his *The World Bewitched* of 1691 (abridged and translated into English in 1700 as *The World turn'd Upside down*) Bekker claims that Scripture and reason together 'prove the Empire of the Devil is but a Chimera, and that he has neither such a Power, nor such an Administration as is ordinarily ascribed to him'.[56] Bekker examines various cases of witchcraft phenomena and concludes that there is not a single example in which there are not grounds for doubt, 'in which one doesn't have good cause to suspect that there is deception'. To the argument (as expressed by Glanvill) that if a large majority of witchcraft phenomena are shown to be fraudulent this does not mean that *all* such phenomena are fraudulent, Bekker responds that on the contrary if just one out of a hundred such cases can be shown to be natural or fraudulent, he considers himself entitled to conclude that the remaining ninety-nine also are. Bekker mocks at the accounts given as to how the Devil can perform marvellous feats; the Devil must work with matter and motion as humans must and the feats of the Devil must be explained in such terms. 'There is no argument so absurd', Bekker writes, 'as that of attributing an unusual effect to an occult or unknown cause, but above all, to these sorts of [spiritual] intellects, as people want to do, in order to draw as a consequence that they have the power and the capacity to do such things. Why not rather investigate deeply into knowledge of Nature, in order to be able to unite things corporeal into things corporeal?'[57] Bekker takes the argument a step further. Since it is absurd to seek explanations of events that really can and do happen in terms of demonic interventions, it is of even greater absurdity to seek demonic explanations for events that have never happened and in the nature of things cannot happen. Bekker wants the nonsense stopped. Christians and mechanical philosophers must relegate the Devil to the wilderness where he belongs and seek explanations in terms of matter and motion for only those events that truly do happen *and which are not imaginary*. In his *History of Oracles* published anonymously in 1686 Bernard de Fontenelle made the same point: 'What in my view brings home the extent of our ignorance', he lamented, 'is not so much the facts which really *are* facts, but which we cannot explain, as the explanations we produce of the facts which are *not* facts at all'.[58] Once again, the mechanical philosopher is called upon to supply explanations of all genuine phenomena.

Does, however, the breakdown of the mechanical philosophy at the hands of Newton threaten such arguments against Satanic intervention in daily life? As we have seen, Newton and his immediate followers believed that his gravitational theory amply demonstrated the existence of God; there was therefore no need to invoke the Devil to uphold Christianity. While his teacher Barrow had been a believer in the reality of demonic witchcraft, Newton himself progressed from a belief in the reality of Satanic intervention to one of total denial. Thus in discussing the language used in the visions of Ezekiel, Daniel and the Apocalypse, Newton eventually noted that it was necessary to allow 'for the changes that have been made in the signification of words'. It was his radical but non-publicly expressed opinion that

Spirits frequently signified the tempers and dispositions of the mind; and evil spirits the diseases and distempers thereof as when Saul was troubled with an evil spirit from the Lord; Devils signified the imaginary Ghosts of dead men whom the heathens worshipped as Gods; Inchanters, Magicians, Sorcerers, Necromancers and Witches signified deceivers and cheats who by certain forms of words and ceremonies and other juggling tricks pretended to supernatural powers and acts of prognosticating for magnifying themselves among the people.[59]

In any case Newton's theory did not become widely accepted until the 1730s and 1740s; when at the hands of Maupertuis and materialist philosophers Newtonian theory was interpreted in terms of remarkable powers immanent to matter, then Christianity was directly threatened. But by that time—the middle of the eighteenth century—it had become socially all but impossible to invoke Satanic witchcraft in defence of God and thereby of the established social order.

The necessity of God
We have traced, then, both the disappearance of belief in the possibility or actuality of Satanic interference in the course of nature *and* the acceptance of the mechanical and experimental philosophies to a common fundamental source: an almost overwhelming confidence displayed by male members of ruling classes in their potential ability to control events and an almost obsessive desire to impose such control. In particular, if nature is to be mechanically appropriated, then the course of nature itself (or 'herself') must be regular and orderly, in no way whimsical or capricious, so that causes of effects can be identified and reproduced at will. Secondly, no interference in the (regular) course of nature must be allowed that is not sanctioned or commanded by the (male) ruling elite; the Devil must consequently be dismissed as a reality or as an active agent in human affairs while God Himself, although Divine Creator of the cosmos, must be relegated to the position of benign spectator and supporter of the affairs of Europe's (male) ruling elites. Satan does not exist; God does. Why, however, had not a clean sweep been made by these ruling elites of the various (ruling-class) beliefs inherited from former centuries? After all, Aristotelian cosmology had been totally dismissed and two centuries of belief in Satanic witchcraft had been firmly jettisoned. Why had not Christianity been likewise jettisoned by ruling elites now apparently brimful of confidence in their masculine powers? It was certainly a step taken by a few individuals.

The answer appears to be two-fold. In the first place, a

powerful institution existed that guaranteed a livelihood and considerable influence to its members; these members would have no reason to challenge all or most of the tenets of Christianity and every reason not to. In the second place, the male ruling elites needed to legitimate their own privileged and ruling position in society and a fundamental prop of their position, as they realized very well, was religion and the support of the Church. They had no reason to challenge publicly all or most of the fundamental tenets of the Christian religion and every reason not to. If in private some of them held serious reservations, it was in no way in their interests to proclaim such reservations to the illiterate and ruled. Since, therefore, social classes remained and men continued to rule over women, the (changing) beliefs of ruling-class men necessarily reflected their need to perpetuate social and sexual inequalities. God consequently remained indispensable in seventeenth and eighteenth-century Europe. This is basically the answer to our second question (at the end of section 1, Chapter 1) as to why the disappearance of witch hunting did not herald the dawn of a new and rational Europe. Class and sex oppression remained. This is not to say that Christian members of ruling elites were hypocrites. It is to say that probably a few of them were and that nearly all of them recognized the desirability of religion in underwriting their own privileged positions. Certainly Sir George Savile and Charles Davenant made the political function of religion very clear to their fellow men of power and privilege.

In 1684 Sir George Savile, First Marquis of Halifax and Lord Privy Seal under both Charles II and William of Orange, appropriately and approvingly noted that in all ages religion 'hath been the foundation of government'. 'And though false gods have been imposed upon the credulity of the world', it was his opinion, just as it had been Jean Bodin's a century earlier, that 'the awe and reverence men had to them and their oracles kept them within bounds towards one another, which the laws alone, with all their authority, could never have effected'.[60] The writer on political and economic matters, Charles Davenant, agreed. In his *Discourse on the Plantation Trade,* published in 1698, Davenant warned that it is 'hardly to be doubted, but that if the common people are once induced to lay aside religion, they will quickly cast off all fear of their rulers'. It is for this reason, he explained, that 'wise lawgivers have therefore endeavoured to keep the inferior rank of men within bounds, by a sense of religion, and a fear of offending that power by which they were created'. Even if, very regrettably, the religion imposed by rulers in earlier times had necessarily to be of a rather crude nature, given the very low intellectual capacity of the masses, Davenant observed that 'the wiser sort had generally one religion for themselves, and another for the vulgar'. This being the case, Davenant strongly urged the English government to maintain a close watch on 'the state of religion in our American colonies' and, while permitting a variety of religious views to flourish, to instruct appointed governors to ensure 'that no doctrines are published, destructive to the very fundamentals of religion itself'.[61]

Men of property and power continually looked over their shoulder to that critical period during the Civil War and Commonwealth when it looked for a time as if, in England, reason might break through the constraints of power and privilege. The Marquis of Halifax himself noted how 'the liberty of the late times gave men so much light, and diffused it so universally among the people, that they are not now to be dealt with as they might have been in an age of less inquiry'. Although he thought it possible that 'good resolute nonsense backed with authority may yet prevail', generally speaking he considered that men had become such 'good judges of what they hear that the clergy ought to be very wary before they go about to impose upon their understandings which are grown less humble than they were in former times. . . '. ('It is a fundamental', he acknowledged, 'that there were witches—much shaken of late'.) Halifax mourned that 'the world is grown saucy, and expecteth reasons, and good ones too, before they give up their own opinions to other men's dictates, though never so magisterially delivered to them'.[62] A man that Halifax might well have had in mind—or ought to have had in mind—was Gerrard Winstanley.

3. *The Question of Private Property*

Against private property: Gerrard Winstanley
We have already remarked that during the English Civil War state censorship broke down so completely that radical groups were able to get their views in print. Particularly striking are the views of Winstanley and the group of 'Diggers' or 'True Levellers' that he led. If, taking our cue from the task Bertolt Brecht set the Gods in *The Good Person of Szechwan,* we have been scouring the sixteenth and seventeenth centuries for a rational human being, our search might well stop here although with only the same problematic success than Brecht's Gods achieved!

Little is known of Winstanley's life. Born in Lancashire in 1609, Winstanley after a meagre education entered a branch of the cloth industry only to become bankrupt during the Civil War. Harsh material conditions made Winstanley reflect critically on the events that had led to his own bankruptcy and which had done nothing to ameliorate the wretched condition of so many of his fellow countrymen. Winstanley's pamphlets began to appear. But not only pamphlets. On 1 April 1649 Winstanley and a group of about twenty men and women began to cultivate some common ground in north Surrey, appealing in their 20 April manifesto *The True Levellers Standard Advanced* for more people to join them in their communal project. On the day the manifesto appeared, Winstanley and another Digger William Everard were brought before General Fairfax to explain and defend their actions. Refusing to take off their hats in the presence of Fairfax who was, they maintained, 'but their fellow creature', they argued that they were breaking no laws and expressed the hope that property owners would voluntarily join them.[63] Although Fairfax, who visited the Digger colony on 26 May, agreed that the Diggers' activities were legal, harassment by local property owners continued. Communal property was destroyed and individuals physically beaten. On 1 June the Diggers published their second manifesto *A Declaration from the Poor Oppressed People of England* (parts of which were quoted in Chapter 3). In the meantime, however, mutinous and radical army regiments had been crushed by Fairfax and Cromwell at the Battle of Burford on 14 May 1649. Finally, exactly a year after it had been founded, the Digger colony was burnt to the ground by landlords and its members dispersed. Two years later Winstanley, not yet silenced, published his famous 'Utopian' manifesto *The Law of Freedom*.

It is my intention to examine only some principal aspects of Winstanley's writings. What I find remarkable about them is their progressively radical nature. While in his first pamphlet Winstanley displays the humanitarian commitment that characterizes his writings, he quickly goes beyond his theologically generous position that the damned shall at the last be saved by God—that there is to be no *eternal* damnation—to argue that perhaps there is no hell at all. Addressing the University Professors of Oxford and Cambridge on their theological claims, he admonishes: '[Y]ou doe not know that but as your Fathers have told you; which may be as well false as true, if you have not better ground than tradition'.[64] Winstanley takes the Devil by the horns. Does the Devil exist? Tradition maintains that he does but Winstanley tells the reader that 'this devil is the four evil angels within you: subtlety, hypocrisy, envy, and cruelty'. Nor is he frightened to ask the most radical question of all. Does God exist? Winstanley informs the reader that it is fundamentally mistaken to imagine God to be in 'a place of glory beyond the sun, moon, and stars, [to] imagine a divine being you know not where'; for rather God is 'the spirit and power that dwells in every man and woman' and indeed in every creature of the creation 'according to his orb'.[65] Winstanley has reached a position of pantheistic materialism. Moreover, his pamphlet entitled proudly and defiantly 'Truth Lifting Up Its Head' confirms not only his rejection of belief in God as a supernatural power but argues that even use of the *word* 'God' is undesirable: 'I am made to change the name from God to Reason', he writes, 'because I have been held under darknesse by that word, as I see many people are'. But what exactly does the word 'Reason' imply? What does it mean to walk righteously, or in the sight of Reason? Winstanley idealistically answers:

When a man lives in all acts of love to his fellow creatures; feeding the hungry . . . relieving the oppressed . . . looking upon himselfe as a fellow creature (though he be Lord of all creatures) to all other creatures of all lands; and so doing to them, as he would have them doe to him; to this end, that the Creation may be upheld and kept together by the spirit of love, tenderness and onenesse, and that no creature may complaine of any act of unrighteousnesse and oppression from him.

It is Winstanley's opinion that man originally lived according to Reason but when (for some reason or other) he fell into living off the objects of the Creation, his Fall also corrupted the earth and 'caused it to bring forth poysonous Vipers, Todes and Serpents, and Thornes and Bryars'.[66] Although 'liberation' is long overdue, Winstanley carefully points out that it is not only necessary for the sake of man but—Winstanley displays his millenarian commitment—necessary for *all* of creation: 'And truly as man might see all creatures in him now, but in a rest-lesse condition, groaning under bondage, waiting for a restauration.'[67]

As Winstanley's thought develops, however, his remaining quasi-Christian beliefs become progressively secularized. In a pamphlet probably written in the months directly preceding the attempt to cultivate St George's Hill in Surrey, Winstanley diagnoses what he sees as the ultimate roots of human conflict: 'And all the strivings that is in mankind is for the earth', he proclaims, 'who shall have it; whether some particular persons shall have it and the rest have none, or whether the earth shall be a common treasury to all without respect of persons.' 'And this is the battle', Winstanley continues, 'that is fought between the two powers, which is property on the one hand, called the devil or covetousness, or community on the other hand, called Christ or universal love'.[68] The issue is joined: private property versus communal ownership of the earth.

Winstanley imparts this information to Fairfax. During the struggle of the Digger colony to survive, the commander of Cromwell's armies is succinctly told that all wars, bloodshed and misery followed the advent of private appropriation of land and that human misery will cease only 'when all the branches of mankind shall look upon themselves as one man, and upon the earth as a common Treasury to all'.[69] As Fairfax's soldiers watched, the Digger colony was sacked and burnt. Two years later, Winstanley published his last message to the English people.

Respectfully Winstanley addresses the Preface of his *Law of Freedom* to Cromwell, pointing out to him that oppression still exists in England, merely that oppressors have been changed, that if he, Cromwell, who has 'the power of the land in your hand', does not use it to bring an end to oppression, then he and his kind will be universally abhorred and must always fear the inevitable rebellion. Winstanley's aim after such an opening skirmish is both to identify the principal causes of oppression and to convince Cromwell and his readers that a non-oppressive society is possible. I begin with Winstanley's treatment of 'this doctrine of a God, a devil, a heaven or a hell, [and] salvation and damnation after a man is dead'.[70] Displayed throughout all of Winstanley's writings and in particular throughout *The Law of Freedom* are hatred of the clergy and rejection of and contempt for their doctrines.

The common people have for centuries, Winstanley asserts, been oppressed by king and gentry, by lords of the manor and their lawyers. Then why have they so seldom rebelled? The explanation Winstanley offers is that the clergy were originally delegated the task of convincing oppressed people that all would be well if they were loyal to the king but that if they were not they would suffer the 'hell of prisons, whips and gallows'. In return for such service to the king the clergy were granted a share of the king's wealth obtained from oppression of the people. When, however, people gradually began to see through the clergy's hypocrisy, Winstanley claims that the clergy then counter-attacked by divining a 'heaven and hell after death', a strategy so successful that it awed not only the common people but the king as well, thus enabling the clergy to 'become the god that rules'. However, it must be obvious, Winstanley maintains, that such successful deceit was possible only by the blinding of the people's reason, only by the success of that insistent demand by the clergy that the 'doctrine of faith must not be tried by reason'. 'No', retorts Winstanley bitterly, 'for if it be, their mystery of iniquity will be discovered, and they would lose their tithes'.[71]

Winstanley insists time and again that it is in no way possible to discover knowledge beyond the creation. If it is the case that anything happens to a man after death, over and above the return of his body to the four elements of earth, water, air and fire, we cannot know it and to pretend otherwise is to 'build castles in the air'. It is to maintain, as the clergy do maintain, only 'imaginary and ungrounded doctrines'.[72] But this they do for very good reasons. Winstanley could scarcely have endeared himself to the clergy of England with his blunt indictments:

So that this divining spiritual doctrine is a cheat; for while men are gazing up to heaven, imagining a happiness or fearing a hell after they are dead, their eyes are put out, that they see not what is their birthrights, and what is to be done by them here on earth while they are living. This is the filthy dreamer, and the cloud without rain.

And indeed the subtle clergy do know that if they can but charm the people, by this their divining doctrine, to look after riches, heaven and glory when they are dead, that then they shall easily be the inheritors of the earth, and have the deceived people to be their servants.[73]

It is obvious that Winstanley cannot and does not believe in the possibility of diabolical magic and witchcraft. Tyranny, he proclaims, is 'the devil and Satan' and although bewitchment of people undoubtedly occurs, Winstanley knows precisely where to look for its source: it is the proud and ignorant clergy who have 'bewitched all the world by their covetousness and pride'; it is that 'mighty city divinity, which hath filled the whole earth with her sorcery and deceived all people'. In Winstanley's ideal Commonwealth witches, it is true, will be put to death. But who are the witches? 'He who professes the service of a righteous God by preaching and prayer', admonishes Winstanley, 'and makes a trade to get the possessions of the earth, shall be put to death for a witch and a cheater'.[74] This is indeed a harsh law but Winstanley believes it is the only way, once a free Commonwealth has been established, to prevent its corruption and the return of oppression. The re-establishment of private property, even at the cost of transgressors' lives, must never be permitted.

Winstanley, then, contemptuously dismisses the idea of a transcendent God, a Devil, heaven and hell; diabolical witchcraft is impossible. Winstanley is concerned with humankind's real existence here on earth, and disputes over possession of the earth. But why do disputes occur? Is it that the earth is inherently incapable of producing enough food so that all people may live sufficiently well? Winstanley argues that sufficient food can easily be produced provided the earth is maintained as a common treasury for all people. It was therefore the buying and selling of the earth that gave rise to both poverty and oppression. Once again Winstanley is not concerned with subtleties. When some people claimed ownership over parts of the earth, others obviously 'gave no consent' or were tricked into agreeing. Mankind was then antagonistically divided into masters on the one hand and servants or labourers on the other. Inevitably, continual buying and selling of the privately owned earth and its produce led to further antagonism and discontent since the whole aim of such trade, Winstanley affirms, is individual betterment at the expense of neighbours. Ensuing disorder then enabled crafty, ambitious individuals to propose an apparently reasonable solution whereby they should rule over all contending people, preserving order and keeping the peace. But, Winstanley argues, this 'solution' merely increased the oppression under which the dispossessed of the earth labour for the benefit of a minority of contending property owners. While, therefore, abolition of the monarchy and its 'government of highwaymen' is necessary there can be no doubt about the true solution: 'The Nations of the world will never learn to beat their swords into plough-shares, and their spears into pruning hooks, and leave off warring, until'—Winstanley is emphatic—'this cheating device of buying and selling be cast out among the rubbish of Kingly power'.[75]

The problem must be faced, however, as to why this buying and selling arose in the first place and here Winstanley is not altogether consistent. In a remarkable passage in *The Law of Freedom* he proclaims:

I speak now in relation between the oppressor and the oppressed; the inward bondages I meddle not with in this place, though I am assured that if it be rightly searched into, the inward bondages of the minde, as covetousness, pride, hypocrisie, envy, sorrow, fears, desperation, and madness are all occasioned by the outward bondage, that one sort of people lay upon another.

Now this begs the question heroically. Covetousness, Winstanley is assured, is one of the consequences of the system of private property, yet private property is not possible without the prior existence of covetousness. If Winstanley wishes to deny (Hobbes' claim) that covetousness is the state of nature, he must give reasons why covetousness should ever have arisen in men's hearts. He is trapped. If he argues that humankind originally lived under conditions of material scarcity, then the ideal Commonwealth he describes in *The Law of Freedom* is impossible unless, or until, techniques for appropriation of the earth have been sufficiently developed to make scarcity eliminable. On the other hand, if he rejects identifying scarcity as the underlying cause of human conflict, then he must identify covetousness as innate or potentially present in men or at least in *some* men. Winstanley considers only the latter possibility and reluctantly accepts that 'the heart of man is so subject to be overspread with clouds of covetousness, pride and vain-glory' that the citizens of his ideal Commonwealth—all free men and whose elected officers serve the people—will have to impose stern laws to defend themselves against potentially vain, proud and covetous men in their midst.[76]

Winstanley, then, does not conceive of the possibility of material scarcity in his Commonwealth; all goods will be communally owned and the store houses will always be full. *Goods, not women.* Winstanley believes it necessary to deny emphatically the opinion of some people—which can result only from 'unreasonable beastly ignorance'—that the Commonwealth will necessarily entail a 'community of all men and women for copulation, and so strive to live a bestial life'.[77] On the contrary, families will remain as they presently exist, with the husband and father as head of the household. It is best to say no more on such an unsavoury topic.

These male heads of households, Winstanley explains, will have the responsibility of collecting what they need for their families' personal consumption from 'particular stores' but they will not collect more than they need, either to look contentedly upon an excess of possession or to waste and squander what they cannot consume or use. Any such 'unrational practice' is to be prevented by the laws and faithful officers of the Commonwealth.[78] The same considerations apply to the activities of tradesmen who draw freely from general stores whatever they need for the practice of their trades.

Discipline is rigidly maintained. Idleness and neglect of duty—should any ever occur—are to be punished according to the laws of the Commonwealth: for the first offence by a verbal reproof in private or in public, for a second offence by whipping, for a third by loss of freedom for a specified period, the offender working under the orders of any freeman engaged in productive activity. Flight from such forced labour is punishable by death. If any accusation against a person is not proved, the accuser must submit to the punishment of the talion. Physical assault is punished according to the law of Moses, 'blow for blow . . . limb for limb, life for life'. Rape of a woman, 'robbery of a woman['s] bodily freedom', is a capital offence; but the offence must be proved by two witnesses or the man's confession.[79] It is significant that the rapist is to be executed for his violation of the woman's freedom, not for violation of the husband's, father's, or brother's honour.

Despite such severe punishment of rapists, Winstanley's Commonwealth is uncritically patriarchal. Otherwise it is totally democratic. Although women neither vote nor serve in office, all men over twenty years of age are eligible to vote while all men over forty, younger men if exceptionally able, are eligible to serve as officials of the people for periods of one year at a time.

Another radical proposal Winstanley makes is that all children are to be educated: boys are to be 'trained up in learning and in trades' and girls 'in reading, sewing, knitting, spinning of linen and woollen, music and all other easy neat works, either for to furnish storehouses with linen and woollen cloth, or for the ornament of particular houses with needlework'. Such a sexual division of education appears to be quite unproblematic for Winstanley. However, he is particularly insistent that no child is to be 'trained up only to book learning and no other employment' as in the system of all oppressive governments; for then, he claims, 'through idleness and exercised wit therein they spend their time to find out policies to advance themselves to be lords and masters above their labouring brethren'.[80]

Although Winstanley maintains that his Commonwealth can and must be founded on a sufficiency of material goods, he is nevertheless anxious that continual investigation should be undertaken into the secrets of nature. Indeed, natural philosophy is to flourish as never before. It is in oppressive governments, Winstanley complains, that men keep their discoveries secret so that they can thereby make a living, and therefore 'kingly bondage' is 'the cause of the spreading of ignorance in the earth'. Conversely, it is only when the Commonwealth's freedom is established, Winstanley proclaims, that knowledge will cover the earth '*as the waters cover the seas*; and not till then'. Certainly one of the most important functions of the 'postmasters' chosen in each parish will be the regular transmission of all recently discovered secrets of nature and of new inventions in any art or trade or techniques in cultivation of the earth 'whereby the Commonwealth may more flourish in peace and plenty'. Discoverers of such new secrets and inventions are not only to be greatly honoured but will have the pleasure of witnessing the rapid diffusion of their ideas and innovations into all corners of the Commonwealth. Winstanley optimistically concludes that 'in time there will not be any secret in Nature, which now lies hid (by reason of the iron age of Kingly oppressing Government) but by some or other will be brought to light, to the beauty of our Commonwealth'.[81] There is no claim in this mature work that thorns, briars, adders and carnivores will all disappear after the achievement of the true Commonwealth; neither is there the same emphasis, as in Winstanley's early works, on liberation of the non-human world. However, it is clear that there is to be no rapacious appropriation of the earth but rather a moderate use of all things for the benefit of the citizens of the Commonwealth. The overall aim is peace, plenty and beauty.

Although this final goal exists only as a dream, yet it is a realizable dream. The alternative is starkly put: 'here is life and death set before you', Winstanley tells the reader, 'take whether you will'.[82] Winstanley has seen and promulgated the truth to the best of his ability but the truth by itself has been insufficient to change oppressive government into a Commonwealth; the struggle must and will be taken up afresh but not by him. Anguished and exhausted Winstanley ends *The Law of Freedom* looking forward to his return to the four Aristotelian elements from which he is made.

The importance of Winstanley is clear. He is seemingly unaware of the Copernican world system, of Paracelsus and Descartes. What he focuses on is injustice: both the social order that incorporates injustice and the beliefs that sustain and legitimate an unjust society. From this viewpoint Winstanley dismisses belief in God, heaven, Satan and hell as concepts with no factual backing at all but which are powerful weapons in the armoury of ruling groups. The elimination of injustice requires first and foremost not so much diligent inquiry into the secrets of nature but the elimination of social stratification and the disappearance of private property: only in such a 'true Commonwealth' would investigation into the secrets of nature contribute towards a consolidation of peace, plenty and beauty. The mechanical philosophers, Winstanley would have wished to argue, hoped to achieve the impossible: the elimination of hunger, disease and brute labour without the prior elimination of private control over resources. While private property and therefore social inequality exist, Winstanley's view is that oppression will only intensify as private control over nature increases.

There is a further aspect of Winstanley's thought that needs emphasis. Nowhere is to be found the desire that mankind will take possession of the earth as a means of displaying man's power and greatness. Although in the true Commonwealth the natural world will (thanks to new inventions) increasingly provide the plenty that guarantees peace, Winstanley seeks to realize a beautiful world in which great emphasis is placed on tenderness and gentleness. To be sure, Winstanley is not a 'feminist' in that he fails to advocate the full and free participation of women in the self-government of the Commonwealth and recommends a sexual division of education and labour; he even in one of his earlier 'Christian' pamphlets claims that 'the branches of mankind have been led by the powers of the curse in flesh, which is the *Feminine* part; not by the power of the righteous Spirit, the *Masculine* power'.[83] Nevertheless in his emphasis on gentleness and tenderness Winstanley emphatically rejects the 'masculinist' emphasis on hardness, toughness and (ever-increasing) power. The ideal—if an unrealizable ideal—is the elimination of pain and suffering throughout not only the human world but the world of all sentient creatures. If punishment for transgression of the Commonwealth's laws is relatively harsh—and it is—one must remember not only that typical punishment was exceedingly severe in seventeenth-century England (and Europe) but that Winstanley witnessed unprovoked and brutal assaults on his pacifist Diggers. Non-violent means—as Winstanley realized —are not always sufficient to achieve and consolidate a non-violent goal.

Winstanley, then, is radical: he is radical in dismissing belief in God, Satan, heaven and hell as superstition; he is radical in believing that the elimination of social classes and private property is necessary (and sufficient) in order to eliminate injustice and the consequences of injustice; above all, he is radical in believing (or wanting to believe) in the possibility of a world in which no sentient creature would have reason for complaint as a result of humanity's mastery over the natural world.

For private property
The radical nature of Winstanley's beliefs and proposals can be highlighted by contrasting them with those of a man who was to be considered 'the philosopher' by the *philosophes* of the following century. Whereas Winstanley had argued for a society qualitatively different from the one being established in mid-century England, John Locke (1632–1704), the son of a Somerset lawyer and Fellow of the Royal Society from 1668, undertook to provide the justification for that very society. Winstanley had argued for the abolition of private property and the use of money; Locke defended both.

In his *Two Treatises on Government,* first published in 1690, Locke forcefully argues his case. A man's person is his own property. The labour of his body and the work of his hands are also rightfully his. 'Whatsoever, then, [a man] removes out of the state that Nature hath provided and left it in, he hath mixed his labour with it, and joined to it something that is his own, and thereby makes his property.' Private property is therefore inherent in the nature of human existence: it is not the existence of money that brings into being private property; it is, argues Locke, 'the condition of human life'. But there is a qualitative

—and momentous—difference between a society that uses money and one that does not. For Locke argues that no man is entitled to possess more property than he can make use of or consume without wastage: 'As much land as a man tills, plants, improves, cultivates, and can use the product of, so much is his property', explains Locke; in a moneyless society an upper limit therefore clearly exists to the amount of property a man may own. In a society that uses money, however, the crucial and all-important difference is that *no upper limit exists*. For gold and silver, 'which have value only from the consent of men', do not perish with time, and therefore a man may produce in a monetary society well beyond what he himself can use or can exchange for other goods, the surplus he produces being exchangeable for (non-perishable) money. Moreover, possession of money makes possible the employment of other men so that a man's production of goods may be increased without limit (Locke explaining that 'a free man makes himself a servant to another by selling him for a certain time the service he undertakes to do in exchange for wages he is to receive'.)[84] More to the point, Locke concludes remorselessly, if somewhat questionably, since men in the state of nature *agreed* to the use of money it follows that they also agreed to a 'disproportionate and unequal possession of the earth', even if as a consequence the vast majority of men (Locke admits elsewhere) now live only 'from hand to mouth', seldom enjoying anything more 'than a bare subsistence'.[85] Since, presumably, such men may not always understand that their ancestors agreed to unequal shares of the earth, civil government is necessary. As Locke explains: 'The great and chief end, therefore, of men uniting into commonwealths, and putting themselves under government, is the preservation of their property.'[86]

Now although reason ought ideally to be sufficient to convince all men to behave virtuously and to obey the laws of civil society, there is no possibility that this will happen in practice. Since the 'greatest part of mankind want leisure or capacity for demonstration', Locke recommends in his *Reasonableness of Christianity* that inculcation of 'plain commands is the sure and only course to bring them to obedience and practice'. After all, Locke writes, where 'the hand is used to the plough and the spade, the head is seldom elevated to sublime notions or exercised in mysterious reasonings'. Philosophy is then impotent: it is a blessing if such men can understand 'plain propositions', to say nothing, Locke gallantly comments, concerning the intellectual capacities 'of the other sex'. It is therefore obvious to Locke why God chose to send His Son to mankind. 'And I ask', Locke puts the question rhetorically, whether one coming from heaven in the power of God, in full and clear evidence and demonstration of miracles, giving plain and direct rules of morality and obedience; be not likelier to enlighten the bulk of mankind, and set them right in their duties, and bring them to do them, by reasoning with them from general notions and principles of human reason?

Locke takes pains to demonstrate that he is far from decrying the achievements of the ancient philosophers; they had certainly demonstrated 'the beauty of virtue' but since inevitably they had had to leave her 'unendowed' very few were prepared to live a virtuous life. Locke sees, however, that by the teachings of Christ 'interest is come about to her, and virtue now is visibly the most enriching purchase, and by much the best bargain'. There is no attempt to mince matters:

The view of heaven and hell will cast a slight upon the short pleasures and pains of this present state, and give attractions and encouragements to virtue, which reason and interest, and the care of ourselves, cannot but allow and prefer. Upon this foundation and upon this only, morality stands firm, and may defy all competition.[87]

Locke is here at one with Halifax and Davenant: religion is the best guarantee that, among other things, the property of the ruling class will remain inviolable.

There are, nevertheless, problems to be faced. For how are men to know that revelation has come from God or the Son of God and not from Satan or evil angels? Even if we accept—as we must—that the genuine sign of a divine revelation is a miracle or a series of miracles, it is still necessary to ask how miracles are to be distinguished from natural but unusual phenomena or from the marvellous events that are within the capacities of Satan and evil angels. Clearly reason—if it is to play a part—can be no guide in assessing the truth of any revelation that concerns matters totally beyond earthly experience: 'Thus', argues Locke in his *Essay Concerning Human Understanding,* 'that part of the angels rebelled against GOD and thereby lost their first happy state, and that the dead shall rise and live again; these and the like, being beyond the discovery of reason, are purely matters of faith, with which reason has, directly, nothing to do'.[88] However, what reason can do—and given the 'odd opinions and extravagant actions *enthusiasm* has run men into', it is imperative that reason be so used—is to determine whether a revelation comes from God or does not come from God; it is only after reason has given its assent that faith is allowed by reason to take over. In his *Discourse on Miracles* Locke quickly cuts through the tangled undergrowth of distinguishing miracles from marvellous feats or unusual natural phenomena: it is simply a question of reason's recognition of superior *power.* Locke gives many examples: for instance, it is true that God turned Aaron's rod into a serpent and that Pharaoh's magicians also made serpents; but Aaron's serpent ate up Pharaoh's and the conclusion follows that the power behind Aaron is superior to the power at Pharaoh's disposal. 'So that', Locke concludes, 'the marks of a superior power accompanying it, always have been, and always will be, a visible and sure guide to divine revelation'. In particular, argues Locke,

the number, variety, and greatness of the miracles wrought for the confirmation of the doctrine delivered by Jesus Christ, carry with them such strong marks of an extraordinary divine power, that the truth of its mission will stand firm and unquestionable, till any one rising up in opposition to him shall do greater miracles than he and his apostles did.[89]

How can one be certain that the events—and the miracles—related in the Four Gospels truly happened? Locke is simply certain that they did! Locke's acceptance of the institution of private property and of unequal ownership of the earth means for him the necessary acceptance of religion in general and Christianity in particular. There are other consequences: this acceptance of belief in the existence of God requires him to uphold, if uneasily, a mind-matter dualism.

In his *Essay Concerning Human Understanding* Locke maintains that all knowledge of the natural world comes from two sources only: there is sensation of the external sensible objects of the world which produce in our minds the ideas we have of these objects, and then there is the operations of our minds which produce from such ideas further sets of ideas. Of the ideas we have of bodies some of them—the so-called 'primary qualities' —correspond to real properties of the objects themselves such as 'solidity, extension, figure, motion or rest, and number' while on the other hand, the so-called 'secondary qualities' 'are nothing in the objects themselves but powers to produce various sensations in us by their *primary qualities* . . . as colours, sounds, taste, etc.'[90] In making this distinction, Locke, friend of Robert Boyle, is, of course, being faithful to the ontology defining the 'mechanical philosophy'. It is furthermore a distinction that upholds the immateriality of God's being. Certainly there is a great danger in supposing that God is a *material* being for then—Locke confesses his fear—those men 'devoted to matter' can all the more easily argue 'all to be matter and so deny a God, that is, an eternal cogitative being'. Locke confidently asserts, however, that even men devoted to matter are reluctant to deny the mind-matter dualism of Descartes and allow that each particle of matter thinks. And yet, Locke points out, 'if they will not allow matter as matter, that is, every particle of matter, to be as well cogitative as extended, they will have [a] hard task to make out to their own reasons a cogitative being out of incogitative particles'. 'For unthinking particles of matter, however put together, can have nothing thereby added to them but a new relation of position, which it is impossible should give thought and knowledge to them.' It follows to Locke's satisfaction that, provided a mind-matter dualism is maintained, God is an *immaterial, eternal, cogitative* being.[91]

Earlier in his *Essay* Locke tackled the objection that it is difficult, if not impossible, to conceive of an immaterial thinking being. The counter-argument is that it is equally difficult, if not impossible, to conceive of a material extended body! For Descartes' theory that cohesion consists solely in the mutual rest of all the body's parts is dismissed by Locke as untenable, together with all theories that attempt to give an explanation of cohesion in terms of an ether pressure surrounding the body. After an elaborate discussion Locke's verdict is unambiguous that '*a solid extended substance [is] as hard to be conceived as a thinking immaterial one*'. But we know from experience, despite the impossibility of conception, that material extended bodies exist, and therefore it cannot be repugnant to reason to conclude that it is possible for an immaterial thinking being to exist, namely God. (The argument is obviously a dangerous one: if matter has inexplicable properties like cohesion, why cannot matter think? Make the slightest concession to matter and God's immateriality is obviously jeopardized, not to say His very existence.) Although Locke does waver on the necessity of maintaining a rigid spirit-matter distinction and will be attacked for it, nevertheless overall he consistently attempts to ascribe qualitatively different properties to spirit and matter: 'Pure spirit, viz. God', Locke declares, 'is only active; pure matter is only passive; those beings that are both active and passive one may judge to partake of both'.[92] While we are on the subject of spirit, it is very reasonable to suppose that angels of all kinds exist—even if we are in absolute ignorance of their various powers. For

when we consider the infinite power and wisdom of the Maker, we have reason to think that it is suitable to the magnificent harmony of the universe and the great design and infinite goodness of the Architect that the *species* of creatures should also, by gentle degrees, ascend upward from us toward his infinite perfection, as we see they gradually descend from us downwards; which if it be probable, we have reason then to be persuaded that there are far more *species* of creatures above us than there are beneath: we being, in degrees of perfection, much more remote from the infinite being of GOD than we are from the lowest state of being and that which approaches nearest to nothing.[93]

It is thus clear that in his public writings Locke accepts belief in the existence of not only God but also Satan, good and fallen angels, and heaven and hell (with eternal life for the blessed and annihilation of the wicked after appropriate torment in hell). If this is a true doctrine, it is also a doctrine necessary to persuade people to live virtuously and the poor and illiterate to respect their betters. However, Locke is seemingly untroubled by questions of witchcraft and Satanic intervention. He is a modern man, brimful of confidence. In practice God and Satan do not intervene in the operations of the natural world; the new men of property are therefore to be unimpeded in their objective of accumulating wealth—and of using the labouring poor as a principal means. The other principal means was to be development of the 'mechanical arts', aided eventually by the maturation of the 'masculine philosophy'.

4 The Ruling Class, Other People and Nature

Working-class people as raw material

If ruling-class confidence in its own powers was the reason why educated belief in the Devil's powers all but vanished—which was clearly a historically progressive step of decisive importance —that very same confidence plus determination to stay in power at the expense of the labouring poor undermined what good intentions the ruling class otherwise professed. If even a minority of people must be regarded as inferior and undeserving vis-à-vis the position of the elite, then the ruling-class cosmology must be such as to violate, either in principle or in practice, an epistemological foundation stone of a rational society, namely that all people must as far as possible be brought into decision-making processes, not excluded from them. If in any sense at all some people are regarded by other people as mere matter or raw material rather than as material, reasoning, sentient beings, then there is no possibility of the realization of a rational society. Since the new philosophers saw themselves and property owners as representing mind and the mass of people as mere matter—as did Henry Power very explicitly—then natural philosophy was undermined at the very outset of the philosophers' bid to free themselves from superstition, falsity and ignorance. It may not be totally impossible but it is very unlikely that truth can be realized on a foundation of oppression—the greater likelihood is that the oppressors will mystify both themselves and, for long periods of time, the oppressed.

At the beginning of the seventeenth century Francis Bacon —hero of the experimental philosophy in England and eventually throughout Europe—proclaimed the desirability of the ruler's deception and mystification of the ruled:

For as in civil actions he is far the greater and deeper politician that can make other men the instruments of his ends and desires and yet never acquaint them with his purpose (so as they shall do what he wills and yet not know that they are doing it), than he that imparts his meaning to those he employs.[94]

By the end of the seventeenth century, the rulers' approach is not essentially different. The majority of people are to be manipulated and used; there is to be no question of the realization of a society of educated equals holding all productive forces in common. That had been Winstanley's communistic dream and that dream had been shattered. How little would Winstanley have agreed with the arguments and sentiments advanced in William Petyt's *Britannia Languens or a Discourse of Trade*. Petyt (1641?–1707), who after taking a degree at Cambridge had been called to the bar in 1670 'for his service done in asserting and defending the rights and privileges of this country',[95] made very clear his opinion of the opportunities people present to their rulers:

People are, therefore, the chiefest, most fundamental and precious commodity, out of which may be derived all sorts of manufactures, navigation, riches, conquests and solid dominion. This capital material being of itself raw and indigested is committed into the hands of supreme authority in whose prudence and disposition it is to improve, manage and fashion it to more or less advantage.[96]

People are here put on basically the same level as mere matter and, if unlike matter, people have needs, they are to be considered by rulers only in so far as the rulers' own needs can thereby be better met. Like Winstanley, Sir William Petty confessed to a dream—'a pleasant and a profitable dream indeed'—but there can scarcely have been two dreams more different. Petty was concerned to increase the national wealth of England with the consequence that in his *Political Arithmetick* (written during the 1670s and published posthumously in 1690) he lamented the cost to the English of 500 years of preventing and suppressing rebellions in Ireland for, he claimed, so little profit to themselves (not the appropriate place for Petty to recall that he had made a fortune for himself by the cheap purchase of lands which Cromwell had 'confiscated' in Ireland). Under the pretence of making 'a jocular, and perhaps ridiculous digression', Petty proposed that the population of Ireland—and that of the highlands of Scotland for good measure—be transplanted into England. The market costs of the land and housing in both Scotland and Ireland Petty estimated at some £13 million, the cost of transplantation at most some £4 million. 'So then', wrote Petty, 'the Question will be, whether the benefit expected from this Transplantation, will exceed Seventeen Millions?' Petty estimated a benefit of some £69,300,000, explaining that 'the advantage will arise in transplanting about Eighteen Hundred Thousand People, from the poor and miserable Trade of Husbandry, to more beneficial Handicrafts'. More calculations followed before Petty made his final point: 'I further add, that the charge of the *Government, Civil, Military,* and *Ecclesiastical* would be more *cheap, safe* and *effectual* in this condition of *closer* co-habitation than otherwise, as not only reason, but the example of the United Provinces doth demonstrate.'[97] Throughout Petty's pleasant and profitable dream to which he returns in his *Treatise of Ireland* (1687) there is no discussion of the wishes of the Irish and Scottish peoples.

Working-class people, property and innovation
If God's existence had been made secure by the omnipresence of design in the world (each of His creatures bearing witness to God's infinite wisdom) and indeed made even more secure by the theory of *emboîtement,* then men of the bourgeois class could consequently turn in security to the mechanical appropriation of that Great Machine of the World. Although the industrial revolution did not get under way as a revolutionary phenomenon until the late eighteenth century, an impressive technical base had already been consolidated in previous centuries. One commentator has, I think not inappropriately, remarked of the sixteenth and seventeenth centuries that the true significance of the age lay 'in countless small technical advances, in the spread of technical knowledge by means of the printed word and illustration, in the training of men technically skilled in the various departments of industrial activity'.[98] Towns in particular grew in importance. Although England remained very much a rural nation run by landed aristocracy and country gentlemen, Clark and Slack emphasize how by 1700 a whole new range of towns had appeared—industrial towns like Halifax and Manchester, dock-yard towns like Chatham and Portsmouth, and the spas such as Bath and Tunbridge Wells—while the population of metropolitan London increased from some 200,000 at the beginning of the seventeenth century to 575,000 by its end. Even though rural industry at the beginning of the eighteenth century became increasingly important, nevertheless, Clark and Slack point out, 'its raw materials were bought in the town, its products finished and sold there'.[99] Factory production developed in momentum. Thomas Lombe's textile factory at Derby in 1717 was followed by other immense structures. Technical expertise increased. During the eighteenth century, David Landes remarks, there existed in

England 'a higher level of technical skill and a greater interest in machines and 'gymcracks' than in any of the other countries of Europe'.[100] Even where English techniques were markedly inferior to Continental ones and 'technological transfer' did not occur, perversely enough such backwardness ultimately proved to be advantageous to the development of English industry. Wood had virtually disappeared as a fuel source in England and the mining of coal required efficient drainage techniques; but nowhere was English technique more backward than in mine-pumping. Efforts by experimental philosophers to construct an effective steam engine proved abortive (as had the attempt by Huygens to make a gunpowder engine) but by 1712 Thomas Newcomen, a literate Devon ironmonger, had constructed his famous engine utilizing the effective pressure of the atmosphere upon creation of a partial vacuum by rapid condensation of steam. English technology was taking off and it was doing so without the direct assistance of experimental philosophers; indeed, despite the early enthusiasm of members of the Royal Society for utilitarian objectives, by 1700 Baconian aims had virtually disappeared from the Society and would not strongly re-emerge among English natural philosophers until the second half of the eighteenth century. For the time being English technology was going ahead under its own steam and the incentive of the profit motive.

Had not belief in the Devil and Satanic witchcraft necessarily to wane and disappear under the combined impact of growing preoccupation with the technical appropriation of matter and also the increasing confidence, not to say comfort, of the political elite? If the Devil necessarily had to be banished from the workfloor, how could he survive elsewhere? The political elite lost any preoccupation they might have had with the machinations of the Devil and turned more of their attention to the discontents of the labouring poor. Keith Thomas records how in England, as witch prosecutions declined towards the end of the seventeenth century, the number of actions taken against malicious damage of property steadily increased. For hedge-breaking and rick-burning Parliament introduced the death penalty, ignoring the advice of a mid-seventeenth-century writer —or at least the first part of it—that malicious actions stemming from such 'unnatural envy' would only be 'removed when oppression and ignorance of the law of God were removed from the shoulders of the poor'.[101] However, the anger of the poor was not directed solely against the agricultural property of the rich.

In his *History of the Royal Society* Thomas Sprat had argued that the 'hands of men employed are true *Riches*' and further that the 'saving of those hands by inventions of *Art,* and applying of them to other *Works,* will increase those *Riches*'. In Sprat's opinion unemployment could not result from labour-saving inventions, since the 'hands' of the labouring class could always be put to work in alternative manufactures; and if 'there be not vent for their productions at home', then, he asserted, 'we shall have it abroad'.[102] Despite Sprat's (unargued) reassurances, the ruling elite found itself forced to pay increasing attention to the opposition of working people to unemployment-creating techni- cal inventions. The historian George Clark has noted how widespread are the records of machine-breaking in this period; in England in particular, 'the first saw-mills had to stop working in 1663 because of popular opposition, and the same thing hap- pened again at Limehouse as late as 1676'.[103] Knitting machines (the so-called stocking frames) were smashed in 1710. As if to enable future historians to be able to locate within a 10-year period the end of one era and the beginning of a new one, the English government introduced the death penalty for frame- breaking in 1726 and abolished the crime of witchcraft from the statute books in 1736. Instead of allowing the prosecution and execution of old women who cursed and railed against an oppressive rural and patriarchal system of control and who were thought to use diabolical means to contribute either to its malfunctioning or the distress of its members, now members of the ruling elite concentrated their attention on the real actions of those who opposed the new, oppressive system of incipient industrial capitalism, whether these were the actions of workers who resisted technological innovation (within a capitalist frame- work) or the actions of the unemployed and destitute who tried to redistribute income and wealth by means proscribed by the ruling elite. As capitalism developed in eighteenth-century England so the English penal code became increasingly severe until Sir Samuel Romilly could tell the English Parliament in 1810 that in no other country in the world were there more capital offences than in England.[104] Burglary of over 40 shillings, shoplifting above 5 shillings, illegal cutting down of trees, destruction of turnpike gates: all were capital offences, together with over 150 other offences. Gerrard Winstanley would not have been surprised.

Neither would he have been surprised at the publication in 1835 of Andrew Ure's famous work on *The Philosophy of Manufactures.* Science for the people? In Ure's own words:

By the infirmity of human nature it happens, that the more skilful the workman, the more self-willed and intractable he is apt to become, and, of course, the less fit a component of a mechanical system, in which, by occasional irregularities, he may do great damage to the whole. The grand object therefore of the modern manufacturer is, through the union of capital and science to reduce the task of his work-people to the exercise of vigilance and dexterity.

Francis Bacon, we recall, had argued that in scientific inquiry weights should be applied to the investigator's understanding and the whole process reduced to a relatively automatic procedure needing no special ability or intelligence; whether or not this has ever been true of scientific inquiry, scientific inquiry has certainly been used and is still being used to de-skill the greater part of the labour process: Ure rejoices how in the factory system and thanks to mechanistic science 'the most expensive element of production [i.e., "skilled labour"] gets progressively superseded and will, eventually, be replaced by mere overlookers of machines'.[105]

Science, Ure continued, can and does help capitalism in other ways. For skilled workers are not only highly paid, but often become 'arrogant' and strike for yet higher pay. However, Ure describes a mechanism especially invented to make striking women in an industry redundant and warns with satisfaction 'how surely science, at the call of capital, will defeat every unjustifiable union which the labourers may form'. Describing another invention made for the same purpose, the so-called *Iron Man,* Ure pronounces: 'This invention confirms the great doctrine already propounded, that when capital enlists science in her service, the refractory hand of labour will always be taught docility.'[106]

If, however, for over a century the Devil by and large has disappeared from the minds of the ruling elite, God has not, and certainly not from the mind of Ure. Manufacturers in particular should be aware, Ure warns, that persons 'not trained up in moral and religious nurture . . . are readily moved to outrage by crafty demagogues, and they are apt to regard their best benefactor, the enterprising and frugal capitalist who employs them, with a jealous and hostile eye'. Ure is therefore in favour of religious instruction to all working people, since they must understand that the 'first and great lesson—one inculcated equally by philosophy and religion—is that man must expect his chief happiness, not in the present, but in a future state of existence'.[107] 'Man' in this case stands for the oppressed men and women of all races.

Women, nature and ruling men:
'the masculine birth of time'
Men of the ruling classes prided themselves on their possession of mind, on their pre-eminence in the faculty of reason; the labouring classes were relegated to the status of matter or raw material to be put to use by those superior to them in reasoning

power. Within the privileged classes men claimed the right to rule over women because of supposed male predominance of intellect; men associated themselves with mind and rational activity, women with matter and carnal instincts. Mind over matter: crudely such a distinction captures an important component of the male ruling classes' attempted legitimation of both class and sex inequalities.

The mental 'inferiority' of women automatically meant in the minds of its practitioners that the 'new philosophy' would be the all but exclusive possession of *male* philosophers. The Secretary of the Royal Society had stated very explicitly that its members aimed to raise a 'Masculine Philosophy'; words are feminine, deeds are masculine, he had agreed. Clergy, natural philosophers (with a few notable exceptions) and especially physicians proclaimed the inability of women to pursue serious study, *The Compleat Midwifes Practice* explaining that although females 'take with appearance of knowledge in sleight and easie matters, [they] seldom reach any farther than to a sleight superficial smattering in any deep Science.'[108] Furthermore, women being essentially emotional, carnal creatures, Glanvill was only stating the obvious when he remarked that mind would not triumph over matter if such lower feminine passions as women represented were ever allowed to gain the upper hand over the new philosophy. The predominantly intellectual nature of the pursuit of truth therefore meant that the new philosophy would necessarily provide privileged males with a further sanctuary from the threatening and forbidding power of females. Moreover, from that masculine sanctuary a whole series of assertions and theories concerning the 'male-female relation' eventually challenged religious and popular conceptions.

Women, we recall, were generally considered throughout the sixteenth and seventeenth centuries to be lascivious, voracious creatures for ever a threat to male self-control, spirituality, and achievement. The soldier in Walter Charleton's *Ephesian Matron* was not stating an idiosyncratic view when he exclaimed:

You are the true *Hiena's,* that allure us with the fairness of your skins; and when folly hath brought us within your reach, you leap upon us and devour us. You are the traitors to Wisdom; the impediment to Industry . . . the clogs to virtue, and goads that drive us to all Vice, Impiety, and Ruine. You are the Fools Paradise, the Wisemans Plague, and the grand Error of Nature.[109]

Women were to pay dearly for such male perception of them. Only recall the typical misogynistic comments of the witch-hunters Kramer and Sprenger. Young or old, women were insatiable. They ought ideally to be sexually passive; 'in reality' they were sexually voracious. 'Of women's unnatural, unsatiable

lust, what country, what village doth not complain', noted Robert
Burton in his *Anatomy of Melancholy*. Age brought even greater
desire. '[T]o see an old lecher, what more odious, what can be
more absurd? and yet so common? . . . Worse it is in women than
in men', indicted Burton; 'whilst she is so old a crone, a beldam,
she can neither see nor hear, go nor stand, a mere carcass, a
witch, and scarce feel, she caterwauls, and must have a
stallion'.[110] It was only too well known how, unfortunately,
through their inordinate sexual desire both young and old women
were easy prey for Satan.

A distressing feature of sexual intercourse, Montaigne had
argued, lay in its 'inevitable' reduction of the male to the level of
a mere beast, in orgasm the male's much vaunted reasoning
powers quite vanishing. 'In everything else [but intercourse] a
man may keep some decorum', Montaigne lamented, challenging
his readers to 'find out, if you can, therein any serious and
discreet procedure'.[111] Worse still, Montaigne believed, women
outstrip men both in sexual capacity and desire so that a woman's
lord and master, particularly when ageing, can easily be exposed
by her as a creature quite inadequate in sexual potency. Male
'superiority' and 'dignity' thus appeared to Montaigne pathetically vulnerable to unrepressed female sexuality. St Augustine, too,
had earlier expressed concern at how 'the crisis of excitement . . .
practically paralyses all power of deliberate thought' and he
particularly stressed how no reasonable man likes another to
observe the 'uncontrollable movements' he makes in orgasm; not
even the male organ was under the control of the owner's mind
and St Augustine looked longingly back to the time before the Fall
when the penis was under its owner's mental control and men
'rationally' impregnated their wives, unemotionally depositing
their semen at the entrance to the vagina in exactly the same spirit
as a farmer ploughs the soil.[112] Equally concerned, Thomas
Browne wrote sadly in 1643 how sexual intercourse is 'the
foolishest act a wise man commits in all his life'. 'I might be
content', he wrote, 'that we might procreate like trees, without
conjunction. . . .'[113] William Petty, too, noted how men made all
aspects of sexual intercourse 'ridiculous, shamefull, and filthy, so
as not to bee seen or spoken of in the company and presence of
others without laughter'.[114] Whatever the underlying causes,
sexuality—and particularly female sexuality—greatly troubled
(some) thinking Christian men.

The Protestant Reformation eventually changed matters somewhat in so far as Protestants believed it better to marry than burn,
always provided no adultery occurred and sexual moderation
prevailed in marriage. Piously one preacher stressed that the

marriage bed 'ought by no meanes to be stained . . . with sensuall excesses'; another cautioned how a man may 'play the adulterer with his own wife . . . by inordinate affection and action'.[115] Eventually capitalism, the Reformation and medical pronouncements were to turn Catholic doctrine on female sexuality upside down: the (bourgeois) woman became perceived as *naturally* sexless and the custodian of spiritual values leading to the happy result that the (bourgeois) husband—more mind than body—no longer needed to fear the marriage bed and the 'insatiable' demands of a 'voracious' wife. Indeed, by the middle of the nineteenth century (male) physicians had pronounced the *healthy* middle-class woman as virtually sexless: male sexual prowess could therefore not easily be challenged. However, not only was any sexual excess deemed religiously wrong, but the medical establishment argued that it was an underlying cause of much disease, the physician Hermann Boerhaave warning as early as 1722 that the 'rash expenditure of semen brings on a lassitude, a feebleness, a weakening of motion, fits, wasting, dryness, fevers, aching of the cerebral membranes, obscuring of the senses and above all the eyes, a decay of the spinal cord, a fatuity, and other like evils'.[116] Even more alarming were the consequences of masturbation. By the nineteenth century the medical profession had decided that masturbation was the disease that threatened the erection of the new industrial civilization with collapse. Severe measures were increasingly taken against young male masturbators and much severer ones against both young and adult female masturbators, including clitoridectomy and ovariotomy.[117]

It is interesting that just as male physicians ultimately came to the opinion that 'nice' women—their class of women—were not only passive but passionless, so in the seventeenth century mechanical philosophers not merely all but banished life conceptually from the cosmos but minimized the role of woman in procreation, declared nature incapable of giving rise to life, and proclaimed matter to be in itself inert and passive—possessing therefore the *ideal* female qualities. According to Robert Hooke, for example, Body and Motion were the 'Female' and 'Male' of Nature, Body being the 'Female or Mother Principle', Hooke explained, 'therefore rightly called by Aristotle and other Philosophers, *Materia,* Material Substance, or *Mater*; this being in itself', he stressed, 'without Life or Motion, without form, and void, and dark, a Power in it self wholly unactive, until it be, as it were, impregnated by the second Principle [Motion], which may represent the Pater, and may be call'd *Paternus, Spiritus,* or hylarchick Spirit. . . . '[118] It is scarcely surprising that bourgeois women would also come to be conceived as essentially passive and inactive. Appropriately enough, as the feminist historian Hilda Smith notes, 'men made some headway during the seventeenth century in becoming accepted as midwives, while the traditional midwives, who were primarily female, were prevented by physicians from securing adequate education or organisation'[119] At the same time the mechanical philosophy upgraded *masculine* creativity: God *the Father* had at one time created the cosmos and all its life forms with no feminine assistance whatever; as befitting her sex, woman's future role was merely to nourish the growing foetus that God the Father had implanted in her (or in her husband according to the animalculist theory of *emboîtement*). Western bourgeois man, made in the image of God the Father and having chosen to cut himself adrift from 'mother earth', had therefore left himself with no alternative but to appropriate the physical world—God's 'great automation'—mechanically and asexually. Asexually?

To the extent that natural philosophy is a life of the mind, it might be argued that it provides an escape from sexuality, the more so the more complete is extirpation of sexual concepts and imagery. Newton himself recommended that the 'way to chastity is not to struggle with incontinent thoughts but to avert the thoughts by some imployment', proceeding to pour scorn on hapless monks who in their idleness fasted themsleves, Newton believed, into seeing 'apparitions of women . . . and of the Devil tempting them to lust'. 'Thus while we pray that God would not lead us into temptation', observed Newton thoughtfully, 'these men ran themselves headlong into it'. At all costs lust was to be avoided. It was with horror that Newton wrote of Simon Magus whose priests, he believed, 'enticed women to lust' and in place of the Eucharist offered—and that after adultery—'the seminal profluvia of men and menstrua of women...saying this is my body and this is my blood'.[120] For Newton, natural philosophy was to be the means of escape from women, carnality and lust. So much so that during a nervous depression in 1693 the 'unfortunate' Newton even wished for John Locke's death after coming to the opinion that this fellow member of the Royal Society had been plotting to 'embroil' him with women![121]

Into their male sanctuary the seventeenth-century practitioners of natural philosophy not surprisingly took with them attitudes and needs reflecting an underlying preoccupation with that dangerous, mysterious, feminine sex, necessarily excluded from the sanctuary because of supposedly inferior mental ability compounded by excessive carnality. Nevertheless, excluded though she might be, the presence of woman as female nature constantly and tantalizingly loomed in the minds of natural philosophers. Thus Francis Bacon wrote that unlike the Aristotelians he could not suppose that men were 'on such familiar terms with nature that in response to a casual and perfunctory salutation she would condescend to unveil for us her mysteries and bestow on us her blessings'.[122] Similarly Thomas Vaughan accused the Aristotelians of having 'Nature before them' but not adopting the right method to 'apprehend her'.[123] Likewise John Webster criticized the Aristotelians for believing, according to him, that pure contemplation would be sufficient to reveal the 'mysteries of mother nature', as if nature would willingly 'follow us into our Chambers and there in idlenesse communicate her secrets unto us'. But 'Dame Nature', he contended, could never be argued out of 'her secrets' and that far more than syllogisms were needed to 'unlock her Cabinet'.[124] What was needed was the 'experimental philosophy' of Francis Bacon and Robert Boyle. Indeed, after Boyle's death, for example, John Evelyn F.R.S. felt himself able to rejoice that, whenever 'stubborn matter' had come under his friend's 'inquisition', Boyle had never failed to extort 'a confession of all that lay in her most intimate recesses'.[125] The 'new philosophers' saw themselves as men equipped to gain for the first time that so elusive and essentially carnal understanding of nature's inner and emphatically feminine secrets. It was Newton's teacher Isaac Barrow who wrote in 1664 how the aim of the new philosophy was to 'search Nature out of her Concealments, and unfold her dark Mysteries'.[126] At best nature was to be wooed in order to be conquered. We have seen how Thomas Sprat, stressing how nature 'is also a Mistress' who yields to the most forward suitor, rejoiced in the expectation that the Royal Society's 'Courtship to Nature' would eventually expose her 'Beautiful Bosom' to the view and satiation of its members.[127] When because of a priority dispute with Hooke Newton threatened to suppress publication of the third book of his *Principia*, Halley expressed to Newton his deepest regret 'that any disgust should make you think of desisting in your pretensions to a Lady, whose favours you have so much reason to boast of. 'Tis not she', Halley comforted Newton, 'but your rivals envying your happiness that endeavour to disturb your quiet enjoyment'.[128] In the minds of the natural philosophers, knowledge of nature was likened to knowledge of woman. In dedicating his *Essay Concerning Human Understanding* to the Earl of Pembroke John Locke expressed his admiration for a man who in his desire for truth had managed to achieve 'so intimate an acquaintance with her in her more retired recesses'.[129] Likewise, a few weeks before the publication of the *Principia*, Halley congratulated Newton on 'exalting humane reason to so sublime a pitch by this utmost effort of the mind' and told him how the world would feel pride in recognizing a man 'capable of penetrating so far into the abstrusest secrets of Nature'. While (male?) pride there has certainly been, nevertheless David Hume went some way to restoring nature's honour when in the following century he perceptively remarked that while Newton had seemed 'to draw off the veil from some of the mysteries of nature', in reality he had only demonstrated the unfathomable obscurity of 'her ultimate secrets'.[130]

However, as Halley's exuberance suggests, the attainment of intimate knowledge of nature is only one aspect of the scientific quest in patriarchal society. Perhaps such a restricted goal suffices for men who want only to return in safety to a surrogate breast or merely to peep at what is hidden away, forbidden and dangerous. But it does not suffice for 'real' men anxious to display their virility for all to see, including themselves. Robert Boyle, it is true, carefully and soberly distinguished between the 'two very distinct Ends that Men may propound to themselves in studying Natural Philosophy. For some Men care only to Know Nature, others desire to Command Her'.[131] More colourfully and more forcefully, on the other hand, Thomas Vaughan urged philosophers to redirect their attentions away from the 'Vomits of Aristotle' and back towards 'the green, youthfull, and flowerie *Bosome* of the *Earth*', combining this advice with the virile injunction that on no account must philosophers be content merely to 'lick the shell' of nature but must 'pierce ... experimentally into the Center of things'. Well might Nature complain, continued Vaughan, that he had 'all most broken her Seale, and exposed her naked to the World'.[132] If a life of the mind—and devotion to the quest for truth—is insufficient to prove social superiority and establish true masculinity, then scientific truth can be appropriated to prove virility, especially if that truth is the *causal* knowledge of nature openly sought by experimental and mechanical philosophers. Aristotelian philosophers had necessarily stood impotent before nature, Francis Bacon jeered, destined 'never to lay hold of her and capture her'. Dissipating his energies in useless contemplation, Aristotle had 'left nature herself untouched and inviolate'. Bacon, on the contrary, felt able to extend an invitation to those 'true sons of knowledge' who aspire 'to penetrate further' and 'overcome ... nature in action' to join with him 'that passing by the outer courts of nature, which numbers have trodden, we may find a way at length into her inner chambers'. Bacon proclaimed his virile intention to inaugurate the 'truly masculine birth of time', the new era in which mankind would increasingly gain the power to 'conquer and subdue [nature], to shake her to her foundations'. In his *Advancement of Learning* Bacon appealed to men to make peace among themselves and join forces against nature 'to storm and occupy her castles and strongholds', an invitation to what might not unreasonably be called gang-rape of nature.[133] Following in Bacon's footsteps, Henry Oldenburg wrote to a future Fellow of the Royal Society that the 'true sons of learning' are those men who do not remain satisfied with well-known truths but strive to 'penetrate from Nature's antechamber to her inner closet'. Not unexpectedly, we find a specialist on the Enlightenment writing how the language of the eighteenth-century *philosophes* was 'redolent with metaphors of battle and the physical act of penetration'.[134] Science was a masculine quest and the earth was female. A final example from the beginning of the nineteenth century: at the start of his career at the Royal Institution Sir Humphry Davy, future President of the Royal Society, explained proudly how the 'man of science', not content with what is found on the surface of the earth, 'has penetrated into her bosom . . . for the purpose of allaying the restlessness of his desires or of extending and increasing his power'. 'And who would not be ambitious of becoming acquainted with the most profound secrets of nature; of ascertaining her hidden operations?' asked Davy rhetorically. Science, he triumphantly proclaimed, has bestowed upon the natural philosopher 'powers which may be called creative; which have enabled him . . . by his experiments to interrogate nature with power, not simply as a scholar, passive and seeking only to understand her operations, but rather as a master, active with his own instruments'.[135]

I have written earlier that liberation of humankind from the many tyrannies of nature that exist is one thing; the desire to achieve total power over nature 'for its own sake' is quite another. For its own sake? It would rather appear that after a long historical development a class of men had emerged in western Europe who would sever ties with 'mother earth' in pursuit of a compulsive drive to prove their masculinity and virility. The means was to be ever-developing technological appropriation of a passive earth so that men might achieve, in Francis Bacon's momentous words, 'the effecting of all things possible'.[136] What was to be the outcome? Bearing in mind men's obsession with female sexuality throughout the period of early modern Europe and with their own fear of inadequacy vis-à-vis female desire and the capacity of non-human demon lovers (Lynn White reminds us that 'no other civilized age anywhere in the world has made the male genitals so conspicuous as the sixteenth century with the codpiece'),[137] I turn very briefly to odd but interesting remarks originating in the main from the middle class of that first European country to undertake on a massive scale the industrial appropriation of the natural world.

The louder the boast, the greater the proclaimed objectives, perhaps the more insecure the would-be dominant male. True, by the middle of the nineteenth century medical pronouncements were, as we have seen, helping to render bourgeois husbands safe from wifely criticism, *healthy* middle-class women being pronounced by physicians as essentially asexual: 'As a general rule, a modest woman seldom desires any sexual gratification for herself. She submits to her husband's, but only to please him . . . No nervous or feeble young man need, therefore, be deterred from marriage by an exaggerated notion of the arduous duties required from him', advised in 1862 the influential physician William Acton. Although that was undoubtedly reassuring for the middle-class male, nevertheless 'low and vulgar women' were perceived as retaining the animal's sexual voraciousness while working-class men constantly threatened to overturn the social order.[138] Not all ruling-class males—particularly bourgeois males —felt as socially and sexually secure as they would have liked. Women were not the only threat they had made to their sexual self-respect.

It is significant that African males, enslaved by white ruling classes from the fifteenth century onwards, were almost immediately regarded by white males as sexually more potent than themselves and considerably better endowed by nature. Indeed, as a consequence of such a 'picture of Negro sexuality which developed so rapidly and in such explicit terms in the sixteenth and early seventeenth century', comments an historian of racism, the idea that the negro's penis was larger than the white man's was to become by the early eighteenth century 'something of a commonplace in European scientific circles'.[139] It was therefore rather fortunate that there could be no questioning the superior intellect of white ruling-class males: 'I am apt to suspect the negroes, and in general all the other species of men . . . to be naturally inferior to the whites', confessed David Hume in 1748. And he explained: 'There never was a civilised nature of any other complexion than white, nor even any individual eminent either in action or speculation. No ingenious manufactures amongst them, no arts, no sciences.[140] Before the end of the eighteenth century Dr Charles White, Fellow of the Royal Society, after noting the 'scientific' fact that 'the PENIS of an African is larger than that of a European [as] has . . . been shewn in every anatomical school in London' (capitals in the original), felt somewhat relieved to find that in '[a]scending the line of gradation, we come at last to the white European; who being most removed from the brute creation, may, on that account, be considered as the most beautiful of the human race'. Moreover, inadequate compensation though this might have seemed, White triumphantly stated that the cavity of the skull, 'which contains the *cerebrum* and *cerebellum*, is less capacious in the African than in the European'—indeed, that there could be no doubting the white man's 'superiority in intellectual powers'.[141] While the African might be more potent than the white man, closer to nature as he was, it was constantly asserted that he was irremediably far behind the white man's level of intelligence. Lacking intelligence, then, it was thought or hoped that he did not attract healthy white middle-class women. As was only to be expected, however, the 'lower class of women in *England,* are remarkably fond of the blacks, for reasons too brutal to mention', indicted the judge and writer Edward Long in his *Candid Reflections . . . on What is Commonly Called the Negro-Cause,* adding for good measure that the women 'would connect themselves with horses and asses, if the laws permitted them' (no longer with demons, one notes, but certainly with negroes, ideally with horses and asses!). This being the case and given the existence of social mobility, both upwards and downwards, the introduction of negro servants into England would mean the presence of a 'venomous and dangerous ulcer' whose malignancy would in time lead to the infection of every family in the country. Such a diabolical conspiracy was to be prevented at all costs. Like Charles White a few years later, Long believed it essential to emphasize the existence of 'gradations of the intellectual faculty', first rudiments appearing in monkeys, more advanced stages in 'the *oran-outang,* that type of man, and the Guiney Negroes', while ascending upwards away from 'varieties of this class to the lighter casts' we reach above all that which must be so carefully cherished—the intellect's 'utmost limit of perfection in the pure White'.[142] Examples could be repeated indefinitely: white males towards the top of the social pyramid rested the legitimation of their privileged position on their claim to intellectual dominance over all below them—over their 'own' women, over all other women, and over all other men, white, non-white, and particularly black—and, moreover, a claim backed by the prestige of science.

As a good Victorian, T.H. Huxley omitted consideration of negroes' special 'lower' capacities in his 1865 essay 'Emancipation: Black and White'. Instead he emphasised the white man's 'superior' mental skills, informing readers that 'no rational man, cognizant of the facts, believes that the average negro is the equal, still less the superior, of the average white man'. This being so, Huxley continued, 'it is simply incredible that, when . . . our prognathous relative has a fair field and no favours, as well as no oppressor, he will be able to compete successfully with his bigger-brained and smaller-jawed rival, in a contest which is to be carried on by thoughts and not by bites'. In the contest between white man and black man, it is, Huxley insisted, brain *not body* that counts. On the other hand, when it came to consideration of the ' "irrepressible" woman question' Huxley chose to emphasize the white man's supposedly mental *and physical* 'superiority' over his potential female competitor. For even after women's emancipation—of which Huxley professed himself an advocate—Darwin's 'bulldog' was confident that the 'big chests, the massive brains, the vigorous muscles and stout frames, of the best men will carry the day, whenever it is worth their while to contest the prizes of life with the best women'.[143] In the contest between white man and white woman it is now brain *and body* that counts. Four years later in 1869 Francis Galton in his *Hereditary Genius* dismissed any suggestion that physical weakness was 'an essential or even usual accompaniment' of genius. On the contrary, Darwin's cousin enthused, a 'collection of living magnates in various branches of intellectual achievement is always a feast to my eyes, being as they are, such massive, vigorous, capable-looking animals'.[144] Charles Darwin himself put the matter very simply in his *Descent of Man*: 'Man is more powerful in body and mind than woman', he affirmed.[145]

Even so, is he more sexually 'powerful' than woman and what of his black rivals seeking emancipation? Thank God, the educated Victorian could rejoice, for the white man's scientific and industrial civilization that lifted his (ruling-class) virility and potency beyond reach and challenge. It might be true, as the relentless Dr Acton had suggested, that the 'intellectual qualities are usually in an inverse ratio to the sexual appetites, . . . almost . . . as if the two were incompatible; the exercise of the one annihilating the other', but science was a white man's pursuit and it was an essentially *virile* one.[146] Thus a man's success in medicine depended 'on his virile courage, which the normal woman does not have nor is expected to have', explained Dr G.H. Simmons, the editor of the *Journal of the American Medical Association* in 1900.[147] Indeed, before the end of the nineteenth century an English physician found himself able to put 'other races' and all women in their inferior place by invoking male accomplishments in science (managing in a few words to correlate science with mind, knowledge, power and the male ability to penetrate): 'the principal feature', wrote Dr J.H. Bennet, 'which appears to me to characterize the Caucasian race, to raise it immeasurably above all other races, is the power that many of its *male* members have of advancing the horizon of science, of penetrating beyond the existing limits of knowledge—in a word, the power of scientific discovery. I am not aware', he continued, 'that the female members of our race participate in this mental power, in this supreme development of the human mind... What right then have women to claim mental *equality* with men?'[148] So argued Dr Bennet in 1870 (emphases in the original). It remained, however, the sad case that men had still to be gestated within and suckled by women even though male physicians had at least managed to gain control of childbirth. Mournfully, therefore, a distinguished New York gynaecologist commented in the 1850s that 'from the foundation of the world man has been born of woman; and not withstanding that his inventive genius has discovered steam... and sends lightning to do his bidding over the almost boundless extent of the world, yet we cannot hope that any change may be affected in this particular'.[149] If the mechanical philosophy had 'liberated' man from intimate and sensuous connection with the earth, it had thus far not been able to 'liberate' men from their reproductive dependence on women. Or from their fear of female sexuality.[150]

In the middle of the seventeenth century Henry Vaughan, twin brother of the Paracelsian-Agrippan Thomas Vaughan, wrote an interesting verse:[151]

> I summoned nature; pierced through all her store:
> Broke up some seals, which none had touched before;
> Her womb, her bosom, and her head,
> Where all her secrets lay a-bed,
> I rifled quite; and having past
> Through all the creatures, came at last
> To search myself, where I did find
> Traces and sounds of a strange kind.

Perhaps the 'male-female relation' ought not to be exluded from a discussion of the scientific revolution. Indeed, throughout this essay I have attempted to demonstrate that the scientific revolution cannot be understood without reference to the consequences of social stratification. And everywhere I have more than hinted that neither can it be understood without reference to sexual stratification as well. Neither, perhaps, for that matter can the industrial revolution. And neither can current problems.

AFTERWORD

The correlation of consciousness with masculinity culminates in the development of science, as an attempt by the masculine spirit to emancipate itself from the power of the unconscious.

> Erich Neumann, *The Origins and History of Consciousness*, 1949

The male ideology of the 'feminine' that we have inherited in the West seems to be rooted in a self-alienated experience of the body and the world, projecting upon the sexual other the lower half of these dualisms....

It is perhaps not too much to say that the Achilles' heel of human civilization, which today has reached global genocidal and ecocidal proportions, resides in this false development of maleness through repression of the female.

> Rosemary R. Ruether, *New Woman, New Earth: Sexist Ideologies and Human Liberation*, 1975

It is difficult not to feel admiration for the men who achieved the multifaceted revolution this essay has described. Above all, mechanical and experimental philosophers expressed confidence in their potential ability to gain power over the natural world. The truth they sought was, as Francis Bacon so crisply put it, the truth whose measurement is power: the knowledge they sought was *causal* knowledge of natural processes. Not for them the privilege of merely uncovering nature's veils and peeping at her secrets.

In so far as nature oppresses humankind, the institutionalized search for causal knowledge is clearly a necessary feature of human society. However, as this essay I hope demonstrates, the institutionalization of the search for power over the natural world occurred in the seventeenth century in a context of extreme social stratification. True, nature was harsh. But social conditions were also very harsh. And since mechanical and experimental philosophers in the main allied themselves with ruling and privileged groups they thereby constrained themselves to interpret the natural world and their findings in a way that at the very least did not undermine the legitimation of class power but rather reinforced that legitimation. Moreover, it was inevitable that the eventual fusion of scientific and industrial revolutions would lead to the application of sophisticated scientific technology in the enhancement of the wealth and power of ruling groups and where

253

necessary—and it was often necessary—in the suppression of the disprivileged.

I have argued that the diabolicentric cosmology against which so many of the natural philosophers contended had been a result not only of the harshness of nature but of social stratification. Although the Copernican revolution undermined this cosmology, it was nevertheless possible for people with no knowledge of the Copernican world system to reject the diabolicentric aspects of a geocentric cosmology and indeed to reject supernatural religion in general; all that had been necessary for Gerrard Winstanley was an awareness of the lack of empirical support for supernatural religion combined with a burning awareness of the unjustness of the social world and of the social function of religion in underwriting the social *status quo*. Moreover, Winstanley was also aware that without the creation of a just society, the acquisition of power over nature would at best prove to be a Janus-faced achievement, at worst a disaster for humanity. History has, I think, confirmed that in an unjust, divided world science cannot in the long run help mankind but only exacerbate the conflict between rich and poor, between developed and underdeveloped. If it is pointless to argue that what seventeenth-century western Europe needed was not so much a scientific revolution but rather a transformation towards a just social order, is it now necessary to insist that what the world needs is not so much more science and technology but societal transformation that eliminates the causes of social, national and racial conflict? In *Liberation and the Aims of Science* I have argued that the principal cause remains class control of productive forces together with the (consequent) maldistribution of wealth, privilege, power and knowledge within and between nations.

But perhaps there is, as this essay has suggested, an equally serious and perhaps even more recalcitrant problem than that of class structure. In many men's eyes it must have appeared in gathering-hunting societies that women could do everything men could do and yet also possessed the magical power of creating and growing babies. Hunting men, born of and suckled by women, whose primary identification was with women, were no doubt helped in securing an elusive 'masculine' identity by means of a friendly and convenient division of labour in which they (and women) placed great value on an all-male activity such as hunting. However, in societies in which men dominate women, whether classless or class-structured, men face the problem of convincing themselves that they are in fact 'superior' to the 'inferior' creatures with whom they necessarily come into intimate contact. Thus the sexual relation between men and 'their' women becomes very problematic in 'sexist' society particularly because women, unless totally sexually repressed, are able to hit back at their 'owners' and sexual 'partners' by taunting their sexual fragility vis-à-vis women's real or feigned sexual voraciousness. Men, it might be argued, have apparently responded by attempting to establish manhood and virility in ways less susceptible to traumatic failure. Negatively, for example, they have downgraded female magical powers by denying any creative female role in the creation of the cosmos or in the creation of offspring. Positively, they have claimed that it is men who possess the magical creative power of the word: Marduk took over from his ancestress Tiamat whom he slew in combat after demonstrating magical oral powers; God the Father created the cosmos by His Word alone with no female help possible or necessary. But male magical power is nonetheless illusory and thus overall in pre-capitalist society the proof of male virility and the means of men's oppression of women remained anchored to men's greater physical strength. In class-structured capitalist society, however, further problems arise in so far as the ruling and privileged classes are no longer 'virile' warriors but calculating, reasoning men. However, ruling-class virility, especially that of bourgeois and scientist (as opposed to the warrior class), can now be demonstrated to (sexually repressed) women and to oppressed classes and races by grandiose technological appropriation of the earth. For since scientific power over natural processes, unlike magical oral power, not only 'works' but is highly efficacious, the scientists, technologists and managers of capitalist society have at their disposal a *real* means of displaying their virility and of reassuring themselves of their 'superior' masculinity. And such a display they have certainly attempted —albeit, as many feminists have unkindly remarked, their display now threatens humanity with total disaster.

Obviously these few lines serve only to suggest the existence of real problems characteristic of sexist society, greatly exacerbated by class structure. It is nevertheless apparent that the transcendence of capitalist society might not bring about the realization of a gentle, non-oppressive world but on the contrary might lead to the realization of a society in which a male-dominant scientific-technocratic elite seeks to achieve ever-increasing power in a perpetual and increasingly catastrophic display of male virility. The transcendence of capitalist society is a necessary but not a sufficient condition for the realization of a just and humanly desirable world. What is also necessary is the transcendence of male sexism (and female counter-sexism). Marcuse is, I believe, correct in arguing that only if patriarchal domination can be transcended will it be possible to realize a sensuously rich, increasingly gentle, and beautiful world. And I think he is also correct in believing that a necessary aspect of such a social world will be a new perception of the non-human world and of the relationship of human beings to that world.

In summary, then, if it remains doubtful that God acted wisely in the 1660s in replacing Christ's Second Coming with the Royal Society and Paris Academy, the millenarian hope still remains that if both capitalism and sexism can be transcended all humankind may yet have good reason to celebrate the coming of the new philosophy.

ABBREVIATIONS

AL	Bacon, *The Advancement of Learning* in Spedding.
AMA	Vaughan, *Anima Magica Abscondita: Or A Discourse of the universall Spirit of Nature* (London, 1650).
AT	Vaughan, *Anthroposophia Theomagica: Or A Discourse of the Nature of Man and his state after death* (London, 1650).
CHO	A.R. Hall and M.B. Hall (eds.), *The Correspondence of Henry Oldenburg* (University of Wisconsin Press, 1965–73; Mansell, 1975), 10 volumes.
CIN	H.W. Turnbull, J.F. Scott, A.R. Hall and L. Tilling (eds.), *The Correspondence of Isaac Newton* (Cambridge UP, 1959–77), 7 vols.
DAL	Bacon, *Of the Dignity and Advancement of Learning* in Spedding.
Dialogue	Galileo, *Dialogue Concerning the Two Chief World Systems,* tr. S. Drake (University of California Press, 1953).
DM	Descartes, *Discourse on the Method of Rightly Conducting the Reason and Seeking Truth in the Sciences,* tr. L.J. Lafleur (Liberal Arts Press, 1956).
DR	Copernicus, *De Revolutionibus.*
DScB	C.G. Gillispie (ed.), *Dictionary of Scientific Biography* (Scribner, 1970–6), 14 volumes.
EM	P. Hazard, *The European Mind 1680–1715* (1935; Penguin, 1964).
EW	E.W. Monter, *European Witchcraft* (Wiley, 1969).
GBWW	Great Books of the Western World (Chicago: Encyclopedia Britannica, 1952).
HRS	Sprat, *The History of the Royal Society of London,* J.I. Cape and H.W. Jones (eds.), (Routledge, 1959).
NNL	M. Boas Hall (ed.), *Nature and Nature's Laws* (Harper, 1970).
NO	Bacon, *Novum Organon* in Spedding.
NS	A. Koyré, *Newtonian Studies* (Chapman and Hall, 1965).
PM	Newton, *Principia Mathematica,* tr. A. Motte, revised F. Cajori (1934; University of California Press, 1966).
PP	Descartes, *Principles of Philosophy.*

RDM K. Thomas, *Religion and the Decline of Magic* (Weidenfeld, 1971; Penguin, 1973).

RPM E. Cassirer, P.O. Kristeller and J.H. Randall, Jr., *The Renaissance Philosophy of Man* (University of Chicago Press, 1948).

SDM D.P. Walker, *Spiritual and Demonic Magic from Ficino to Campanella* (1958; Notre Dame Press, 1975).

Spedding J. Spedding, R.L. Ellis and D.N. Heath (eds.), *The Works of Francis Bacon* (London, 1858–61; reprinted Friedrich Frommann Verlag, 1963), 7 vols.

SPSK E. Mendelsohn, P. Weingart and R. Whitley (eds.), *The Social Production of Scientific Knowledge* (Reidel, 1977).

VTPM E.J. Aiton, *The Vortex Theory of Planetary Motions* (Macdonald-Elsevier, 1972).

WGW G.H. Sabine (ed.), *The Works of Gerrard Winstanley* (Cornell UP, 1941).

WJL *The Works of John Locke* (London, 1823; reprinted Scientia Verlag Aalen, 1963), 10 vols.

WRB T. Birch (ed.), *The Works of the Honourable Robert Boyle* (London, 1722), 6 vols.

WTUD C. Hill, *The World Turned Upside Down* (Temple Smith, 1972; Penguin, 1975).

ACKNOWLEDGEMENTS

By permission of Chatto and Windus Ltd: Quotation from *Malleus Maleficarum*, by Kramer and Springer, translated by Montague Summers. By permission of Random House, Inc.: Excerpt from *Cows, Pigs, Wars and Witches*, by Marvin Harris, ©Random House, Inc. 1974. Reprinted by permission of Princeton University Press: Excerpts from *Colloquium of the Seven about Secrets of the Sublime*, by Jean Bodin, Translation, Annotations and Critical Readings, by Marion Leathers Daniels Kuntz, © Princeton University Press 1975. By permission of Mouton Publishers: Extracts from *The Ash Wednesday Supper*, by G. Bruno, translated by S. L. Jaki (1975). By permission of University of California Press: Extracts from *Concerning the Two Great World Systems*, by Galileo, translated by S. Drake (1953). By permission of University Books, Inc.: Extracts from *Demonolatry*, by N. Remy, translated by E. A. Ashwin (1974). By permission of the Royal Astronomical Society: Extract from *Occasional Notes of the Royal Astronomical Society, No. 10*, translated by J. F. Dobson and S. Brodestsky (1947).

NOTES

Preface
Some works of authors mentioned in the Preface but which are not referred to
explicitly in the Notes are:
A.G. Debus, *Man and Nature in the Renaissance* (Cambridge UP, 1978).
E.J. Dijksterhuis, *The Mechanization of the World Picture,* tr. C. Dikshoorn
(1950; Oxford UP, 1961).
B. Easlea, *Liberation and the Aims of Science* (Sussex UP, 1973).
J. Farley, *The Spontaneous Generation Controversy: From Descartes to Oparin*
(Johns Hopkins UP, 1972).
R.S. Westfall, *Science and Religion in Seventeenth-Century England* (1958; Ann
Arbor, 1973); *The Construction of Modern Science: Mechanisms and
Mechanics* (Wiley, 1971; Cambridge UP, 1977).

Chapter **1** *The Existence of Witches*
1. Book of Revelation, The Bible, 13:18 and 20:2,3; see, for example, E.L.
   Tuveson, *Millenium and Utopia: A Study in the Background of the Idea of
   Progress* (1949; Harper, 1964), pp. 39–40.
2. H. Kamen, *The Iron Century: Social Change in Europe 1550–1660* (1971;
   Sphere, 1976).
3. Exodus, 22:18
4. E.W. Monter, 'Pedestal and Stake: Courtly Love and Witchcraft', in R.
   Bridenthal and C. Koonz (eds), *Becoming Visible: Women in European
   History* (Houghton Mifflin, 1977), p. 133
5. *A History of the Rise and Influence of the Spirit of Rationalism in Europe*
   (1865; London, 1904), Vol. 1, pp. 137–8
6. *HRS,* pp. 339–41
7. *A Philosophical Dictionary* (London: Truelove, no date), Vol 1, pp. 436–7;
   Vol. 2, p. 59
8. P. Smith, *A History of Modern Culture* (1930; Harvard UP, 1957), Vol. 1,
   pp. 450–1; *The European Witch-Craze* (Penguin, 1969), p. 108
9. Marcuse writes that 'rational' is a 'mode of thought and action . . . geared to
   reduce ignorance, destruction, brutality, and oppression'; in *One-
   Dimensional Man* (Routlege, 1964), p. 142
10. *Malleus Maleficarum,* tr. M. Summers (Pushkin Press, 1948), Pt I, Question
    2, pp. 16 and 21
11. *Ibid,* Pt. I, Qu. 6, p. 47.
12. *Ibid,* Pt. II, Qu. 1, Ch. 1, pp. 97–8; Ch. 13, p. 143
13. *Ibid,* Pt. I, Qu. 6, p. 41.
14. *Ibid,* Pt. II, Qu. I, Ch. 3, p. 108.
15. *Ibid,* p. 107.
16. *Ibid,* Pt. I, Qu. 12, p. 69; Qu. 18, p. 87.
17. *Ibid,* Pt. III, Qu. 1, p. 206
18. *Ibid,* Pt. III, Qu. 8, p. 215; Qu. 22, p. 243

19. *Ibid*, Pt. II, Qu. 1, Ch. 15, p. 149
20. *Ibid*, Pt. III, Qu. 14, p. 226; Qu. 25, p. 249
21. *EW*, p. 59
22. *On the Tricks of Demons (De Praestigiis Daemonum)*; references are to the French translation of the enlarged edition, *Histoires, disputes et discovrs, des illusions et impostures des diables* (Geneva, 1579); Bk 3, Ch. 3, p. 212, tr. in *EW*, p. 42
23. Tr. H.C.E. Midelfort in R.M. Kingdon (ed.), *Transition and Revolution* (Burgess, 1974), p.223.
24. *Tricks of Demons*, Bk. 6, Ch. 6, p. 640 and Ch. 4, pp. 628–9, quoted in H.C. Lea, *Materials toward a History of Witchcraft* (Yoseloff, 1957), Vol. 2, pp. 524, 523.
25. *Tricks of Demons*, Bk. 3, Ch. 4, p. 213, tr. in *EW*, p. 43.
26. *Tricks of Demons*, Bk. 6, Ch. 17, p. 674; see *EW*, p. 37.
27. *EW*, p. 47.
28. *Drama of Universal Nature*, quoted in P. King, *The Ideology of Order: A Comparative Analysis of Jean Bodin and Thomas Hobbes* (Allen and Unwin, 1974), p. 21; K.D. McRae (ed.), *The Six Bookes...*, tr. R. Knowles (Harvard UP, 1962), p. 539.
29. *De la Demonomanie des Sorciers (On the Demonic Madness of Witches)* (Chez Arnould Coninx, 1586), p. 411, quoted in G. Zilboorg, *A History of Medical Psychology* (Norton, 1941), p. 240; *Colloquium of the Seven..*, tr. and ed. by M.L.D. Kuntz (Princeton UP, 1975), p. 82; *Demonomanie*, p. 405, quoted in Zilboorg, p. 238.
30. *Demonomanie*, pp. 402–4; *EW*, pp. 53–4; for a discussion of Simon Magus, see E.M. Butler, *The Myth of the Magus* (1948; Cambridge UP, 1979).
31. *Demonomanie*, Preface, tr. H.C.E. Midelfort, 'Were There Really Witches?' in R.M. Kingdon (ed.), *Transition and Revolution* (Burgess, 1974), p. 229; see also *Demonomanie*, pp. 425–6.
32. *Colloquium*, ref. 29, pp. 21–2.
33. *Demonomanie*, pp. 385–6, tr. J. O'Faolain and L. Martines (eds.), *Not in God's Image: Women in History* (Fontana, 1974), p. 222.
34. *Demonomanie*, Bk. 4, Ch. 1, p. 283; C. Baxter, 'Johann Weyer's *De Praestigiis Daemonum*' in S. Anglo (ed.), *The Damned Art* (Routledge, 1977), p. 54.
35. *EW*, p. 69.
36. *The Discoverie of Witchcraft* (1584; EP Publishing, 1973), pp. x, 396, xii, xxii.
37. *Ibid*, pp. 11, 2.
38. *Ibid*, p. 30.
39. *Ibid*, pp. 43, 44.
40. *Ibid*, pp. 68, 46, 82.
41. *Ibid*, pp. 313, 363, 374.
42. *Ibid*, pp. 254–5, 237.
43. *Ibid*, pp. 245, 237–8, 247.
44. *Ibid*, p. 406.
45. *Ibid*, pp. 411, 428, 429, 459.
46. 'On Books', Bk. 2, in *Essays*, tr. J.M. Cohen (Penguin, 1958), p. 171.
47. 'A Defence of Seneca and Plutarch', Bk 2, *ibid*, p. 228.
48. 'That it is folly to measure truth and error by our own capacity', Bk 1, *ibid*, pp. 87, 89.
49. 'On Cripples', Bk. 3, in *the Essential Montaigne*, tr. S. Hughes (Mentor, 1970), p. 315.
50. *Ibid*, pp. 313, 311, 315–16.

51. *Ibid,* pp. 315–16.
52. *Ibid,* p. 316.
53. 'On Physiognomy', Bk 3, *Essays,* p. 343.
54. 'On the Affection of Fathers for their Children', Bk 2, *ibid,* p. 142.
55. 'On Cruelty', Bk 2, *ibid,* pp. 184, 189, 190.
56. 'Upon Some Verses of Virgil', Bk 3, in W.C. Hazlitt (ed.), tr. C. Cotton, GBWW Vol. 25, pp. 413, 429.
57. 'On the Power of the Imagination', Bk. 1 in *Essays,* p. 42.
58. See M.H. Ilsley, *A Daughter of the Renaissance* (The Hague, Mouton, 1963), especially Ch. 14. Reacting to (male) criticisms of her work, de Gournay made the memorable comment, 'That one who says thirty absurdities will still win the prize because of his beard'; Ilsley, pp. 71, 209.
59. *Demonolatry,* tr. E.A. Ashwin (University Books, 1974), p. xii.
60. *Ibid,* pp. 56, 14.
61. *Ibid,* pp. 48–51.
62. *Ibid,* p. 53.
63. *Ibid,* p. 74.
64. *Ibid,* p. 182.
65. *Ibid,* p. 183.
66. *Ibid,* p. 183–4.
67. *Ibid,* pp. 185, 178, 185–6, 188.
68. J.O'Faolain and L. Martines, ref. 33, pp. 145, 141; quoted in V.L. Bullough, *The Subordinate Sex* (Baltimore, Penguin, 1974), p. 115. For a general discussion see R.R. Ruether, 'Misogynism and Virginal Feminism in the Fathers of the Church' in R.R. Ruether (ed.), *Religion and Sexism* (Simon and Schuster, 1974).
69. W.H. Wagner, 'The Demonization of Women' in *Religion in Life* (Spring, 1973), pp. 56–74, p. 73; J.E. Hunter, 'Images of Women', *J. of Social Issues* Vol. 32 (1976), pp. 7–17, p. 12.
70. Quoted in R.W. Southern, *Western Society and the Church in the Middle Ages* (Penguin, 1970), p. 314.
71. K. Casey, 'The Cheshire Cat: Reconstructing the Experience of Medieval Women' in B.A. Carrol (ed.), *Liberating Women's History* (University of Illinois, 1976), p. 226.
72. 'Women and the Civil War Sects', *Past and Present,* No. 13 (1958); reprinted in T. Ashton (ed.), *Crisis in Europe 1560–1660* (Routledge, 1965), p. 330.
73. E. Power, *Medieval Women,* M.M. Postan (ed.), (Cambridge UP, 1975), p. 30.
74. Midelfort, *Witch Hunting in Southwestern Germany 1562–1684* (Stanford UP, 1972), p. 187.
75. Kamen, ref. 2, pp. 366, 276.
76. 'Les Paysans de Languerdoc', *EW,* pp. 165, 170.
77. *Cows, Pigs, Wars and Witches* (Random House, 1974), pp. 239–40.
78. *AL,* Vol. 3, Bk 2, p. 372; *DAL,* Vol. 4, Bk 4, p. 388.
79. P. Kibre, 'The Faculty of Medicine at Paris, Charlatanism, and Unlicensed Medical Practices in the Later Middle Ages', *B. of the History of Medicine,* Vol. 27 (1953), pp. 1–20.
80. Quoted in M.J. Hughes, *Women Healers in Medieval Life and Literature* (1943; Libraries Press, reprinted 1968), pp. 85–6 note 21.
81. Quoted in V.L. Bullough, *The Development of Medicine as a Profession* (Hafner, 1966), p. 95.
82. Quoted in Hughes, ref. 80, p. 86; see also J. Donnison, *Midwives and Medical Men* (Heinemann, 1977), pp. 1–15, B. Ehrenreich and D. English, *Witches, Midwives, and Nurses* (The Feminist Press, 1973).
83. Quoted in W. Pagel, *Paracelsus* (S. Karger, 1958), p. 296.

84. *Discourse* (Cambridge, 1608) pp. 174, 256, 175–6.
85. *RDM,* p. 646.
86. *Ibid,* pp. 579, 646.
87. Tr. in D. Stimson, *The Gradual Acceptance of the Copernican Theory* (Hanover, New Hampshire, 1917), pp. 46–7.

Chapter 2   The Status of the Earth
1. T.S. Healy, (ed.), *Ignatius His Conclave* (Oxford UP, 1969), p. 15.
2. *Dialogue,* p. 328.
3. Ref. 5 (Ch. 1), p. 9.
4. M.G. Evans, *The Physical Philosophy of Aristotle* (U of New Mexico Press, 1964).
5. *On the Generation of Animals,* tr. A.L. Peck (Heinemann, 1953), 716a, p. 11. See especially M.C. Horowitz, 'Aristotle and Women', *J. Hist. Biology* Vol. 9 (1976), pp. 183–213.
6. *Generation of Animals,* ref. 5, 732a, p. 133.
7. *The Politics of Aristotle,* tr. E. Barker (Oxford UP, 1946), 1254b, p. 13 and 1335b, p. 327.
8. *Metaphysics,* tr. W.D. Ross (Oxford UP, 1928), 1041b; *De Generatione et Corruptione,* tr. H.H. Joachim in D. Ross (ed.), *The Works of Aristotle* (Oxford UP, 1930), Vol. 2, 322a.
9. *De Generatione . . . ,*336b.
10. *Physica,* tr. R.P. Hardie and R.K. Gaye in Ross, ref. 8, Vol. 2, 192a.
11. *De Caelo (On the Heavens),* tr. J.L. Stocks in Ross, ref. 8, Vol. 2, 310a.
12. *De Partibus Animalium,* tr. D.M. Balme (Oxford UP, 1972), 727b, p. 49.
13. *Historia Animalium,* tr. D'Arcy W. Thompson (Oxford UP, 1910), 582a.
14. *On the Generation of Animals,* 737a, p. 175.
15. *Historia Animalium,* 559a.
16. *De Caelo,* ref. 11, 292a.
17. *The Almagest,* Bk. 1, Sec. 7, tr.R.C. Taliaferro in GBWW, Vol. 16, p. 12.
18. 'Commentary on Aristotle's Physics' in M.R. Cohen and I.E. Drabkin (eds.), *A Source Book of Greek Science* (1948; Harvard UP, 1958), pp. 217–23, p. 223.
19. Quoted in V.L. Bullough, *The Subordinate Sex* (Baltimore, Penguin, 1974), p. 174.
20. See J. Taylor, 'Copernicus on the Evils of Inflation...', *J. of the History of Ideas* Vol. 16 (1955), pp. 540–7.
21. Quoted in R. Wittkower, *Architectural Principles in the Age of Humanism* (Tiranti, 1962), pp. 21–2.
22. *Ibid,* pp. 20–1.
23. *DR,* tr. J.F. Dobson and S. Brodestsky, *Occasional Notes of the Royal Astronomical Society,* No. 10 (1947), reprinted in M.K. Munitz (ed.), *Theories of the Universe* (Free Press, 1957), Preface, p. 150.
24. *Narratio Prima* in E. Rosen (ed.), *Three Copernican Treatises* (Dover, 1959), pp. 146, 145. According to Rosen, p. 21, Copernicus nowhere distinguishes between real and imaginary spheres.
25. *DR,* Bk. 1, Chs 10 and 5 in Munitz, ref. 23, pp. 169, 157.
26. *Ibid,* Ch. 10, p. 169; see especially the classic account by T.S. Kuhn in *The Copernican Revolution* (Harvard UP, 1957).
27. *DR,* Ch. 8, in Munitz, ref. 23, p. 161.
28. *Ibid,* Ch. 8, p. 163.
29. Periods and average distances are calculated from the results given by Copernicus in Ch. 5 of *DR* and are taken from A.P. French, *Newtonian Mechanics* (MIT Press, 1971), p. 252.

30. *DR,* Bk. 1, Ch. 10, p. 170; Preface, p. 151.
31. *DR,* tr. C.G. Willis in GBWW, Vol. 16, p.732.
32. *DR,* Bk. 1, Ch. 10, in Munitz, ref. 23, p. 169.
33. *Ibid,* Preface, p. 152.
34. Quoted in R. Dugas, *A History of Mechanics* (Routledge, 1957), p. 109.
35. 'On the Most Recent Phenomena of the Aetherial World', in *Occasional Notes of the Royal Astronomical Society,* No. 21 (1959), reprinted in *NNL,* pp. 59–61.
36. 'In Defense of Raymond Sebond', Bk. 2, *The Essential Montaigne,* pp. 233–4.
37. 'On Presumption', Bk. 2, *Essays,* pp. 217–18.
38. 'In Defense of Raymond Sebond', p. 125.
39. Quoted in A. Koestler, *The Sleepwalkers* (Penguin, 1964), p. 364.
40. Bk. 5, tr. C.G. Wallis, in GBWW, Vol. 16, p. 1050.
41. Quoted in A. Koyré, *The Astronomical Revolution* (1961; Methuen, 1973), pp. 153, 144. (Each face of a perfect solid has equal sides and all its faces are identical. It had been proved in antiquity that there are only five such solids: the cube, tetrahedron, docahedron, icosahedron, and octahedron.)
42. *Astronomia Nova,* tr. A.R. Hall, *NNL,* p. 73.
43. Quoted in Koyré, ref. 41, pp. 261, 288, 296, 152. For a clear elementary account of Kepler's derivation of his first two laws, see C. Wilson, 'How Did Kepler Discover His First Two Laws?', *Scientific American,* Vol. 226 (1976), pp. 93–106.
44. *Conversation with the Sidereal Messenger,* tr. E. Rosen (Johnson, 1965), p. 39. (I am indebted to Robert McCutcheon for first drawing my attention to this quotation).
45. J. Lear (ed.), *Kepler's Dream,* tr. P.F. Kirkwood (University of California Press, 1965), p. 103.
46. *Ibid,* pp. 90–1 note 8 and p. 103 note 60.
47. Quoted in *The Sleepwalkers,* ref. 39, p. 361.
48. *The Starry Messenger* in S. Drake (ed.), *Discoveries and Opinions of Galileo* (Doubleday, Anchor, 1957), p. 45.
49. Quoted in E.L. Tuveson, ref. 1 (Ch. 1), p. 51.
50. *The Fall of Man* (London, 1616), pp. 23, 378; see the discussion in R.F. Jones, *Ancients and Moderns* (1936; University of California Press, 2nd edn., 1961), pp. 25–9.
51. *The Starry Messenger* in Drake, ref. 48, pp. 27–9.
52. *Second and Third Letters on Sunspots,* in *ibid,* pp. 119, 142.
53. Donne, ref. 1, p. 17.
54. *On the Sense and Feeling in All Things and on Magic* in A.B. Fallico and H. Shapiro (eds.), *Renaissance Philosophy* (Random House, 1967), Vol. 1, p. 370.
55. *The Defense of Galileo,* tr. G. McColley (Smith College Studies in History Vol. XXII, Nos. 3–4, 1937), p. 41.
56. Quoted in Drake, ref. 48, p. 163.
57. Quoted in C. Ginzburg, 'High and Low: The Theme of Forbidden Knowledge in the Sixteenth and Seventeenth Centuries', *Past and Present* Vol. 73 (1976), 28–41, p. 35.
58. *First Letter on Sunspots* in Drake, ref. 48, p. 97.
59. *Dialogue,* p. 6.
60. *Ibid,* pp. 36–7, 268.
61. *Ibid,* pp. 58–60.
62. *Ibid,* pp. 113, 166–7.

63. *Ibid,* pp. 334, 373, 334.
64. *Ibid,* pp. 327–8.
65. *Ibid,* p.' 432; for this interpretation of Galileo's theory of tides, see H.I. Brown, 'Galileo, the Elements, and the Tides', *Studies in History and Philosophy of Science* Vol. 7 (1976), pp. 337–51.
66. *Dialogue,* p. 440.
67. *Ibid,* pp. 445, 447, 455.
68. *Ibid,* pp. 445, 462.
69. Quoted in J.J. Langford, *Galileo, Science and the Church* (Ann Arbor, 1966), p. 132.
70. Quoted in W.R. Shea, *Galileo's Intellectual Revolution* (Macmillan, 1972), p. 176.
71. *Dialogue,* pp. 449, 464.
72. Quoted in Langford, ref. 69, p. 154.
73. *A Discourse concerning a New World and anoth[er] Planet* (London, 1640), pp. 108 [107], 205.

Chapter 3 The Barrenness of Matter

1. *De Magnete* (Dover, 1968), p. 309.
2. *Ibid.,* pp. 333, 321–2.
3. *New Philosophy of Our Sublunary World,* quoted in P. Duhem, *The Aim and Structure of Physical Theory,* tr. P.P. Wiener (1914; Atheneum, 1962), p. 230.
4. *De Magnete,* pp. xlviii, 171, 136, 97.
5. W.F. Whitehead (ed.), *Three Books of Occult Philosophy* (1897; The Aquarium Press, 1971), Bk. 1, Ch. 10, pp. 61, 60, 76.
6. F. Yates, *Giordano Bruno and the Hermetic Tradition* (1964; Vintage, 1969) pp. 31, 34 (Yates' quotations are 'in the nature of *précis'*).
7. Ficino, *Commentaire sur le Banquet de Platon,* tr. R. Marcel (Paris, 1956), p. 220; see also Yates, p. 126.
8. Ref. 5, Bk. 1, Ch. 68, p. 206.
9. According to Morton Smith, 'Jesus the magician' was the figure seen by most ancient opponents of Jesus, whereas 'Jesus the son of God' was the figure seen by that party of his followers whose eventual triumph led to the destruction of the works which pictured the former Jesus; see M. Smith, *Jesus the Magician* (Gollancz, 1978).
10. Quoted by J.H. Randall, Jr. in *RPM,* p. 277.
11. *Immortality of the Soul,* tr. W.H. Hay II in *RPM,* pp. 364, 375, 277, 368.
12. *SDM,* p. 111; Del Rio quoted in D.C. Allen, *Doubt's Boundless Sea: Skepticism and Faith in the Renaissance* (Johns Hopkins UP, 1964), p. 10.
13. *Tricks of Demons,* ref. 22 (Ch. 1), Bk. 2, Ch. 3, pp. 127 (i), (ii) (three consecutive pages are numbered '127'):*Colloquium,* ref. 32 (Ch. 1), p. 37 (D.P. Walker writes that Bodin was no longer a Christian by the end of his life but believed 'in a kind of simplified, archaic Judaism', *SDM,* p. 171). H.C. Lea recounts that as late as 1660 in Saxony a hapless 'conjurer' who produced 24 mice from a concealed bag was convicted of sorcery and executed 'by a slow fire'; his two young children were also executed as certain sorcerers; Lea, ref. 24 (Ch. 1), Vol. 2, p. 902.
14. *Of the Laws of Ecclesiastical Polity,* Bk. 1, sect. 4 (1594; Dent, 1907), Vol. 1, p. 164.
15. See especially J.G. Burke, 'Hermetism as a Renaissance World View' in R.S. Kinsman (ed.), *The Darker Vision of the Renaissance* (University of

California Press, 1974) and C. Butler, *Number Symbolism* (Routledge, 1970), especially Ch. 4.

16. *Oration on the Dignity of Man*, tr. E.L. Forbes in *RPM*, p. 224.
17. Agrippa, Bk. 3, Ch. 6, quoted in C.G. Nauert, Jr., *Agrippa and the Crisis of Renaissance Thought (University of Illinois Press, 1965), p. 251.*
18. *The Complete Plays* (Penguin, 1969), pp. 267–8.
19. W. Pagel, 'Paracelsus', *DScB*, Vol. 10, pp. 304–13, p. 307; J. Jacobi (ed.), *Paracelsus: Selected Writings* (1951; Princeton UP, 2nd edn. 1958), pp. 122–3, 137.
20. F. Hartmann, *The Life and Prophecies of Paracelsus* (R. Steiner, 1973), pp. 90–1.
21. H.M. Pachter, *Magic to Science: The Story of Paracelsus* (Henry Schuman, 1951), p. 313 note 7; Jacobi, ref. 19, pp. 168, 176–8.
22. *The Ash Wednesday Supper,* tr. S.L. Jaki (The Hague; Mouton, 1975), p. 67.
23. *Ibid,* pp. 59–61.
24. J.A. Symonds, *The Sonnets of Michael Angelo Buonarroti and Tommaso Campanella* (London, 1878), p. 135.
25. H. Morley (ed.), *Ideal Commonwealths* (London, 1885), p. 229.
26. Ref. 24, p. 143.
27. Ref. 54, (Ch. 2), pp. 371, 362.
28. Ref. 24, p. 126.
29. Tr. Thomas Vaughan, reprinted in F. Yates, *The Rosicrucian Enlightenment* (Routledge, 1972), pp. 249, 240, 241, 243, 256.
30. Quoted in O. Hannaway, *The Chemists and the Word: The Didactic Origins of Chemistry* (Johns Hopkins UP, 1975), p. 99.
31. For an apologist's account of Fludd's cosmology, see J. Godwin, *Robert Fludd: Hermetic Philosopher and Surveyor of Two Worlds* (Thames and Hudson, 1979).
32. Quoted in M. Caspar, *Kepler,* tr. C.D. Hellman (Abelard-Schuman, 1959), p. 292; W. Pauli, 'The Influence of Archetypal Ideas on the Scientific Theories of Kepler' in C.G. Jung and W. Pauli, *The Interpretation of Nature and the Psyche* (1952; Routlege, 1955), pp. 197, 200; see also C. Butler, ref. 15, pp. 90–1.
33. Quoted in A.C. Crombie, 'Mersenne' in *DScB*, Vol. 9, p. 317.
34. *SDM,* p. 156.
35. *PP,* Pt. 4, §187, tr. from F. Alquié (ed.) *Oeuvres Philosophiques de Descartes* (Garnier Frères, 1973), Vol. 3, p. 502n.
36. *Le Monde*, Ch. 7 in Alquié, Vol. 1, p. 349; quoted in J. Collins, *Descartes' Philosophy of Nature* (Blackwell, 1971), p. 26.
37. *DM,* Pt. VI, p. 40.
38. *Ibid.,* Pts. II and V, pp. 14, 38.
39. *Ibid.,* Pt. I, p. 6.
40. *PP* in *NNL,* pp. 120, 110.
41. Quoted in R. M. Blake, 'The Role of Experience in Descartes' Theory of Method' in E.H. Madden (ed.), *Theories of Scientific Method: The Renaissance through the Nineteenth Century* (Washington UP, 1966), p. 76.
42. *DM,* Pt. VI, p. 41.
43. *PP,* Pt. 4, §205 in E.S. Haldane and G.R.T. Ross (eds), *The Philosophical Works of Descartes* (Cambridge UP, 1931), Vol. 1, p. 301.
44. *Ibid.,* Pt. 2, §4, pp. 255–6.
45. *Primae Cogitationes circa Generationem Animalium* (1701), quoted in J. Roger, *Les Sciences de la Vie dans la Pensée Française du XVIIIe Siècle* (Armand Collin, 1963), p. 146.

46. *Descartes on Method, Optics, Geometry and Meteorology*, tr. P.J. Olscamp (Bobbs-Merrill, 1965), p. 361.
47. *PP*, Pt. 4, §187, tr. from Alquié, ref. 35, Vol. 3, p. 502.
48. *Ibid.*, Pt. 4, §171, Vol. 3, p. 486; see, for example, J.F. Scott, *The Scientific Work of René Descartes* (Taylor and Francis, 1952), pp. 188–93; see also the account given by Jacques Rohault, *System of Natural Philosophy* (1723; Johnson Reprint, 1969), Vol. 2, 'Of the Load-stone', pp. 163–87.
49. See, for example, *VTPM*, pp. 53–4; Scott, ref. 48, pp. 186–7; Rohault, ref. 48, Vol. 2, 'Of the Flux and Reflux of the Sea', pp. 114–21.
50. 'Scientific Treatises', tr. R. Scofield in GBWW, Vol. 33, pp. 383, 429.
51. Letter to Mersenne, in C. Adam and G. Milhaud (eds.), *Correspondance* (Paris; Presses Universitaires de France, 1960), Vol. 6, p. 51; quoted in P. Duhem, ref. 3, pp. 15–16.
52. See *VTPM*, pp. 76–9 and *NS*, pp. 119–21.
53. See, for example, C. Lougee, *Le Paradis des Femmes: Women, Salons, and Social Stratification in Seventeenth-Century France* (Princeton UP, 1976).
54. Quoted in J. Bouten, *Mary Wollstonecraft and the Beginnings of Female Emancipation in France and England* (1922; reprinted, Porcupine Press, 1975), p. 39; Madame de Sevigné, *Correspondance* (Gallimard, 1978), Vol. 3, p. 955, quoted in J.S. Spink, *French Free Thought from Gassendi to Voltaire* (London UP, 1961), p. 229.
55. *RDM*, pp. 169–71; *WTUD*, pp. 22–3. See especially G.E. Aylmer, 'Unbelief in Seventeenth-Century England' in D. Pennington and K. Thomas (eds.), *Puritans and Revolutionaries, Essays in Seventeenth-Century Hisory Presented to Christopher Hill* (Oxford UP, 1978).
56. *The Mathematical Preface*, with Introduction by A.G. Debus (Science History Publication, 1975); for a general discussion of Dee, see especially P.J. French, *John Dee: The World of an Elizabethan Magus* (Routledge, 1972) and the Introduction by J. Heilbron in *John Dee on Astronomy* (University of California Press, 1978).
57. Quoted in R.H. Kargon, *Atomism in England from Hariot to Newton* (Oxford UP, 1966), pp. 27–8; see also J.W. Shirley, 'Sir Walter Raleigh and Thomas Harriot' in J.W. Shirley (ed.), *Thomas Harriot Renaissance Scientist* (Oxford UP, 1974), p. 23.
58. R[obert] B[ostocke], *the Difference betweene the Auncient Phisicke... and the Latter Phisicke* (London, 1585), Ch. 24.
59. Quoted in A.G. Debus, *The English Paracelsians* (Oldbourne, 1965), pp. 121–2.
60. Ref. 84 (Ch. 1), p. 11.
61. *The Great Instauration*, Spedding, Vol. 4, p. 21.
62. *AL*, Vol. 3, p. 381; Spedding, Vol. 4, p. 33.
63. *DAL*, Vol. 4, p. 365; *NO*, Vol. 4, p. 47; *DAL*, Vol. 4, p. 366; *NO*, Vol. 4, p. 84; *AL*, Vol. 3, p. 289. See especially the discussion in P. Rossi, *Francis Bacon: From Magic to Science*, tr. S. Rabinovitch (1957; Routledge, 1968).
64. *NO*, Vol. 4, pp. 109, 62–3, 97; *DAL*, Vol. 4, p. 298.
65. 'Thoughts and Conclusions' in B. Farrington, *The Philosophy of Francis Bacon* (Liverpool UP, 1970), pp. 93, 92, 96, 92, 62.
66. *NO*, Vol 4, p. 42; *DAL*, Vol. 4, p. 373; 'Thoughts and Conclusions', ref. 65, p. 59.
67. Quoted in C. Webster, *The Great Instauration* (Duckworth, 1975), p. 324; see especially E. Mendelsohn, 'The Social Construction of Scientific Knowledge' in *SPSK*.
68. *WTUD*, p. 20.
69. *WGW*, pp. 105–6; *WTUD*, p. 139.

70. *WGW*, pp. 269, 271, 276–7; see also C. Hill, *Winstanley: The Law of Freedom and Other Writings* (Penguin, 1973), pp. 99, 101, 107–8.

71. See, for example, P.M. Rattansi, 'Paracelsus and the Puritan Revolution, *Ambix*, Vol. 11, (1963), pp. 24–32; *RDM*, pp. 227, 270; A.G. Debus, *The Chemical Dream of the Renaissance* (Heffer, 1968), pp. 26–7; J.R. Jacob, 'Robert Boyle and Subversive Religion in the Early Restoration', *Albion* Vol. 6, (1974), pp. 275–93, p. 278.

72. *AMA*, p. 6; *AT*, pp. 50, 48 (Agrippa, *Three Books of Occult Philosophy* (London, 1651), Bk. 3, Ch. 44, pp. 498–9); *AT*, p. 30; *AMA*, p. 13.

73. *The Second Lash of Alazonomastix* (Cambridge, 1651), p. 11; *Observations upon AT and AMA* (London, 1650), pp. 2, 88, 49, 56.

74. *The Second Lash*, p. 35.

75. *The Man-Mouse Taken in a Trap* (London, 1650), p. 114.

76. *The Second Lash*, pp. 41, 151.

77. A.G. Debus (ed.), *Science and Education in the Seventeenth Century* (Macdonald, 1970), pp. 69, 199, 210.

78. *Ibid.*, pp. 34, 106, 46, 36.

79. P.M. Rattansi, ref. 71, p. 30.

80. *PHYSIOLOGIA Epicuro-Gassendo-Charltoniana: Or a Fabrick of Science Natural, Upon the Hypothesis of Atoms* (Johnson Reprint, 1966), pp. 58, 275, 344.

81. *Darknes of Atheism...*(London, 1652), pp. 97, 201.

82. N.R. Gelbart, 'The Intellectual Development of Walter C. Charleton,' *Ambix*, Vol. 18 (1971) pp. 149–68, p. 166; I am indebted to this article for an illuminating analysis of Charleton's philosophy.

83. See especially J.R. Jacob, *Robert Boyle and the English Revolution* (Franklin, 1977) for biographical details of Boyle and for (what I find) a convincing analysis of Boyle's philosophical, religious and political commitments.

84. *WRB*, Vol. 1, p. 356.

85. *Ibid.*, Vol. 4, pp. 69, 73; Vol. 5, p. 514; Vol. 2, p. 61.

86. *Ibid.*, Vol. 5, p. 532; Vol. 1, p. lxxix (letter to Henry Stubbe, 1665–6).

87. *A History of Magic and Experimental Science* (Columbia UP, 1958), Vol. 8, Ch. 28.

88. *WRB*, Vol. 5, p. 165.

89. Quoted in J.R. Jacob, 'The New England Company, the Royal Society and the Indians', *Social Studies of Science*, Vol. 5 (1975), pp. 450–5, p. 453.

90. T.C. McLuhan (ed.), *Touch the Earth* (Abacus, 1972), p. 56; P. Farb, *Man's Rise to Civilization* (Avon, 1968), p. 333.

91. *Experimental Philosophy*, Introduction by M. Boas Hall (1664; Johnson Reprint, 1966), pp. 184, 193.

92. G. Rodis-Lewis (ed.), tr. from *Oeuvres de Malebranche* (Paris; Libraire Philosophique J. Vrin, 1962), Vol. 1, pp. 266–7; quoted in L. Stone, *The Family, Sex and Marriage in England 1500–1800* (Weidenfeld, 1977), p. 357; M. Albistur and D. Armogathe, *Histoire du feminisme Francais* (Paris; Editions des femmes, 1977), p. 170.

93. P. Bayle, *Les pensées diverses sur la comète* (1683: Paris; Droz, 1939), Vol. 2, pp. 80–1; D.A.L. Backer, *Precious Women* (Basic Books, 1974), pp. 177, 209.

94. L.D. Cohen, 'Descartes and Henry More on the Beast Machine', *Annals of Science*, Vol. 1 (1936), pp. 48–61, p. 50.

95. *Ibid.*, pp. 52–3.

96. Ref. 92, Vol. 2, p. 394; quoted in D. Harwood, *Love for Animals and How It Developed in Great Britain* (New York, 1928), p. 87.

97. Quoted in C.E. Raven, *John Ray, Naturalist* (1942; Cambridge UP, 1950), pp. 49–50, 375.
98. 'On the Modern Theory of Generation', *Phil. Transactions of the Royal Society*, Vol. 17 (1691), No. 192 in Vol. 16 (1862–92) (Johnson Reprint, 1963), pp. 474–83, p. 476.
99. *Experiments on the Generation of Insects* (1688), tr. M. Bigelow (Chicago, 1909), p. 116.
100. *The Book of Nature or the History of Insects* (London, 1758), tr. T. Flloyd, Pt. 2, pp. 71, 69.
101. 'On the Formation of the Chick in the Egg' (1672) in H.B. Adelmann, *Marcelo Malpighi and the Evolution of Embryology* (Cornell and Oxford UP, 1966), Vol. 2, pp. 935, 945.
102. Ref. 100, p. 3 (and see p. 16).
103. *Oeuvres de Malebranche*, ref. 92, Vol. 1, p. 83.
104. Ref. 98, p. 476.
105. *Contemplation de la nature* (1764, 2nd edn. 1769), quoted in T.S. Hall, *Ideas of Life and Matter* (University of Chicago Press, 1969), Vol. 2, p. 36; E.B. Gasking, *Investigations into Generation 1651–1828* (Hutchinson, 1967), p. 120.
106. *Collected Letters*, Vol. 2 (Amsterdam, 1941), p. 335; L. Poliakov, *The Aryan Myth* (Chatto and Windus and Heinemann for Sussex UP, 1974), p. 160.
107. J. Farley, 'The Spontaneous Generation Controversy', *J. Hist. Biology*, Vol. 5 (1972), pp. 95–125, p. 103.
108. *Leibniz: Philosophical Writings*, tr. M. Morris (Dent, 1934), p. 239.
109. *WRB*, Vol. 5, p. 251; see also R. Lenoble, *Histoire de l'idée de nature* (Paris; Albin Michel, 1969), pp. 315, 334.
110. 'Publisher to the Reader', in R. Boyle, *Experiments and Considerations Touching Colours* (London, 1664).
111. J. Roger, ref. 45, pp. 390, 432–3.

Chapter 4 Gravitational Attraction

1. *Leviathan* (Penguin, 1968), Pt. I, Ch. 11, pp. 160–1.
2. *Ibid*, Pt. I, Ch. 13 p. 186.
3. *Ibid*, Pt. III, Ch. 38, p. 478 and Ch. 43, p. 609.
4. *Ibid*, Pt. III, Ch. 32, pp. 411, 414.
5. *Ibid*, Pt. I, Ch. 2, p. 93.
6. *Ibid*, Pt. III, Ch. 43, p. 612.
7. *Ibid*, Pt. II, Ch. 30, pp. 378–9.
8. See especially S.I. Mintz, *The Hunting of Leviathan* (Cambridge UP, 1962).
9. *Enthusiasmus Triumphatus* (1656, with additions 1662; Los Angeles, William Andrews Memorial Library, 1966), pp. 38, 29.
10. *Immortality of the Soul* (London, 1659), Bk. 1, Ch. 10, p. 64.
11. *Ibid*, Bk. 1, Ch. 9, p. 56.
12. Hobbes, *English Works*, W. Moleworth (ed.) (London, 1839–45), Vol. 1, pp. 513, 531.
13. Ref. 10, Bk. 3, Ch. 13, pp. 463, 465.
14. *The True Intellectual System of the Universe*, T. Birch (ed.) (London, 1820), Vol. 3, p. 310.
15. Ref. 10, Bk. 3, Ch. 13, p. 469.
16. Ref. 14, Vol. 3, p. 315; Vol. 1, pp. 56–8.
17. Ref. 10, Bk. 2, Ch. 2, p. 124.
18. Printed in Glanvill, *A Praefatory Answer to Mr Henry Stubbe* (London, 1671), p. 155.
19. Printed in Glanvill, *Sadducismus Triumphatus* (London, 1681), p. 16.

20. C. Webster, 'Henry More and Descartes: Some New Sources', *Br. J. for the History of Science* Vol. 4 (1969), pp. 359–77, p. 370.
21. Quoted in P.H. Osmond, *Isaac Barrow: His Life and Times* (London: Society for Promoting Christian Knowledge, 1944), pp. 28, 30, 31.
22. *Ibid*, p. 31; quoted in B.J.T. Dobbs, *The Foundations of Newton's Alchemy, or, the Hunting of the Green Lyon* (Cambridge UP, 1975), p. 101.
23. *The Usefulness of Mathematical Learning Explained and Demonstrated* (1734; Frank Cass, 1970), pp. 64, 61, 59, 239; see also the discussion in R.H. Kargon, ref. 56 (Ch. 3), pp. 118–121.
24. *Dialogues Concerning Two New Sciences*, tr. H. Crew and A. de Salvio (1638; Dover, 1954), p. 167. Galileo then proceeds to make an erroneous argument in attempting to demonstrate that the velocity of a falling body is not proportional to the *distance* of descent.
25. I.B. Cohen, 'Isaac Newton', in *DScB*, Vol. 10, p. 61; see also I.B. Cohen, *The Birth of a New Physics* (Heineman, 1961) for a clear, elementary discussion of the Copernican revolution and Newtonian physics.
26. 'On the Gravity and Equilibrium of Fluids', in A.R. and M.B. Hall (eds.), *Unpublished Scientific Papers of Isaac Newton* (Cambridge UP, 1962), pp. 142–3, 127, 137, 139, 142.
27. 'An Experimental Discussion of Quicksilver, growing hot with Gold', *WRB*, Vol. 4 pp. 219–30, p. 228; I am indebted to B.J.T. Dobbs (ref. 22) for this discussion of Newton's alchemy.
28. *CHO*, Vol. 2, pp. 1–2.
29. Quoted in O. Hannaway, ref. 30 (Ch. 3), p. 51. Newton possessed in his library a copy of Oswald Croll's *Basilica Chymica*.
30. Quoted in Dobbs, ref. 22, p. 178.
31. *Ibid*, p. 212; see also P.M. Rattansi, 'Some Evaluations of Reason in Sixteenth and Seventeenth-Century Natural Philosophy' in R.M. Young and M. Teich (eds.), *Changing Perspectives in the Historiography of Science* (Heinemann, 1973), p. 159.
32. 'The Role of Alchemy in Newton's Career' in M.L. Righini Bonelli and W.R. Shea (eds.), *Reason, Experiment and Mysticism in the Scientific Revolution* (Macmillan, 1975), p. 195.
33. Quoted in F.E. Manuel, *Isaac Newton Historian* (Cambridge UP, 1963), pp. 14, 4; J.M. Keynes, *Essays in Biography* (Hart-Davis, 1951), p. 311.
34. Quoted in L.T. More, *Isaac Newton A Biography* (1934; Dover, 1962), pp. 301, 313.
35. *PM*, p. xviii.
36. *Ibid*, p. 12.
37. This is proved in most textbooks on Newtonian theory; see, for example, A.P. French, ref. 29 (Ch. 2), pp. 261–5.
38. For a general discussion of the phenomenon of tides, see, for example, A. Defant, *Ebb and Flow: The Tides of Earth, Air and Water*, tr. A.J. Pomerans (Michigan UP, 1958).
39. *PM*, pp. 395, 394.
40. *PM*, p. 543.
41. I have followed the treatment given by French, ref. 29 (Ch. 2), pp. 583–5.
42. *PM*, p. 396.
43. *PM*, p. 547.
44. Quoted in *NS*, p. 144.
45. *PM*, p. 400; see especially the polemical essay 'Newton's effect on scientific standards' in I. Lakatos, *Philosophical Papers*, J. Worrall and G. Currie (eds.) (Cambridge UP, 1978), Vol. 1.
46. Quoted in *NS*, 117–18.

47. *Treatise on Light* (Dover, 1962), p. 3.
48. Quoted in R. Dugas and P. Costable 'The Birth of a New Science: Mechanics', in R. Taton (ed.), *The Beginning of Modern Science* (Thames and Hudson, 1964), p. 265.
49. Quoted in M.C. Jacob, *The Newtonians and the English Revolution 1689–1720* (Harvester, 1976), p. 181.
50. *CIN,* Vol. 3, p. 280; see also Ch. 5 this essay, Sec. 4 (ref. 121, Ch. 5).
51. H.S. Thayer (ed.), *Newton's Philosophy of Nature* (Hafner, 1953), p. 46.
52. *Ibid,* p. 54.
53. *Opticks* (4th edn 1730; Dover, 1952), pp. 401–2; *PM,* p. 668.
54. *PM,* pp. xxvii, xxviii, xxxii.
55. See Rohault, ref. 48 (Ch. 3) and M. Hoskin, ' "Mining All Within," Clarke's Notes to Rohault's *Traité de Physique*', *The Thomist,* Vol. 24 (1961), pp. 357–63.
56. Ref. 49, pp. 248, 189.
57. H.G. Alexander (ed.), *The Leibniz-Clarke Correspondence* (Manchester UP, 1956), pp. 11, 12, 29, 30.
58. *Ibid,* pp. 94, 72, 93, 85, 93.
59. *Ibid,* pp. 118, 116.
60. *NS,* p. 147.
61. *VTPM,* pp. 106, 109.
62. *Ibid,* p. 97–8.
63. I.B. Cohen (ed.), *Isaac Newton's Papers and Letters on Natural Philosophy* (Cambridge UP, 1958), p. 457.
64. *VTPM,* p. 204; P.L.M. de Maupertuis, *Oeuvres* (Lyon, 1768; Georg Olms Verlag, 1974), Vol. 1, p. 124. I am indebted to E.J. Aiton's essay for this discussion of Maupertuis' work.
65. *VTPM,* p. 203; see also *NS,* p. 162; *Oeuvres,* Vol. 1, p. 99.
66. *VTPM,* p. 247.
67. *The Earthly Venus,* tr. S.B. Boas (Johnson Reprint, 1966), pp. 10, 15, 53, 56.
68. Quoted in S.A. Roe, 'The Development of Albrecht von Haller's Views on Embryology', *J. of the History of Biology* Vol. 8 (1975), p. 169 note 9.
69. *The Art of Hatching and Bringing up Domestick Fowls* (London, 1750), pp. 462–3; quoted in E. Gasking, ref. 105, (Ch. 3), pp. 83–4.
70. Quoted in B. Glass, 'Maupertuis, Pioneer of Genetics and Evolution', in B. Glass, O. Temkin and W.L. Strauss, Jr. (eds.) *Forerunners of Darwin* (Johns Hopkins UP, 1959) p. 68; *Oeuvres,* Vol. 2, pp. 158–9.
71. *Ibid,* p. 58; *Oeuvres,* Vol. 1, p. 12.
72. Quoted in T.S. Hall, ref. 105 (Ch. 3), p. 28; *Oeuvres,* Vol. 2, p. 177.
73. *Oeuvres,* Vol. 2, Letter VI, pp. 255–6; see also H. Hastings, *Man and Beast in French Thought of the Eighteenth Century* (Johns Hopkins UP, 1936), p. 243.
74. Epitaph, J. Butt (ed.) *The Poems of Alexander Pope* (Methuen, 1965), p. 808.
75. *History of England* (Edinburgh, 1792), Vol. 8, p. 334.
76. K.G. Denbigh, *An Inventive Universe* (Hutchinson, 1975), p. 7.
77. *Chance and Necessity,* tr. A. Wainhouse (Collins, 1972), p. 113.
78. 'On Chance and Necessity' in F. Ayala and T. Dobzhansky (eds.), *The Philosophy of Biology* (Macmillan, 1974), pp. 357–8.
79. 'Beyond Freedom and Dignity: Skinner's Behaviourism', *Cambridge Review* (19 Nov., 1971), p. 61.
80. See especially M' Espinasse, 'The Decline and Fall of Restoration Science' in *Past and Present* Vol. 14 (1958), pp. 71–89; M. Berman, ' "Hegemony"

and the Amateur Tradition in British Science', *J. Social History* Vol. 8 (1975) 30–50; T.S. Kuhn, 'Mathematical vs Experimental Traditions in the Development of Physical Science', *J. Interdisciplinary History* Vol. 7 (1976), 1–31; J.L. Heilbron, *Electricity in the Seventeenth and Eighteenth Centuries: A Study of Early Modern Physics* (University of California Press, 1979).

Chapter 5 The Appropriation of Nature

1. *RDM*, p. 579; A. Dyce (ed.), *The Works of Richard Bentley* (London, 1838; AMS Press, 1966), Vol. 3, p. 320.
2. *Cautio Criminalis (Precautions for Prosecutors)* in A.C. Kors and E. Peters, *Witchcraft in Europe 1100–1700* (Dent, 1973), pp. 352–7.
3. *Witchcraft...* (Cornell UP, 1976), pp. 106–7.
4. Ref. 74 (Ch. 1) pp. 194, 192.
5. Ref. 3, p. 37.
6. *RDM*, p. 663.
7. *The Vanity of Dogmatizing: The Three Versions,* Introduction by S. Medcalf (Harvester, 1970) title Ch. 19 (1661 edn.); see especially J.I. Cope, *Joseph Glanvill, Anglican Apologist* (Washington University Studies, 1956).
8. *Vanity,* Ch. 25, p. 49.
9. *Ibid,* Ch. 25, p. 155 (1665 edn.) and Ch. 21, pp. 211–12 (1661 edn.).
10. *An Antidote against Atheism* (London, 1652), Bk. 3, Ch. 16, p. 142 in *A Collection of Several Philosophical Writings* (4th edn., London, 1712).
11. Subsequent editions were entitled:
Some Philosophical Considerations Touching the Being of Witches and Witchcraft (1667),
A Blow at Modern Sadducism (1668),
Against Modern Sadducism in the Matter of Witches and Apparitions (1675), *Saducismus Triumphatus* (1681).
12. *Against Modern Sadducism* in *Essays on Several Important Subjects in Philosophy and Religion* (facsimile edn., Friedrich Frommann Verlag, 1970), pp. 4, 58, 38, 3, 59.
13. *Ibid,* p. 6.
14. *Ibid.*
15. *Ibid,* pp. 7, 9, 10, 14.
16. *Ibid,* pp. 38, 60.
17. *Vanity,* ref. 7, (1661 edn.), Ch. 19, p. 182.
18. *Displaying...* pp. 17–18, 27–8, 268, 227; *Sadducismus Triumphatus* (1681), 'The Postscript', p. 29.
19. The diversity of beliefs displayed by members of the Royal Society is discussed by K. Theodore Hoppen in his two papers 'The Nature of the Early Royal Society', *British J. for the History of Science*, Vol. 9 (1976), pp. 1–24, 243–73.
20. See M. Purver, *The Royal Society: Concept and Creation* (Routledge, 1967), p. 165.
21. 'To the Reader'; see, for example, *The Mathematical and Philosophical Works of... John Wilkins* (London, 1708).
22. Quoted in H.C. Lyons, *The Royal Society, 1660–1940* (1944; Greenwood, 1968), p. 41.
23. *A Letter... to Peter du Moulin concerning Natural experimental Philosophie* (Cambridge, 1669), p. 30.
24. *HRS*, pp. 62, 94, 113.

25. *Ibid*, pp. 62, 339, 110.
26. *Ibid*, p. 348.
27. *Ibid*, pp. 352–5.
28. *Ibid*, pp. 361, 62.
29. *Ibid*, p. 429.
30. *Ibid*, pp. 339–41.
31. *Ibid*, p. 122.
32. *Ibid*, pp. 123–4, 327.
33. Ref. 110, Ch. 3.
34. *Vanity*, ref. 7, (1661), Ch. 2, p. 11, Ch. 15, p. 118.
35. Quoted in H. Brown, *Scientific Organizations in Seventeenth-Century France* (1934; Russell, 1967), p. 101; see also *CHO*, Vol. 1, p. 287.
36. *Vanity*, ref. 7, 'Preface to the Royal Society' (1665).
37. *HRS*, p. 415.
38. *WRB*, Vol. 5, p. 179.
39. *Vanity*, ref. 36.
40. Quoted in J.E. King, *Science and Rationalism in the Government of Louis XIV 1661–83* (1949; Octagon, 1972), p. 220.
41. C.M. Cipolla, *European Culture and Overseas Expansion* (Penguin, 1970), p. 61.
42. Quoted in R. Hahn, *The Anatomy of a Scientific Institution: the Paris Academy of Sciences 1666–1803* (University of California Press, 1971), pp. 11, 12, 16.
43. *NNL*, p. 226.
44. Cipolla, ref. 41, p. 62.
45 *EW*, p. 127; M. Summers, *The Geography of Witchcraft* (Citadel, 1973), pp. 422–9.
46. P. Rossi, *Philosophy, Technology and the Arts in the Early Modern Era,* tr. S. Attanasio (Harper, 1970), p. 128.
47. Cipolla, ref. 41, p. 62.
48. Summers, ref. 45, p. 429; see also R. Mandrou, *Magistrats et sorciers en France au XVIIe siècle*(Paris: Plon, 1968), pp. 425–564 and extract in *EW*, pp. 128–43.
49. *Vanity*, ref. 7, (1661), Ch. 19, p. 178.
50. Ref. 36 (Ch. 1), p. xxii.
51. *EM*, p. 188; *Pensées Diverses sur la Cométe* (Paris; Droz, 1939), Vol. 1, p. 271.
52. Ref. 91 (Ch. 3), p. 192.
53. *EM*, p. 362.
54. Ref. 7 (Ch. 1), Vol. 1, p. 207.
55. Extract from *Recherche de la Vérité* in *EW*, pp. 123–6.
56. *The World Bewitched* (London, 1695), 'An Abridgement of the Whole Work', no page numbers; Vols 2–4 have not been translated in unabridged form.
57. Kors and Peters, ref. 2, pp. 373–5.
58. *EM*, p. 197; *Histoire des Oracles* (Paris; Union Générale d'Editions, 1966), p. 21.
59. Manuel, ref. 33 (Ch. 4), p. 149.
60. J.P. Kenyon (ed.), *Halifax Complete Works* (Penguin, 1969), p. 67.
61. *The Political and Commercial Works of Charles Davenant* (Gregg Press, 1967), pp. 45–47.
62. Halifax, ref. 60, pp. 73, 194.
63. C. Hill (ed.), *Winstanley: The Law of Freedom and Other Writings* (Penguin,

1973), p. 27; also G. Juretic 'Digger No Millenarian: The Revolutionizing of Gerrard Winstanley', *J. History Ideas 36* (1975), pp. 263–80; J.C. Davis, 'Gerrard Winstanley and the Restoration of True Magistracy', *Past and Present* No. 70 (1976), 76–93.

64. 'Truth Lifting Up Its Head', *GWG*, p. 100.
65. 'The Saints Paradice', *GWG*, pp. 96, 44.
66. *GWG*, pp. 105–6, 111, 113–14.
67. 'The New Law of Righteousness', *GWG*, p. 156; compare H. Marcuse, *Counterrevolution and Revolt* (Allen Lane, 1972), Ch. 2.
68. 'Fire in the Bush', *GWG*, p. 493; Hill (ed.), ref. 63, p. 268.
69. 'To the Lord Fairfax', *GWG*, p. 290.
70. *The Law of Freedom in a Platform or True Magistracy Restored, GWG*, pp. 502, 568; Hill (ed), pp. 276, 351.
71. *GWG*, p. 523; Hill, p. 299.
72. *GWG*, pp. 565, 504; Hill, pp. 349, 279.
73. *GWG*, p. 569; Hill, p. 353.
74. *GWG*, pp. 537, 564, 570, 597; Hill, pp. 316, 347, 354, 385.
75. *GWG*, pp. 511, 529, 511; Hill, pp. 287, 306–7, 287.
76. *GWG*, pp. 520, 540; Hill, pp. 296, 319.
77. *GWG*, p. 526; Hill, p. 302.
78. *GWG*, p. 583; Hill, p. 369.
79. *GWG*, pp. 591–2, 599; Hill, pp. 379, 388.
80. *GWG*, pp. 579, 577; Hill, pp. 365, 362.
81. *GWG*, pp. 564, 571; Hill, pp. 347, 355–6.
82. *GWG*, p. 585; Hill, p. 372.
83. 'The New Law of Righteousness', *GWG*, p. 157.
84. *Two Treatises* (Dent, 1924), pp. 130, 133, 132, 140, 157–8, 140; see especially C.B. Macpherson, *The Political Theory of Possessive Individualism: Hobbes to Locke* (Oxford UP, 1962).
85. 'Some Considerations of the Consequences of the Lowering of Interest and Raising the Value of Money' (1691), *WJL*, Vol. 5, pp. 57, 71.
86. *Two Treatises* (Dent), p. 180.
87. 'The Reasonableness of Christianity' (1695), *WJL*, Vol. 7, pp. 146, 157, 146, 150.
88. *An Essay Concerning Human Understanding* (1690, 5th edn, 1706; Dent, 1964–5), Vol. 2, Bk. 4, Ch. 18, p. 285.
89. 'A Discourse on Miracles', *WJL*, Vol. 9, pp. 262, 261.
90. *Essay*, Vol. 1, Bk. 2, Ch. 8, p. 104.
91. *Ibid*, Vol. 2, Bk. 4, Ch. 10, pp. 223–5. See also the sermon preached by Richard Bentley in 1692 entitled 'Matter and Motion Cannot Think' in A. Dyce (ed.), ref. 1, Vol. 3, pp. 27–50.
92. *Essay*, Vol. 1, Bk. 2, Ch. 23, pp. 258–9.
93. *Ibid*, Vol. 2, Bk. 3, Ch. 6, p. 50; see also Bk. 4, Ch. 3, p. 162.
94. *DAL*, Vol. 4, p. 364.
95. Quoted in T. Cooper, 'William Petyt' in S. Lee (ed), *Dictionary of National Biography* (London, 1908–9), Vol. 15, pp. 1018–9
96. Quoted in E.S. Furniss, *The Position of the Labourer in a System of Nationalism* (Kelly and Millman, 1957), pp. 16–17n.
97. C.H. Hull (ed.), *The Economic Writings of Sir William Petty* (Augustus M. Kelley, 1963), Vol. 1, pp. 287, 285, 288, 289, 290.
98. H. Kellenbenz, 'Technology in the Age of the Scientific Revolution 1500–1700', in C.M. Cipolla (ed.), *The Fontana Economic History of Europe: The Sixteenth and Seventeenth Centuries* (Fontana, 1974), p. 265; see also A.R. Hall, 'Scientific Method and the Progress of Techniques' in

E.E. Rich and C. Wilson (eds), *The Cambridge Economic History of Europe* (Cambridge UP, 1967), Vol. 4.
99. P. Clark and P. Slack, *English Towns in Transition 1500–1700* (Oxford UP, 1976), pp. 10, 1.
100. *The Unbound Prometheus* (Cambridge UP, 1969), p. 61.
101. *RDM,* pp. 533–4.
102. *HRS,* p. 400.
103. *Science and Social Welfare in the Age of Newton* (Oxford UP, 1969), p. 97.
104. Quoted in L. Radzinowicz, *A History of Criminal Law* (Stevens, 1948), Vol. 1, p. 4.
105. *The Philosophy of Manufactures or An Exposition of the Scientific, Moral, and Commercial Economy of the Factory System of Great Britain* (Frank Cass, 1967) p. 20.
106. *Ibid,* pp. 40, 368.
107. *Ibid,* pp. 407, 423.
108. Quoted in H. Smith, 'Gynecology and Ideology in Seventeenth-Century England' in Carroll, ref. 71 (Ch. 1), p. 103.
109. *Ephesian Matron* (1659; William Andrews Clark Memorial Library, 1975), pp. 70–1.
110. *Anatomy of Melancholy* (1621; Dent, 1932), Vol. 3, pp. 55–6.
111. 'Upon Some Verses of Virgil', GBWW, Vol. 25, p. 425.
112. *The City of God*, tr. G.G. Walsh and G. Monahan (Catholic U of America, 1952), Bk. 14, Chs 16, 19, 23, pp. 388, 394, 401–2.
113. *The Religio Medici and Other Writings* (Dent, 1931), p. 65.
114. H.W. Lansdowne (ed.), *William Petty: Papers* (London, 1927), Vol. 1, pp. 155–6.
115. C.H. George and K. George, *The Protestant Mind of the Renaissance* (Princeton UP, 1961), p. 272.
116. *Institutiones medicae*, §776; quoted in V.L. Bullough, *Sexual Variance in Society and History* (Wiley, 1976), p. 496.
117. See, for example, G.J. Barker-Benfield, 'Sexual Surgery in Late-Nineteenth-Century America', *Int. J. of Health Services,* Vol. 5 (1975), pp. 279–98.
118. 'A Discourse on the Nature of Comets' (1682) in R. Waller (ed.), *The Posthumous Works of Robert Hooke* (London, 1705), pp. 171–2.
119. Ref. 108, p. 109.
120. F.E. Manuel, *The Religion of Isaac Newton* (Oxford UP, 1974), pp. 13, 73; for Simon Magus, see E.M. Butler, ref. 30 (Ch. 1).
121. Ref. 34, (Ch. 4), p. 385 and *CIN,* Vol. 3, p. 280.
122. 'The Refutation of Philosophies' in Farrington, ref. 73 (Ch. 3), p. 129.
123. *AMA,* p. 6.
124. Ref. 77 (Ch. 3), p. 68.
125. *Diary and Correspondence of John Evelyn* (H.G. Bohn, 1859), Vol. 3, p. 348.
126. Ref. 23 (Ch. 4), pp. xxix-xxx.
127. *HRS,* pp. 124, 327.
128. Ref. 34 (Ch. 4), p. 312; see also *CIN,* Vol. 2, p. 441.
129. Ref. 88, Vol. 1, p. xxvii.
130. *CIN,* Vol. 2, p. 474.
131. 'Certain Physiological Essays' *WRB,* Vol. 1, p. 310.
132. *Magia Adamica* (London, 1650), p. 86; *AMA,* pp. 8, 13.
133. Ref. 65 (Ch. 3), pp. 130, 83; *NO,* Vol. 4, p. 42; ref. 65 (Ch. 3), pp. 92–3; AL Vol. 4, p. 373.

134. *CHO*, Vol. 1, p. 113; P. Gay, *The Enlightenment* (Weidenfeld, 1970), Vol. 1, p. 132.
135. *A Discourse Introductory to a Course of Lectures on Chemistry* (London, 1802), pp. 14, 17, 16.
136. *The New Atlantis,* Spedding, Vol. 3, p. 156.
137. 'Death and the Devil', in Kinsman (ed.), Ref. 15 (Ch. 3), p. 33. Times have apparently not changed! According to P. Robinson in *The Modernization of Sex* (Elek, 1976), p. 152 the two books by W. Masters and V. Johnson, *Human Sexual Response* and *Human Sexual Inadequacy* 'could almost be retitled *Female Sexual Response* and *Male Sexual Inadequacy*'.
138. *The Functions and Disorders of the Reproductive Organs* (1857; London, 3rd edn., 1862), p. 102.
139. W.D. Jordan, *White over Black: American Attitudes Toward the Negro* (Penguin, 1969), p. 158.
140. Note to 1753–4 edn. 'Of National Characters' (1748); quoted in Jordan, ref. 139, p. 253.
141. *An Account of the Regular Gradation in Man* (London, 1779), pp. 61, 134, 63, 134; see Jordan, pp. 501–2.
142. *Candid Reflections . . .* (London, 1772), pp. 48–9; *History of Jamaica* (London, 1774), Vol. 2, p. 372. Edward Long (1734–1813), born and educated in England, served as judge of the vice-admiralty court in Jamaica until 1769 when he returned to England to devote himself to writing.
143. *Lectures and Lay Sermons* (Dent, 1910), pp. 115, 116, 119.
144. *Hereditary Genius* (1869, 1892; Peter Smith, 1972), pp. 387–8.
145. *The Descent of Man and Selection in Relation to Sex* (1871, 2nd edn. 1874; London 1901), Ch. 20, p. 911.
146. Ref. 138, p. 50.
147. Quoted in M. Fishbein, *A History of the American Medical Association* (W.B. Saunders, 1947), p. 218.
148. *The Lancet,* 1870, Vol. 1, p. 888.
149. A.K. Gardner, *History of the Art of Midwifery* (Stringer and Townsend, 1852), p. 12; quoted in G.J. Barker-Benfield, *The Horrors of the Half-Known Life* (Harper, 1978), p. 293.
150. According to the social historian Charles E. Rosenberg, 'Evidence indicating male anxieties in regard to female sexuality are as old as history itself and have attracted an elaborate, if dissonant, body of discussion; whatever metapsychological interpretation one places upon this phenomenon, its existence seems undeniable,' in 'Sexuality, Class and Role in Nineteenth-Century America', *American Quarterly*, Vol. 25 (1973), pp. 131–53, p. 147.
151. 'Vanity of Spirit', *Henry Vaughan: The Complete Poems* (Penguin, 1976), p. 172.

NAME INDEX

Names appearing in the Notes but not in the text are included in the Index only where the notes in question substantially augment the text. Principal references are shown in italicized page numbers.

SUBJECT INDEX